Arab Background Series

Editor: N. A. Ziadeh, Emeritus Professor of History,
American University of Beirut, Beirut

Origins and Early Development of Shiʿa Islam

S. Husain M. Jafri

Longman, London and New York
Librairie du Liban

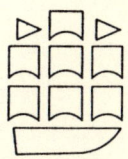

LONGMAN GROUP LTD
London and New York
Associated companies, branches and representatives throughout the world
LIBRAIRIE DU LIBAN
Beirut

First published 1979
ISN 0 582 78080 2

British Library Cataloguing in Publication Data

Jafri, Husain M
Origins and early development of Shiʿa Islam.
1. Shiites—History
I. Title
297'.82'09021 BP192.4 78-40611
ISBN 0-582-78080-2

Typeset by CCC and printed and bound at William Clowes & Sons Limited Beccles and London.

To
the Memory
of my Beloved Mother

Contents

Abbreviations		viii
Editor's Preface		ix
Preface		xi
Chapter 1	Conceptual Foundations	1
Chapter 2	Saqīfa: The First Manifestations	27
Chapter 3	ʿAlī and the First Two Caliphs	58
Chapter 4	The Re-emergence of the ʿAlid Party	80
Chapter 5	Kūfa: Stage of Shīʿī Activities	101
Chapter 6	The Abdication of Ḥasan	130
Chapter 7	The Martyrdom of Ḥusayn	174
Chapter 8	The Reaction after Karbalā	222
Chapter 9	The Struggle for Legitimacy	235
Chapter 10	The Imamate of Jaʿfar aṣ-Ṣādiq	259
Chapter 11	The Doctrine of the Imamate	289
Bibliography		317
Index		323

Abbreviations

BM	British Museum
BSOAS	*Bulletin of the School of Oriental and African Studies*
EI[1]	*Encyclopaedia of Islam,* 1st edition, Leiden 1913–38
EI[2]	*Encyclopaedia of Islam,* new edition, Leiden 1960-proceeding
IC	*Islamic Culture*
JAOS	*Journal of the American Oriental Society*
JBBRAS	*Journal of the Bombay Branch of the Royal Asiatic Society*
JRAS	*Journal of the Royal Asiatic Society*
REI	*Revue des Études Islamiques*
RSO	*Rivista degle Studi Orientali*
SOAS	School of Oriental and African Studies, University of London
ZDMG	*Zeitschrift der Deutschen Morgenländischen Gesellschaft*

Editor's preface

The Arab World has, for some time, been attracting the attention of a growing public throughout the world. The strategic position of the Arab countries, the oil they produce, their sudden emancipation and emergence as independent states, their revolutions and *coups d'état*, have been the special concern of statesmen, politicians, businessmen, scholars and journalists, and of equal interest to the general public.

An appreciation of the present-day problems of Arab countries and of their immediate neighbours demands a certain knowledge of their geographical and social background; and a knowledge of the main trends of their history—political, cultural and religious—is essential for an understanding of current issues. Arabs had existed long before the advent of Islam in the seventh century AD, but it was with Islam that they became a world power. Arab civilization, which resulted from the contacts the Arabs had with other peoples and cultures, especially after the creation of this world power, and which reached its height in the ninth, tenth and eleventh centuries, was, for a few centuries that followed, the guiding light of a large part of the world. Its rôle cannot, thus, be ignored.

The Arab Background Series provides the English-speaking, educated reader with a series of books which attempt to clarify the historical past of the Arabs and to analyse their present problems. The contributors to the series, who come from many parts of the world, are all specialists in their own fields. This variety of approach and attitude creates for the English-speaking reader a unique picture of the Arab World.

N. A. ZIADEH

Preface

The rise and development of Islam has been the subject of numerous studies, both general and specialized, but a major question, that of the origins and early growth of Shīʿa Islam, has received insufficient attention. So far, the approach to this subject has been largely through the works of heresiographers such as Baghdādī, Ibn Ḥazm, and Shahrastānī; and the picture that has emerged has been that of a heresy founded on political and economic considerations. Indeed, valuable as the heresiographies are for an understanding of the problems involved, over-dependence on such polemical works can only be expected to result in such conclusions.

A much more reliable basis for research may be found in the historical texts, many of which preserve contemporary documents and fragments of older and more trustworthy accounts; but in their studies of Shīʿa Islam, scholars have seldom turned to these more objective works. For many years, of course, these texts were accessible only in ancient manuscripts preserved in isolated collections scattered throughout the world. And within the works themselves, a passage relevant to our subject may often appear only after the perusal of an entire volume. Now, however, the great upsurge of scholarly interest in the Islamic world in both the East and the West has borne fruit, and the researcher has at his disposal modern critical editions of early sources and a plethora of invaluable reference aids.

In the light of the evidence now available, it is possible to undertake a critical reassessment of the origins and development of Shiʿa Islam. In these pages, therefore, an attempt is made to trace out and reconstruct those earliest tendencies and ideas which gave Shīʿa Islam its distinctive character. As these factors came to focus on the question of religious leadership, our discussion will largely concentrate on the Shīʿī response to this problem, from its origins among a group of early Muslims until the Imamate of Jaʿfar aṣ-Ṣādiq. By this time, all the fundamental elements of Shīʿism had appeared, and were being formulated into what would eventually become the Twelver system of doctrine and legal practice.

My aim has been to reconstruct and present the development of an Islamic ideal—that of a particular vision of religious leadership that first appeared after the Prophet's death—based on the testimony of the historical sources. In this sense my work may be seen as completing itself with Chapter Eight, dealing with the movement of the *Tawwābūn*. Chapter Nine deals with a problem within the Shī'a itself, and here certainly historical sources cannot be of much help. A solid historical foundation can be restored once again with Chapter Ten, which provides a background for the Imamate of Ja'far aṣ-Ṣādiq. The last chapter does not, in fact, mark the culmination of the main theme of this work, but rather offers to the reader an assessment of a developed stage of a concept of religious leadership as it emerged from its rudimentary foundations.

With these few words about the work, it is my pleasant duty to acknowledge the valuable help which has been rendered to me in the preparation of this study. Professor Nicola A. Ziadeh kindly offered me the opportunity to write in his series. Much of the research work involved was made possible by a generous grant from the American University of Beirut. Mr Lawrence I. Conrad rendered patient and perseverant assistance during the course of my work, and Miss Lamia Awad typed the manuscript with diligence and care. Numerous colleagues and friends have read parts of the text and have made valuable comments and suggestions. To all of them I extend my utmost gratitude and sincere thanks.

American University of Beirut SYED HUSAIN M. JAFRI
27th August 1976

Chapter 1

Conceptual Foundations

The division of the community of Islam into Sunnī and Shīʿī branches has commonly been explained in terms of purely political differences. Its origins have been attributed to basically political partisanship with regard to the leadership of the Umma, a partisanship which later exploded into conflict in the civil war between ʿAlī and Muʿāwiya. This war not only established the Umayyads in power, but also supposedly marked the advent of Shīʿism as a religious movement divergent from the main body of believers. Such an interpretation grossly oversimplifies a very complex situation. Those who thus emphasize the political nature of Shīʿism are perhaps too eager to project the modern Western notion of the separation of church and state back into seventh century Arabian society, where such a notion would be not only foreign, but completely unintelligible. Such an approach also implies the spontaneous appearance of Shīʿism rather than its gradual emergence and development within Islamic society. The recent occidental conception of "a purely spiritual movement" is exceptional. Throughout most of human history religion has been intimately involved in the whole life of man in society, and not least in his politics. Even the purely religious teaching of Jesus—as it is commonly regarded—is not without its political relevance.[1]

Just as the Prophet was basically a religious and spiritual teacher and messenger and, at the same time, due to the circumstances, a temporal ruler and statesman, Islam has been since its very birth both a religious discipline and, so to speak, a socio-political movement. It is basically religious because of the status Muḥammad attained as the Apostle of

God appointed and sent by Him to deliver His message to mankind, and political because of the environment and circumstances in which it arose and grew. Likewise Shīʿism, in its inherent nature, has always been both religious and political, and these co-existing aspects are found side by side throughout its history. It is therefore difficult to speak, at any stage of its existence, about the "political" Shīʿa as distinct from the "religious" one. Throughout the first three or four centuries of Islamic religious and institutional development, one cannot fail to see that all religious discussions among Muslims had both political and social relevance. When we analyse different possible relations which the religious beliefs and the political constitution in Islam bear to one another, we find the claims and the doctrinal trends of the supporters of ʿAlī more inclined towards the religious aspects than the political ones; thus it seems paradoxical that the party whose claims were based chiefly on spiritual and religious considerations, as we shall examine in detail presently, should be traditionally labelled as political in origin.

The term Shīʿa, keeping in view its historical development, must strictly be taken throughout this chapter in its literal meaning as followers, party, group, associates, partisans, or in a rather looser sense, the "supporters".[2] In these meanings the word Shīʿa occurs a number of times in the *Qurʾān.*[3] In its applied meaning as a particular designation for the followers of ʿAlī and the people of his house, and thereby a distinct denomination within Islam against the Sunnī, the term Shīʿa was a later usage. In the infant years of Islamic history, one cannot speak of the so-called "orthodox" Sunna and the "heretical" Shīʿa, but rather only of two ill-defined points of view that were nevertheless drifting steadily, and finally irreconcilably, further apart. With this meaning of the term Shīʿa in mind, our main purpose here is to trace the background of this support to ʿAlī and to investigate its origins in the Arabian society of the day in the midst of which Islam arose. Consequently it will be illustrated how this attitude became manifest as early as the death of the Prophet Muḥammad.

The starting point in any study of Shīʿī Islam must, by historical necessity, be the nature and composition of the Muslim community which emerged at Medina under the leadership of Muḥammad. This community was homogeneous neither in cultural background and traditions nor in politico-social institutions. The unification of different people or groups of people in a new system does not imply a complete elimination or even a change in some of their deep-rooted values and traditions. It was therefore natural that certain values, ideas, and inclinations of different component parts of the Umma should reflect themselves in certain aspects of the new religious order. Consequently, rather than a homogeneous approach to all issues, especially of a non-fundamental nature, one must expect to find in the Umma a multiplicity of approaches and points of view, with the acceptance of Muḥammad and his mission being the fundamental factor binding the various groups together.

The inclination of some of the Arabs from among the Companions of the Prophet to support ʿAlī was thus a natural corollary of the already existing ideas prevalent among the various Arab tribes who together constituted Muḥammad's Umma at Medina. This Umma consisted of the Meccans, both from the Quraysh al-Biṭāḥ (those who inhabited the district immediately around the Kaʿba) and Quraysh aẓ-Ẓawāhir (those whose quarters were in the outskirts); of Medinese, who were divided into Aws and Khazraj, both tribes of the South Arabian stock and still preserving many of the characteristics of their original land; of the desert Arabs surrounding Medina; and even of some Arabs and non-Arabs from distant places, such as Bilāl of Abyssinia and Salmān of Persia. All of them together formed a common society under Islam, but when we consider a problem common among them we have to take into consideration the different temperaments and inclinations of each group, and not those of only one single people, group, or locality. We must presume that the Arabs of different origins and socio-cultural backgrounds understood Islam, at least in its early stage, according to their own social and moral ideas.

Arab society, both nomadic and sedentary, was organized on a tribal basis, and of all the social bonds, loyalty to the tribe (*al-ʿaṣabīya*) was considered the most important. This feeling of *al-ʿaṣabīya,* along with other aspects of tribal life, provides the most emphatic expression of and a constant theme for pre-Islamic poetry. The tribal system was based on the actual or fictitious descent from a common ancestor through whom the social and moral status of the members of the tribe was determined. People who could not boast of their ancestors as a symbol of greatness were of little social standing and often subject to contempt. Knowledge and awareness of the common ancestor was therefore the central point in Arab social consciousness, and honour and glory of a tribe in comparison with any other tribe consisted of the honour and glory of its ancestors. Any claim to prestige and honour of the individual members as well as the whole tribe was perhaps exclusively dependent on that of the ancestors. The word used for such claims is *ḥasab,* which is commonly explained by the Arab philologists in the meaning of enumeration of the famous deeds of ancestors.[4] This does not mean that the word *ḥasab* excludes the enumeration of those ancestors themselves who figure in the genealogical tree in both paternal and maternal descent.[5] If the noble deeds of one's ancestors are numerous enough to be cited and boastfully enumerated by their descendants, the richer is their *ḥasab* or *sharaf,* as is evident from a popular expression, *al-ḥasab* or *sharaf al-ḍakham.*[6] This means a nobility which becomes "thicker" and stronger through accumulated noble deeds of ancestors generation after generation.[7] Thus sings the famous Arab poet Nābigha adh-Dhubyānī:

> "His father before him and his father's father
> built the glories of life as models."[8]

A tribe with large numbers but few deeds of fame to its credit coming down from its ancestors was not only of less social standing but also subject to mockery from those who could enumerate more of their ancestors' noble deeds. So we hear from the poet Ḍamra as he says:

> "And the joint stock which they have begotten
> among the race of Saʿd and Mālik:
> but some of the fire-sticks of the tribe fail to light
> and are nothing worth."[9]

In a rigidly tribal system such as that of the Arabs, the fame of ancestors for noble deeds was the foremost source of pride and of claim to superiority. Nobility thus derived, a tribe considered it a constellatory factor in claiming its higher position in relation to other tribes. Within a tribe a particular clan had higher claim to glory, and therefrom to leadership, if its direct line of ancestors was more distinguished by their noble deeds in relation to other clans of the same tribe. This fame of ancestors was not mere genealogical ornament to the descendants but had individual relevance to each man and was of great significance in the claim of individual honour.[10] Thus, for example, Nuʿmān b. al-Mundhir, King of Ḥīra, askedʿ Āmir b. Uḥaymir b. Bahdala, who had claimed the highest rank among all present, "Are you then the noblest of all Arabs in respect of your tribe?" He replied, "The Maʿadd excel in nobility and number, and amongst them the Nizār, and amongst them the Muḍar, and amongst them the Khindif, amongst whom the Tamīm, and amongst these the ʿĀwf, within ʿĀwf the family of Bahdala. He who does not admit this may contest with me."[11]

Not only physical characteristics were considered by the Arabs to be hereditary;[12] they firmly believed that noble qualities as well were inherent in certain stocks. Moral qualities thus being genetically transmitted, the best virtues for an individual were therefore only those which were handed down to him from his noble ancestors. The Arabs made a clear distinction between inherited nobility and nobility claimed only on account of personal merit, the former being a source of great social prestige while the latter was of little consequence. In other words, personal fame and merit counted for little in securing for oneself an exalted position; it was inherited fame and inherited merit which confirmed proper estimation in the society.[13] There are numerous references in pre-Islamic poetry where ancestral nobility and virtues are described as a strong and lofty building which they built for their descendants[14] and which it would be shameful for the latter to destroy.[15] Ancestral fame of nobility and virtuous deeds must therefore be preserved as the strongest and most continuous incentive to be adopted by the descendants. It was in this sense that the term *Sunna* had frequently been used long before Islam.[16] After Islam the institution of *Sunna* remained as forceful as ever, but its content was drastically replaced by the Prophetic *Sunna*. Nevertheless certain trends of the original *Sunna* did persist, at least in certain sections of the Arab-Muslim community.

The most privileged in Arab society, in the midst of which Islam arose, was therefore the one who could boast publicly that he was destined to have ancestors who had nothing undistinguished to leave to him as their *Sunna*. A word commonly used to express the idea of ability to trace moral qualities back to one's noble ancestors is *'irq*, (pl. *a'rāq* and *'urūq*). *'Irq* means root, origin of a man, and its plural *a'rāq* signifies ancestors of a man. Thus frequent expressions of a man's inheritance from noble ancestors are found in phrases such as, "he has an hereditary share in generousness or nobleness,"[17] or "noble blood lifted him up to his ancestors."[18]

It is clear that in the religious sentiments of the Arabs, ancestral piety, noble deeds, and moral qualities as *Sunna* played an important role. The religion of the Arabs, which varied in strength and importance from locality to locality throughout the peninsula, was originally the worship of tribal symbols, which later became identified with certain forces of nature represented by numerous deities. The tribal deity, symbolized in the sacred stone (*nasab*), was called the lord (*rabb*) of its temple. Allāh, the supreme deity of the Meccan sanctuary, was described as *Rabb al-Ka'ba* or *Rabb Hādha al-Bayt.*[19] It is important to note that the word *rabb* often referred not to the deity but to the person in charge of the sanctuary.

There was no organized priestly hierarchy, but certain clans acted as guardians of the sanctuaries. This guardianship passed from one generation to another, together with the reputation for hereditary sanctity.[20] This sanctity, which had its original source in the magical power attributed to the idol which they served, was strictly connected with the idea of nobility of race (*sharaf*) synonymous with the pride of descent from noble ancestors. The nobility of the clan being hereditary, the priestly clans of long standing represented the highest aristocracy in pre-Islamic Arabia. Traces of this sort of aristocracy are to be found in the belief of the Arabs, especially of the South, that members of certain families have a charisma or spiritual power, or *sharaf*. The guardianship of a sanctuary, a "house" (*bayt*), and "honour" (*sharaf*) came to be understood as being inseparable.[21] As a result, priesthood in Arabia was very often combined with tribal leadership, even with kingship. We may go even further by stating that political leadership there was originally of a religious and priestly nature. The South Arabian monarchial institution of the *mukarrib* is a clear proof of the office of the priest-king who embraces at once religious and temporal authority.

The clans of political rulers could have attained the status of great nobility after first acquiring power by political means, but nevertheless, they could not equal the sacerdotal lineages; for example, the kings of Kinda ranked only after the three most noble priestly houses. These three houses, "after the house of Hāshim b. ʿAbd Manāf amongst the Quraysh", were: Az-Zurara b. ʿUdas of the Tamīm, Al-Ḥudhayfa b. Badr of the Fazārī tribe, and Dhū'l-Jaddayn b. ʿAbd Allāh b. Hammām of the Shaybān tribe. "And as far as the Kinda were concerned they were not counted amongst the *ahl-al-buyūtāt,* even though they were the kings."[22]

It is apparent that not only was priestly status the foundation of political leadership, but when the latter was attained by men of non-priestly clans, it imposed upon them religious functions. They were also mediators between men and deities. As a result, the idea of tribal leadership and service to the God became synonymous. Those who led the tribe were of necessity the guardians of the tribal *bayt.* They were the *ahl al-bayt,* the "people of the house", or the *bayt* of such and such a tribe.[23] Together these leading clans formed the noble estate of Arabia, the *buyūtāt al-ʿArab.*[24] Even later, when the meaning of the *ahl al-bayt* became limited to the descendants of the Prophet, the term *Buyūtāt al-ʿArab* survived into later centuries in the sense of the tribal aristocracy and nobility.[25]

It is against this background that we have to consider the status of the Banū Hāshim, not only among the people of Mecca but in a wider circle due to their vast contacts with the people of different places through the yearly fair of ʿUkāẓ and the pilgrimage to the Kaʿba. Some western scholars have sceptically questioned whether the ancestors of Muḥammad were really as important in dignity, nobility, and influence as the sources suggest, and they usually claim that the importance of the Banū Hāshim has in fact been grossly exaggerated. The basis of this doubt is that the ʿAbbāsids were descendants of Hāshim, whereas the rivals whom they ousted, the Umayyads, were the descendants of ʿAbd Shams, and that the latter have been treated unsympathetically by the historians who happened to write under the ʿAbbāsid regime. For this reason, it is claimed that Hāshim and his family, the ancestors of the ʿAbbāsid caliphs, had been given greater prominence in extant histories than they really possessed. This entire hypothesis, however, is open to considerable criticism. Scrutiny of the sources suggests that this has not happened to any appreciable extent, and that there are no grounds for assuming any serious falsification or large scale invention in presenting Muḥammad's ancestry.[26]

There is no need to go as far back as Quṣayy, father of ʿAbd ad-Dār and ʿAbd Manāf, whom unanimous historical testimony presents as the unrivalled supreme authority of Mecca both in religion and in political matters.[27] After the death of Quṣayy, ʿAbd ad-Dār inherited his father's authority, but he died early and his sons were too young to effectively maintain their rights. ʿAbd Manāf, the younger son of Quṣayy, had been the powerful rival of his elder brother and ultimately concentrated some of the chief offices of his father in his person after the death of ʿAbd ad-Dār.[28] Eventually the sons of ʿAbd Manāf inherited their father's influence; among them, Hāshim, though the youngest, was entrusted with the most honourable offices pertaining to the Kaʿba, *ar-rifāda* and *as-siqāya:* providing food and water to the pilgrims.[29] There are no serious grounds to doubt the accounts given by the early tradition that Hāshim achieved great success and glory in his lifetime by his acts of public welfare and by his splendid hospitality extended to the pilgrims visiting the Kaʿba from all parts of Arabia.[30] When Hāshim died, he was replaced by his brother Al-Muṭṭalib. For a short time it seems that the fortunes of the family were declining under the leadership of Al-Muṭṭalib, but they soon recovered under Hāshim's son ʿAbd al-Muṭṭalib, who had been brought up in Medina with his mother and then brought to Mecca by his uncle Al-Muṭṭalib.[31]

The other sons of Hāshim having died without male issue, ʿAbd al-Muṭṭalib took charge of the family's affairs, which meant the *de facto* merger of the Banū Hāshim and Banū ʿAbd al-Muṭṭalib. This is not the place to discuss whether or not the family of Hāshim at that time was as prosperous and influential in Meccan internal affairs as it used to be. The same sources which are too often suspected of being biased in presenting Muḥammad's ancestors in unduly favourable circumstances do not hesitate to relate how ʿAbd al-Muṭṭalib faced serious set-backs at the beginning of his career. The grand offices of *ar-rifāda* and *as-siqāya* secured for the house of Hāshim a commanding and permanent influence, and it seems natural that by the virtue of these offices a widespread fame abroad must have guaranteed to the family at least some regard in Mecca. ʿAbd al-Muṭṭalib seems to have been a man of initiative and energy,[32] necessary prerequisites to become a man of consequence in the Meccan merchant aristocracy. He greatly enhanced his position by restoring the ancient well of Zamzam. In the course of time, he became the chief custodian of the Kaʿba and was also regarded as a renowned judge of the customary law. Because of his position as the sole person in charge of the main services pertaining to the most respected sanctuary of the Peninsula, he became one of the most, if not the most, prominent figures of Mecca. We are told by Ibn Saʿd and Ibn Hishām that "he was the leader of the Quraysh until his death," and that "his greatness in honour (*sharaf*) attained an exalted position which no one from amongst his fathers had reached before him. He commanded great respect and the love of his people."[33]

After ʿAbd al-Muṭṭalib's death, his eldest surviving son Abū Ṭālib inherited his father's position. It seems, however, that Abū Ṭālib did not prove himself to be of that same calibre and energy as his father and grandfathers, and consequently the family lost much of that power and command which it had previously enjoyed in the inner circle of Meccan aristocratic society.[34] Nevertheless it does not necessarily follow that the material decline of the family's fortunes should have deprived it, in the minds of the people, of the memory of their immediate past. The regard for a successor of three or four illustrious generations could not have faded so soon, especially among groups beyond Mecca. The sanctuary of the Kaʿba, a shrine of extreme antiquity, was a highly important and popular centre of worship in the Peninsula,[35] and its offices of *as-siqāya* and *imārat al-bayt* (keeper of the Kaʿba) are noted in the *Qurʾān*.[36] Supplying the pilgrims with water must have been a lucrative job in Mecca, where water is so scarce, and the water of Zamzam, which soon shared in the sacredness of the sanctuary, was required not only by the yearly pilgrims but also by the huge trade caravans halting at Mecca.[37] Many early writers have recorded detailed accounts of the universal influence of the Kaʿba, of the vast contacts of the people of Mecca due to its being a centre for the trade caravans from Yaman in the South, from Dūmat al-Jandal in the extreme North, and from other far-off places, and of the ʿUkāẓ, the greatest of the Arabs' yearly fairs. It is therefore natural that the honorific services attached to the sanctuary and rendered by the house of Hāshim for such a long period must have extended the family's fame and prestige over a very wide area as the pilgrims and the caravans left Mecca. We can thus conclude that at the time of Muḥammad's emergence, his family must have retained the glory and memory of the long-standing sacerdotal lineage of Hāshim even though the family's material and political fortunes were at a low ebb at that time. Psychologically at least, the works and deeds of three generations cannot be obliterated from the consciousness of the people abroad by the sudden decline in wealth and political power of the present generation at Mecca. The Banū Hāshim were commonly recognized by the Arabs as the guardians of the Temple, the *Ahl al-Bayt*, of Mecca.[38]

It was in this family background that Muḥammad arose as the Messenger of God and restorer of the true religious *Sunna* of Abraham and Ishmael[39] which had been corrupted and distorted by the people through the ages. Abraham was not only recognized by the Arabs as their tribal father and progenitor but was also acknowledged by them as the founder of the sanctuary of the Kaʿba and of Mecca. This tradition was no Muslim legend. If it had not been an accepted truth long before Muḥammad's time, it could not have been referred to in the *Qurʾān* as an acknowledged fact; nor could certain spots around the pre-Islamic Kaʿba have been connected, as we know them to have been, with the names of Abraham and Ishmael.[40] Muḥammad was fully conscious of this popular and deep-rooted tradition of Abraham's association with the Kaʿba, with which the Arabs in general and Muḥammad's four generations of predecessors in particular were so closely linked. Ibn Khaldūn points out that it was regarded as something extraordinary and most honourable if the leadership continued in one and the same family for four generations.[41]

All the factors discussed above combine to form an inseparable background against which the problem of succession to Muḥammad has to be considered. As has been pointed out above, this problem must not be considered only from the point of view of seventh century Meccan society, for the Umma of Muḥammad at the time of his death was composed of people of a variety of background, values, and ideas, drawn from different parts of Arabia. It was, therefore, natural that different people should view the problem from different angles. The way in which the problem of succession was solved in the assembly of Saqīfa between the death and the burial of the Prophet will be discussed below. It will suffice here to note in passing that the decision taken in Saqīfa was also in conformity with the common practice and ancient tradition of the Arabs, at least of one important group from among them.

The two main constituent groups of the Umma at the time of Muḥammad's death were the Arabs of northern and central Arabia, of whom the tribe of the Quraysh was the most important and dominant, and the people of South Arabian origin, the Banū Qayla, whose two major branches, the Aws and the Khazraj, were settled in Yathrib. They were known as the *Anṣār*, or "helpers", because they gave Muḥammad and Islam a shelter and a home at the most critical moment of the Prophet's mission. Differences in almost all aspects of life—social, cultural, economic, religious, geographical, and even presumably racial and ancestral—between the Arabs of the South and the North are too well known to need elaboration here at length. Goldziher,[42] Wellhausen,[43] Nicholson,[44] and many other outstanding scholars have thoroughly studied the subject in depth. It should, however, be pointed out that to consider all the Arabs as one single cultural group is a grave mistake. They had never been so. The North was cut off from the centre by the desert as the South was separated from the rest of Arabia by the Rubʿ al-Khālī. Widely different geographical and economic conditions played their inevitable and natural role in every aspect of development of the two kindred races. The Arabs of northern and central Arabia, the Ḥijāz, and the highlands of Najd, developed along different lines from the southern Arabs of Al-Yaman in character, way of life, and socio-political and socio-religious institutions. As in all other aspects of life, the two groups differed widely from each other in religious sensitivity and feelings. Among the people of the much more advanced and civilized provinces of South Arabia there was a clear predominance of religious ideas, whereas among the people of the North religious sentiments were evidently lacking. A South Arabian prince, for example, in his votive inscriptions thanked the gods who made him victorious over his enemies, and warriors erected votive memorials to their divine helper for any success they achieved. In general the thankful and submissive feeling towards the gods is the basic theme of the existent South Arabian monuments. In sharp contrast to this, the warriors of northern Arabia boasted of their heroic courage and the bravery of their companions. They did not feel obliged to thank divine powers for their success, though they did not altogether refuse to acknowledge such powers.[45] Even the scanty traces of lukewarm religious sentiments amongst the northern Arabs cannot be dissociated from the influence of the southern Arabs settled down in the North.[46] This difference in religious sentiments was naturally reflected in their pattern of tribal leadership. The chiefs or the sheikhs in the North had always been elected on a principle of seniority in age and ability in leadership. There might sometimes be other considerations, such as nobility and lineal prestige, but in the North these were of less importance. The Arabs in the South were, on the other hand, accustomed to hereditary succession in leadership based on hereditary sanctity. Because of this fact the South Arabian tribes of the Aws and the Khazraj at Yathrib presented an atmosphere more easily conducive to the religious thought which was of great importance in Muḥammad's success. Thus we may assume that the majority of the North Arabians understood Islam, at least at the first stage of their acceptance of it, as a socio-political discipline based on the religion taught by the Prophet, since they had been lukewarm to religious impulses. The Aws and the Khazraj, South Arabian in origin, understood Islam as basically a religious discipline coupled with a socio-political movement, since in their cultural past, though remote, they had been more sensitive to religion. It was only a matter of emphasis in approach and understanding, at least at the first spontaneous response.

When the Prophet died the question of his succession was therefore understood to combine in it both political and religious leadership, a principle well known to the Arabs though naturally with different degrees of emphasis on one or the other of these two aspects. To some it was more political than religious; to others it was more religious than political. The majority of the Muslims, who readily accepted Abū Bakr, laid more emphasis on the socio-political side in accepting the customary procedure of succession to the chieftainship in its new interpretation given by the first caliph, as we shall examine below. They largely, if not solely, disregarded the religious principle and the idea of the hereditary sanctity of a certain house. This assumption is strongly supported by the statement of ʿUmar b. al-Khaṭṭāb to Ibn ʿAbbās, "The people do not like having the prophethood and caliphate combined in the Banū Hāshim."[47] We must assume that both ʿUmar and Abū Bakr were well aware of the importance which the idea of inherited sanctity held in one section of the Umma. At the same time they must have realized that should the election of Abū Bakr be open to doubt, the unity of the Umma would be seriously endangered. They nevertheless considered it necessary to dissociate the caliphate from the priesthood of the Kaʿba, which was enshrined in the hereditary sanctity of the Banū Hāshim.

There were others, especially of South Arabian origin, who felt that in Mecca leadership, together with priestly prerogatives, was inherited in the clan of ʿAbd Manāf by the Hāshimites,[48] though after the death of ʿAbd al-Muṭṭalib they were overshadowed by the clan of Umayya in political matters. The rise of Muḥammad as the Prophet of God and the supreme authority in Arabia again brought the Banū Hāshim to power, a fact acknowledged by Abū Sufyān's surrender to the Prophet at the fall of Mecca. To some of the Companions, therefore, a normal logical choice of successor would have been another Hāshimite, and the entire question of succession to the leadership of the Muslim community was, for them, a problem of great religious significance. In addition to political expediency, deep-rooted religious considerations had to be taken into account by certain of the Companions. These, whom we may call more legalistically minded individuals, could not agree to the interpretation given by Abū Bakr and his supporters, because, as we shall see below, they understood the leadership of the community as above all a religious office. To them Muḥammad was the restorer of the true religion of Abraham and Ishmael, and so in him the hereditary sanctity of his clan reached its highest level. This idea was also strongly supported by the *Qur'ān* when it declared, for example, "Verily, God has chosen Adam and Noah, the family of Abraham and the family of ʿImrān above all people."[49] The commentators have all unanimously explained that Muḥammad belonged to the "family of Abraham" referred to in this verse. Thus when he died his successor could only be a man from the same family and endowed with the same qualities by the same principles.

In this respect, there must be noted the Qur'ānic concept of the exalted and virtuous family, whose favour in the eyes of God derives from their righteous deeds and services in the cause of God. In all ages the prophets have been particularly concerned with ensuring that the special favour of God bestowed upon them for the guidance of man be maintained in their families and pass to their progeny. The *Qur'ān* repeatedly speaks of the prophets praying to God for their progeny and asking Him to continue His guidance in their lineages. In the answer to these prayers, the verses of the *Qur'ān* bear direct testimony to the special favour of God being granted to the direct descendants of the prophets to keep their fathers' covenants intact, to become true examples of their fathers' righteousness, and to keep fast to the path of righteousness set by these prophets. Four terms are repeatedly used in the *Qur'ān* to express God's special favour for the descendants of the prophets: *Dhurrīya, Āl, Ahl,* and *Qurbā.*

The word *Dhurrīya,* meaning offspring, progeny, or direct descendant, has been used in thirty-two verses of the *Qur'ān.* It is used either in direct connection with the prophets' own concern that their children should remain on their path or that their work of guidance should be continued through their own progeny. Often the word is used in verses where the prophets claim that God had selected them to become models of righteousness based on their direct descent from other prophets. This concern for a prophet's progeny is reflected in a verse (II, 124) where Abraham was told by God: "I will make you an Imam of the people." Whereupon Abraham pleads, "And what about my offspring (*Dhurrīyatī*)?" God replies, "My covenant will not go to evildoers." In a similar verse (XIV, 37) Abraham prays to God:

> "Oh my Lord God! I have made some of my offspring to dwell in a valley without cultivation by the Sacred House, in order, Oh Lord, that they may establish regular prayer: so fill the hearts of some among men with love towards them and feed them with fruits: so that they may give thanks."

This prayer is favourably answered when God declares (XIX, 58):

> "There are they on whom God bestowed His bounties from the prophets of the posterity of Adam; and of those whom we carried with Noah [in the Ark] and of the posterity (*Dhurrīya*) of Abraham and Israel and of those whom we guided and chose."

The term *Āl*, meaning nearer or nearest relations by descent from the same father or ancestor or a man's family or kinsmen, is used in the *Qur'ān* twenty-six times in connection with the descendants of the prophets or those who succeeded them in guidance and special favour from God. A verse describing Muḥammad as belonging to the descendants of Abraham has been quoted above. In another verse (IV, 54) we read:

> "Or do they envy the people for what God has given them of His grace: But indeed we have given to Abraham's children (*Āl Ibrāhīm*) the book and the wisdom and we gave them a great kingdom."

The word *Ahl*, which is used many times in the *Qur'ān*, has almost the same meaning as *Āl*, though it is also used in a broader sense in referring to the people of a town or inhabitation, a group, or followers. When used in conjunction with the term *bayt*: *Ahl al-bayt*, it refers to the immediate descendants of a family or such a family of the same "house", or *bayt*. In this compound form, *Ahl al-bayt* is used in the

Qur'ān especially in reference to the immediate family of Muḥammad. In verse XXXIII, 33, we hear:

> "And God only wishes to remove from you [all kinds of] uncleanliness, O members of the family [of Muḥammad] and thoroughly purify you."

All the commentators of the *Qur'ān* are unanimous in the opinion that the term *Ahl al-bayt* in this verse refers to Muḥammad's daughter Fāṭima, his cousin and son-in-law ʿAlī, and his two beloved grandsons, Ḥasan and Ḥusayn.

The fourth term, *Qurbā* (from the root *qaruba*, nearness), means near or blood relationship, relatives, or kinsmen. As is the case with the term *Ahl al-bayt*, the term *Qurbā* was also used specifically for the immediate relatives of Muḥammad. Thus the *Qur'ān* (XLII, 23) reads:

> "That is the bounty whereof God gives glad tidings to his servants who believe and do righteous deeds.
>
> "Say, [O Muḥammad] I do not ask any reward from you for this [apostleship] except the love of [my] relatives."

Commenting on this verse, the commentators are again unanimous in their opinion that the word *Qurbā* refers to Muḥammad's relatives—Fāṭima, ʿAlī, Ḥasan, and Ḥusayn. The only point of disagreement arises in that the Sunnī commentators include the wives of the Prophet, whereas the Shīʿī writers do not.

The total number of verses that mention special favour requested for and granted to the families of the various prophets by God runs to over a hundred in the *Qur'ān*. From this we may draw two conclusions. If one accepts the axiom that the *Qur'ān* was revealed in terms understandable in the cultural atmosphere of seventh-century Arabia, then it is obvious that the idea of the sanctity of a prophet's family was a commonly accepted principle at that time. Even more important is the fact that the *Qur'ān's* constant repetition of this idea must have left the impression among some of the Muslims that Muḥammad's family had a religious prerogative over others.

Neither Banū Taym b. Murra, the clan of Abū Bakr, nor Banū ʿAdī b. Kaʿb, the people of ʿUmar, had ever been regarded with esteem on any religious grounds, thus those who laid stress on the religious principle could not accept them as candidates for succession to Muḥammad. The candidate could come only from the Banū Hāshim, and amongst them the figure of ʿAlī was by far the most prominent. He too was the great-grandson of Hāshim and the grandson of ʿAbd al-Muṭṭalib. He was the son of Abū Ṭāliḅ, Muḥammad's uncle, who had given the Prophet the care and love of the father Muḥammad had lost before birth. ʿAlī was the nearest and closest associate of Muḥammad, for the Prophet had acted as his guardian during the famine of Mecca, and he had subsequently adopted him as a brother both before the Hijra and again in Medina.[50] He was the first male to embrace Islam,[51] Khadīja being the first woman. He was also the husband of Fāṭimá, the Prophet's only surviving daughter, and by her fathered two of the Prophet's grandsons, Al-Ḥasan and Al-Ḥusayn, both of whom Muḥammad loved dearly.

It seems that these inherent personal qualities and virtues secured ʿAlī a unique and advantageous place over all other family members and companions of Muḥammad, and earned him a group of friends who were devoted to him with a special zeal and consideration even during the lifetime of the Prophet. Perhaps it is because of this that the Shīʿa claim the existence of Shīʿism even in the lifetime of the Prophet; the earliest heresiographers, Saʿd al-Ashʿarī and An-Nawbakhtī, clearly state that Shīʿism (in the sense of a particular regard and appreciation of ʿAlī's personal merits) had already appeared in Muḥammad's lifetime.[52] Moreover, this idea of ʿAlī's superior qualifications for the caliphate was further strengthened by a series of events which took place during the Prophet's life in which he showed some special consideration for ʿAlī. A few of these should be pointed out as illustrations of ʿAlī's growth in prestige and favour:

1 At the very beginning of his mission, when the verse "Warn your tribe, the nearest kinsmen" (XXVI, 214) was revealed (about three years after Muḥammad's first revelation and the conversion of Khadīja, ʿAlī, and Abū Bakr), the Prophet gathered all the Banū ʿAbd al-Muṭṭalib and informed them of his mission. Explaining his task, he asked for support and help in furthering the cause. Instead of assistance, the Prophet received only ridicule; the only exception was ʿAlī, who,

though only thirteen years old, gave the Prophet his enthusiastic support.[53]

2 The prerogative of the religious brotherhood between ʿAlī and Muḥammad, which has already been mentioned above, must be taken into special account in this series of events. The Prophet adopted ʿAlī as his brother in faith (*ukhūwwa*) both before the Hijra and again in Medina. This was such a recognized historical fact that no historian has denied it.

3 ʿAlī's position can only have been elevated in the eyes of the Companions when he was appointed by Muḥammad as the standard bearer at both Badr and Khaybar and in other wars.[54]

4 The nomination of ʿAlī by the Prophet as his deputy at Medina during the expedition to Tabūk was another important record to ʿAlī's credit.[55] It was on this occasion that the famous tradition is reported in which Muḥammad said to ʿAlī, "You are to me what Aaron was to Moses except that there will be no Prophet after me."[56] This tradition attached to the event of Tabūk has been recorded by almost all historians and traditionists, and when we see that Muḥammad was referring to many similarities in his person and mission with other great prophets of the past, we find no difficulty in accepting this tradition. In one of the several Qur'ānic passages dealing with this subject (XX, 29–32), Moses asks of God: "And give me a minister from my family, Aaron, my brother; add to my strength through him, and make him share my task." Muḥammad's comparison of himself with Moses would thus have been incomplete without an Aaron, and obviously no other person in his family but ʿAlī could serve him as Aaron.

5 Yet another very important event was the communication of the chapter of *al-Bara'a* (*Qur'ān*, IX). In the ninth year of the Hijra, the Prophet sent Abū Bakr to lead the people in the *Hajj*. After Abū Bakr's departure to Mecca the chapter of *Bara'a* was revealed to the Prophet to communicate to the people, especially to the polytheists. When people asked the Prophet whether he would dispatch the chapter to Abū Bakr to deliver it on his behalf, he replied, "No, I will not send it except through someone from amongst the people of my family (*rajul-un min ahli baytī*)." The Prophet then called 'Alī and ordered him to take his own camel and go to Mecca at

once and deliver the Qur'ānic message to the people on his behalf.[57]

There are no serious grounds to doubt the authenticity of these events, which have been recorded by writers of all schools of thought and which also seem plausible in their context. Even if one is inclined to extreme caution and scepticism, it cannot be denied that these events in favour of ʿAlī were in such wide circulation that the majority of historians and traditionists from the earliest times had to record them. In this series of events, the famous but controversial tradition of Ghadīr Khum, upon which the Shīʿa place the utmost importance, has been intentionally ignored. This event is named after a place called Ghadīr Khum, a pool or a marsh with some shady trees, situated only a few miles from Mecca on the road to Medina, from where people disperse to their different destinations. When Muḥammad was returning from his Farewell Pilgrimage he stopped at Ghadīr Khum on 18 Dhū'l-Ḥijja (10 March 632) to make an announcement to the pilgrims who accompanied him from Mecca and who were to disperse from this junction. By the orders of the Prophet, a special dais or pulpit made of branches of the trees was erected for him. After the noon prayer the Prophet sat on the pulpit and made his last public address to the largest gathering before his death three months later. Taking ʿAlī by the hand, Muḥammad asked his followers whether he was not superior in authority and person (*awlā*) to the believers themselves. The crowd cried out in one voice: "It is so, O Apostle of God." He then declared: "He of whom I am the *mawlā* [the patron, master, leader, friend?], of him ʿAlī is also the *mawlā* (*man kuntu mawlāhu fa ʿAlī-un mawlāhu*). O God, be the friend of him who is his friend, and be the enemy of him who is his enemy (*Allāhumma wāli man wālāhu wa ʿādi man ʿādāhu*)."

As far as the authenticity of the event itself is concerned, it has hardly ever been denied or questioned even by the most conservative Sunnī authorities, who have themselves recorded it. Most noteworthy among them are Imam Aḥmad b. Ḥanbal in his *Musnad*, Tirmidhī, Nasā'ī, Ibn Māja, Abū Dā'ūd and almost all other *Sunan* writers, Ibn al-Athīr in his *Usd al-Ghāba*, Ibn ʿAbd al-Barr in his *Istīʿāb*, followed by all other writers of biographical works and even Ibn ʿAbd Rabbih in his *ʿIqd al-Farīd*, and Jāḥiẓ in his *ʿUthmānīyya*.[58] The traditions of Ghadīr are so abundantly reported and so commonly attested by hundreds of different transmitters belonging to all schools of thought that it would be futile to doubt their authenticity. Ibn Kathīr,[59] a most staunch supporter of the Sunnī viewpoint, has devoted seven pages to this subject and has collected a great number of different *isnāds* from which the tradition is narrated. It is also Ibn Kathīr who informs us that the famous historian aṭ-Ṭabarī, in a two-volume unfinished work entitled *Kitāb al-Faḍā'il* (mentioned also by Yāqūt in his *Irshād*, VI, p. 452), wrote in full details the Prophet's discourse in favour of ʿAlī at Ghadīr Khum. A modern scholar, Ḥusayn ʿAlī Maḥfūẓ, in his penetrating researches on the subject of Ghadīr Khum, has recorded with documentation that this tradition has been narrated by at least 110 Companions, 84 *tābiʿūn*, 355 *ʿulamā'*, 25 historians, 27 traditionists, 11 exegesists, 18 theologians, and 5 philologists.[60] Most of them were later counted by the Sunnīs as among their own number.

Horovitz[61] and Goldziher,[62] in their studies on the tradition of Ghadīr Khum, state that the oldest evidence of this tradition is the verses of Kumayt (died 126/743–4), which they consider undoubtedly genuine. The refusal of these two scholars to accept any evidence before Kumayt is based on their sceptical assumption that the verses of the Prophet's poet, Ḥassān b. Thābit, composed on the spot, might not be genuine. However, the Shīʿī sources, and also some of the Sunnī authorities, claim that the oldest evidence is the verse of Ḥassān b. Thābit, which the poet, with the Prophet's approbation, instantly composed and recited[63] when the people were congratulating ʿAlī on the occasion. Keeping in view the fact that Ḥassān was accompanying the Prophet at his historical first pilgrimage after the migration, and the fact that the poet used to compose and recite verses on all noteworthy occasions of the Prophet's activities, it is highly improbable that this event should have passed unrecorded by Ḥassān, the official poet-reporter of Muḥammad.

The event is, however, not recorded by some of those sources which are commonly used for the study of the life of the Prophet, such as Ibn Hishām, Ṭabarī, and Ibn Saʿd. They either pass in silence over Muḥammad's stop at Ghadīr Khum, or, if they mention it, say nothing of this tradition. Veccia Vaglieri explains the attitude of these few writers in that they "evidently feared to attract the hostility of the Sunnīs, who were in power, by providing material for the polemic of the Shīʿīs, who used these words to support their thesis of ʿAlī's right to the caliphate. Consequently, the western biographers of Muḥammad, whose work is based on these sources, equally make no reference to what happened at Ghadīr Khum. It is, however, certain that Muḥammad did speak in this place and utter the famous sentence, for the account of this event has been preserved, either in concise form or in detail, not only by Yaʿqūbī, whose sympathy for the ʿAlid cause is well known, but also in the collections of traditions which are considered as canonical, especially in the *Musnad* of Ibn Ḥanbal; and the *ḥadīths* are so numerous and so well attested by the different *isnāds* that it does not seem possible to reject them."[64]

The bone of contention between the Sunnīs and the Shīʿīs is not, however, and never has been, the authenticity of the event of Ghadīr Khum, nor the declaration of the Prophet in favour of ʿAlī, as quoted above; the real disagreement is in the meaning of the word *mawlā* used by the Prophet. The Shīʿa unequivocally take the word in the meaning of leader, master, and patron, and therefore the explicitly nominated successor of the Prophet. The Sunnīs, on the other hand, interpret the word *mawlā* in the meaning of a friend, or the nearest kin and confidant.[65] No doubt the richness of meaning of many an Arabic word and the resulting ambiguity does render both the interpretations equally valid. The Sunnīs, while accepting the tradition, assert that in that sentence the Prophet simply meant to exhort his followers to hold his cousin and the husband of his only surviving daughter in high esteem and affection. Further, the Sunnīs explain the circumstance which necessitated the Prophet's exhortation in that some people were murmuring against ʿAlī due to his harsh and indifferent treatment in the distribution of the spoils of the expedition of Al-Yaman, which had just taken place under ʿAlī's leadership, and from where he, along with those who participated in the expedition, directly came to Mecca to join the Prophet at the Ḥajj. To dispel these ill-feelings against his son-in-law, the

Prophet spoke in this manner.[66] Accepting this explanation as such, the fact still remains that this declaration of the Prophet in such an extraordinary manner, equating ʿAlī in authority and person with himself, does provide a strong basis for the Shīʿī claims.

Taking for granted the controversial character in interpretation of the Ghadīr tradition, the events mentioned above could have been understood by some of the Prophet's Companions as indicative of his inclination towards ʿAlī, though he did not or could not nominate him explicitly, perhaps because of the old North Arabian custom of leaving the selection of a leader to the people. A commonly suggested obstacle in the way of ʿAlī is said to have been his comparatively young age at the time of Muḥammad's death. However, our sources do not fail to point out that, though the "Senate" (*Nadwa*) of pre-Islamic Mecca was generally a council of elders only, the sons of the chieftain Quṣayy were privileged to be exempted from this age restriction and were admitted to the council despite their youth. In later times more liberal concessions seem to have been in vogue; Abū Jahl was admitted despite his youth, and Ḥākim b. Ḥazm was admitted when he was only fifteen or twenty years old.[67] Ibn ʿAbd Rabbih tells us, "There was no monarchic king over the Arabs of Mecca in the Jahilīya. So whenever there was a war, they took a ballot among chieftains and elected one as 'King', were he a minor or a grown man. Thus on the day of Fijār, it was the turn of the Banū Hāshim, and as a result of the ballot Al-ʿAbbās, who was then a mere child, was elected, and they seated him on the shield."[68] At the time of Muḥammad's death ʿAlī was at least thirty-three years old, though in some other sources his age is given as thirty-six.

In conclusion, the idea that the question of the succession was primarily religious, rather than merely political, the popular notion of the hereditary sanctity of the Banū Hāshim, coupled with the events which took place during the lifetime of the Prophet in favour of ʿAlī, led to the crystallization of a point of view concerning the succession to the leadership of the community in which a number of Muḥammad's Companions felt that ʿAlī was the most suitable person to keep the covenant intact. In the heated debates of the Saqīfa incident, right after the Prophet's death, these Companions did not hesitate to voice their opinions. The resulting disagreement, to which we now turn, marks the beginning of what was eventually to develop into a permanent division of the Umma into Sunnī and Shīʿī.

Notes to Chapter 1

[1] W. Montgomery Watt, *Islamic Political Thought* (Edinburgh, 1968), p. 26

[2] See Lane, *Lexicon,* IV, pp. 1632 f.

[3] e.g. XIX, 69; XXVIII, 15; XXXVII, 83

[4] Ibn Qutayba, *Rasā'il al-Bulaghā'*, p. 360

[5] *Aghānī,* I, p. 45

[6] *Aghānī,* I, p. 72; Yāqūt, *Mu'jam al-Buldān,* III, p. 519

[7] *Aghānī,* X, p. 300

[8] *Dīwān an-Nābhiga adh-Dhubyānī,* ed. Shukrī Fayṣal (Beirut, 1968), p. 165

[9] *Mufaḍḍalīyāt,* XCIII, v. 14

[10] *Mufaḍḍalīyāt,* XXXI, v. 4: "By God, my cousin, thou art not better in stock than I, (*Lā afḍalta fī ḥasabī*)"

[11] Ibn Qutayba, op. cit., p. 348; *'Iqd,* III, p. 332

[12] *Aghānī,* I, p. 31

[13] 'Amr b. Kulthūm, *Mu'allaqa,* vv. 40, 52, 55; *Mufaḍḍalīyāt,* XL, v. 44; LXXXVII, v. 2; Zuhayr b. Abī Salma, *Mu'allaqa,* v, p. 26; *Aghānī,* X, p. 300

[14] Labīd, *Mu'allaqa,* v. 83; 'Amr b. Kulthūm, *Mu'allaqa,* v. 52

[15] *Aghānī,* XXII, p. iii

[16] Labīd, op. cit., v. 81

[17] Lane, *Lexicon,* V, pp. 2020 ff.

[18] Yāqūt, op. cit., III, p. 471

[19] *Qur'ān,* CVI, 3

[20] Ibn Hishām, I, p. 126; *'Iqd,* III, p. 333

[21] On this see R. B. Serjeant's "Ḥaram and Ḥawṭah, The Sacred Enclave in Arabia", in *Mélanges Ṭāḥa Ḥusain,* ed. 'Abd al-Raḥmān Badawī (Cairo, 1962), pp. 42 f.; and "The Saiyids of Haḍramawt", *BSOAS,* XXI (London, 1957); also Ibn Durayd, *Ishtiqāq,* p. 173

[22] Ibn Durayd, op. cit., p. 238; *Aghānī,* XIX, p. 128; *Iqd,* III, pp. 331 ff.

[23] Ibn Hishām, I, pp. 143, 145; *'Iqd,* III, pp. 313, 333 ff.; Ibn Durayd, loc. cit.; Serjeant, "Ḥaram and Ḥawṭah", p. 43

[24] *EI*² articles "Ahl al-Bayt" and "Buyūtāt al-'Arab"

[25] Serjeant, loc. cit.

[26] See W. Montgomery Watt, *Muḥammad at Mecca* (Oxford, 1953), p. 31; Serjeant, "The Saiyids of Haḍramawt", p. 7

[27] Ibn Hishām, I, pp. 131 ff.; Azraqī, *Akhbār Makkah,* I, pp. 64 ff.; Ibn Sa'd, I, pp. 69 ff.; *'Iqd,* III, pp. 312 f.

[28] Ibn Saʿd, I, p. 74. Azraqī, *Akhbār,* I, p. 66, states that ʿAbd Manāf possessed not only *ar-rifāda* and *al-siqāya,* but also *al-qiyāda,* leadership of Mecca.

[29] Ibn Hishām, I, pp. 143 f.; Ibn Saʿd, I, p. 78. Azraqī, *Akhbār,* I, p. 67, says that after ʿAbd Manāf, the offices of *ar-rifāda* and *as-siqāya* passed to Hāshim, and that of *al-qiyāda* was given to ʿAbd Shams.

[30] Ibn Hishām, loc. cit.; Ibn Saʿd, loc. cit.

[31] Ibn Hishām, I, pp. 145 f.; Ibn Saʿd, I, pp. 81 ff.

[32] Cf. Montgomery Watt, *Muḥammad at Mecca,* p. 31

[33] Ibn Saʿd, I, p. 85; Ibn Hishām, I, p. 150

[34] Cf. *EI*² article "Abū Ṭālib"

[35] A recurrent theme in the *Qurʾān,* best illustrated in II, 126–7

[36] IX, 19

[37] See Muḥammad Ḥamīdullāh, "The City State of Mecca", *IC,* XII (1938), p. 266

[38] Ibn Hishām, I, p. 145; Ṭabarī, I, pp. 2786 f.

[39] *Qurʾān,* II, 135–7

[40] ibid., II, 125

[41] Ibn Khaldūn, *Proleg.,* I, p. 289. Cf. Von Kremer, *Staatsidee des Islam*; trans. Khuda Bukhsh, *Politics in Islam* (Lahore, 1920), p. 10

[42] *Muhammedanische Studien,* trans. S. M. Stern and C. R. Barber, *Muslim Studies* (London, 1967), I, pp. 79–100

[43] *The Arab Kingdom and Its Fall,* trans. M. Weir (Calcutta, 1927), *passim*

[44] *A Literary History of the Arabs* (Cambridge, 1969), pp. 1 ff.

[45] Goldziher, *Muslim Studies,* I, pp. 12–13

[46] ibid., p. 14

[47] Ṭabarī, I, p. 2769 f.

[48] Most of the supporters of ʿAlī in the early disagreement over the caliphate were of South Arabian origin and were quite clear in their defence of ʿAlī's claims on religious grounds.

[49] III, 33

[50] Ibn Hishām, I, pp. 262 f.; II, pp. 150 f.; Balādhurī, I, p. 270; Ibn Ḥabīb, *Muḥabbar,* p. 70

[51] According to Ibn Isḥāq, ʿAlī was ten years old at the time when Muḥammad received his first revelation and was the first who prayed with the Prophet and Khadīja (Ibn Hishām, I, p. 262; Balādhurī, I, p. 112). Those comparatively few early writers who mention Abū Bakr as the first Muslim among men do so because of ʿAlī's young age. See *Istīʿāb,* III, pp. 1090 ff., which gives numerous traditions with different *isnāds* supporting the view that ʿAlī was the first male to accept Islam and to pray with Muḥammad, whereas Abū Bakr was the first to publicly announce his Islam.

[52] Saʿd al-Ashʿarī, *Firaq,* p. 15; Nawbakhtī, *Firaq,* p. 23

[53] Masʿūdī, *Murūj*, II, p. 277. Also see commentaries of Ṭabarī, Ibn Kathīr, and Thaʿlabī under verse 214, *Sūra* XXVI

[54] Ibn Hishām, II, p. 264; III, p. 349; *Istīʿāb*, III, p. 1097; *ʿIqd*, IV, p. 312

[55] Ibn Hishām, IV, p. 163

[56] Ibn Hishām, loc. cit.; Bukhārī, *Ṣaḥīḥ*, II, p. 194; Nawbakhtī, *Firaq*, p. 19; *ʿIqd*, IV, p. 311; *Istīʿāb*, III, pp. 1099 f.

[57] Ibn Hishām, IV, p. 190 (repeated by the majority of historians and traditionists)

[58] See Veccia Vaglieri, *EI*[2] Art. "Ghadīr Khum", where there are mentioned exact references to all of the above works except *ʿIqd*, IV, p. 311

[59] *Al-Bidāya wa 'l-Nihāya* (Cairo, 1348–51 AH), V, pp. 208–14

[60] *Ta'rīkh ash-Shīʿa* (Karbala, n.d.), p. 77. In modern times numerous voluminous works on Ghadīr Khum have appeared, thus Amīnī's *Al-Ghadīr* in 38 volumes, and Al-Mūsawī's *ʿAbāqāt al-Anwār*, in 34 volumes; all dealing with the *rijāl* of the tradition.

[61] *EI*[1] article "Kumayt"

[62] Cf. *EI*[2] article "Ghadīr Khum", Bibliography

[63] Amīnī, *Ghadīr*, II, p. 32; also see ʿĀmilī, *Āʿyān ash-Shīʿa*, III/i, pp. 524–32

[64] *EI*[2] article "Ghadīr Khum"

[65] Ibn Kathīr, loc. cit.

[66] ibid.

[67] Azraqī, *Akhbār Makkah*, I, p. 65; Ibn Durayd, *Ishtiqāq*, p. 97

[68] *ʿIqd*, III, p. 315

Chapter 2

Saqīfa: The First Manifestations

In any attempt to determine the origins of Shīʿī feelings in Islam, one must try to examine in detail the earliest incident in which such feelings manifest themselves. The history of a people in every branch, be it political, cultural, religious, or constitutional, is an unbroken continuity. No religious or political organization nor any particular viewpoint within a religious tradition can be properly understood without due reference to its first tangible appearance.

Historically the event of the Saqīfa is inextricably connected with the emergence of the Shīʿī viewpoint. The Saqīfa, after which the event is named, was an old assembly hall in Medina where the people used to discuss and resolve their crucial problems. It was there that, as soon as the news of the Prophet's death came out, the people of Medina gathered together to choose their leader. It was there that a group of Muhājirūn forced on the Anṣār their wish for the acceptance of Abū Bakr as the sole leader of the community. In this meeting at the Saqīfa, some voices were raised in support of ʿAlī's claims to the caliphate; thus "Saqīfa" should be taken as a generic name for the first split among the Muslims. To ignore it in tracing out Shīʿī history and subsequent development in Islam would certainly lead to misunderstanding and wrong conclusions. It is thus an historical imperative to examine the proceedings of the Saqīfa and attempt to ascertain the points raised therein which ultimately found expression in the establishment of the Shīʿī discipline in Islam.

A characteristic historiographical problem has to be seriously taken into consideration before any attempt can be made to outline the Saqīfa incident. One may well question the authenticity of the reports in ascertaining the exact details of what occurred in the selection of the first successor of the Prophet. The controversial nature of the subject itself and the difficulty inherent in the source material make the task of this investigation far from easy. This difficulty becomes still more serious when we note that the earliest extant report on the event was committed to systematic writing not before the first half of the second century of Islam, and during the reign of the first two ʿAbbāsid caliphs. This was the time when the division of the Muslim community into Shīʿī and Sunnī groupings had set deep into the hearts of Muslims, and both camps were accusing each other of deviation from the true path of Islam. In these circumstances it seems quite possible that the different reports describing the proceedings of Abū Bakr's selection would have been circulated from different quarters according to their respective interests. One might, therefore, suspect the reports of the historians of Shīʿī sympathies such as Ibn Isḥāq, Yaʿqūbī, and Masʿūdī as being biased in favour of the Shīʿīs; and similarly the writings of Ibn Saʿd, Balādhurī, and even Ṭabarī as reporting in Sunnī colour. Nevertheless, a close scrutiny of all early sources named above shows that the event of the Saqīfa is reported, in its broad outline and essential points, in very similar ways, with of course some differences in details, in treatment of the material, and in emphasis on one report or the other. These differences are clearly indicative of the inclinations of the respective writers or their informants towards one side or the other, and can be discerned, though not without some difficulty. Similarly those reports of the very few writers who take extreme positions to support one particular view can also be easily distinguished when compared with other accounts.

For a study of this nature, it would be most appropriate to extract and examine the earliest known coherent tradition as a basis for comparison with accounts recorded by other writers. The earliest extant work which reports the Saqīfa episode is that of Muḥammad b. Isḥāq b. Yasār (born 85/704, died 151/768), whose *Sīrat Rasūl Allāh* was the first comprehensive biography of the Prophet. His report, though concise and brief, gives almost all the essential information of the event without dwelling on many of the details and different reports given by the writers who immediately followed him. The shortness of Ibn Isḥāq's account of the Saqīfa is easily understandable in that his work deals mainly with the life and career of the Prophet. The event of the Saqīfa in all its details is thus beyond the scope of his work; that the incident is mentioned at all is probably due to the fact that it took place before the burial of the Prophet. This is evident from the arrangement of the closing chapters of his biography, which deal with: 1: The illness of the Prophet, 2: His death, 3: The affair of the Saqīfa of Banī Sāʿida, 4: Funeral preparations and burial of the Prophet.

Ibn Isḥāq first introduces the event in only a few lines and without citing his authorities.[1] It is Ibn Isḥāq's usual technique to introduce first a collective tradition by combining different reports into a simple narrative which serves as an introduction to the detailed account which follows. In this he proves himself to be a loyal pupil of his master Az-Zuhrī, who was the first to introduce collective traditions.[2] Thus what appears to be simply an introductory paragraph in Ibn Isḥāq's narrative of the Saqīfa is given by others with different *isnāds* (chain of transmitters) and with slightly varying words and lengths. After this brief introduction Ibn Isḥāq relates the whole event in one single tradition of considerable length, which runs to about three and a half pages[3] and covers almost all the essential points of the event. This tradition deserves a few observations. Firstly, the whole story is related in the very words of the second caliph, ʿUmar b. al-Khaṭṭāb, from one of his Friday sermons in the mosque of Medina. ʿUmar being a strict disciplinarian in observance of religious formalism, Friday prayers must have been attended by a great number of people in Medina, and his exposition must have had such a wide circulation among both the Muhājirūn and the Anṣār that it could not be a later fabrication attributed to him. Secondly, this speech is reported almost unanimously by the majority of the historians who followed Ibn Isḥāq, such as Ṭabarī and even Balādhurī, who often wrote selectively to support the Sunnī viewpoint of his day. Thirdly, it is beyond any doubt true that ʿUmar b. al-Khaṭṭāb himself played the most important role at that crucial moment, took the initiative in the fateful event of the Saqīfa, and indeed was the moving spirit in the selection of Abū Bakr. A unanimously accepted report in his own words is therefore of the greatest historical importance. Fourthly, Ibn Isḥāq begins the tradition by prefixing the words "in connection with these events (Saqīfa) ʿAbd Allāh b. Abī Bakr told me . . . " This indicates that, besides 'Umar's account, Ibn Isḥāq was aware of other reports and detailed accounts, but for the sake of brevity picked out the one which he considered the most reliable and at the same time comprehensive enough to cover the entire event.

The *isnād* of this tradition in Ibn Isḥāq is direct, short, based solely on Medinese informants, and prefixed with the verb of certainty and personal contact, *haddathanī*, "he told me". The *isnād* reads: "ʿAbd Allāh b. Abū Bakr told me from (1) Ibn Shihāb az-Zuhrī (2) from ʿUbayd Allāh b. ʿAbd Allāh b. 'Utba b. Masʿūd (3) from ʿAbd Allāh b. al-ʿAbbās." Both ʿAbd Allāh b. Abī Bakr[4] (born ca. 60/679–80, died ca. 130/747–8) and Zuhrī[5] (born ca. 51/671, died 124/742) belonged to the third generation (*Tabʿi Tābiʿūn*) after the Prophet, and to the second generation of traditionists. Both were pioneers of Muslim historiography, and both received their material from the *Tābiʿūn*, who in turn were either eye-witnesses to the events while in their early youth or had received the information from the Companions of the Prophet. With the recent researches in Islamic historiography by Nabia Abbott[6] and others, it is now established beyond any doubt that the life, wars, and career of the Prophet, collectively known as *Sīra*, along with subsequent events, became an object of historical research beginning with the generation that followed Muḥammad. In this connection there appear names such as Abān[7] (born ca. 20/641, died ca. 100/718–19), the son of the Caliph 'Uthmān; 'Urwa b. az-Zubayr b. al-ʿAwwām[8] (born 23/644, died 94/712–13); Wahb b. Munabbih[9] (born 34/654–5, died 110/728–9); and others. This interest in historical research gathered great momentum by the third generation and reached its climax in the *Sīra* or *Maghāzī* works of two of Ibn Isḥāq's most prominent teachers, Zuhrī and ʿAbd Allāh b. Abī Bakr. It is reasonable to assume that these two pioneers of historical writing in Islam must have interested themselves in the event of the Saqīfa, which was certainly the most important event that took place at the time of the death of the founder of Islam. It is equally reasonable to assume that Ibn Isḥāq preferred to narrate the event as it was handed down to him from his two most intimate and respected teachers rather than to quote from other sources, especially when his interest in the Saqīfa was limited to the events related to the death of the Prophet. It is also important to note that these two authorities, especially Zuhrī, appear in almost all the later works which describe the Saqīfa incident. Balādhurī and Ṭabarī, whose interest in the event is not confined to the events connected with the death of the Prophet, quote these two sources in their accounts of what they consider to be one of the most important historical events in Islamic history.

In Ibn Isḥāq's narrative, Zuhrī's authority is ʿUbayd Allāh b. ʿAbd Allāh b. ʿUtba b. Masʿūd,[10] one of Zuhrī's four most trusted and esteemed teachers. These four were Saʿīd b. al-Musayyib[11] (died 94/712–13), under whom Zuhrī sat for ten years as a faithful student, ʿUrwa b. az-Zubayr, Abān b. ʿUthmān, and ʿUbayd Allāh b. ʿAbd Allāh. All four are among the most distinguished and recognized authorities on *Fiqh, Sīra,* and *Maghāzī.* Zuhrī is frequently quoted as expressing his highest regard for them, and described them as the "four seas of knowledge" and "the four seas of the Quraysh".[12] Three of them, with the exception of Abān, are also among the famous illustrious seven lawyers of Medina. All these four have been credited with leaving written works for the following generations in addition to what they had transmitted orally to their pupils. Our interest in these four celebrated scholars of Islamic history is due not only to the fact that one of them appears in Ibn Isḥāq's *isnād*, but also to the fact that their names frequently appear in many of the *isnāds* of the Saqīfa event recorded by other writers.

A word must be said concerning ʿAbd Allāh b. al-ʿAbbās[13] (born three years before the Hijra, died 68/687–8), who appears as the last authority in Ibn Isḥāq and in many other Saqīfa accounts written by the historians and traditionists who followed Ibn Isḥāq. It will suffice to say that he has always been respected as one of the most trustworthy authorities in all periods and among all schools of thought in Islam, not only in Qur'ānic exegesis but in other branches of learning cultivated at Medina. He was in fact one of the distinguished founders of the Medinese school of learning and scholarship, which devoted itself mainly to religious sciences. Bukhārī, Muslim, Abū Dā'ūd, Tirmidhī, An-Nasā'ī, Ibn Māja, followed by many others, unanimously accepted his traditions. In the scholarly research for which he was well known, he gathered information concerning the life of the Prophet by questioning senior companions.[14] Not only did he witness the event of the Saqīfa as a young man, but he also must have carefully preserved the information received from his father Al-'Abbās, the uncle of the Prophet, who was undoubtedly involved in the controversy which engulfed Medina immediately after the death of the Prophet. It is not surprising therefore that 'Abd Allāh b. al-'Abbās appears in almost all the sources describing the Saqīfa.

The second author of note who deals with the Saqīfa is Abū 'Abd Allāh Muḥammad b. Sa'd (born ca. 168/784–5), who wrote the first systematic and comprehensive biographical work, *Kitāb aṭ-Ṭabaqāt al-Kabīr* (The Book of Classes), dealing with important personalities from the Prophet down to the time of his own death in 230/844–5. In arranging his material he deals in detail with the lives and careers of the first generation of Muslims, especially the Companions and close associates of the Prophet. One would have expected that Ibn Sa'd, while writing a long forty-one page[15] biography of Abū Bakr, would have discussed the event of Saqīfa in much greater detail than his predecessor Ibn Isḥāq. As it was perhaps one of the most important and most crucial events in the entire career of Abū Bakr, it is surprising that Ibn Sa'd does not seem to be interested in the proceedings as such. He clearly attempts to hush up all those reports which might reflect on the controversial character of the selection of Abū Bakr, and carefully selects only those traditions which exalt Abū Bakr's undisputed excellence and qualifications for the leadership of the community at the death of the Prophet. He makes every effort to praise and glorify the first caliph's virtues, his services to Islam, and the qualities which befitted him for immediate succession to Muḥammad. Indeed he uses the same technique in writing 'Alī's biography to show that he was the best candidate for the office in his time. In this he proves himself the true representative of the Sunnī tradition in Islam of the early third century and of the piety of the Medinese school, both of which were built on the Murji'a doctrine. This doctrine, in its more refined and developed form in the third century, required a Muslim to refrain from any discussion which might tarnish the respect and honour with which the early personalities of Islam, especially the Companions, were regarded. Anyone reading Ibn Saʿd's biography of Abū Bakr will immediately notice that the writer is interested in presenting only the best qualities and virtues of his subject. A brief summary of Ibn Saʿd's arrangement of the material will help in understanding how he wishes his reader to look at Saqīfa.

Ibn Saʿd begins by writing two pages on the clan, family name, and title of Abū Bakr.[16] Even in this biographical data his main emphasis is on his title of *Aṣ-Ṣiddīq*, the truthful. He inserts a tradition to the effect that after Muḥammad's ascent to heaven (*Miʿrāj*), which he feared people would not accept, the angel Gabriel assured him that Abū Bakr would do so since he was a *Ṣiddīq*. The second section, entitled "Abū Bakr's Conversion to Islam",[17] contains five traditions all to the effect that Abū Bakr was the first among men to believe in Muḥammad's Prophethood and completely ignores many traditions which describe ʿAlī as the first man to become Muslim.[18] This is followed by the third section, with the heading, "Description of the Cave and the Migration to Medina",[19] in which Ibn Saʿd records twenty-six traditions. These traditions emphasize Abū Bakr's close friendship with Muḥammad, that he was "only one of the two" when Muḥammad took refuge in the cave on his way to Medina, and that his services were invaluable at that critical moment. Then, after a few traditions about Abū Bakr's abode at Medina, he immediately records Abū Bakr's brotherhood in faith with ʿUmar b. al-Khaṭṭāb and the Prophet's declaration that Abū Bakr and ʿUmar were the leaders or Lords of the adults of Paradise of all times, with the exception of the Prophets and the apostles. This is followed by the traditions which describe Muḥammad's special favour to Abū Bakr when he ordered the latter's house to be built adjoining the mosque in Medina while others were denied this honour, that Abū Bakr defended Muḥammad in all the battles, and that the Prophet appointed him as his standard-bearer at Tabūk. The last five traditions in this section describe Muḥammad's statements that if he was to choose a friend

(*Khalīl*) for himself he could name no one other than Abū Bakr, that "No one is more beloved to me in my entire community than Abū Bakr," and that "The most zealous and vigilant after me in my community is Abū Bakr."

The fourth section, entitled "Description of the Prayer which the Prophet Ordered Abū Bakr [to lead] before his Death",[20] is perhaps the most indicative of Ibn Saʿd's attitude. Here he gives ten traditions, the first five of which describe the Prophet's insistence that only Abū Bakr must lead the prayer while Muḥammad was sick. The following three traditions describe Muḥammad's request for writing material to write down his will and command to the effect that Abū Bakr should succeed him, so that people should not doubt or disagree on this question. When ʿAbd ar-Raḥmān, the son of Abū Bakr, went out to bring the writing material, people said, "Sit down. Who could dispute over Abū Bakr?" In the ninth tradition, ʿĀ'isha the widow of the Prophet is reported to have replied when she was asked: "O mother of the faithful, who did the Prophet appoint to succeed him?" "Abū Bakr," she replied. "Who after Abū Bakr?" she was asked. "ʿUmar," she answered. "Who after ʿUmar?" again she was asked. "Abū ʿUbayda b. al-Jarrāḥ," she answered, on which the enquirer kept silent. The section closes on the tenth tradition, coming back to the topic given to the heading, saying, "The Prophet was sick for thirteen days; whenever he felt better he led the prayer, but whenever his condition was not so well Abū Bakr led the prayer." It is interesting to note here that except for two rather unimportant reports, all of these traditions are reported from ʿĀ'isha, the daughter of Abū Bakr, whose rivalry with and dislike for both ʿAlī and Fāṭima are well known.

Anyone who reads this section of Ibn Saʿd will immediately feel that the author has a specific task set before him. The entire section is carefully planned to show that Abū Bakr, by the special favours and indications shown by the Prophet, was beyond any doubt the only deserving candidate to succeed the dying Prophet. The author becomes so impatient that he even abandons the main theme of the section, and in the second tradition, which would have otherwise been under the event of the Saqīfa, describes ʿUmar's argument against the Anṣār in favour of Abū Bakr, based on the latter's being the leader of the prayer. The tradition reads: "When the Prophet died, and the Anṣār suggested [in the assembly of the Saqīfa], 'Let us have a leader from among ourselves and a leader from among yourselves (*Muhājirūn*),' 'Umar said, 'Did not you know, O people of Anṣār, that the Prophet appointed Abū Bakr to lead the people in prayer?' The Anṣār said 'Yes.' 'Then would you like to prefer yourselves to Abū Bakr?' 'We take refuge in God, to prefer ourselves over Abū Bakr,' said the Anṣar."[21]

Immediately after this section, Ibn Saʿd comes to the event of the Saqīfa. Unlike other writers before and after him, he does not name this section "Affair (*amr*) of the Saqīfa", but gives the heading, "Description of the Homage [paid] to Abū Bakr" (*Dhikr bayʿat Abī Bakr*). One cannot fail to see that in the four preceding chapters Ibn Saʿd has carefully prepared a psychological background for his reader to accept his account of the undisputed selection of Abū Bakr on the basis of his merits and qualities so far enumerated. On the Saqīfa he records a total of fifteen traditions[22] of which only six directly or indirectly are related to the Saqīfa. The first tradition reports that when the Prophet died 'Umar came to Abū 'Ubayda b. al-Jarrāḥ and said, "Open your hand and I will pay homage to you (*Li ubayaʿuka*) because the Prophet declared you trustworthy of this community." Abū 'Ubayda replied, "O 'Umar, I never found you so misled since you accepted Islam. Would you do me fealty while there is among you *Āṣ-Ṣiddīq*, only second of the two [in the cave]?" The second tradition is almost identical.

The third tradition is a peculiar example of Ibn Saʿd's treatment of the subject. In this report he extracted a small sentence from the lengthy three-page tradition reported by Ibn Isḥāq and others in the form of 'Umar's speech in the mosque of Medina. Ibn Saʿd's fragment reads: "Ibn 'Abbās said, 'I heard 'Umar saying, while describing Abū Bakr's *bayʿa*, "There is none among you to whom people would devote themselves as they did to Abū Bakr."'" In the fourth tradition Ibn Saʿd can no longer completely ignore the controversy which arose on the question, but even this is presented as an argument in favour of Abū Bakr. It reads: "When people held back from Abū Bakr, he said, 'Who could be more deserving for this thing (*amr*) than I? Was I not the first to pray with the Prophet?' Then he mentioned those good deeds [*lit.* attributes] which he performed with the Prophet." The fifth tradition is, in fact, the only one which, on the authority of Abū Bakr's grandson, Qāsim b. Muḥammad b. Abī Bakr,[23] refers to the debate of the Saqīfa. It is hurriedly hushed up in only seven lines; the rest of the tradition deals with the distribution of some goods by Abū Bakr. The rest of the ten traditions have hardly anything to do with the Saqīfa event as such, and are mainly devoted to Abū Bakr's excellence, frugality, simplicity, devotion, and piety.

There is hardly any need for further comments on Ibn Saʿd's treatment of the Saqīfa. It should suffice here to note that an historical investigation into the controversial nature of the subject was outside the scope of his work. Nevertheless, his importance as an early writer cannot be overemphasized. He is one of the foremost authorities of his time and represents a school of biographer-traditionists of great importance; in any study of the Saqīfa he cannot be ignored. Ibn Saʿd becomes much more important when we notice his adherence to the "pious" traditional technique and the adoption of many a tradition given by him in this subject by those who followed him. He represents a school which came to dominate the development of the Sunnī point of view in Islam. His presentation of the Saqīfa leads his reader to believe that Abū Bakr's selection went smoothly, without any noticeable opposition or controversy, and that it was readily and instantly accepted by everyone, including ʿAlī, who himself admitted the former's superior claims and merits.

We now must turn to Ibn Saʿd's younger contemporary Aḥmad b. Yaḥyā b. Jābir al-Balādhurī[24] (died 279/892–3), whose voluminous *Ansāb al-Ashrāf* is perhaps the most important historico-biographical work of the third century. On the one hand, he follows Ibn Saʿd in technique and incorporates much of his material; on the other, he goes much deeper and collects every possible report and version of the Saqīfa event from divergent sources and different schools. While Ibn Saʿd depends mainly on Medinese informants, Balādhurī finds them unsatisfactory; he goes further and frequently quotes Madāʾinī, who takes up a kind of middle position between Kūfan and Medinese traditionists. He also narrates from Ibn al-Kalbī, Abū Maʿshar, ʿAwāna, and, in at least two cases, even from the Shīʿī Abū Mikhnaf.[25] He thereby demonstrates not only his keen historical interest in investigating the event of the Saqīfa but also its great importance in the annals of early Islam. The pietistic attitude which was a dominant characteristic of the Medinese schools, especially when dealing with the differences among the prominent companions, was not so prominent with the more historically-minded authors of the Kūfan and Baṣran schools. Balādhurī's preservation of the latter tradition is thus of considerable importance for the present discussion.

In Balādhurī's scheme, the Saqīfa is treated in a manner similar to that of Ibn Isḥāq, with the events connected with the death of the Prophet. In the chapter entitled "Affair of the Saqīfa", Balādhurī records a total of thirty-three traditions,[26] seven of which are exactly identical to material in Ibn Saʿd. In this Balādhurī shows his great respect for his elder contemporary, whom he always quotes with the direct verb, *ḥaddathanī* (he told me), indicating that he took Ibn Saʿd's material not from the *Ṭabaqāt* but by direct dictation from Ibn Saʿd himself.[27] The rest of the twenty-six traditions deal with the controversy over the question of succession, the heated debates which took place in the Saqīfa, rival claims of the *Anṣār* and the *Muhājirūn*, ʿAlī's protest over the selection, the opposition of Banū Hāshim and some of the Anṣār to Abū Bakr, and Abū Bakr's own statement that though he was not the best candidate, he accepted the caliphate to save the community from dissension. Eleven of these twenty-six traditions are taken from Madā'inī, who frequently quotes Zuhrī, whose own *isnāds* often go back to the sources of the "four seas of the Quraysh" discussed above.[28] The most revealing point here is that four of these twenty-six traditions (1: a complete description of the controversial debate in the Saqīfa; 2: Abū Sufyān's offer of help to ʿAlī; 3: Abū Bakr's statement that though he was not the best candidate, he accepted the caliphate only to avoid dissension; and 4: a small part of ʿUmar's speech that even if Abū Bakr's selection was a hasty affair, it did save the community from evil) are narrated by Balādhurī from Ibn Saʿd with the verb "he told me". Ibn Saʿd knew these traditions and found them important enough to transmit them orally to Balādhurī, but he himself shrank from including them in his *Ṭabaqāt.*

The long speech of ʿUmar which describes the Saqīfa in full and comprises the comprehensive account in Ibn Isḥāq, as we have seen above, is reported by Balādhurī three times; first (No. 1173) from Ibn Saʿd, where only a small sentence justifying Abū Bakr's merits (as in *Ṭabaqāt*) is reported; a second time (No. 1176) when only the first part of it is given; then finally the full text (No. 1181), as in Ibn Isḥāq, is recorded. In all three places the final three authorities are the same as in the *Sīra*: Zuhrī, ʿUbayd Allāh, and Ibn ʿAbbās, though the first authorities change in all three instances. In No. 1173 Zuhrī's narrator is Ṣāliḥ b. Kaysān;[29] in No. 1176 it is Muʿammar b. Rashīd[30] and in No. 1181, the full text is taken by Balādhurī from Madāʾinī through Ibn Juʿdaba.[31] There are a few differences between the text of Madāʾinī quoted by Balādhurī and that of ʿAbd Allāh b. Abī Bakr quoted by Ibn Isḥāq. To conclude it will suffice to say that although Balādhurī displays a tendency in favour of Abū Bakr's excellence for the office, as is evident from the order of preference in the arrangement of the material, he does not suppress many traditions which show the inclination of some of the important companions towards ʿAlī.

The picture of the Saqīfa still remains rather incomplete until one takes into consideration Balādhurī's younger contemporary Ibn Wāḍih al-Yaʿqūbī (died 284/897). Anyone reading Yaʿqūbī's rendering of the Saqīfa immediately after Ibn Saʿd and Balādhurī will notice a sharp contrast both in substance and in emphasis. Whereas Ibn Saʿd would have us believe that Abū Bakr faced hardly any opposition from those who favoured ʿAlī, Yaʿqūbī would impress upon his reader that there was rather serious opposition to Abū Bakr from a group which supported ʿAlī's rights to the caliphate.

Unlike Ibn Saʿd and Balādhurī, Yaʿqūbī does not give separate traditions prefixed by *isnād*, nor does he follow his sources verbally except in quotations and direct speeches. This is his method throughout his history, the Saqīfa being no exception. Opening with the heading, "Information (*khabar*) of the Saqīfa of Banū Sāʿida and the Fealty to Abū Bakr", he writes a cohesive, uninterrupted four-page narrative from all the sources available to him.[32] It of course paraphrases many traditions into one continuous account, but all the quotations and speeches are faithfully preserved without any transformation. This is evident from comparisons with other sources before and after him.

As regards his sources, we know that, as a general rule and perhaps for the sake of a literary cohesive text, he rarely cites his authorities. Nevertheless, it is usually not difficult to ascertain their identity.[33] In the case of the Saqīfa, some of his sources, such as Madā'inī and Abū Mikhnaf, are the same as those used by Ṭabarī. Here we must point out that it is beyond any doubt an historical fact that the event of the Saqīfa became an object of keen historical interest right from the very beginnings of historical writing in Islam. This is evident from Ibn Nadīm's and Ṭūsī's *Fihrists*, Najāshī's *Rijāl*, and other bibliographical works which list numerous treatises on the Saqīfa under the names of a great many writers beginning from the early second century onward. For example, both Abū Mikhnaf[34] and Madā'inī[35] are reported to have written independent treatises on the subject, and when we read the Saqīfa account in Ṭabarī, Balādhurī, and others, we find a number of traditions on their authority. Ibn Abī 'l-Ḥadīd (died ca. 656/1258) in his voluminous *Sharḥ Nahj al-Balāgha*, a mine of valuable historical material composed with the help of a rich library of rare manuscripts in his possession, writes forty pages on the Saqīfa[36] that incorporate some of these rare treatises which survived until his time. Among these is a text by Abū Bakr Aḥmad b. ʿAbd al-ʿAzīz al-Jawharī[37] (died 298/910–11), who cites many early authorities in his treatise on the Saqīfa. A modern scholar of note, Aghā Buzurg at-Tehrānī, records in his exhaustive work on Shīʿī literature a great number of treatises written down on the Saqīfa in the early centuries of Islam.[38] Many of them considerably predate Yaʿqūbī; a few of them even originate from the circle of traditionists who gathered around the Imam Jaʿfar aṣ-Ṣādiq (died 148/765–6).

By the time Ibn Saʿd, Balādhurī, and other Sunnī writers set out to write, Sunnī Islam had already defined and fixed its attitudes and loyalties based on the Murji'ī principles of synthesis and tolerance. It was, therefore, natural for these writers to suppress or ignore any report that might clash with the accepted norms of the day. Most of that material which could support the Shīʿī position in favour of ʿAlī was thus either suppressed or conveniently suspected of being fabricated. This was exactly what happened to Yaʿqūbī. There is a common tendency to suspect his accounts, which could support the Shīʿī cause, mainly because he himself was a Shīʿī. But quite logically, if Yaʿqūbī can be suspected of bias in favour of the Shīʿī position, why cannot other historians of the opposite affiliation be equally suspected of suppressing those reports which serve the Shīʿī purpose? In this situation, we feel that Yaʿqūbī's history should be considered a valuable compendium of historical documents which survived the tendentious efforts of the historians of the majority party. The argument for the overall authenticity of his material is enhanced by the fact that most of his Saqīfa material is also reported in fragmentary fashion by his non-Shīʿī successors. We may thus conclude that certain data handed down to us by Yaʿqūbī, but omitted by his three predecessors, are of immense historical importance for the reconstruction of the Saqīfa event. These four writers cover every point of view and leave little to be added by the encyclopaedic annalist Muḥammad b. Jarīr aṭ-Ṭabarī (died 311/923–4). He generally displays a remarkably unbiased and uncommitted attitude in his history, undoubtedly the most comprehensive that has survived to us. He does not base his selection of sources on religious affiliations, but uses them according to his own historical judgement in relation to each event. He builds his narrative by recording several parallel and co-ordinated traditions or, wherever necessary, by giving divergent reports coming to him from different sources. In the latter case he gives his own historical opinion either by explaining how each event is to be placed and interpreted or by arranging his material in order of preference. This second method he uses when reporting on the Saqīfa. He completely ignores Ibn Saʿd's account of the event, incorporates most of the material of Ibn Isḥāq, Yaʿqūbī, and Balādhurī through his own sources, and makes some additions of his own. He reports ʿUmar's speech on the Saqīfa in full, exactly as did Ibn Isḥāq, but the former's authority is ʿAbbād b. ʿAbbād[39] (Al-Muhallabī) from ʿAbbād b. Rāshid,[40] while the last three authorities are the same as in Ibn Isḥāq. He is also the one who, alone among all the historians of Islam, preserves Abū Mikhnaf's treatise on the Saqīfa.[41] On the whole, Ṭabarī's history presents a balanced and unbiased account of the Saqīfa. He makes it absolutely clear that there was a strong body of support for ʿAlī, but on the other hand, emphasizes that Abū Bakr was duly elected by the majority of the people.

There is little need to examine in detail the works of those writers who followed these five early sources. Subsequent authors, such as Masʿūdī[42] (died 344/955–6), Ibn Athīr[43] (died 630/1232–3), Ibn ʿAbd Rabbih[44] (died 327/938–9), and even Suyūṭī (died 911/1505–6) in his specialized work on the subject of the caliphate,[45] add hardly anything substantially important to our knowledge on the event. Later Shīʿī works by authors such as aṭ-Ṭabrasī[46] and al-Majlisī[47] are mainly polemic in nature and give a very tendentious pro-Shīʿī account of no historical value.

In an attempt to reconstruct the events at the Saqīfa, the best approach is to take, as a basis, Ibn Isḥāq, who is not only the earliest authority, but also the one whose work has reached us in the recension of Ibn Hishām (died 218/833), himself a die-hard Sunnī and earlier than the other four writers mentioned above. Moreover, Ibn Hishām never hesitates in his task of editing Ibn Isḥāq's *Sīra* to correct or comment on any point with which he disagrees, and he often inserts some additional information he thinks was overlooked or omitted by the author.[48] Ibn Hishām makes none of these comments, additions, or corrections in the account of the Saqīfa, however. The tradition of the Saqīfa in the *Sīra* is thus an account recorded by a writer of Shīʿī leaning,[49] approved by an editor-critic of Sunnī belief, and also reported by the majority of the writers following Ibn Isḥāq through different authorities, as we have seen above. For other necessary details not presented by Ibn Isḥāq, we must draw from our other four authorities. It is our intention here to base our reconstruction of the Saqīfa on a translation of ʿUmar's speech as recorded by Ibn Isḥāq.[50] Since a speech of this sort naturally is not supposed to cover every detail, frequent breaks will be utilized to draw in other sources and attempt to form a complete picture of the proceedings. Sources of the additions filling the gaps will be given within the narrative so that the reader will be able to notice them immediately.

Before narrating ʿUmar's speech, Ibn Isḥāq opens with an introduction, without *isnād*, which can be found in Balādhurī (I, p. 583) on the authority of Aḥmad b. Muḥammad

b. Ayyūb[51] from Ibrāhīm b. Saʿd[52] from Ibn Isḥāq from Zuhrī. It reads as follows:

"When the Apostle died, this clan of the Anṣār gathered round Saʿd b. ʿUbāda in the hall of Banū Sāʿida; and ʿAlī and az-Zubayr b. al-ʿAwwām and Ṭalḥa b. ʿUbayd Allāh separated themselves in Fāṭima's house while the rest of the Muhājirūn gathered round Abū Bakr accompanied by Usayd b. Ḥuḍayr with the Banū ʿAbdu'l-Ashhal. Then someone came to Abū Bakr and ʿUmar telling them that this clan of the Anṣār had gathered round Saʿd in the hall (*saqīfa*) of Banū Sāʿida: 'If you want to have command of the people, then take it before their action becomes serious.' Now [the dead body of] the Apostle was still in his house, the burial arrangements not having been completed, and his family had locked the door of the house. ʿUmar said, 'I said to Abū Bakr "Let us go to these our brothers of the Anṣār to see what they are doing."'"[53]

After this Ibn Isḥāq records ʿUmar's famous speech, for which the chain of transmitters has been examined in each of our sources above. Passing over those parts which do not deal with the Saqīfa, it reads:

"In connection with these events [selection of Abū Bakr] ʿAbd Allāh b. Abū Bakr told me from Ibn Shihāb az-Zuhrī from ʿUbayd Allāh b. ʿAbd Allāh b. ʿUtba b. Masʿūd from ʿAbd Allāh b. ʿAbbās who said, 'I was waiting for ʿAbd ar-Raḥmān b. ʿAwf in his station in Minā while he was with ʿUmar in the last pilgrimage which ʿUmar performed. When he [ʿAbd ar-Raḥmān] returned he found me [ʿAbd Allah b. alʿAbbas] waiting, for I was teaching him to read the *Qurʾān*. ʿAbd ar-Raḥmān said to me: "I wish you could have seen a man who came to the Commander of the Faithful [ʿUmar] and said, 'O Commander of the Faithful, would you like a man who said, "By God, if ʿUmar were dead I would do fealty to so-and-so."? Fealty given to Abū Bakr was an unpremeditated affair (*falta*) and was ratified.'"'"

Here we must point out that this speech, though recorded by the vast majority of writers, includes neither the name of the person who talked to ʿUmar nor the name of the one to whom he wished to pay fealty, except in Balādhurī, I, pp. 581, 582. In tradition No. 1176 Balādhurī quotes ʿUmar as saying that the person speaking to ʿUmar was Zubayr, and that the person Zubayr wanted to hail as caliph was ʿAlī. In tradition No. 1181, Balādhurī gives only one name: "ʿUmar delivered a sermon in which he said that 'so-and-so says if ʿUmar dies we will pay our homage (*bāyaʿnā*) to ʿAlī.'" Balādhurī's report can be confirmed by later writers such as Ibn Abī 'l-Ḥadīd, who gives the name of ʿAlī on the authority of al-Jāḥiẓ.[54] It is, however, of great importance to note that it was ʿAlī's name which caused ʿUmar to deliver such an important and fiery speech.

"ʿUmar was angry [when he heard this] and said, 'God willing, I shall get up among the men tonight and warn them against those who desire to usurp power over them.' I (ʿAbd ar-Raḥmān) said, 'Do not do it, Commander of the Faithful, for the festival brings together the riff-raff and the lowest of the people; they are the ones who will be in the majority in your proximity [assembly] when you stand among the people. I fear lest you should stand and say something which they will repeat everywhere, not understanding what you say or interpreting it correctly; so wait until you come to Medina, for it is the home of the Sunna and you can confer privately with the jurists (*fuqahā'*) and the nobles of the people. You can say what you like and the jurists will understand what you say and interpret it properly.' ʿUmar replied, 'By God, if He wills, I will do so as soon as I reach Medina . . .'

"We came to Medina at the end of Dhū'l-Ḥijja and on the Friday I (Ibn ʿAbbās) returned [to the mosque] quickly when the sun had set . . . ʿUmar sat on the pulpit, and when the muezzins were silent he praised God, as was fitting, and said: 'Today I am about to say to you something which God has willed that I should say and I do not know whether perhaps it is my last utterance. He who understands and heeds it let him take it with him wherever he goes; and as for him who fears that he will not understand it, he may not deny that I said it.'

". . . I have heard that someone [Zubayr as in Balādhurī] said, 'If ʿUmar were dead I would do fealty to so-and-so [ʿAlī].' Do not let a man deceive himself by saying that acceptance of Abū Bakr was a hasty mistake (*falta*) which was ratified. Admittedly it was that, but God averted the evil of it. There is none among you to whom people would devote themselves as they did to Abū Bakr. He who accepts a man as ruler without consulting the Muslims, such acceptance has no validity for either of them: and they are subject to death [punishment].

"What happened was that when God took away His Prophet [from among us], the Anṣār opposed us and gathered with their leaders in the Saqīfa [hall] of Banū Sāʿida, and ʿAlī and az-Zubayr and their companions [and those who were their supporters] withdrew from us, while the Muhājirūn gathered to Abū Bakr."

From ʿUmar's own statement, it is clear that there was serious opposition to Abū Bakr's candidacy not only from the Anṣār, but also from ʿAlī and his supporters. Thus, no sooner had the news of Muḥammad's death come out than the Anṣār of Medina, undoubtedly fearful of Meccan domination and perhaps aware of their designs, hastily assembled in the Saqīfa Banū Sāʿida to elect a leader from among themselves. ʿUmar b. al-Khaṭṭāb, upon hearing people saying that Muḥammad was dead, stood and furiously remonstrated that the Prophet could not die. Claiming that Muḥammad had simply disappeared for a time, he threatened he would kill anyone who claimed that Muḥammad was dead.[55] Abū Bakr, who had been at his house in Sunḥ, a suburb of Medina, then arrived on the scene. Hearing ʿUmar's altercations, he went straight into the Prophet's house. Discovering that Muḥammad had passed away, Abū Bakr came back and confirmed his death to the people gathered around ʿUmar.

At this point we have three different versions. The first reports that when Abū Bakr was addressing the people, an informant came and told him and ʿUmar about the Anṣār's meeting in the Saqīfa. Both Abū Bakr and ʿUmar, along with those around them, then rushed to the Saqīfa. This version must be rejected on the simple grounds that Abū ʿUbayda b. al-Jarrāḥ does not appear anywhere in this tradition, contradicting all other reports, where he is one of the three most important persons in the whole drama. The second version reports that after confirming the death of the Prophet to the people, Abū Bakr and ʿUmar went to the house of the Prophet and joined his relatives, who were busy with the burial preparations. Two informants then came and told them about the Saqīfa, whereupon the three—Abū Bakr, ʿUmar, and Abū ʿUbayda—ran to the Saqīfa. This version also does not appear to be correct because: 1: it presupposes that these three most important companions were completely unaware of both the serious tension, often conflict, which had been developing over the last few years between the Muhājirūn and the Anṣār, and the gravity of the situation under the circumstances; 2: it contradicts ʿUmar's statement that ʿAlī and his supporters separated themselves from the others and locked the door of the house; 3: it is a tradition recorded only by Balādhurī (I, p. 581), and on a rather weak *isnād.* The third version, which is repeatedly narrated by all of our sources with the exception of Ibn Saʿd, reports that after addressing the people regarding Muḥammad's death, Abū Bakr, along with ʿUmar and Abū ʿUbayda, went to the house of, most probably, Abū ʿUbayda. There they met to deliberate on the critical leadership crisis which had arisen owing to the death of the Prophet, and certainly keeping in view the resentful feelings of the Anṣār which had been developing for quite some time.[56] It was there that the council of the Muhājirūn was interrupted by an informant who rushed in to tell them what the Anṣār were doing. Hearing that, Abū Bakr, ʿUmar, and Abū ʿUbayda rushed to the Saqīfa to prevent any unexpected development. Returning again to ʿUmar's speech, we are told:

> "I told Abū Bakr that we should go to our brothers the Anṣār, so we went off to go to them when two honest fellows [ʿUwaym b. Sāʿīda[57] and Maʿn b. ʿAdī[58]] met us and told us of the conclusion the people had come to. They asked us where we were going, and when we told them they said that there was no need for us to approach them and we must make our own decision. I said, 'By God, we will go to them.' And [when we arrived] we found them [the Anṣār] in the hall of Banū Sāʿida. In their midst was a man wrapped up. In answer to my inquiries, they said that he was Saʿd b. ʿUbāda and that he was sick. When we sat down there, a speaker pronounced the *Shahāda* and praised God as was fitting and then continued: 'We are God's Helpers and the squadron of Islam. You, O Muhājirūn, are a family of ours and a company of your people have come to settle down [among us].' I [at this point ʿUmar interrupted and] said: 'And look, they were trying to cut us off from our origin and wrest authority from us.' When the Anṣār's speaker finished, I wanted to speak, for I had prepared a speech in my mind which pleased me much. I wanted to produce it before Abū Bakr and to repulse the roughness and asperity of the speaker of the Anṣār. But Abū Bakr said, 'Gently, ʿUmar!' I did not like to anger him and so he spoke. He was a man with more knowledge and dignity than I, and by God he did not omit a single word which I had thought of and he uttered it in his inimitable way better than I could have done. Abū Bakr said: 'All the good that you have said about yourselves you duly deserve. But the Arabs will not recognize authority except in this tribe [*lit.*

clan] of Quraysh. They are the best and the noblest of the Arabs in descent, blood, and country [i.e. settled in the centre].'"

An addition from Balādhurī (I, p. 582) completes Abū Bakr's speech and shows further how he argued against the Anṣār: "We are the first people in Islam; and among the Muslims, our abode is in the centre, our descent is noblest, and we are nearer to the Prophet in relation; and you [Anṣār] are our brothers in Islam and our partners in religion; you helped us, protected us and supported us, may God reward you His best. So we are the rulers (*umarā'*) and you are the deputies (*wuzarā'*). The Arabs will not submit themselves except to this clan of the Quraysh. Certainly a group from among you [present] knows well that the Prophet said, 'The leaders are from the Quraysh (*al-a'immat-u min al-Quraysh*), therefore, do not compete with your Muhājir brothers in what God has bestowed upon them.'"

Now we return again to ʿUmar's speech.

"[Abū Bakr said,] 'So I offer you one of two men; accept whichever you please.' Thus saying he took hold of my hand and that of Abū ʿUbayda b. al-Jarrāḥ, who was sitting between us. Nothing he ever said displeased me more than that. By God, I would rather have come forward and have had my head struck off—if that were no sin—than rule over a people of whom Abū Bakr was one . . ."

In Yaʿqūbī's account (II, p. 123), "[Abū Bakr said] 'The Quraysh are closer to Muḥammad than you, so here is ʿUmar b. al-Khaṭṭāb, for whom the Prophet prayed, "O God, confirm his faith," and the other is Abū ʿUbayda, whom the Prophet declared "a trustee of this umma"; choose either one whom you like and pay homage to him.' But both of them refused and said, 'We cannot take preference over you, you are the companion of the Prophet and only second of the two [in the cave at the time of the *hijra*].'" In one of Balādhurī's accounts (I, p. 582), when Abū Bakr suggested the name of ʿUmar, the latter exclaimed: "And while you are alive? Who could set you aside from your place in which the Prophet had installed you?" Yaʿqūbī (II, p. 123) describes Abū ʿUbayda as saying: "O people of Anṣār, you were the first to help [Islam] so do not be the first to differ and change." Yaʿqūbī continues: "Then ʿAbd ar- Raḥmān b. ʿAwf stood and said: 'You have your merits, but you do not have [any one among you] like Abū Bakr, ʿUmar, and ʿAlī.' On this, one of the Anṣār, Al-Mundhir b. Arqam,[59] sharply replied: 'We do not reject the merits you have mentioned; indeed there is among you one with whom no one can dispute, if he seeks this authority, and that man is ʿAlī b. Abī Ṭālib.'"

It was at this stage of suggestions and counter suggestions by Abū Bakr, ʿUmar, and Abū ʿUbayda for each other that Al-Ḥubāb b. Mundhir[60] from the Anṣār offered a compromise solution. Thus continues ʿUmar:

> "One of the Anṣār said, 'I am the rubbing post and the fruitful propped-up palm [i.e. a man who can cure people's ills and is held in high esteem because of his great experience]. Let us have one ruler from among ourselves, and another ruler from among yourselves, O Quraysh.' Altercations waxed hotter and voices were raised until, when a complete breach was to be feared, I said, 'Stretch forth your hand, Abū Bakr.' He did so and I paid him homage; the Muhājirūn followed and then the Anṣār. [In doing so] we jumped on Saʿd b. ʿUbāda and someone said that we had killed him. I said, 'God kill him.'"

Here ends ʿUmar's historic speech, accepted by almost all of those who wrote on the Saqīfa. Before we proceed further it might be of interest to note ʿUmar's reply to Ḥubāb's suggestion as it is recorded by Ṭabarī (I, p. 1841) in a separate account narrated by Abū Mikhnaf: "ʿUmar said: 'How preposterous; two swords cannot be in one sheath. By God, the Arabs will never agree to your authority while their Prophet is from others [i.e. from ourselves].'"

It is also Ṭabarī (I, p. 1818) who records for us from one of his most trusted and frequently cited authorities, Abū Maʿshar, that even after ʿUmar's homage to Abū Bakr, there were still some of the Anṣār who protested against the decision and exclaimed: "We will not pay our homage to anyone except ʿAlī." But this and some other similar voices were lost in the tumult and, following the examples of ʿUmar and Abū ʿUbayda, those of the Muhājirūn present paid homage to Abū Bakr, and were followed by the Anṣār for one reason or another, as we shall see presently.

Before we describe the events which followed the assembly of Saqīfa, it would be helpful to examine briefly the complex situation and unique circumstances which made Abū Bakr's selection possible. Firstly, clan rivalries among the Quraysh, or among the Muhājirūn in particular, made it easier for them to accept the leadership of Abū Bakr—a man of an insignificant branch, Banū Taym b. Murra.[61] Because of its inconspicuous place among Meccan ruling clans, Banū Taym had never been involved in the power struggle and political conflicts that had plagued the rival clans of the Quraysh. Secondly, the Muhājirūn, as a whole, were also fearful of the possibility of Medinan domination should the Muhājirūn involve themselves in their own clannish rivalries and internecine fighting. To them Abū Bakr was thus the best compromise candidate. Thirdly, as far as the Anṣār were concerned, we should take note of the deep-rooted and old enmity between the Banū Aws and the Banū Khazraj. Saʿd b. ʿUbāda[62] was the chief of the Khazraj; the Banū Aws accordingly found it much more tolerable and profitable to submit themselves to a Qurayshite leader than to allow a chief of the rival tribe to rule over them. This is evident from the fact that the first among the Anṣār to pay homage to Abū Bakr was one of the chiefs of the Banū Aws, Usayd b. Ḥuḍayr.[63] According to Ṭabarī (I, p. 1843), "Some of the Aws, among them Usayd b. Ḥuḍayr, spoke among themselves, saying, 'By God, if the Khazraj become rulers over you once, they will continue to maintain this superiority over you and will never let you have any share in it, so stand up and pay homage to Abū Bakr.' Then they [the Aws] stood and paid homage to Abū Bakr." We may also recall that this Usayd b. Ḥuḍayr was the only one from the Anṣār who took part in the deliberations of the Muhājirūn, certainly knowing of Saʿd b. ʿUbāda's candidacy and thus acting against him and the Khazraj.

As for the Banū Khazraj, they realized that their position was far too weak to face a united front of the Muhājirūn and the Banū Aws, their old rivals, or rather enemies, in the city politics of Medina. The constant wars and deadly feuds between the Aws and the Khazraj are commonplace stories of the *ayyām al-ʿArab* ("Battle Days") literature. Thus the Khazraj found it unwise to lag behind in giving support to and gaining the favour of the ruling authority upon which agreement had very nearly been reached. Moreover, Saʿd b. ʿUbāda was envied by some of his own cousins or clansmen, as was a common feature of the Arab clans; and according to some the first who paid homage to Abū Bakr was Saʿd's own cousin Bashīr b. Saʿd.[64] It is thus clear that as a result of group politics, clan rivalries, and personal jealousies, Abū Bakr was able to exact homage from most of the people. To these factors must be added the overall impression in the sources that Abū Bakr did enjoy a certain prestige and was held in high esteem for his sobriety, old age, his close association with and support of Muḥammad, and his valuable services to Islam from the very advent of the Prophet's mission. Thus the impact of his personality, which grew over the years under the Prophet, should not be ignored in analysing the results of the Saqīfa. The material preserved in the sources also strongly suggests that Abū Bakr and ʿUmar had formed an alliance long before, possibly with Abū ʿUbayda b. al-Jarrāḥ as a third member, and that these three did carry considerable weight and influence in the newly emerging Islamic nobility, as well as in group politics against the old Meccan aristocracy.[65] Finally, it must also be noted that Abū Bakr's succession was realized neither through a free election in any sense of the term nor through a free choice of the community. It was simply a decision by a particular group from among the Muhājirūn which was hastily forced or thrust upon all others. Its success was due only to the delicate existing group conflicts in Medina. This is obvious from ʿUmar's own statement quoted above that, "Admittedly it was a hasty affair (*falta*) but God averted the evil of it." The arguments advanced by ʿUmar and Abū ʿUbayda in favour of Abū Bakr—lineage in the Quraysh, early conversion to Islam, long companionship to the Prophet, services to the cause of Islam, and lastly his close relationship to and the esteem in which he was held by Muḥammad—are in effect of the same nature as those advanced in favour of ʿAlī against Abū Bakr, and they certainly lend more strength to ʿAlī's claims than to those of Abū Bakr. Abū Bakr's only exclusive claim to the succession—his leadership of the prayer during the Prophet's illness—reflects later theological colour, and the traditions pertaining to it are often confused and contradictory.

Keeping in view the arguments and counter-arguments at the Saqīfa, the choice of Abū Bakr seems to have been an accident of circumstances. The conflict between the supporters and the opponents of Abū Bakr centred on considerations of *what is necessary under the circumstances*, and *what ought to be*. The former principle soon resulted in the establishment of a mighty and sweeping caliphate-empire. The latter principle of *what ought to be* led a group of the community, though small, to develop its own interpretation of Islamic ideals and polity.

The task of consolidation of Abū Bakr's authority as the successor to the Prophet, however, was still far from complete after the Saqīfa meeting. ʿAlī b. Abī Ṭālib, the most important candidate from the Prophet's family, as is unanimously attested by Sunnī and Shīʿī sources alike, along with his close associates and the family of Hāshim, was not even aware of the decision taken in the Saqīfa. They came to hear about it only when, after securing homage at the Saqīfa, Abū Bakr, along with his supporters, came to the mosque of the Prophet and an unusual tumult arose from the gathered mob. Though the timing of the events which followed is confused,[66] it is perhaps at this point that ʿAlī and a number of his supporters both from the Anṣār and the Muhājirūn assembled in Fāṭima's house and started deliberating on what was to be done. Besides numerous references to this effect, it is also supported by the first part of ʿUmar's speech when he said, "And ʿAlī and Zubayr with their companions withdrew from us." Abū Bakr and ʿUmar, fully aware of ʿAlī's claims and also of the respect he commanded in a certain group of the companions, and fearing lest there be some serious reaction on his and his partisans' part, summoned them to the mosque to pay homage. They refused to come. ʿUmar, with his cut-and-thrust policy, advised Abū Bakr to act promptly before it was too late. The two men marched to ʿAlī's house with an armed party, surrounded the house, and threatened to set it on fire if ʿAlī and his supporters would not come out and pay homage to the elected caliph. ʿAlī came out and attempted to remonstrate, putting forward his own claims and rights and refusing to honour Abū Bakr and ʿUmar's demands. The scene soon grew violent, the swords flashed from their scabbards, and ʿUmar with his band tried to pass on through the gate. Suddenly Fāṭima appeared before them in a furious temper and reproachfully cried:

"You have left the body of the Apostle of God with us and you have decided among yourselves without consulting us, and without respecting our rights. Before God, I say, either you get out of here at once, or with my hair dishevelled I will make my appeal to God."

This made the situation most critical, and Abū Bakr's band was obliged to leave the house without securing ʿAlī's homage.[67] He could not, however, resist for long and had to yield before the growing pressure. The traditions vary and are often contradictory as to when he was reconciled with Abū Bakr. According to one or two very weak and isolated traditions, which clearly reflect later theological tendency, ʿAlī paid homage to Abū Bakr instantly, only complaining that he had not been consulted; according to some others he did so the same day but under compulsion and with the conviction that he had better claims to the office. But according to the most commonly reported traditions, which must be accepted as authentic because of overwhelming historical evidence and other circumstantial reasons, ʿAlī held himself apart until the death of Fāṭima six months later.[68]

Insisting that ʿAlī should have been chosen, a number of his partisans from among both the Anṣār and the Muhājirūn who had delayed for some time in accepting Abū Bakr's succession were fain to yield, however. They gradually, one after the other, were reconciled to the situation and swore allegiance to Abū Bakr. Their names and number vary in different sources, but the most distinguished among them and most commonly recorded by the majority of the sources are as follows.[69]

1 Ḥudhayfa b. al-Yamān,[70] a Medinese *ḥalīf* of the Aws and a most distinguished Companion of the Prophet. Known as a great warrior who fought at Uḥud and served the Prophet as a special counsellor at Khandaq, his personal loyalty and attachment to ʿAlī remained unchanged even after his allegiance to Abū Bakr. Before his death, he asked his two sons to support ʿAlī, which they did until they were killed at the battle of Ṣiffīn while fighting for ʿAlī against Muʿāwiya.

2 Khuzayma b. Thābit,[71] from the tribe of Aws, whom the Prophet called "*Dhu'sh-Shahādatayn*", the one whose testimony was worth that of two men. He fought alongside ʿAlī at

the battles of Al-Jamal and Ṣiffīn and was killed in the latter by Muʿāwiya's army.

3 Abū Ayyūb al-Anṣārī,[72] whose father, Khālid b. Kulayb, belonged to Banū Najjār and whose mother was from the Khazraj. He was one of the most important Companions among the Anṣār and was the host of the Prophet in Medina until his house was built. He fought for the cause of ʿAlī in the battles of Al-Jamal, Ṣiffīn, and Nahrawān.

4 Sahl b. Ḥunayf,[73] from the tribe of Aws, who fought for the Prophet at Badr and other battles. He was a great friend of ʿAlī, came with him from Medina to Baṣra, and fought at Ṣiffīn. ʿAlī appointed him governor of Persia.

5 ʿUthmān b. Ḥunayf,[74] brother of Sahl and a great favourite of ʿAlī, who appointed him governor of Baṣra.

6 Al-Bara'a b. ʿĀzib al-Anṣārī,[75] from the tribe of Khazraj and one of the aristocrats of Medina representing pro-ʿAlid Anṣār. He came with ʿAlī to Kūfa and fought for him at Al-Jamal, Ṣiffīn, and Nahrawān.

7 Ubayy b. Kaʿb,[76] from a branch of the Banū Khazraj and one of the leading jurists and *Qur'ān* readers among the Anṣār.

8 Abū Dharr b. Jundab al-Ghifārī,[77] one of the earliest followers of Muḥammad, an ascetic, and extremely devoted to piety. He had always been a most vocal supporter of ʿAlī and is one of the four pillars of the first Shīʿa. The Caliph ʿUthmān exiled him to his birthplace, a small village known as Rabdha, where he died.

9 ʿAmmār b. Yāsir,[78] a south Arabian affiliated with the clan of Makhzūm of the Quraysh, an early convert to Islam, and one of the four pillars of the first Shīʿa.

10 Al-Miqdād b. ʿAmr,[79] a south Arabian either from Kinda or Bahra, adopted by a certain Aswad b. ʿAbd Yathūth of the Banū Makhzūm. He was one of the seven early converts to Islam and one of the four pillars of the first Shīʿa.

11 Salmān al-Fārisī,[80] a Persian by origin and an ardent follower and companion of the Prophet, who ransomed him from slavery and adopted him as his *mawla* and member of the *Ahl al-Bayt*. He had always been an ardent supporter of ʿAlī, and his support to ʿAlī at the time of Abū Bakr's selection has been mentioned distinctly even by Balādhurī.

12 Az-Zubayr b. al-ʿAwwām,[81] one of the most distinguished Companions of the Prophet from the Quraysh. He was the

most energetic supporter of ʿAlī and no doubt sincere in his enthusiastic attitude. He came out of the house of Fāṭima, sword in hand, when ʿUmar arrived there and tried to force those in the house to pay homage to Abū Bakr. A serious encounter between him and ʿUmar is recorded by almost all of our historians. It was, however, only twenty-five years later that ambition made him strive for the caliphate, which resulted in the battle of al-Jamal between him and ʿAlī.

13 Khālid b. Saʿīd,[82] from the clan of Umayya, only third or fourth after Abū Bakr to become Muslim, and the only one from this clan who seriously resisted Abū Bakr's succession in favour of ʿAlī. As the representative of the Prophet, he was at Ṣanʿā' when Muḥammad died. When he reached Medina a few days after Abū Bakr's selection, he offered his allegiance to ʿAlī saying, "By God, no one among all the men is more entitled to take the place of Muḥammad than you." Though ʿAlī declined to accept his homage, Khālid refused to recognize Abū Bakr for three months.

The seriousness of their opposition to or resentment of Abū Bakr before they become reconciled to him is almost impossible to ascertain, since the Shīʿī sources exaggerate this to the extreme[83] whereas the Sunnī sources try to ignore or minimize it as much as possible.[84] Historically it cannot be denied, however, that these men formed the nucleus of the first ʿAlid party, or the Shīʿa. It cannot be claimed that all were equally enthusiastic and warm supporters; some of them were lukewarm supporters who recognized ʿAlī's position as the most worthy for the office of the caliphate because of his personal merits, but nevertheless paid homage to Abū Bakr without much resentment. The attitude of ʿAmmār, Miqdād, Abū Dharr, and Salmān must have been different from that of the others. These four companions are regarded by all the Shīʿīs as "the Four Pillars" (*al-arkān al-arbaʿa*) who formed the first Shīʿa of ʿAlī. After ʿAlī's compromise with Abū Bakr, however, reasons for further opposition on the part of his supporters ceased to exist and this élite of the first Shīʿa dwindled away physically. But can ideas, once introduced, ever die out? The later years in the history of the development of Islamic thought provide an answer to this question.

Notes to Chapter 2

[1] Ibn Hishām, IV, pp. 306 f.

[2] ʿAbd al-ʿAzīz ad-Dūrī, "Al-Zuhrī, A Study on the Beginnings of History Writing in Islam", *BSOAS*, XIX (1957), p. 8

[3] Ibn Hishām, IV, pp. 307–10

[4] *Tahdhīb*, V, p. 164

[5] *Wafayāt*, IV, pp. 177 f.; *Tahdhīb*, IX, p. 445

[6] *Studies in Arabic Literary Papyri* (Chicago, 1957–72), I, pp. 5–31; II, pp. 5–64

[7] *Tahdhīb*, I, p. 97

[8] *Wafayāt*, III, pp. 255 ff.

[9] ibid., VI, pp. 35 f.

[10] *Tahdhīb*, VII, p. 23; *Aghānī*, IX, pp. 135 ff.

[11] Ibn Saʿd, II, pp. 379 ff.

[12] Ibn Saʿd, II, p. 382; *Aghānī*, IX, p. 137

[13] Ibn Saʿd, II, pp. 365 ff.

[14] See W. Montgomery Watt, "ʿAbd Allāh b. al-ʿAbbās", *EI*²

[15] Ibn Saʿd, III, pp. 169–213

[16] ibid., pp. 169–71

[17] ibid., pp. 171–2

[18] See Ch. 1, footnote 51

[19] Ibn Saʿd,III, pp. 172–8

[20] ibid., pp. 178–81

[21] ibid., p. 179

[22] ibid., pp. 181–5

[23] Ibn Saʿd, V, p. 187; Ibn Ḥajar, *Tahdhīb*, VIII, p. 333; *Wafayāt*, IV, pp. 59 f.

[24] For the life and work of Balādhurī, see Goitein's introduction to Volume V of the *Anṣāb*, pp. 9–32

[25] On these early writers, see, respectively, Ibn Nadīm, *Fihrist*, pp. 100 ff., 95, 277, 91, 93

[26] *Ansāb al-Ashrāf*, ed. Muḥammad Ḥamīdullāh (Cairo, 1960), I, pp. 579–91

[27] Goitein, op. cit., p. 18

[28] See footnote 12

[29] Dhahabī, *Mīzān*, II, p. 299

[30] ibid., IV, p. 154

[31] ibid., p. 436

[32] *Ta'rīkh* (Beirut, 1960), II, pp. 123–6

[33] E. L. Petersen, *ʿAlī And Muʿāwiya In Early Arabic Tradition* (Copenhagen 1964), pp. 169 ff.

[34] Najāshī, *Rijāl*, p. 245

[35] Ibn Nadīm, *Fihrist*, p. 101

[36] *Sharḥ Nahj al-Balāgha*, ed. Muḥammad Abū'l-Faḍl Ibrāhīm, 2nd ed. (Beirut, 1965), II, pp. 21–60

[37] ibid., pp. 44–60. For Al-Jawharī see *Adh-Dharī'a*, XII, p. 206

[38] *Adh-Dharī'a ilā Taṣānīf ash-Shī'a*, 24 volumes, Najaf, *passim*

[39] Dhahabī, *Mīzān*, II, p. 367

[40] ibid., p. 365

[41] Ṭabarī, I, pp. 1837–45

[42] *Murūj adh-Dhahab*, ed. Dāghir (Beirut 1965), II, p. 301, and *at-Tanbīh wa'l-Ishrāf* (Beirut 1965), p. 284, in both of which he mentions Saqīfa only in passing, referring his reader to his exclusive work on the subject, which unfortunately is lost.

[43] *Al-Kāmil fi't-Ta'rīkh*, II, pp. 221 ff. in which his account of Saqīfa is almost the same as that of Ṭabarī

[44] *Al-'Iqd al-Farīd*, IV, pp. 257 ff.

[45] *Ta'rīkh al-Khulafā'*, ed. 'Abd al-Ḥamīd, (Cairo, 1964), pp. 61–72

[46] *Al-Iḥtijāj*, ed. Muḥammad Bāqir al-Khursān (Najaf 1966), I, pp. 89–118

[47] *Bihār al-Anwār*

[48] A. Guillaume, translating the *Sīra*, collected all the assertions and comments of Ibn Hishām and arranged them separately at the end of the book under the heading, "Ibn Hishām's Notes". There are 922 notes of various length, some of them are as long as a page or more. See A. Guillaume, *The Life of Muḥammad* (Oxford, 1955), pp. 690–798

[49] This is a common accusation levelled against Ibn Isḥāq. See, however, Nabia Abbott's comments on this subject in *Studies in Arabic Literary Papyri* (Chicago, 1957–72), I, p. 97. The remarkable lack of any partiality in a fragment of the *Ta'rīkh al-Khulafā'* leads Abbott to question the accuracy of such accusations.

[50] For the translation of Ibn Isḥāq's account, I have largely drawn on Guillaume's translation of the *Sīra*.

[51] Dhahabī, *Mīzān*, I, p. 133

[52] ibid., p. 33

[53] Ibn Hishām, IV, pp. 306 f.

[54] Ḥadīd, *Sharḥ*, II, p. 25

[55] Later he explained to Ibn 'Abbās that he wrongly understood the Qur'ānic verse (II, 143) which says, "Thus we have made you a middle people that you may be a witness against men, *and that the Apostle may be a witness against you.*" Ibn Hishām, IV, pp. 311 f.

[56] e.g. Ṭabarī, I, p. 1683

[57] *Istī'āb*, III, p. 1248

[58] ibid., IV, p. 1441

[59] ibid., p. 1449. His father's name must be ʿArfaja.

[60] ibid., I., p. 316

[61] On these rivalries, see Montgomery Watt, *Muḥammad at Mecca*, pp. 4–8, 16–20, 141–4; idem, *Muḥammad at Medina* (Oxford, 1956), pp. 151–91

[62] *Istīʿāb*, II, p. 594

[63] ibid., I., pp. 92 ff. Yaʿqūbī's description of him (II, p. 124) as a Khazrajī leader must be a scribal error.

[64] *Istīʿāb*, I., pp. 172 ff. Our sources are not clear on who paid homage first. Yaʿqūbī, loc. cit., says it was Bashīr b. Saʿd, while according to Balādhurī, I, p. 582, it was Usayd b. Ḥuḍayr.

[65] See Henri Lammens, "Le 'triumvirat' Aboû Bakr, ʿOmar, et Aboû ʿObaida", *Mélanges de la Faculté Orientale de l'Université St Joseph de Beyrouth*, IV (1910), pp. 113–44

[66] From here on, our sources are utterly confused about the timing of the sequence of events, since each tradition is recorded separately. We are not, therefore, sure whether the demand of homage from ʿAlī and his supporters was made immediately after they came to the mosque from the Saqīfa, or after the burial of the Prophet on the following day when general homage was being paid to Abū Bakr. A careful reading of the sources (e.g. Balādhurī, I, p. 582) strongly suggests, however, that it was demanded as soon as they came to the mosque from the Saqīfa.

[67] Many versions of this tradition may be found in Balādhurī, I, pp. 585 f.; Yaʿqūbī, II, p. 126; Ṭabarī, I, p. 1818; Abū Bakr al-Jawharī in Ḥadīd, *Sharḥ Nahj al-Balāgha*, II, pp. 47, 50, 56 f.; *ʿIqd*, IV, pp. 259 f. *Al-Imāma Wa's-Siyāsa*, I, pp. 12–13, (though its attribution to Ibn Qutayba is incorrect, it is certainly a very early work extremely rich in sources) gives a very detailed account of the episode of ʿUmar and Abū Bakr's attack on the house of Fāṭima and the force used to secure ʿAlī's homage. Also L. V. Vaglieri, *EI*[2] article "Fāṭima", who, commenting on these events, says "Even if they have been expanded by invented details, they are based on facts."

[68] Yaʿqūbī, II, p. 126; Balādhurī, I, p. 586; Ṭabarī, I, p. 1825; *ʿIqd*, IV, p. 260; Ḥadīd, II, p. 22

[69] For the details and certain differences in names see Yaʿqūbī, loc. cit.; Balādhurī, I, p. 588; *ʿIqd*, IV, p. 259; Ḥadīd, II, pp. 50 ff.

[70] Ibn Saʿd, VI, p. 15; *Istīʿāb*, I, p. 334

[71] Ibn Saʿd, IV, pp. 378 ff.; *Istīʿāb*, II, p. 448

[72] Ibn Saʿd, III, pp 484 ff.; *Istīʿāb*, II, p. 424; IV, p. 1606

[73] Ibn Saʿd, III, pp. 471 f.; *Istīʿāb*, II, p. 662

[74] *Istīʿāb*, III, p. 1033

[75] Ibn Saʿd, IV, p. 364; *Istīʿāb*, I, pp. 155 f.

[76] Ibn Saʿd, III, p. 498; *Istīʿāb*, I, pp. 65 f.

[77] Ibn Sa'd, IV, p. 219; *Istī'āb*, IV, pp. 1652 f.
[78] Ibn Sa'd, III, p. 246; *Istī'āb*, III, pp. 1135 ff.
[79] *Istī'āb*, IV, pp. 1480 ff.
[80] Ibn Sa'd, IV, p. 75; *Istī'āb*, II, p. 634
[81] *Istī'āb*, II, p. 510
[82] Ibn Sa'd, IV, p. 97. *Istī'āb*, II, pp. 420 ff. For his support to 'Alī, see Balādhurī, I, p. 588; Ya'qūbī, p. 126; Ḥadīd, II, p. 58
[83] e.g. see Ṭabarsī, *Iḥtijāj*, I, pp. 118–89
[84] e.g. see Ibn Sa'd, III, pp. 181–5

Chapter 3

ʿAlī and the First Two Caliphs

The discussion above will suffice to elucidate our view that the origins of Shīʿī feelings and inclinations may be found in the conception of the sanctity for which the Banū Hāshim were widely known, in the special consideration with which ʿAlī was held by Muḥammad (who was, above all, fully conscious of his family's traditionally religious heritage and exalted position), and lastly, in the events in favour of ʿAlī which took place during Muḥammad's lifetime. Since the first convergence of these convictions focused on the questions and issues involved in the Saqīfa incident, this episode marks both the first open expression of and the point of departure for what ultimately developed into the Shīʿī understanding of Islam. However, after the initial defeat of ʿAlī's supporters and his own recognition of Abū Bakr's administration six months later, circumstances were such that Shīʿī tendencies lost most of their open and active manifestations. The period of the caliphates of Abū Bakr and ʿUmar, between the Saqīfa episode and the *Shūrā* (the election of ʿUthmān), is thus one of comparative dormancy in the history of the development of Shī ʿism.

Nevertheless, a close scrutiny of the early sources, and especially a careful comparison of the Shīʿī and Sunnī early records, reveals two distinct and important undercurrents in operation throughout this period; firstly, ʿAlī's passive attitude towards the ruling authorities; and secondly, the attempts of Abū Bakr and ʿUmar to displace Banū Hāshim, and especially ʿAlī, from their prerogative claims to the leadership of the community according to their own understanding of the new order and the form they felt it should take. Both of these trends apparent in this period form an inseparable phase in the development of Shī'ī ideas and therefore should be taken into consideration.

'Alī's passive attitude can easily be illustrated by comparing the active role played by him during the lifetime of Muḥammad with his completely inactive and withdrawn life in the period immediately following the Prophet's death. The most active and enthusiastic participant in all the enterprises in the cause of Islam and a great warrior in the forefront of all the battles fought under Muḥammad,[1] 'Alī suddenly reverted to leading a quiet life, almost confined to the four walls of his house. This marked contrast cannot have been without serious causes.[2] Seeing 'Alī's firm conviction that he had the best claims to succeed Muḥammad, as is evident from all the sources, one would have expected him to fight for his rights to the bitter end. He did not resort to this course of action, however, even though such opportunities presented themselves. He declined to make use of the strong military support offered to him by Abū Sufyān to fight for his rights, for he considered that such action would lead to the destruction of infant Islam.[3] At the same time, on the other hand, he did not recognize Abū Bakr and refused to pay him homage for six months. In addition to the demoralizing factor of Fāṭima's death, which occurred six months after the succession of Abū Bakr, what perhaps compelled 'Alī to reconcile his position with the existing order was the serious eruption of apostasy and rebellion among the Arab tribes in the peninsula. This coincidence of Abū Bakr's succession and the rebellion of the tribes naturally forced people in Medina to forget whatever ideological or personal differences they had and to unite themselves against a common danger. Such a serious external threat to the very existence of the Islamic order proved to be a great advantage to Abū Bakr in reducing internal opposition to his rule. The character of 'Alī as presented by both Sunnī and Shī'ī sources alike suggests that his feelings of love, dedication, sincerity, and undivided loyalty to the cause of Islam were above personal considerations. From the age of thirteen he had been committed to the service of the mission of the Prophet; seeing such a dangerous and widespread rebellion of the tribes against Islam, 'Alī had no choice but to reconcile himself with the existing order. This he did. But he did not take any active part in any of the apostasy wars, thus still preserving his withdrawn attitude; nor did Abū Bakr ask him to participate in the wars outside Medina.

In spite of maintaining his withdrawn and passive attitude towards Abū Bakr and ʿUmar, ʿAlī did occasionally help the caliphs. This co-operation rendered to the ruling caliphs appears to have been of the same nature as that expected of any reasonable opposition leader. He recognized that, under the circumstances, the solidarity, security, and integrity of the community could only be preserved if the diverse groups which it comprised were willing to co-operate and maintain harmonious relations among themselves. Yet within this framework he attempted, again as was to be expected, to correct what he regarded as mistakes of the government, and criticized policies which differed from his viewpoint.

The points of difference in religious and political matters between ʿAlī on the one hand, and Abū Bakr and ʿUmar on the other, are difficult to ascertain because both the Sunnī and the Shīʿī source materials are extremely tendentious. The Sunnī sources, such as the works of Ibn Saʿd and those who followed him, were written in the period when the recognition of the first four caliphs as the *Rāshidūn* was firmly established in the *Jamāʿa*. (The English term "orthodoxy", which is usually used for the central body of the Muslims, is in an Islamic context not only incorrect but misleading; we shall therefore use the Arabic term *Jamāʿa* for this so-called orthodoxy.) Naturally, every effort was made to show as much agreement as possible, at least between ʿAlī, Abū Bakr, and ʿUmar. ʿUthmān tends to be excluded in religious and political matters, though attempts were nevertheless made to save even ʿUthmān's position by blaming the abuses of his caliphate on Marwān, his notorious secretary. On the other hand, the Shīʿī sources give a completely different and extreme view of ʿAlī's disagreement, not only with ʿUthmān, but also with Abū Bakr and ʿUmar, on almost every matter, whether religious or political. In short, according to the Sunnī sources, ʿAlī was a valued counsellor of the caliphs who preceded him; according to the Shīʿī sources, he was the person who, dominated by his heroic love and sense of sacrifice for the faith and disregarding his personal grievances, saved the caliphs from committing the serious mistakes to which they were often prone and which would otherwise have been suicidal for Islam. ʿUmar is thus often reported to have said: "Had there not been ʿAlī, ʿUmar would have perished." It is very interesting to note that this statement is reported by some of the important early Sunnī authors too.[4]

Apart from some of the serious points of disagreement between ʿAlī and his first two successful rivals, for which there is unanimous historical testimony, as we shall point out below, exactitude in the determination of the mass of this material is probably beyond our reach. The truth, however, seems to have been, as Veccia Vaglieri suggests, that "ʿAlī was included in the council of the caliphs, but although it is probable that he was asked for advice on legal matters in view of his excellent knowledge of the *Qurʾān* and the *Sunna,* it is extremely doubtful whether his advice was accepted by ʿUmar, who had been a ruling power even during the caliphate of Abū Bakr."[5] Moreover, evidence of ʿAlī's opinions not being accepted on religious matters is manifested in the fact that his decisions very seldom find a place in the later-developed Sunnī schools of law, whereas ʿUmar's decisions find common currency among them. On the other hand, ʿAlī is a frequently quoted authority on matters of law in all Shīʿī branches.[6] On political and administrative matters, his disagreement with ʿUmar on the question of *dīwān* (distribution of stipends) and his absence from all the wars fought under ʿUmar can be well cited. Without further elaboration, it may safely be assumed from our evidence that, regardless of the exact nature of his feelings and aspirations, ʿAlī maintained a passive and withdrawn attitude towards the caliphates of both Abū Bakr and ʿUmar.

ʿAlī accepted the political realities of his day, but nevertheless remained convinced of the fact that he was better qualified for the caliphate and that he had been unjustly deprived of the leadership of the community. ʿAlī's feelings regarding his predecessors are best expressed in his own words in one of his famous speeches at the mosque of Kūfa during his own caliphate. This historic exposition of ʿAlī, known as *ash-Shaqshiqiyya,* is recorded by Ash-Sharīf ar-Raḍī in the *Nahj al-Balāgha,*[7] which contains ʿAlī's sermons, speeches, letters, and maxims. As with most of the material presented in this valuable work, there can hardly be any doubt as to the authenticity of this speech, since it was reported by many early authors long before Ash-Sharīf ar-Raḍī. ʿAlī says:

"Nay, by God, the son of Abū Quḥāfa [Abū Bakr] had exacted the caliphate for himself while he knew full well that my position in it was like that of the pivot in a mill; the flood waters flow down beneath me and the birds do not soar high up to me; yet I hung up a curtain before it and turned aside from it [the caliphate]. I then started thinking whether I should attack with a severing hand or should watch patiently the blind darkness in which the old man becomes decrepit and the young man old, in which the believer tries his utmost till he meets his Lord, and I came to the conclusion that patience in a situation like this was wiser. So I adopted patience, although there was a mote rankling in my eye and a bone sticking in my throat on seeing my heritage being plundered, till the first one [Abū Bakr] died and handed over the reins of the caliphate to another person [ʿUmar] after him. [Here ʿAlī quotes a verse from the poet Āʿsha, which reads] 'How vast is the difference between this day of mine when I am on the back of the camel [i.e. suffering from the hardship of a rough journey] and the day of Ḥayyān, brother of Jābir [i.e. when he was comfortably placed under the power and prestige of Ḥayyān].'[8] How hard did they [Abū Bakr and ʿUmar] squeeze its udders and how they made it [the caliphate] travel on a rugged path, which inflicts deep wounds and is rough to the touch, in which one stumbles frequently and has to offer excuses, so that its rider is like the rider of a difficult mount: if he draws its reins tight, its nose is pierced, and if he relaxes it, he plunges into destruction. And so the people were afflicted, by God, with stumbling, refractoriness, capriciousness, and cross-purposes. But I kept patience in spite of the length of time and the severity of the ordeal, until he [ʿUmar] went his way."[9]

ʿAlī thus describes his feelings towards the reign of his two predecessors and summarizes their periods in the caliphate. Ibn Abī 'l-Ḥadīd, writing a long commentary on this speech, explains major characteristics of the first two caliphs, their policies in arranging the affairs of the community, their attitude towards ʿAlī, and ʿAlī's reservations about the handling of matters by them.

We may now turn to the second observation made above concerning this interim period in the development of Shīʿism: the attempts made by both Abū Bakr and ʿUmar to displace the Banū Hāshim in general and 'Alī in particular from prerogatives in the leadership of the *Umma.* The first and most important step in this direction was taken by Abū Bakr on the day following the Prophet's death, when Fāṭima came to claim the estate of Fadak. She asserted that this estate was given to her father unconditionally as his share of the spoils of Khaybar.[10] Quoting Muḥammad's words: "We [the Prophets] do not leave as inheritance what we make legal alms," Abū Bakr refused her claim, maintaining that Fadak belonged to the community as a whole and that Fāṭima, although entitled to the usufruct, could not hold the right of ownership.[11]

This question of inheritance soon became one of the most debated problems in the conflict between the Shī'a and their opponents.[12] It might seem that Abū Bakr's refusal in effect meant that no claims would be justified on family grounds. To acknowledge the justice of one claim of inheritance based on family ties would open the door to further and more extensive claims, and Abū Bakr felt that to accept the rights of the family of 'Alī to the inheritance of Fadak might be regarded as equal to admitting their rights to the succession of the Prophet in all spheres, spiritual as well as material. This fear was perhaps based on the grounds that Muḥammad, as leader of the community, was entitled to one fifth of the spoils of war (*Khums*), and by this special right he became owner of the Fadak. To inherit a property as a token of an exalted position and prerogative was somewhat different from an ordinary inheritance. It is almost unanimously reported that after this event Fāṭima did not speak to either Abū Bakr or 'Umar till her death six months later. She asked 'Alī to have her buried at night, and not to allow Abū Bakr and 'Umar to take part in her funeral. 'Alī accordingly carried out her wishes and buried her at night, with only the family members accompanying her coffin.[13]

The caliphate of Abū Bakr lasted just over two years, and on his deathbed he explicitly appointed 'Umar, already a ruling power behind him, as his successor. The way he arranged the problem of succession after him leaves us in no doubt that Abū Bakr had made up his mind in favour of 'Umar since his assumption of the caliphate. He took careful measures to preclude any possibility of opposition to his nomination of ʿUmar and made sure that the latter should not face any difficulty. He was fully aware of ʿAlī's claims to the caliphate and the support and respect he enjoyed from a certain group. Abū Bakr therefore first called ʿAbd ar-Raḥmān b. ʿAwf, told him about his decision, and after some persuasion secured his consent. The only other person whom the dying caliph called in to make his decision known was ʿUthmān b. ʿAffān. When the news of Abū Bakr's decision came out, some of the prominent Companions of the Prophet became extremely disturbed and apprehensive. Under the leadership of Ṭalḥa, they sent a delegation to protest against the decision and tried to persuade the Caliph not to nominate ʿUmar.[14] Nothing could change Abū Bakr's mind, and he asked ʿUthmān to write down his testament in favour of ʿUmar. The community at large had no share in the choice and was told by the Caliph to accept his nomination and obey ʿUmar as the new caliph after him, for he could not think of anyone more suitable than him. The testament he announced before the people reads:

> "This is a testament of Abū Bakr, the successor of the Prophet of God, to the believers and the Muslims . . . I have appointed as ruler over you ʿUmar b. al-Khaṭṭāb, so listen to him and obey him. I have not made him your ruler except for [your] good."[15]

Anyone reading the account of ʿUmar's nomination by Abū Bakr will immediately notice that the decision was neither based on the method of consultation with the élite of the people, nor was the opinion of the community in general sought before the choice was made. It was simply Abū Bakr's own personal and arbitrary decision, which he wanted to be endorsed by only those of the Companions whom he considered most important from a clannish point of view, as will be seen below.

For our interest, however, at once the most important and revealing point is that in this entire process of the nomination of ʿUmar by Abū Bakr, ʿAli was totally ignored and excluded from the ranks of those the dying Caliph called for consultation, if consultation it was, and whose support he tried to secure. In fact, as all of our sources unanimously report, from all the Companions of the Prophet only two, ʿAbd ar-Raḥmān b. ʿAwf and ʿUthmān, were selected by Abū

Bakr for consultation and then were entrusted with the charge of wholehearted support for ʿUmar.[16] This in all probability must have been on the suggestion of ʿUmar himself, who planned to counteract any possible opposition from the Banū Hāshim by appealing to this branch of the Quraysh. ʿAbd ar-Raḥmān belonged to the Banū Zuhra and ʿUthmān to the Banū Umayya, both of which had been serious rivals of Banū Hāshim before Islam. The emergence of these two Companions was very characteristic in many ways, especially for the development of the later history of the caliphate, for they represented the wealthiest circles of the Muslim community.[17] ʿAbd ar-Raḥmān was ʿUthmān's brother-in-law, and the two men could be expected to support each other. The former also had the wholehearted support of Saʿd b. Abī Waqqās, a fellow clan member and cousin from the Banū Zuhra. In this way the direct support and influence of the most important political elements among the Muhājirūn were secured to oppose any possible activity from the Banū Hāshim and their partisans in favour of ʿAlī's candidacy.

ʿAlī's serious disagreements with the policies of ʿUmar in both political and religious matters will be discussed below in connection with the selection of ʿUthmān. Here it may be pointed out in passing that during the most active and eventful ten years of ʿUmar's caliphate, in which the most spectacular conquests of Persian and Byzantine provinces took place and in which all the prominent Companions of the Prophet took active part, ʿAlī remained uninvolved. Nor did ʿAlī hold any office under ʿUmar, as had been the case under Abū Bakr and would continue later under ʿUthmān. The only exception was his being in charge of Medina during ʿUmar's journey to Palestine, when he took with him all the other leading Companions of the Prophet and military commanders to approve regulations of the conquest and the *dīwān*. ʿAlī alone was absent from the historic surrender of Jerusalem and Syria. ʿUmar is reported to have strictly prevented the Banū Hāshim from going out of Medina.[18] This is evident from the very fact that neither ʿAlī nor any other member of the Banū Hāshim has been reported to have taken part in any activity outside the capital.

ʿUmar's attitude towards ʿAlī is best illustrated by a dialogue which took place between the former and Ibn

ʿAbbās. On a certain occasion ʿUmar asked Ibn ʿAbbās, "Why did ʿAlī not join us and co-operate with us? Why did the Quraysh not support your family while your father is the uncle and you are the cousin of the Prophet?" "I do not know," replied Ibn ʿAbbās. "But I know the reason," said ʿUmar. "Because the Quraysh did not like to allow both the Prophethood and the caliphate to be combined in your house, for with this you would feel arrogant and rejoice."[19] In another version, when ʿUmar heard some verses of Zuhayr b. Abī Sulma which described the glory, nobility of descent, and virtues of the clan of Banū ʿAbd Allāh b. Ghaṭfān, he said to Ibn ʿAbbās: "I do not know any other clan among the Quraysh to whom these verses can be better applied than the Banū Hāshim, because of their relationship and superior claims to the Prophet, but the people did not like to allow the Prophethood and the caliphate in your family so that you would become arrogant and rejoice at it among the people. The Quraysh, therefore, preferred to choose the leader for themselves and they made the right choice and were guided by God in that." "O, Prince of the Faithful," said Ibn ʿAbbās, "as for your statement that the Quraysh chose their own leader and were guided in the right choice, it may be correct if the choice of Quraysh for their leader was in the same sense as the choice of God from among the Quraysh. As for your statement that the Quraysh did not like to allow both the Prophethood and the caliphate to be with us, it is not surprising, for God has described many people who disliked 'what God has sent down to them and thus render their deeds fruitless'."[20] At this point ʿUmar became angry and said: "I have heard many things about you but I ignored them because of my regard for you. I am told that you think that we have taken away the caliphate from you through oppression and because of envy." "As for oppression, it is evident," said Ibn ʿAbbās, "and as concerns envy, so it is obvious; Satan envied Adam and we are the children of Adam." ʿUmar lost his temper and retorted, "Alas, O Banū Hāshim, your hearts are full of hatred, rancour, and false pretensions." "Be gentle, O Prince of the Faithful," said Ibn ʿAbbās, "and do not describe the hearts of the people from whom God has removed all kinds of uncleanliness and purified them with complete purification.[21] Moreover, the Prophet himself belonged to the Banū Hāshim." "Let us leave this topic," said 'Umar.[22] The dialogue speaks for itself and needs no comment. It will suffice to say that it is one of the most revealing statements in explaining the attitude of 'Umar towards 'Alī on the one hand, and the Hāshimite attitude towards 'Alī's predecessors in the caliphate on the other.

However, the dominating personality of 'Umar and his realistic understanding of the tides of the time were strong enough not to allow any manifestation of discontent during his rule, which was continuously involved in the conquest of rich new lands for Islam. The occupation of Abū Bakr with quelling the rebellion of the apostate tribes within the Arabian peninsula, and of 'Umar in conquering foreign lands, served, consciously or unconsciously, to keep internal feuds at rest. On the whole, the caliphate of 'Umar, as that of his predecessor Abū Bakr, characterizes a period in which Islamic ideals of simplicity, justice, equality, devotion to the cause, zeal for the faith, and a socio-economic equilibrium according to their understanding of these, were best represented. After a successful rule of ten years, however, the powerful caliph met his end by the dagger of a Persian slave and died on 26 Dhū'l-Ḥijja 23/3 November 644.

Unlike Abū Bakr, 'Umar during his long caliphate could not develop complete trust and confidence in any one person to justify nominating him as his successor.[23] He nevertheless restricted the choice to six of the early Companions among the Muhājirūn, who had to choose one of themselves as the new caliph. The members of this committee, later referred to by the Muslim jurists and theorists as the *Shūrā* or electorate body, were: 'Uthmān, 'Abd ar-Raḥmān b. 'Awf, Sa'd b. Abī Waqqāṣ, 'Alī, Zubayr, and Ṭalḥa, with 'Umar's own son 'Abd Allāh only in the capacity of an advisor, not as a candidate.[24] Two conspicuous factors are to be observed here. First, the community at Medina as a whole had no say in the selection of the new leader, as both candidacy and decision-making power were confined to the six persons nominated by the Caliph; thus the principle of so-called democracy or election by the people in choosing their leader cannot be applied. Second and more important is the fact that the Anṣār of Medina were completely excluded from expressing their opinion in the affair of the leadership. Perhaps this was due either to their pro-ʿAlid sympathies manifested at the Saqīfa, or to ʿUmar's desire to eliminate any possibility of an Anṣāri being suggested as a candidate. This proved to be a serious blow to the political influence of the Anṣār, and one from which they were never able to recover.

It is not intended to record here in detail the events of the *Shūrā* as such, but rather to recall what had a direct bearing on the development of Shīʿīsm. According to the unanimous account given by our sources, ʿUmar meticulously laid down the regulations which had to be followed by the committee. These regulations were that: 1: the new caliph must be one of this committee, elected by the majority vote of its members; 2: that in the case of two candidates having equal support, the one backed by ʿAbd ar-Raḥmān b. ʿAwf was to be nominated; 3: that if any member of the council shrank from participating, he was to be beheaded instantly; and lastly, 4: that when a candidate had been duly elected, in the event of one or two members of the conclave refusing to recognize him, this minority, or, in the case of equal division of three members on each side, the group opposed to ʿAbd ar-Raḥmān, were to be slain. To enforce this order ʿUmar called in Abū Ṭalḥa al-Anṣārī[25] of the tribe of Khazraj, commanding him to select fifty trusted persons from his tribe to stand at the door of the assembly with swords in hand to ensure that the members of the committee should follow these orders.[26] By appointing the Khazrajites, who immediately after the death of the Prophet had wanted the leadership for themselves, ʿUmar guaranteed that his orders would not be taken lightly.

There is hardly any room to doubt the authenticity of the report that ʿUmar imposed such stern regulations on the members of the committee. Few accounts in the early history of Islam have received such unanimous historical testimony as that of ʿUmar's arrangements of the *Shūrā* and the regulations laid down by him. A comparison of the texts of Balādhurī, Yaʿqūbī, Ṭabarī, and Masʿūdī, followed by numerous other historians such as Dhahabī and Ibn al-Athīr, shows that the basic account is the same in all of them. All these writers cite different authorities belonging to different and often conflicting schools of thought and inclination.[27] Nabia Abbott[28] has recently published a papyrus fragment of Ibn Isḥāq's *Taʾrīkh al-Khulafāʾ* (with valuable commentary) which deals with the *Shūrā* and the terms fixed by ʿUmar. Ibn Isḥāq wrote at least one hundred years before any one of the historians cited above, and it is of great importance to note that the account given by Ibn Isḥāq is strikingly the same. This confirms the account of our historians. Besides this unanimous historical testimony, the circumstances of the time and other guiding factors strongly attest to the accuracy of the account. When we compare ʿUmar's characteristic sternness dominant in his personality and the decisive policies that characterized his rule, with the nature of the regulations imposed by him on the members of the electorate council at such a critical moment, the two factors are in conformity with each other. In addition, the manner in which all the historians record the conditions makes it clear that, on the one hand, ʿUmar was sure that only one of these six companions could become the next caliph, but, on the other hand, he was certain that they would oppose each other in order to avail themselves of the opportunity for leadership. He was therefore afraid of critical dissension among the possible candidates and the disastrous consequences this would have for the young community. This is clearly evident from the report that ʿUmar called in the members of the *Shūrā* and said: "I looked around and found that you are the leaders of the people and the caliphate cannot go except to one of you; but I am afraid that dissension will arise among you and [because of your dissension] the people will also split among themselves."[29] Thus motivated, he laid down such stringent restrictions as he deemed necessary to protect the community from the effects of disastrous schism.

These measures, however, did simultaneously accomplish two main purposes which seem to have been in the mind of the dying Caliph, and which he must have thought to be in the best interests of the community. On the one hand, these measures saved the young *Umma,* though only for the time being, from serious dissension; on the other hand, through these meticulous arrangements ʿUmar completed the task of keeping the caliphate away from the Banū Hāshim, an endeavour he had undertaken immediately after the Prophet's death. Being fully aware of ʿAlī's claims and remembering that he had not even recognized Abū Bakr for six months, ʿUmar knew that ʿAlī would not agree to make his claims the subject of debate in a self-instituted council of electors unless he was bound to do so under compulsion. Though aware of the considerable ambitions of both Zubayr and Ṭalḥa, ʿUmar also realized that ʿAlī and ʿUthmān, among all other members of the council, carried much more weight and realistically were the only ones who had the support necessary to advance themselves as serious candidates, each backed by his own clan, the Banū Hāshim and the Banū Umayya respectively. ʿUmar also seems to have realized that ʿAlī stood a much better chance of success now than ʿUthmān on the grounds which have been discussed in Chapter I. It was no longer possible for the Caliph to simply ignore the claims of ʿAlī, and had he not forced him to become a member of the *Shūrā*, he would have given the Prophet's cousin and the candidate of the Banū Hāshim a free hand to strive for office for himself.[30]

By bestowing both the chairmanship and the final authority of the committee on ʿAbd ar-Raḥmān b. ʿAwf, ʿUmar effectively blocked the chances of ʿAlī and virtually guaranteed the nomination of ʿUthmān. This was such an obvious fact that almost all of our sources record it in the very words of ʿAlī himself. When he heard the regulations laid down by ʿUmar and that ʿAbd ar-Raḥmān was given the casting vote, ʿAlī remonstrated, saying:

> "By God, the caliphate (*Amr*) has again been taken away from us because the final authority rests in the hands of ʿAbd ar-Raḥmān, who is an old friend and brother-in-law of ʿUthmān, whereas Saʿd b. Abī Waqqāṣ is ʿAbd ar-Raḥmān's cousin from the Banū Zuhra; naturally these three will support each other, and even if Zubayr and Ṭalḥa vote for me it would be of no use."[31]

In this way, ʿUmar dealt a final blow to the superior claims of the Banū Hāshim by giving their old rivals, the Banū Umayya, a new lease of power. The clan of Umayya, on its part, saw this as its golden opportunity, and Abū Sufyān in particular regarded the accession of ʿUthmān as the return of the entire clan to a position of power which they should at all costs preserve.[32]

ʿAbbās b. ʿAbd al-Muṭṭalib, the Prophet's uncle and head of the Banū Hāshim, is reported to have warned ʿAlī not to participate in the *Shūrā* and to maintain his freedom of action,[33] but ʿUmar's provisions precluded such a course of action. All of our sources agree that 'Alī yielded only under direct pressure, threatened by fear of arms if he declined to abide by 'Umar's will.[34] When one recalls 'Alī's protests twelve years earlier against the nomination of Abū Bakr after the death of the Prophet, it is not difficult to imagine how deeply disappointed 'Alī must have been to see, for a third time, another man given preference over him. This he describes in his speech of Ash-Shaqshiqiyya, the first part of which has been quoted above:

> "'Umar [from his death-bed] entrusted it [the choice of caliph] to six persons among whom he claimed one was I. By God, and what a council [i.e., "what chance did I stand in it?"]. When did doubt about me cross anyone's mind, even in the case of the first of them [Abū Bakr] so that I was associated to a member of his like?[35] But I went along with them in all situations and I dropped low when they dropped and flew up when they flew. Then one of them [Sa'd] inclined towards his companion ['Abd ar-Raḥmān] while 'Abd ar-Raḥmān swayed in favour of his brother-in-law ['Uthmān], and they did other unmentionable things."[36]

It is by no means easy to establish what really transpired in the deliberations and debates of the council which resulted in the appointment of 'Uthmān. In the mass of the material handed down to us, there is, however, a commonly reported tradition, at once very important and most revealing. It is said that, after three days of long debates and wrangling, at the time of the morning prayer when the Muslims assembled in the mosque to hear the decision of the electoral body, 'Abd ar-Raḥmān b. 'Awf first offered the caliphate to 'Alī on two conditions: one, that he should rule in accordance with the *Qur'ān* and the *Sunna* of the Prophet; and two, that he must follow the precedents established by two former caliphs. Accepting the first condition, 'Alī declined to comply with the second, declaring that in all cases in which he found no positive law of the *Qur'ān* or decision of the Prophet, he would only rely on his own judgement. 'Abd ar-Raḥmān then turned to 'Uthmān and put the same conditions before him. 'Uthmān readily consented to them, whereupon 'Abd ar-Raḥmān declared him caliph.[37] As will be discussed below, this point was later made the basis of the differences between Sunnī and Shī'ī legal theory and practice, whereby the Shī'ī jurists rejected the decisions of the first three caliphs.

This tradition bears the unanimous testimony of both Sunnī and Shīʿī historians alike, and therefore its authenticity can hardly be questioned, as has been done by some scholars. If later Sunnī theologians attempted to ignore it, it was simply because of the fact that the tradition compromised the newly established concept of the acceptance of the first four caliphs as the *Rāshidūn* (rightly guided), and their decisions as precedents for the foundation of the *Jamāʿa*. Apart from this historical evidence, the most convincing factor in support of the accuracy of this tradition lies in ʿAlī's own independent nature and in the marked individuality of his character. When we try to delineate ʿAlī's character from his conversion to Islam at the age of ten or so until his death, the following characteristics emerge. He was uncompromising in his principles, straightforward, and above all too stern in his religious outlook, a factor which may have contributed to the later failure of his own caliphate. These features predominate throughout his career. It is not possible here to go into the details of his biography, but the clearest expressions of his independent attitude are to be found in instances such as when he insisted that *ḥadd* (punishment) be carried out on ʿAbd Allah b. ʿUmar for the murder of Hurmuzān.[38] On another occasion, when all others refused to administer the flogging punishment on Walīd b. ʿUqba, guilty of drunkenness, ʿAlī took this task on himself.[39] A still stronger manifestation of his rigid adherence to principles was when he issued orders of dismissal to Muʿāwiya and other Umayyad governors, though advised by his friends to first consolidate his strength in the capital.[40]

As has been discussed above, even during ʿAlī's period of general inactivity there were points of serious disagreement between him and the Caliphs Abū Bakr and ʿUmar. He was entirely opposed to ʿUmar on the question of *dīwān,* and recommended the distribution of the entire revenue, holding nothing in reserve, a policy which ʿUmar did not accept.[41] Involving, as it did, so many administrative and financial questions, this disagreement can hardly be considered insignificant, and in fact it was only one of several major disputes to which the sources allude. Naṣr b. Muzāḥim al-Minqarī (died 212/827), one of the earliest writers of great importance and credibility, preserved for us the revealing correspondence exchanged between 'Alī and Mu'āwiya. Mu'āwiya, in his letter to 'Alī, besides accusing him of responsibility for the murder of 'Uthmān, which is the main theme of the letter, levelled other charges against him as well. One of them was that 'Alī tried to rebel against Abū Bakr, delayed in recognizing him as the caliph, did not co-operate with the first two caliphs during their caliphates, and continually disagreed with them.[42] 'Alī in his reply, while rejecting all other accusations as false, argued that his delay in recognizing Abū Bakr and his resentment towards him was due to the fact that he considered himself better qualified for the leadership of the community on the same grounds as Abū Bakr had put forward against the Anṣār. That is, if the Quraysh had better claims as against the Anṣār because of the former's relationship to the Prophet, then the Banū Hāshim had the strongest rights, being nearest to the Prophet in relationship.[43]

'Abd ar-Raḥmān knew these differences full well and at the same time he also knew equally well 'Alī's independent and uncompromising nature. But this time, with the deaths of the dominating personalities of Abū Bakr, 'Umar, and Abū 'Ubayda b. al-Jarrāḥ, it was not so easy to set 'Alī aside without serious cause, for his possible rivals (or rival in the person of 'Uthmān) were much inferior to him in many ways. The deed was, however, accomplished by involving 'Alī in an elective committee in which he had no chance of gaining solid majority support, and then offering him the caliphate on terms which would be unacceptable to him.

'Uthmān was a weak man; apart from considerations of family relationships and personal friendship, this weakness was probably one of the reasons why 'Abd ar-Raḥmān supported him. Realizing the weakness of his own claims to the office, 'Abd ar-Raḥmān wanted to establish as caliph a man who would rely on him and serve his interests, which were those of the Quraysh aristocracy and the rich. 'Alī, who belonged to the poor and ascetically minded (*zuhhād*) class, had little in common with such interests and is reported to have repeatedly denounced worldly comforts by saying, "O gold and silver, try to tempt someone other than me."[44] In contrast to this attitude, 'Abd ar-Raḥmān and other members of the *Shūrā* were men of prosperity and wealth, and now, with the conquests of the Byzantine and Persian empires, they were avidly seeking the tremendous new opportunities opened up before them. ʿUthmān's caliphate provided them with such an opportunity and within a few years they had accumulated enormous wealth and had become the richest people of the community. ʿUthmān himself left at his death 100,000 dinars, 1,000,000 dirhams, and estates worth over 100,000 dinars in addition to herds of horses and camels. Similarly the riches of ʿAbd ar-Raḥmān, Zubayr, Ṭalḥa and Saʿd b. Abī Waqqāṣ are described as running into millions.[45] Apart from group politics and party partisanship, it was therefore quite natural for such men to elect someone representing their own class.

The selection of ʿUthmān did not pass without serious protest from ʿAlī himself and opposition from some of his old and ardent partisans. Keeping in view the long-standing disputes between the Banū Hāshim and the Banū Umayya, going back to the days of Hāshim b. ʿAbd Manāf and his brother ʿAbd ash-Shams over the religious and political leadership of the Quraysh, one can well imagine Banū Hāshim's feelings now that the new authority stemming from Muḥammad, a Hāshimite, had been taken over by an Umayyad. The speeches made and the harsh words exchanged between the supporters of ʿAlī and those of ʿUthmān, following ʿAbd ar-Raḥmān's announcement of the selection of the latter, manifest not only partisanship for one or the other, but the trends of thinking and the fundamental differences in approach. Ibn Abī Sarḥ, a notorious Umayyad, once condemned to death by the Prophet,[46] spoke enthusiastically in support of ʿUthmān, with whom he had been suckled by the same wet-nurse, and said to ʿAbd ar-Raḥmān, "If you desire that the Quraysh should not split among themselves, then appoint ʿUthmān." On this ʿAmmār b. Yāsir, an ardent supporter of ʿAlī, rebuking Ibn Abī Sarḥ and referring to his past anti-Islamic career, reproachfully said, "Since when have you become an advisor to the Muslims?"[47] A heated exchange of words followed between the Banū Hāshim and the Banū Umayya. Here the statement of ʿAmmār is worth noting, when he said, "O people, God has made us most honourable through His Prophet and distinguished us through His religion, but you are turning away from the people of the house (*Ahl al-Bayt*) of your Prophet." In reply to this, someone from the clan of Makhzūm, an old rival of the Banū Hāshim, retorted, saying: "This is a matter to be settled among the Quraysh themselves [ʿAmmār was a South Arabian]. Who are you to interfere in our affairs?"[48] The protest of Miqdād in favour of ʿAlī was even stronger than that of ʿAmmār. He said: "It is very hard to see how the people are paying their respect to the members of the family (*Ahl al-Bayt*) of their Prophet after him. It is indeed shocking to see that the Quraysh have forsaken and by-passed the man who is the best among them." Then someone asked Miqdād: "Who are these *Ahl al-Bayt,* and who is that man from them?" "*Ahl al-Bayt* means Banū ʿAbd al-Muṭṭalib and the man is ʿAlī b. Abī Ṭālib," replied Miqdād.[49] These protests may be taken as some of the documented remnants of much more serious vocal disputes: fragments that survived the dominant trends in the history of this critical period of Islam. What must particularly be noted here is the frequent use of the term *Ahl al-Bayt* of the Prophet in relation to the leadership of the community. Keeping in mind the importance of the noble families and the concept of sacerdotal lineages among some sections of the Arabs, as discussed in Chapter 1, it is easily understandable that some people were shocked to see the family of the Prophet so deprived after his death.

The most significant point in this whole event of the *Shūrā,* however, lies in ʿAlī's historic refusal to follow the precedents established by the first two caliphs. This intransigent declaration of ʿAlī forms the most important and the earliest theoretical point which ultimately gave rise to the later development of two different schools of law under the titles of Shīʿī and Sunnī, the former including the Ithnā ʿAsharī, Ismāʿīlī, and Zaydī, the latter including the Ḥanafī, Mālikī, Shāfiʿī and Ḥanbalī. If ideological differences between the two schools date back to the event of the Saqīfa, the differences, in legal matters at least theoretically, must be dated from ʿAlī's refusal to follow the precedents of the first two caliphs. This refusal thus serves as a cornerstone in the development of Shīʿī legal thought. An exponent of the history of ideas would tell us that it often takes a considerably long time for a given idea to present itself in a complete form, and as we shall see later, the idea expressed by ʿAlī in the

Shūrā took at least fifty years to become manifest in a distinguishable independent form and was not fully developed until the imamate of Jaʿfar aṣ-Ṣādiq.

To conclude this phase, we can remark that the selection of ʿUthmān was very largely based on economic, social, and tribal considerations, as exemplified by the speeches made on his behalf. On the other hand, the protests against ʿUthmān's nomination and in support of ʿAlī from men like ʿAmmār and Miqdād were very largely based on religious aspirations. The arguments put forward by these supporters of ʿAlī, as quoted above, concerning his relationship with the Prophet and his unsurpassed services to Islam, practically echo the statements made in favour of ʿAlī's cause at the Saqīfa over a decade earlier. Despite his passive and withdrawn attitude, ʿAlī still retained a devoted core of supporters in the Muslim community.

Notes to Chapter 3

[1] For 'Alī's active participation and unceasing services in furthering the cause of Islam during Muḥammad's lifetime, the fullest and most reliable source is Ibn Hishām's *Sīra.*

[2] This contrast is pointed out by Veccia Vaglieri, in *EI*[2] article "'Alī".

[3] Ṭabārī, I, p. 1827; Balādhurī, I, p. 588

[4] e.g. *Istī'āb,* III, p. 1104. For Shī'ī sources see Majlisī, *Bihār,* VIII, p. 59; *Iḥtijāj,* I, p. 103

[5] L.V. Vaglieri, *EI*[2] article "'Alī"

[6] For the Ithnā 'Asharites, see Kulaynī, *Uṣūl al-Kāfī* and *Furū' al-Kāfī*; for the Ismā'īlites, see Qāḍī Nu'mān, *Da'ā'im al-Islām*

[7] Some scholars have questioned the authenticity of the *Nahj al-Balāgha* and have suggested that it was written by Ash-Sharīf ar-Raḍī himself and attributed to 'Alī. This allegation, in light of my own research on the subject, is absolutely without foundation. Ash-Sharīf ar-Raḍī, the compiler of the *Nahj al-Balāgha,* died in 406/1115, but most of the material of the *Nahj al-Balāgha* I have found word-for-word in sources written long before the fifth century of Islam. These sources include, for example, Naṣr b. Muẓāḥim al-Minqarī's *Waq'at Ṣiffīn,* Ya'qūbī's *Ta'rīkh,* Jāḥiẓ' *Al-Bayān wa'l-Tabyīn,* Mubarrad's *Kāmil,* Balādhurī's *Ansāb al-Ashrāf,* and many other standard works of the second, third, and fourth centuries. I am currently preparing a critical translation of the *Nahj al-Balāgha* in which these sources will be fully analysed and cited.

[8] Ḥayyān had a princely estate in Al-Yamāma where he used to keep the poet A'sha, of the tribe of Banū Qays, under his protection and in luxury and comfort. After the death of Ḥayyān the poet lost all those privileges and was stricken by poverty, wandering about from place to place. By quoting A'sha, 'Alī compares his prestigious status and active life during the lifetime of the Prophet with the negligent attitude of the people towards him after the death of the Prophet. See Ḥadīd, *Sharḥ,* I, pp. 166 f.

[9] *Nahj al-Balāgha,* ed. Muḥammad Abū'l-Faḍl Ibrāhīm (Cairo, 1963), I, p. 29. For other references before Ash-Sharīf ar-Raḍī see Ibn Abī'l Ḥadīd, *Sharḥ,* I, pp. 205 f. and passim, where Abū Ja'far Aḥmad b. Muḥammad (d. 274/887) *Kitāb al-Maḥāsin,* Ibrāhīm b. Muḥammad ath-Thaqafī (d. 283/896) *Kitāb al-Ghārāt,* Abū 'Alī Muḥammad b. 'Abd al-Wahhāb al-Jubbā'ī (d. 303/915), and Abū 'l-Qāsim al-Balkhī (d. 502/1108) *Kitāb al-Inṣāf,* are quoted. Also see

Ṣadūq (d. 381/991), *ʿIlal ash-Sharaʾiʿ*, p. 68; Maʿānī, *Al-Akhbār*, p. 132; Mufīd (d. 413/1022), *Irshād*, p. 166; Ṭūsī (d. 460/1067), *Amālī*, p. 237

[10] Ibn Saʿd, II, pp. 314 ff; Ibn Hishām, III, pp. 352, 368; Yaʿqūbī, II, p. 127; *Istīʿāb*, II, p. 571. Also cf. Vaglieri, *EI*[2] article "Fadak". For the Shīʿī position see Ṭabarsī, *Iḥtijāj*, I, pp. 131–149

[11] Various versions in Ibn Saʿd, II, pp. 314 ff; Bukhārī, *Ṣaḥīḥ*, II, p. 435. For the Shīʿī position, see Yaʿqūbī, II, p. 127, also Amīnī, *Aʿyān*, II, pp. 461 ff.

[12] Jāḥiẓ, *Rasāʾil*, ed. Sandūbī, "Min Kitābihi fīʾl-ʿAbbāsiyya", p. 300

[13] Ṭabarī, I, p. 1825; Bukhārī, *Ṣaḥīḥ*, V, p. 288; Ibn Saʿd, VIII, p. 29; Masʿūdī, *Tanbīh*, p. 288; Ibn Ḥajar, *Ṣawāʿiq*, pp. 12 f.

[14] See the whole account in Ṭabarī, I, pp. 2137 ff.; Yaʿqūbī, II, p. 136 f.; Ḥadīd, *Sharḥ*, I, p. 163 ff.

[15] Yaʿqūbī, ibid.; also see Ṭabarī, I, p. 2138; *ʿIqd*, IV, p. 267, with slight variations in wording

[16] Ṭabarī, I, p. 2137; Yaʿqūbī, loc. cit.; Ḥadīd, *Sharḥ*, I, p. 164. Also see Mubarrad, *Kāmil*, I, p. 7

[17] cf. Masʿūdī, *Murūj*, II, pp. 332 f.

[18] cf. Vaglieri, *EI*[2] article "ʿAlī"

[19] Ṭabarī, I, p. 2769

[20] Reference to *Qurʾān*, XLVII, 9

[21] Reference to *Qurʾān*, XXXIII, 33

[22] Ṭabarī, I, pp. 2770 f.

[23] Abū ʿUbayda b. al-Jarrāḥ, in whom ʿUmar had full confidence and who was one of the triumvirate, had died in the plague of 639–640.

[24] Ibn Saʿd, III, pp. 61 f., pp. 331 ff.; Balādhurī, V, pp. 16 ff.; Yaʿqūbī, II, pp. 160 ff.; Ṭabarī, II, pp. 2778 ff.; Masʿūdī, *Tanbīh*, pp. 290 f.; Dhahabī, *Taʾrīkh*, II, pp. 74 ff.; Ḥadīd, *Sharḥ*, I, pp. 163 ff.; pp. 185 ff.; *ʿIqd*, IV, p. 275

[25] *Istīʿāb*, IV, pp. 1697–9; *Tahdhīb*, III, p. 414

[26] Ibn Saʿd; III, pp. 341 ff.; Balādhurī, V, p. 18; Yaʿqūbī, II, p. 160; Ṭabarī, I, pp. 2779 ff.; Masʿūdī. *Tanbīh*, p. 291; *ʿIqd*, IV, p. 275; Ḥadīd, *Sharḥ*, I, p. 187

[27] e.g., see different *isnāds* in Ṭabarī, loc. cit., and Balādhurī, loc. cit., where the reports of Muḥammad b. Saʿd from Wāqidī, a die-hard pro-ʿUthmānid, are exactly the same as that of Abū Mikhnaf, a confirmed Shīʿī. Even reports going back to ʿUmar's son ʿAbd Allāh and that of Ibn ʿAbbās are the same.

[28] *Studies*, I, pp. 80–99

[29] Ibn Saʿd, III, pp. 344 ff.; Balādhurī, V, pp. 16, 18; Ṭabarī, I, p. 2778; *ʿIqd*, IV, p. 275

[30] See ʿUmar's conversation with the members of the *Shūrā* and especially with ʿAlī and ʿUthmān in Ṭabarī, I, p. 2779; Balādhurī, V, p. 16. The oldest source on this subject, the fragment of the *Taʾrīkh al-Khulafāʾ,* records the same conversations of ʿUmar with the electors and indicates at least ʿUmar's awareness (though not his acceptance) of the strength of ʿAlī's claims. See Abbott, *Studies,* I, p. 81. Also see Ibn Saʿd, III, pp. 62 and 339 ff., where a later version incorporates some dramatic changes in the tradition at the expense of ʿAlī.

[31] Balādhurī, V, p. 19; Ṭabarī, I, p. 2780; *ʿIqd,* IV, p. 276; Ḥadīd, *Sharḥ,* I, p. 191

[32] *Aghānī,* VI, pp. 334 f.

[33] Balādhurī, V, p. 19; Ṭabarī, I, p. 2780; *ʿIqd,* IV, pp. 275 f.

[34] Balādhurī, V, pp. 21 f.; Ṭabarī, I, pp. 2779 f.

[35] i.e. "When my personal excellence was not questionable in comparison to Abū Bakr, how can it be then compared to men like Saʿd b. Abī Waqqās, ʿAbd ar-Raḥmān, and ʿUthmān etc.?"

[36] See note 8 above

[37] Balādhurī, V, p. 22; Yaʿqūbī, I, p. 162; Ṭabarī, I, p. 2793; *ʿIqd,* IV, p. 279; Ḥadīd, *Sharḥ,* I, pp. 188, 194

[38] Balādhurī, V, p. 24; Ṭabarī, I, p. 2796

[39] Balādhurī, V, p. 33; Masʿūdī, *Murūj,* III, p. 225

[40] Ṭabarī, I, pp. 3082 ff., 3085; Dīnawarī, *Akhbār,* p. 142; Masʿūdī, *Murūj,* II, pp. 353 f.; Yaʿqūbī, II, p. 180

[41] See Vaglieri, *EI*² article "ʿAlī"

[42] Minqarī, *Waqiʿat Ṣiffīn,* p. 87

[43] ibid., p. 89

[44] Ibn Khaldūn, *Muqaddima,* pp. 542 f; *ʿIqd,* IV, p. 313; also see Masʿūdī, *Murūj,* II, pp. 425 ff

[45] For the details of each one's wealth, see Ibn Khaldūn, loc. cit.; Masʿūdī, *Murūj,* II, p. 332

[46] Balādhurī, V, p. 49; Ṭabarī, I, p. 2871

[47] Ṭabarī, I, p. 2785; *ʿIqd,* IV, p. 279

[48] ibid.

[49] Ṭabarī, I, pp. 2786 f.; *ʿIqd,* loc. cit.

Chapter 4

The Re-emergence of the ʿAlid Party

The sixteen-year period beginning with the caliphate of ʿUthmān (24/644) and ending with the assassination of ʿAlī (41/661) represents a marked difference from the preceding period of the caliphate of Abū Bakr and ʿUmar in the development of Shīʿism in Islam. It was a turning point in many ways. Firstly, this period created an atmosphere which encouraged Shīʿī tendencies to become more evident and conspicuous. Secondly, the events which took place gave an active and sometimes violent character to the hitherto inactive Shīʿī movement. Finally, the circumstances which prevailed involved the Shīʿī outlook, for the first time, in a number of political, geographical, and economic considerations. The period was therefore one in which the desire of the first Shīʿīs to express their ideas on the succession of ʿAlī, the religious zeal of the Companions, personal hatreds, provincial and economic interests, political intrigues, and the discontent of the poor against the rich were fused together. This fusion not only provided a new sphere of activity for the Shīʿī movement, but also widened its circle of influence to those who needed an outlet for their political grievances, especially those against Muʿāwiya, the representative of the Umayyad aristocracy and Syrian domination. Seeing in ʿAlī a champion of the political independence of Iraq, as opposed to this Syrian domination, these groups supported him and were for the time being of the same mind as the religious supporters of ʿAlī, who believed in his right to the caliphate based on the theocratic principle. The emergence of the political Shīʿa is characterized both by the increase in its influence and its numbers and by the sudden rapidity with which it henceforth grew. An examination of the period in which this emergence occurred will result in a clearer insight into the split which developed within the main body of Islam.

Abū Bakr and 'Umar did not give their respective clansmen any particular share in the rule of the Muslim community, nor were their clans of much political consequence. Such was not the case with 'Uthmān. His clan wanted to regain its past political importance after having taken second place to the Hāshimites after the victory of Muḥammad. When 'Uthmān was elected, the Umayyads regarded this as a triumph for the whole clan, not solely as 'Uthmān's personal success.[1] They considered it natural that the Caliph should give them a share of the profits, and their demands could hardly be refused by the new caliph, who felt that his strength lay in the support and good will of his powerful clansmen. He did what he could to satisfy their demands, and the people were painfully disillusioned when they found the Caliph committed to the improvement of the lot of his own family and clan rather than to the welfare of the community as a whole. 'Uthmān made no secret of bestowing favours on his kinsmen, and justified this action by saying: "The Prophet used to bestow offices on his kinsmen, and I happen to belong to people who are poor. So I let my hands a bit loose in regard to that with which I have been entrusted by virtue of the care I take of it."[2]

It is an historical fact that within a few years of 'Uthmān's accession the Umayyads claimed among themselves the governorships of Kūfa, Baṣra (capital of a vast territory including Iran and Central Asia and extending to Sind), Syria, and Egypt: all the important provinces of the empire. These Umayyad governors, in turn, relied on the support of their own kinsmen, whom they placated and allowed to dominate the caliphal councils.[3] The critical problem here was not so much that the Umayyads dominated all positions of power and advantage, but rather that they were allowed enough latitude to use their powers arbitrarily and unfairly for the benefit of themselves and their kinsmen, thus incurring the dissatisfaction and hatred of many Muslims. 'Abd Allah b. Sa'd b. Abī Sarḥ, 'Uthmān's milk-brother, who administered Egypt, was an extremely unpopular man, whom the Prophet had ordered to be killed during the conquest of Mecca.[4] Al-Walīd b. 'Uqba, 'Uthmān's half-brother, was even more intensely hated by the Kūfans, whom he treated in brutal fashion. He divided lands among his favourites and finally disgraced himself by drunkenness.[5] ʿUthmān was obliged to recall him and appointed another close relative, Saʿīd b. al-ʿĀṣ, who infuriated the local notables by his high-handed treatment of them, then alarmed them by declaring that the *Sawād* of Kūfa would become a "Garden of the Quraysh". Provoked by such abuses, a group of the *Qurʿān* readers in Kūfa, such as Mālik b. Ḥārith an-Nakhaʿī, Sulaymān b. Ṣurad al-Khuzāʿī, Ḥujr b. ʿAdī al-Kindī, Shurayḥ b. ʿAwf al-ʿAbsī, and others, protested in vain against Saʿīd's behaviour. Instead of making proper inquiries, ʿUthmān ordered the agitators to be sent to Syria for Muʿāwiya to deal with.[6]

The names of these distinguished *Qur'ān* readers are to be taken seriously as they afterwards appeared as the leaders of the Shīʿī movement in Kūfa. They stood at the forefront of ʿAlī's army at the battles of Al-Jamal and Ṣiffīn, and even after ʿAlī's assassination they never reconciled themselves with Muʿāwiya. Similarly, the groups of the *Qur'ān* readers from Egypt and Baṣra were not less violent in their protests against the free hand given by the Caliph to his Umayyad governors and their highhanded treatment of the people. This clash with the *Qur'ān* readers set the seal on ʿUthmān's unpopularity in religious circles in the provinces. Here we must point out that the word *qurrā'* (*Qur'ān* readers) used by our sources implies those who distinguished themselves and were recognized by the people as learned in religious matters, and who taught the people the *Qur'ān* and religious observances. Naturally they carried great prestige among the masses and were regarded as the intelligentsia of the people.

In addition to appointing many of his clansmen to lucrative posts, ʿUthmān made large gifts to others.[7] At the same time, he treated some of the Companions of the Prophet very harshly. ʿAbd Allāh b. Masʿūd, then in charge of the treasury in Kūfa, was recalled after a quarrel with Al-Walīd b. ʿUqba, and the Caliph allowed him to be manhandled in his presence.[8] Even worse was the treatment received by ʿAmmār b. Yāsir, who was reviled and beaten into unconsciousness when he arrived from Egypt with a letter of complaint against Ibn Abī Sarḥ.[9]

During the last few years of ʿUthmān's reign, the major part of the population was seething with discontent over the spectacle of Umayyad aristocrats seated in high offices, enjoying wealth and luxury, indulging in debauchery, and lavishly spending the immense wealth which they appropriated to themselves illegitimately. The resulting disequilibrium in the economic and social structure naturally aroused the jealousy of various sections of the population and provided ample combustible material for an explosion. One outspoken leader of the criticism against ʿUthmān's regime was Abū Dharr, a fearless and uncompromising partisan of frugality and asceticism who violently protested against the accumulation of wealth in the hands of a few and demanded the distribution of lands among the community. ʿUthmān, who did not like the idea of Abū Dharr thundering against the wealthy in the mosque of Medina, sent him to Syria. Before long, the Caliph received a letter from Muʿāwiya complaining of Abū Dharr's dangerous activities and ordered that Abū Dharr be bound to a wooden camel saddle and be sent back to Medina under escort. He arrived in the city half dead, with the flesh torn off his thighs, and he was shortly thereafter exiled to Ar-Rabdha, where he soon died.[10] His misadventures were widely related throughout the provinces, awakening an echo of bitterness against ʿUthmān and the class of the rich concurrently with the propagation of ʿAlī's claims to the caliphate.

In this connection the speeches of Abū Dharr, frequently delivered in the mosque of Medina, are of special interest. Gathering people around himself, he used to say:

> "... ʿAlī is the legatee (*waṣī*) of Muḥammad and the inheritor (*wārith*) of his knowledge. Oh you bewildered and perplexed community after its Prophet, if you give preference [in leadership] to those whom God has given preference, and set aside those whom God has set aside, and if you firmly place the succession and inheritance in the people of the house of your Prophet, you will certainly be prosperous and your means of subsistence will be made ample."[11]

We must strongly dissent from the viewpoint of such writers as have laboured to present the rebellion against ʿUthmān as being due to only the evil machinations of some mischief-mongers, and the grievances they voiced as being all forged and artificial. Such writers ignore the fact that these mischief-mongers—if such they were—had real grievances to protest and the tacit support of the *Ṣaḥāba* to provide the necessary sanction. For discontent to develop into open rebellion, two things are essential: leadership, which must come from those who command respect in society, and the time and opportunity to organize and concert action. Both of these prerequisites were present in the last few years of ʿUthmān's caliphate.[12] The attitude of the *Ṣaḥāba,* prominent among them being ʿAlī, Ṭalḥa, and Zubayr, is quite clear. There is ample material to prove that almost all of them, and especially these three, were equally loud in their opposition to the ways of ʿUthmān. Even ʿAbd ar-Raḥmān b. ʿAwf (died 32/652), who had played an all-important role in the election of ʿUthmān, is reported to have hinted long before the outbreak of disturbances that he held ʿUthmān's actions to be a violation of the pledge given by him at the time of his election.[13] Even if we disagree with the reports that they wrote letters to the provincials or actually incited them in a systematic manner, the fact remains that they made no secret of their views and moral support for the rebels.

ʿAlī's attitude towards the situation in this period is clearly illustrated by his reaction to the punishment given to Abū Dharr. When ʿUthmān ordered the latter to be exiled, he gave strict orders that no one should see him off except Marwān, who was to escort him out of Medina. Despite these orders, ʿAlī, accompanied by Ḥasan, Ḥusayn, and his partisan ʿAmmār b. Yāsir, went along with Abū Dharr for quite a long distance. When reminded of the Caliph's directive by Marwān, ʿAlī replied by cursing him and striking the head of Marwān's beast with his stick. When it was time to part, Abū Dharr wept and said, "By God, whenever I see you, I remember the Prophet."[14] To console Abū Dharr, ʿAlī said to him:

> "You were annoyed for the sake of God, so entertain hope from Him for whom you were angry. These people were afraid of you for the sake of their world, and you feared them for the sake of your religion. So leave in their hands that by reason of which they were afraid of you, and flee away with that by reason of which you feared them; for how badly do they need what you have denied them, and how little do you need what they have denied

you. If you had accepted their world they would have loved you; and if you had appropriated to yourself some part of it, they would have felt more secure in your presence."[15]

Marwān reported the entire matter to ʿUthmān, who became quite indignant at such a breach of orders. When he questioned ʿAlī, the latter replied that he was not obliged to obey orders that were not compatible with common sense and justice. "My merits and excellences are far beyond yours; I am far superior to you in every respect."[16] Later these points were more commonly argued by supporters of ʿAlī. The Shīʿī poet Sayyid al-Ḥimyarī availed himself of these arguments to express his extreme Shīʿī views.

After his acceptance of Abū Bakr and the subsequent weakening of his initial party of supporters, ʿAlī remained aloof from all government activities until the end of ʿUmar's rule, as mentioned above. The protest raised after the selection of ʿUthmān demonstrated that ʿAlī's candidacy still had many partisans, but these acted only as individuals and did not form any particular group. Once the caliphate of ʿUthmān gained widespread acceptance in the community, the spontaneous protests of men such as Al-Miqdād and ʿAmmār ceased, though their dissatisfaction remained. As the Caliph gradually began to lose popularity, the old partisans of ʿAlī soon revived their grievances and gave full rein to their long-suppressed desires to see ʿAlī as caliph. Fresh support rallied to the Hāshimite candidate as discontented elements in the empire began to crystallize into factions that needed an effective and acceptable leader. Though Ṭalḥa and Zubayr had considerable local followings in Kūfa and Baṣra respectively, they were far less important than ʿAlī, and their support was doomed to remain limited in character. ʿAlī found himself surrounded by groups of protesters arriving from the provinces, men who called upon him to support their cause, while at the same time ʿUthmān approached ʿAlī and appealed to him to mediate with the rebels. Perhaps compelled by the demands of justice, ʿAlī had no choice but to stand in defence of the offended Companions and demand punishment for the blame-worthy. He himself protested against the rich gifts made by the Caliph to his kinsmen. From this position, he was urged by the *qurrāʾ* to act as their spokesman, which he did to help meet the just demands of the people on the one hand, and to extricate the Caliph from his difficulties on the other.[17]

Two groups, different in outlook but with the same goals, were working simultaneously and serving each other's purposes, though not consciously. One group consisted of the discontented provincial elements discussed above which had been hardest hit by the disequilibrium in the economic structure of the empire, while the other mainly comprised the loyal partisans of ʿAlī. This latter group, led by men like Abū Dharr, Miqdād, ʿAmmār, Ḥudhayfa, and several of the Anṣār, enlisted a number of new activist supporters such as Kaʿb b. ʿAbda an-Nahdī, Mālik b. Ḥabīb ath-Thaʿlabī and Yazīd b. Qays al-Arḥabī.[18] Also included in this circle were the Hāshimites as well as ʿAlī's clients and servants. Among the latter were Qanbar b. Kadam,[19] Mītham b. Yaḥyā at-Tammār, and Rushayd al-Ḥujurī. Due to their religious zeal for and devotion to the person of ʿAlī as the custodian of Muḥammad's message and the true exponent of Islam, these men are symbolic of this stage in the growth of Shīʿism. Both Mītham at-Tammār[20] and Rushayd al-Ḥujurī[21] were crucified in Kūfa in 61/680 by ʿUbayd Allāh b. Ziyād because they refused to curse ʿAlī and continued their zealous adherence to him and to his house even after his death. Their hands, legs, and tongues were cut off and their bodies were hanged, a typical example of Ibn Ziyād's brutal behaviour. Besides these supporters, later writers mention the name of ʿAbd Allāh b. Wahb b. Sabā, known as Ibn as-Sawdā', as having become a great supporter of ʿAlī, travelling from place to place sowing discontent against the rule of ʿUthmān.[22] He is described as a former Jewish rabbi converted to Islam; however, modern Muslim scholars such as ʿAlī al-Wardī strongly suggest that ʿAbd Allāh b. Sabā never existed, and that the activities attributed to him were carried out by ʿAmmār b. Yāsir, whose nickname was also as-Sawdā'.[23] Modern European scholars have also expressed their doubts as to the historical personality of Ibn as-Sawdā' and tend to agree that he is a legendary figure.[24]

It is an interesting phenomenon that both the hatred against ʿUthmān and the numbers of the supporters of ʿAlī grew side by side. The pious opposition to the Umayyad aristocracy became eagerly involved with the partisanship for

'Alī.[25] In addition to 'Alī's ardent supporters, Ṭalḥa and Zubayr also conducted propaganda activities against 'Uthmān. When Muḥammad b. Abī Bakr and Muḥammad b. Abī Ḥudhayfa went to Egypt to rouse the people against the Caliph, they met Muḥammad b. Ṭalḥa, sent there by his father for the same task.[26] Even the widows of the Prophet opposed the Caliph, and 'Ā'isha was especially loud in her denunciations of "Na'thal" (of the big beard and the hairy chest), as she nicknamed him.[27]

The simmering discontent exploded into revolt in 35/656, when rebel contingents from Kūfa, Baṣra, and Egypt marched on Medina under the leadership of the *qurrā'*. It is interesting to note that most of the activists leading these contingents happen to have been of Yemenī origin. These were joined by some of the pro-'Alid Medinese Muhājirūn and Anṣār such as 'Ammār and others. The situation soon became chaotic. The events leading to the murder of 'Uthmān are beyond the scope of this study, but it seems fairly certain that his assassination exceeded the desires of even those of the *Ṣaḥāba* who were openly opposed to the Caliph. Their objectives had been only to depose 'Uthmān, not to kill him. It also seems clear that even during these last tumultuous days 'Alī continued to play his conciliatory and mediatory role. He many times did succeed in dispersing the unruly mob that wanted to hurt the Caliph, and during the siege he appointed his sons Ḥasan and Ḥusayn to stand at the house of 'Uthmān and protect him from the angry crowd. They were, however, jostled and pushed aside by the mob, and the Caliph was killed. Hearing the news, 'Alī was the first to reach the scene and was so furious at what had transpired that he slapped the face of Ḥusayn and hit Ḥasan for failing to save the life of the Caliph.[28]

In the confused atmosphere following the murder of the Caliph, the only candidate for the caliphate that was acceptable to the Muhājirūn and the Anṣār, as well as to the rebellious *qurrā'*, was 'Alī.[29] After three previous but unfulfilled aspirations to gain the office, however, 'Alī was now reluctant to accept the responsibility of leading a community so badly entangled in the question of regicide, and thus to implicate himself in the murder. Ibn 'Abd Rabbih has preserved for us 'Alī's own statement on the situation in the form of an address delivered at the time of the battle of Al-Jamal. In it, ʿAlī says:

> "After ʿUthmān was killed, you came to me saying that you wanted to pay homage to me. I said, 'I do not want it.' I pulled back my hand, but you stretched it forth. I tried to snatch it [my hand] away from you, but you seized it. You said, 'We will accept no other than you, and we would not have gathered together except around you.' You thronged around me like thirsty camels on their watering day, set loose by their keeper who had unfastened their tethers, until I thought you would kill me [by rushing upon me] or that some one of you would kill the other [by jumping one over the other]. In this way all of you paid me your homage, and so did Ṭalḥa and Zubayr."[30]

Pressed by the demands from almost all quarters, ʿAlī finally agreed to accept the office, but he specified that he would rule strictly according to the *Qur'ān* and the *Sunna* of the Prophet and that he would enforce justice and law regardless of any criticism or clash with the interests of any group. Ṭalḥa and Zubayr, though they both had some followings from Baṣra and Kūfa, realized that they had no chance of mustering enough support to contest ʿAlī's candidacy, and they were the first to swear allegiance to him. The Medinese, joined by multitudes of those from the provinces present in the capital, acclaimed ʿAlī as caliph.[31] Through this election, ʿAlī became the first and the only caliph in whose selection a great majority of the community took an active part. He was also the first among the caliphs who, because of the circumstances of his birth, combined in his person both the dynastic and the theocratic principles of succession.

From the very start, ʿAlī inherited great problems which none of his three predecessors had had to face. Marwān b. al-Ḥakam, ʿUthmān's secretary, along with some other members of the clan of Umayya, managed to escape to Syria to join Muʿāwiya, carrying ʿUthmān's blood-stained shirt and the severed fingers of Nā'ila, the murdered caliph's widow, to use for propaganda purposes. From Syria then came the call for vengeance for ʿUthmān's death and a continuous propaganda campaign against ʿAlī.

The murder of ʿUthmān was not a simple assassination committed by an individual to settle personal grievances, as had been the case in 'Umar's death. 'Uthmān's murder was the result of a popular revolt of the poor, discontented, suppressed, and deprived people against the economic, political, and feudalist domination of an old aristocratic family. The more religiously-minded people revolted to safeguard the Islamic ideals of socio-economic justice and equality taught by the *Qur'ān,* enforced by the Prophet, and jealously maintained by Abū Bakr and 'Umar. 'Alī's role as the mediator between the rebel *qurrā'* and the Caliph demonstrates that, on the one hand, he himself was convinced that the resistance movement had been based on just and right demands (and thus asked the Caliph to redress their grievances), while, on the other hand, he had tried his best to save the Caliph from the hands of the unruly mob. Tempers had flared beyond anyone's control, however, and the Caliph was killed by extremists who escaped in the midst of the utter confusion that followed. 'Alī found himself in a hopeless situation. The actual murderers had fled, and it was impossible for him to locate them for punishment; yet the fact remained that many of the *qurrā'* around 'Alī had been nearly as responsible for the tragedy as the murderers themselves. 'Alī himself repeatedly declared that:

> ". . . the murder of 'Uthmān was an act of the days of ignorance [*al-Jāhilīya*: the common term for the pre-Islamic period in Arabia]. I am not indifferent to the demand [of 'Uthmān's blood], but at present [the murderers] are beyond my power. As soon as I get hold of them, I will not hesitate to punish them."[32]

Even Ṭalḥa and Zubayr agreed on this point and said "the insolent and imprudent people overcame the gentle and sober ones and killed ['Uthmān]."[33] In vain, however, did 'Alī try to find a peaceful solution to the problem. The paradoxical position of deploring the murder of 'Uthmān while supporting the justified demands of the *qurrā'*, and cursing the murderers of the Caliph while surrounding himself with their associates, would have been a serious challenge to even the shrewdest and most cunning politician, and this was even more so in the case of 'Alī, whose rigid adherence to principles so often prevented him from adopting a practical political policy.

Before long, it became obvious that 'Alī's attempts to resolve the crisis by peaceful means had failed. Challenges to his authority included even ʿĀʾisha, who refused to return to Medina from the *ʿUmra* (lesser pilgrimage) and turned back to Mecca when informed of the nomination of ʿAlī. Some time later, Ṭalḥa and Zubayr saw an opportunity to dissociate themselves from ʿAlī, and asked permission to perform the *ʿUmra*. Though aware of their plans, ʿAlī granted their request. The two joined ʿĀʾisha in the Holy City and then announced that they had been compelled to swear allegiance to ʿAlī under duress.[34] Though both men were ambitious for the caliphate, neither of them had been a real leader of the masses with great popular support at his command; they could never have concerted their efforts had it not been for ʿĀʾisha, who now shifted from the position of an extreme critic of ʿUthmān to assume the role of his avenger. By marching to Baṣra in 36/656, the triumvirate threatened to cut ʿAlī off from the east and compound the problem of a rebellious Syria by creating a similar problem in Iraq. After much hesitation, ʿAlī finally marched to Kūfa, where he succeeded in gathering a force strong enough to defeat ʿĀʾisha and her associates in the battle of Al-Jamal. Ṭalḥa and Zubayr were slain, and ʿĀʾisha was taken prisoner and sent safely back to Medina.

Having secured his position in Iraq for the moment, ʿAlī then turned to deal with the much more dangerous problem of Muʿāwiya, who, as ʿUthmān's kinsman, called for vengeance,[35] a protest which ʿAlī rejected on the grounds that the sons of ʿUthmān were more entitled to this right.[36] Muʿāwiya realized that if ʿAlī managed to consolidate his authority he would dislodge the former from his position as governor of Syria. The only way to avoid this was to question the validity of ʿAlī's title to the caliphate; given the circumstances in which the new caliph had been installed in office, this was not difficult. ʿAlī's supporters, especially the *qurrāʾ*, were vigorously opposed to any compromise with Muʿāwiya, and Mālik al-Ashtar advised the Caliph not to enter into correspondence with the governor of Syria. Nevertheless, ʿAlī tried peaceful means in dealing with his adversary; only when this failed and it became obvious that Muʿāwiya had resolved to fight did ʿAlī march with his forces to meet the Syrians.

The conflict of Ṣiffīn and the resulting arbitration have been thoroughly and critically studied by a number of scholars, and it is not our purpose here to re-cover well-trodden ground. It will suffice to note that ʿAlī's position rapidly became critical as the emergence of the Khārijites and the arbitration of Adhruh steadily eroded his strength. While he was preparing for a final struggle against Syria, a Khārijite fanatic, ʿAbd ar-Raḥmān b. al-Muljam, struck him with a poisoned sword in the mosque of Kūfa. The fourth caliph died on 21 Ramaḍān 40/25 January 661.

This entire period is discussed by ʿAlī in the last part of his speech of Shaqshiqīyya, and his own comments are useful in examining this confused era:

> "In the end, the third of them [ʿUthmān] stood up shrugging his shoulders arrogantly; and there stood with him the sons of his father, eating up the property of God as the camels eat up the springtide verdure, until what he had twisted became untwisted. His destruction was complete, and his greediness made him fall to the ground. Then all of a sudden I was frightened to see a crowd of people around myself, thick as the hyena's mane, thronging towards me from every direction until [my sons] Ḥasan and Ḥusayn were mobbed and my two sides were split, gathering around me like a herd of goats.
>
> "But when I took up the government, one group broke its pledge, another rebelled, and some others transgressed, as if they had not heard the words of God, who says: 'That is the abode hereafter which we allot to those who do not seek greatness and corruption on the earth, and the end is for those who fear.' (XXVIII, 83) Nay, by God, they have heard these words and comprehend them, but the world is sweet in their eyes and they are pleased by its gaudiness.
>
> "Nay, by Him who has split the seed and created the soul, but for the presence of those who are present and the establishment of the arguments by the existence of the helpers, as also the fact that God has disliked for the knowing ones to watch idly the fullness of the oppressor and the hunger of the oppressed, I would have thrown back its [the caliphate's] rope on its shoulder and made its last drink from the cup of the first one, and you would have found that your world is as distasteful to me as the dripping from the nose of a goat."[37]

With this brief summary as a foundation, we will attempt to analyse the causes and consequences of the major events of ʿAlī's short-lived caliphate. It must be remembered that his succession was greatly resisted by some of the Companions of the Prophet and resulted in the first civil war in Islam; but at the same time, his so-called "failures" proved to be epoch-making in the history of the development of Shīʿism. The bitterness of the supporters of ʿAlī created by his defeats and disappointments provided an historical foundation for the development of their sectarian tendencies, and the destruction done to him gave the later Shīʿa enough material for the formation of their own discipline within the body of Islam.

An attempt to grasp the situation as a coherent whole reveals the fact that the selection of ʿAlī was at once a triumph for a particular view of succession hitherto frustrated, and a great shock to all those who had successfully adopted a principle of leadership devoid of notions of primacy based on hereditary sanctity after the death of the Prophet. With the succession of ʿAlī, these two rival views came into genuine conflict for the first time and crystallized into definite forms. The former view, soon defeated again, was to find expression in a separatist tendency towards a, so to speak, sectarian organization; the latter re-emerged victoriously and more vigorously, and eventually shaped itself in such a way as to become the centre of the Islamic *Umma,* or *Jamāʿa.*

Yaʿqūbī records for us those speeches with which ʿAlī was hailed by his enthusiastic supporters, mostly from the Anṣār, on the occasion of his installation, and which illustrate those tendencies and sentiments with which he was viewed by this group. For example, Mālik b. al-Ḥārith al-Ashtar pledged his allegiance with the declaration that ʿAlī was the *waṣī al-awṣiyā',* the legatee from among the legatees [of the prophets], and the *wārith ʿilm al-anbiyā',* heir to the knowledge of the prophets.[38] Hodgson doubts whether these terms were really used in reference to ʿAlī at such an early date.[39] In the first place, we must bear in mind that Mālik b. al-Ashtar was of Yemenite origin. South Arabia was a land of ancient civilization where for a thousand years kings had succeeded one another according to a dynastic principle and had been regarded as having extraordinary qualities. Even if the seventh-century Arabs had no personal experience of kingship, they must have been unconsciously influenced by this continuing tradition.[40] In this case, the use of terms like *waṣī* and *wārith* by a man of Yemenite origin occurs as a natural and spontaneous corollary of a deep-seated cultural tradition.

In the second place, there are numerous references in contemporary writings which reflect the same spirit. In praise of ʿAlī, Abū'l-Aswad ad-Du'alī sings:

> "Thou art the noblest of the Quraysh in merit and religion.
> I see God and the future state through my love for ʿAlī.
> ʿAlī is the Aaron, ʿAlī is the *waṣī*."[41]

Still more informative is the fact that the term *wārith* appears frequently in the *Qur'ān,* especially in connection with the family of ʿImrān and Ismāʿīl, and Muḥammad uses it as a proof in his efforts to attract the "peoples of the book".[42] It is thus very likely that some of the partisans of ʿAlī could have used the same terminology to express their views.

Moreover, in reading the accounts of the battles of Al-Jamal and Ṣiffīn, one encounters a great bulk of war poetry exchanged between combatants of both sides in which *waṣī* and such expressions are repeated by the partisans of ʿAlī. Extensive quotations here would be cumbersome, and it will suffice to refer the reader to Ibn Abī'l-Ḥadīd, who collected the verses describing ʿAlī as the *waṣī*[43] from the *Kitāb al-Jamal* of Abū Mikhnaf[44] (died 157/774). Another very early work wherein these verses are abundantly quoted is the *Kitāb Waqʿāt Ṣiffīn* by Naṣr b. Muzāḥim (died 212/827), who also frequently quotes Abū Mikhnaf in addition to other early sources.[45]

Apart from these considerations, we have already seen that there had been a devoted party which from the very beginning had expressed personal enthusiasm for ʿAlī largely based on religious considerations. That this group should express its allegiance in appropriately religious terms is only to be expected. Later generations of Shīʿī poets, best represented by Kumayt, Kuthayyir, Sayyid al-Ḥimyarī, and Farazdaq, frequently used the terms *waṣī* and the like in reference to ʿAlī, especially when describing the battles of Al-Jamal and Ṣiffīn.

The purpose of the preceding discussion has been to demonstrate that there was a party who viewed ʿAlī's accession to the caliphate from an angle quite different from the viewpoint of the rest of the community. His rise to power was a great victory for his party, which held a particular conception regarding the leadership of the community, and thus it raised questions that had not arisen under the three previous caliphs, therefore causing him to face serious opposition from various quarters almost right from the start. The initial resistance came from ʿĀ'isha, Ṭalḥa and Zubayr, who raised the call for vengeance and offered themselves as the agents for exacting satisfaction for the murder of ʿUthmān. But the question to be raised here is whether this was really the reason for their revolt. How could ʿAlī alone be held responsible for the killing when Ṭalḥa and Zubayr themselves had been equally active in supporting the grievances of the people? Was ʿĀ'isha not an equal participant in arousing people against ʿUthmān?[46] For the highly emotional and violent atmosphere in Medina at that time, we can do no more and no less than hold all the dissident groups and critics of the Caliph about equally responsible. In one of his speeches, ʿAlī questions these pretenders, saying:

> "By God, they have shown their dislike against me for anything unpleasant and have not appointed an arbitrator between me and themselves; yet they are demanding a right which they had themselves given up and revenge for a blood for which they themselves are responsible. Even if I had a share in it with them, they would still have a share of it; but if they were held responsible for it without me, the blame lies only with them: thus their strongest argument goes only against them. They are still suckling a mother who has already weaned them, and they are reviving an innovation which had been made to die."[47]

In the final analysis, it would appear that the vengeance for ʿUthmān was made an easy pretext both by the triumvirate and later by Muʿāwiya for efforts to check the obvious danger of the rule of the ascetic group in Islam, supported by the lower classes of society and by some of the Anṣār of Medina, of whom ʿAlī happened to be the representative. The emergence of these groups was a real threat to the old Meccan aristocracy, which had been suppressed by Muḥammad's victory and his concept of society and had been kept under strict control by Abū Bakr and ʿUmar. When ʿUthmān, a member of the wealthiest clan of Umayya, came to power, the old aristocratic ideals of his clan and other ruling families of Mecca found an opportunity to re-establish their power and aristocracy. Ironically enough, the impetus given to the ideas of unity and organization by Islam were brought to the service of this group to revitalize itself and re-emerge in power. The revolt of the triumvirate represents Ṭalḥa and Zubayr's last struggle to protect their interests. ʿĀ'isha served as a symbol behind which they could unify their forces, and it certainly was not difficult to involve her in an attack on ʿAlī. Her dislike for him is said to have been based on several factors, one of which was ʿAlī's advice to Muḥammad that he inquire with ʿĀ'isha's slave girl concerning an incident wherein ʿĀ'isha's late return after having been left behind on a journey caused people to start talking maliciously about her.[48] ʿĀ'isha's quarrels with Fāṭima and ʿAlī's questioning of the election of Abū Bakr, ʿĀ'isha's father, also contributed to the hostility.[49] It is therefore clear that in the battle of Al-Jamal the triumvirate was fighting for personal reasons rather than for the blood of ʿUthmān, which was only a convenient pretext. Though they failed in their objectives, they made the task of Muʿāwiya, the unseating of ʿAlī and the reassertion of the ideals threatened by his succession, much easier. The fact that the claim of Muʿāwiya for the blood of ʿUthmān was only an excuse to enable him to remove ʿAlī from power is further evident from a conversation between ʿAmr b. al-ʿĀṣ and ʿĀ'isha soon after the battle of Al-Jamal. ʿAmr said to ʿĀ'isha:

> "I wish you could have been killed on the day of Jamal, and thereby you would have entered Paradise and we would have used your death as our strongest means for reviling and defaming ʿAlī."[50]

The conflict at the battle of Al-Jamal brought about a serious split in the Muslim community. All of our sources reporting on these events use a number of particular designations to express the position adopted henceforth by different groups. These designations are important in that they indicate how the religious outlook, personal loyalties, regional interests, and politico-economic considerations became involved with one another. Those who supported ʿAlī at the battle of Al-Jamal and later at Ṣiffīn were at first called the "people of Iraq" (*ahl al-ʿIrāq*) as well as the "party of ʿAlī" (*shīʿat ʿAlī* or *al-ʿAlawīya*). Their opponents were called *shīʿat ʿUthmān,* or more commonly *al-ʿUthmānīya.* They included the faction of ʿĀ'isha, Ṭalḥa, and Zubayr (called the "people of the camel," or *aṣḥāb al-jamal*) and the Syrians (*ahl ash-Shām*), who were also known as the *shī'at Mu'āwiya*. According to the tendency of the epoch, their positions were also described in more religiously oriented terms through the use of the word *dīn*, which was used in reference to both 'Alī and 'Uthmān in expressions such as *dīn 'Alī* and *dīn 'Uthmān*. Another way of expressing this was to assert that one held the 'Alawī or 'Uthmānī opinion, *ra'y al-'Alawīya* or *ra'y al-'Uthmānīya*.[51] However, besides these general terms used to describe opposing factions, the more precise titles of *Shī'at Ahl al-Bayt* and *Shī'at Āl Muḥammad* were frequently used from this time onwards by the religiously enthusiastic followers of 'Alī. Occasionally the nickname *at-Turābīya* was also used. This title was derived from 'Alī's *kunya* Abū Turāb, Father of Dust, given to him by Muḥammad.[52] More revealing is the fact that 'Alī himself called his opponents by names which indicated their being misled from the true religious path. Those who fought against him at Al-Jamal he referred to as *An-Nākithūn*, "those who break their allegiance". This is a derivation from the Qur'ānic verse which says: "Then anyone who violates his oath (*nakatha*) does so to the harm of his soul."[53] 'Alī named his opponents at Ṣiffīn *Al-Qāsiṭūn*, "those who act wrongfully", taken from the Qur'ānic verse which reads: "Those who swerve (*al-qāsiṭūn*) are fuel for Hell-fire."[54] Lastly, referring to a tradition of the Prophet, 'Alī referred to the Khārijites of Nahrawān as *al-Māriqūn*, "those who missed the truth of religion".[55] Obviously these names became common among 'Alī's followers to describe their opponents.

Throughout this period, however, the followers of 'Alī were developing a continuously broadening base of support. Until the battle of Al-Jamal, the *Shī'at 'Alī* consisted only of a small personal following who from the very beginning regarded him as the most worthy person for the office of the caliphate to lead the community after the death of the Prophet. After the battle of Al-Jamal the term *Shī'at 'Alī* came to include all those who had supported 'Alī against 'Ā'isha, and from this point onwards the original Shī'a group was confusingly included with other groups and individuals who supported 'Alī for other than religious reasons. It was in this wider sense that the term *Shī'a* was used in the document of arbitration at Ṣiffīn.[56] A few decades later, when the Shīʿa started to formulate their official position, some attempts were made to sort out the various groups of ʿAlī's supporters which had been so confusingly mixed up at that earlier stage. The ranks of the Shīʿa were divided into four categories: *Al-Aṣfīya,* the "sincere friends"; *Al-Awliya,* the "devoted friends"; *Al-Aṣḥāb,* the "companions"; and the *Shurṭāṭ al-Khamīs,* the "picked division".[57] To whom the first three terms refer is not quite clear, though various Shīʿī sources indicate the group of earlier followers—Miqdād, Salmān, ʿAmmār, Ḥudhayfa, Abū Hamza, Abū Saṣān, and Shutayr—as belonging to the *Aṣfīya.*

The idea of these classes is certainly of a later date. Nevertheless, we must make some distinction between those followers of ʿAlī who emphasized the religious factor of his succession as the *waṣī* and those who supported his cause mainly on political grounds, especially after he made Kūfa his capital. In addition to a large political following, ʿAlī left behind him a zealous personal party which had sworn to him that they would be "friends to those whom he befriended, and enemies of those to whom he was hostile."[58] Insisting that ʿAlī was "in accordance with truth and guidance" (*ʿala'l-ḥaqq wa'l-huda*) and his opponents consequently in error, they maintained that ʿAlī, by the circumstances of his birth, was specially qualified to bear supreme authority in the community. The existence of this devoted band of religious supporters largely explains how Shīʿism managed to survive the multitude of decisive political defeats inflicted on the movement over the years.

Notes to Chapter 4

[1] *Aghānī,* VI, pp. 334 f.; Mas'ūdī, *Murūj,* II, pp. 342 f.

[2] Ṭabarī, I, pp. 2948 f. For other versions, see Ibn Sa'd, III, 64; Balādhurī, V, p. 25; Ya'qūbī, II, pp. 164 ff.; Dīnawarī, *Akhbār,* p. 139; Mas'ūdī, *Murūj,* II, pp. 334 ff.; *'Iqd,* IV, pp. 280 ff.

[3] See Ṭabarī, I, pp. 2932–3; Mas'ūdī, *Murūj,* II, p. 337

[4] Ṭabarī, I, p. 2871; Balādhurī, V, p. 49

[5] Balādhurī, V, pp. 31 ff.; Ṭabarī, I, p. 2845; Mas'ūdī, *Murūj,* II, p. 335; *'Iqd,* IV, p. 307

[6] Balādhurī, V, pp. 40 ff.; Mas'ūdī, *Murūj,* II, p. 337; Ṭabarī, I, pp. 2916 f.

[7] Balādhurī, V. pp. 27 f.; Ṭabarī, I, pp. 2953 f.; Ash'arī, *Tamhīd,* p. 99

[8] Balādhurī, V, pp. 36 f.; Ya'qūbī, II, p. 170

[9] Balādhurī, V, pp. 48 f.; *'Iqd,* IV, p. 307. Also see Mowdūdī, Abu'l-A'lā, *Khilāfat wa Mulūkīyat,* pp. 105 ff., 321 ff., which gives an admirable exposition of 'Uthman's weakness for his kinsmen and of their misdeeds.

[10] Balādhurī, V, pp. 52 ff.; Ṭabarī, I, pp. 2858 ff.; Mas'ūdī, *Murūj,* II, pp. 339 ff.; Ya'qūbī, II, p. 171

[11] Ya'qūbī, loc. cit.

[12] For these comments see S. M. Yusuf, "The Revolt Against 'Uthmān", *Islamic Culture,* XXVII (1953), pp. 4–5

[13] Balādhurī, V, pp. 26, 57; Ṭabarī, I, pp. 2955, 2980; *'Iqd,* IV, p. 280

[14] Balādhurī, V, pp. 53 ff.; Mas'ūdī, *Murūj,* II, pp. 341 f.; Ya'qūbī, II, pp. 172 f.; Ḥadīd, *Sharḥ,* VIII, pp. 252 ff.

[15] *Nahj al-Balāgha,* I, p. 303

[16] Cf. sources in note 14 above

[17] Balādhurī, V, pp. 26, 60–61; Ṭabarī, I, pp. 2948 f., pp. 2955 ff.; Mas'ūdī, *Murūj,* II, p. 344; Ash'arī, *Tamhīd,* p. 54

[18] Balādhurī, V, p. 40

[19] Kashshī, *Rijāl,* p. 72

[20] ibid., pp. 79–87

[21] ibid., pp. 75–78

[22] Ṭabarī, I, p. 2942; Ash'arī, *Tamhīd,* pp. 55 f.

[23] *Wa'āz as-Salāṭīn* (Baghdad, 1954), pp. 148 ff.

[24] Bernard Lewis, *Origins of Ismā'īlism* (Cambridge, 1940), p. 25; Marshal G. S. Hodgson, "How Did the Early Shī'a Become Sectarian?" *JAOS,* LXXV (1955), p. 2. For further sources, see *EI*[2] article "Abd Allāh b. Sabā".

[25] Hodgson, "Early Shīʿa", p. 3

[26] Balādhurī, V, p. 49. The son of Abū Bakr, Muḥammad was a devoted follower of ʿAlī and a bitter critic of ʿUthmān. Cf. Hodgson, "Early Shīʿa", p. 2

[27] Balādhurī, V, pp. 34, 48–49; Ṭabarī, I, p. 3112; Yaʿqūbī, II, p. 175; *Al-Imāma wa's-Siyāsa,* I, p. 30

[28] Balādhurī, V, pp. 62 ff., 69; Ṭabarī, I, pp. 2988 f.; Masʿūdī, *Murūj,* II, p. 232; *ʿIqd,* IV, p. 290

[29] Balādhurī, V, pp. 70 f.; Ṭabarī, I, pp. 3066 ff.; *ʿIqd,* IV, pp. 291, 310

[30] *ʿIqd,* IV, p. 318

[31] Balādhurī, V, p. 70; Ṭabarī, I, p. 3068; Yaʿqūbī, II, p. 178; Ashʿarī, *Tamhīd,* p. 107; Dīnawarī, *Akhbār,* p. 140

[32] Ṭabarī, I, p. 3080

[33] Ṭabarī, I, p. 3127

[34] Ṭabarī, I, pp. 3091, 3112 ff.; Yaʿqūbī, II, p. 180; Ḥadīd, *Sharḥ,* I, p. 232

[35] Ṭabarī, I, p. 3255

[36] *ʿIqd,* IV, p. 334. Also see Balādhurī, IVA, p. 108, where some companions rejected Muʿāwiya's right to call for the blood of ʿUthmān while there were other nearer relatives of ʿUthmān to claim it.

[37] See Chapter 3, n. 8, above

[38] Yaʿqūbī, II, p. 179

[39] Hodgson, "How Did the Early Shīʿa Become Sectarian?", *JAOS*, p. 2

[40] W. Montgomery Watt, "Shīʿism Under the Umayyads", *JRAS,* 1960, p. 161. Cf. J. Ryckmans, *L'institution monarchique en Arabia avant l'Islam* (Louvain, 1951), pp. 229 ff.

[41] Mubarrad, *Kāmil,* III, p. 205; Masʿūdī, *Murūj,* II, p. 416; *Aghānī,* XII, p. 326. R. Strothmann agrees that there are distinguishable religious honours accorded to ʿAlī in the poetry of ad-Du'alī (cf. *EI*[1] article "Shīʿa"). Also see similar verses composed by Kumayt and Kuthayyir in Mubarrad, *Kāmil,* III, pp. 204 f.

[42] e.g. *Qur'ān,* XIX, 6

[43] Ḥadīd, *Sharḥ,* I, pp. 144–9

[44] Ibn Nadīm, *Fihrist,* p. 93

[45] e.g. pp. 18, 23 f., 43, 49, 365, 382, 385. See also Askāfī, *Naqd al-ʿUthmānīya,* p. 84

[46] Balādhurī, V, p. 34. Even the verses of Ibn Umm Kilāb attribute to ʿĀ'isha the responsibility for the murder of ʿUthmān. Cf. Ṭabarī, I, p. 3112

[47] Mufīd, *Irshād,* p. 146; *Nahj al-Balāgha,* i, p. 63

[48] This incident is known as the *Ḥadīth al-Ifk,* and Bukhārī

records a detailed account of it (See *Ṣaḥīḥ,* III, pp. 25 ff.). Cf. other *ḥadīth* works under the heading "*Ḥadīth al-Ifk*".

[49] ʿUmar Abū Naṣr, *ʿAlī wa ʿĀʾisha* (Baghdad, n.d.), pp. 25 ff.

[50] Mubarrad, *Kāmil,* I, p. 267

[51] These expressions are frequently used in the Arabic sources: e.g. Ṭabarī I, pp. 3196, 3199; Yaʿqūbī, II, pp. 183, 184, 199; *Aghānī,* XII, p. 334; XIV, p. 219

[52] Ṭabarī, I, p. 1272

[53] XLVIII, 10. See Ḥadīd, *Sharḥ,* I, p. 201

[54] LXXII, 15. See Ḥadīd, loc. cit.

[55] Ḥadīd, loc. cit.; Yaʿqūbī, II, p. 193

[56] Minqarī, *Waqʿāt Ṣiffīn,* p. 504; Ṭabarī, I, pp. 3336 f.

[57] *Fihrist,* p. 175; Ṭabarī, II, p. 1; Kashshī, *Rijāl,* pp. 4 f.

[58] Ṭabarī, I, pp. 3350 f. Cf. W. Montgomery Watt, "Shīʿism Under the Umayyads", *JRAS* (1960), pp. 160–161

Chapter 5

Kūfa: Stage of Shīʿī Activities

From the time ʿAlī moved to Kūfa in 36/656, or even earlier, the city became the main centre of Shīʿī movements, aspirations, hopes, and sometimes concerted efforts. It was in and around Kūfa that so many of the stormy events which make up the early history of Shīʿī Islam took place: events such as the mobilization of forces by ʿAlī for the battles of Al-Jamal and Ṣiffīn, the election and abdication of Ḥasan, the uprising of Ḥujr b. ʿAdī al-Kindī, the massacre of Ḥusayn and his companions, the movement of the Tawwābūn, and the revolt of Mukhtār. Yet Kūfa also proved to be a source of setbacks, disappointments, frustrations, and even treachery and failure in the Shīʿī desire to see the house of ʿAlī in command of the affairs of the Muslim community. This chapter, therefore, endeavours to examine in brief the nature and composition of the city of Kūfa and the characteristic tendencies of its people.

The city of Kūfa was founded in the year 17/638, about three years after ʿUmar b. al-Khaṭṭāb assumed the caliphate at Medina.[1] After the Muslim victories at the battles of Al-Qādisīya in 15/636 and that of Jalūlāʾ in the following year, the Caliph ordered Saʿd b. Abī Waqqāṣ, the commander of the Muslim armies in Iraq, to remain where he was, no doubt with the idea of consolidating Muslim control of Iraq and then making further advances into Persia whenever this might prove advisable. Saʿd b. Abī Waqqāṣ therefore stationed the Arab armies at the newly conquered Sassanian capital of Al-Madāʾin, which soon proved to be unsatisfactory to the Arabs because of its damp climate, crowded living conditions, and the lack of a desert environment providing pure air and open pastures for grazing cattle. Informed of the hardships the Arab troops were experiencing in a strange environment, the Caliph wrote to Saʿd to remove the armies from Al-Madā'in and find a place which would suit the Arab way of life and meet their requirements. After two or three places had been tried, and with the help of Salmān al-Farisī and Ḥudhayfa b. al-Yamān, the choice fell on a plain lying on the west bank of the Euphrates close to the old Persian city of Al-Ḥīra.[2] Subsequently Saʿd ordered his forces to encamp there and make it their home. This was the beginning of Kūfa. The choice of the place for the envisaged city was not a hasty one, but was made after careful consideration and a thorough search of the area lasting almost two years.[3]

The description of the founding (*Khiṭaṭ*) of Kūfa given by the sources leaves us in no doubt that at first it was not meant so much to develop a township as to establish a strong, permanent, and strategically located garrison for the Arab armies in the newly conquered distant territory of Iraq. This is clear from ʿUmar's directive when he wrote to Saʿd: "Choose for the Muslims a place for migration (*dār hijra*) and a centre [for carrying out] war (*manzil jihād*)."[4] By *dār hijra* at this particular time, ʿUmar meant a permanent home for those of the fighters of Al-Qādisīya who came for the conquest of Iraq from far-off places and who were supposed to stay there to maintain Muslim control over the new territory; by *manzil jihād* he most probably indicated that these settlers would be expected to undertake further military actions into Persia. Balādhurī gives a slightly different version of ʿUmar's directive in which besides "a place to which Muslims could migrate" he adds the phrase "and which the Muslims could use as a meeting place (*qayrawān*)."[5] This again means that in ʿUmar's mind Kūfa was meant as a garrison town where different contingents from distant places could stay and should be readily available whenever required. The first settlers in this garrison town were, therefore, those hurriedly collected contingents who fought at the battle of Al-Qādisīya and were known as *ahl al-ayyām wa 'l-Qādisīya*.

The planning of the new city and the organization of the quarters for the first inhabitants, especially when they were drawn from such a great variety of tribes, as will be seen presently, must have been a great task for Saʿd b. Abī Waqqāṣ.

Except for Baṣra, which had been founded only a year earlier and was still in the formative stages, the Arabs of northern and central Arabia had little experience in establishing townships. The conception of a town as a political or social unit was still something foreign to the Arab sense of belonging. Even in old cities in northern and central Arabia such as Ṭā'if, Mecca, and Medina, socio-political units were not the cities, but the tribes.

With the beginning of ʿUmar's caliphate and the thrust of outward expansion, those Arabs who seized the first opportunity to fight, and accordingly migrated to Syria, were organized in relatively cohesive groupings since they belonged to large and homogeneous tribes. Similarly, in the Baṣran territories there were mainly two predominant tribes, Tamīm and Bakr, and only a negligible number of 300 other people who came from distant areas.[6]

At Kūfa, on the other hand, the number of those who came to live from far-off places ranged between 15,000 and 20,000, and were exceedingly heterogeneous in tribal composition. There was a marked absence of large dominating clans or groups of clans. At first, Saʿd found the solution in dividing them not into individual clans or tribes, but into their broader tribal categories of Nizārī (North Arabs) and Yemeni (South Arabs). The Nizārīs were therefore quartered on the western side of the plain, and the Yemenis on the eastern side, according to the lots drawn with arrows, as was the custom of the Arabs.[7] The large plot of land which he demarcated for the mosque was to be the centre of the city. Adjoining the mosque the governor's residence and the treasury were built. This first arrangement of the population of Kūfa, however, had to go through three successive reorganizations in the following 33 years.

The organization of the Kūfan population into the two broad groupings of the Nizārīs and the Yemenis soon proved to be unsatisfactory. Firstly, neither the various tribes of the Nizārīs nor the different groups of the Yemenis found it congenial to put up together and soon encountered serious problems. Secondly, such an arrangement presented serious difficulties in forming compact military contingents. Kūfa was founded as a garrison town intended to furnish well-organized contingents ready for action. This was difficult when people were grouped into two broad divisions. Finally, the lack of small groupings into clans or groups of allied clans made it difficult to organize the distribution of stipends on which the population depended. Experiencing these difficulties, Saʿd, after consulting the Caliph ʿUmar, reorganized the population into seven groups. This reshuffling or balancing out, *ʿaddāla, taʿdīl,* was made on the basis of genealogies and alliances with the assistance of two recognized experts in Arab genealogies (*nussāb*).[8] The guiding principle employed in the reorganization was clearly the pre-Islamic or traditional Arabian pattern of tribal organization in which tribes or clans of tribes made political alliances in the form of loose confederacies.

The entire population of Kūfa was thus divided into seven groups, described as *asbāʿ*, in the following units:[9]

1 Kināna with their allies from the *aḥābisḥ* and others and the clan of Jadīla. Kināna was a Meccan tribe and Quraysh was one of its branches, whereas Jadīla, a branch of Qays ʿAylān, was also from the Hijaz and had some connections with Kināna. Both of them were regarded as people of prestige (*ahl al-ʿāliya*). Kināna and Quraysh, along with some other tribes, had in the past formed a group known as *Khindif.* It was natural that in Kūfa both Kināna and Jadīla should enjoy a close relationship and collaborate with the Qurayshi governors and, even though small in number, maintain a privileged position.[10]

2 Quḍāʿa, Ghassān, Bajīla, Khathʿam, Kinda, Ḥaḍramawt, and Azd,[11] combined together, formed a strong Yemeni contingent. Two of them, the Bajīla, led by their chief Jarīr b. ʿAbd Allāh,[12] who was a personal friend of the Caliph ʿUmar, and Kinda, whose leader was Ashʿath b. Qays,[13] had dominating positions in this group.

3 Madhḥij,[14] Ḥimyar,[15] Hamdān,[16] and their allies. This was another powerful Yemeni group, in which the Hamdān attained a significant position in Kūfa and played an important role and produced some staunch supporters of the Shīʿī cause.[17]

4 Tamīm, Rihāb, and Hawāzin, all three belonging to the Muḍar group.[18]

5 Asad, Ghatfān, Muḥārib, Nimr, Ḍubayʿa, and Taghlib,[19]

most of these belonging to the Nizārī group from Rabīʿa and Bakr.

6 Iyād, ʿAkk, ʿAbd al-Qays, Ahl al-Ḥajar, and Ḥamrāʾ. Iyād[20] and ʿAkk,[21] of Nizārī ʿAdnānī origin, had long been resident in the Iraqi region and had joined the Muslim forces against the Sassanian armies. ʿAbd al-Qays,[22] also an ʿAdnānī branch, had migrated to Bahrayn and was known as Ahl al-Ḥajar. They sent a large delegation from Bahrayn to Medina in the year 9/630 and accepted Islam, many of them distinguishing themselves as Companions of the Prophet.[23] Though composed of a hodge-podge of Arab tribes, their importance can hardly be under-estimated, as the ʿAbd al-Qays came to Al-Qādisīya under a powerful Tamīmī chief, Zuhra b. Ḥawiya, one of the chief architects of the Muslim victory at Al-Qādisīya, who solidly united these three tribes under his command to inflict heavy losses on the Persians. Soon after Al-Qādisīya, the strength of this group was immensely increased when 4,000 Persian slaves under their leader Daylam (hence the name Daylamites) accepted Islam on special terms secured from Saʿd, and joined this Tamīmī dynastic chief, who became their patron. They were thus united in a confederacy with the Iyād, ʿAkk, and the ʿAbd al-Qays. The name Ḥamrāʾ in this group refers to these 4,000 Persians.[24] This group, however, at least numerically, formed one of the strongest units at Kūfa, and consequently their numerically advantageous position was bound to come into direct conflict, in the not too distant future, with the interests and superior claims of the tribes of high social standing in the Kūfan socio-political complex. Elements of this group, especially the ʿAbd al-Qays, are particularly noted by the sources for their strong support for ʿAlī at both Al-Jamal and Ṣiffīn.[25]

7 The seventh group, *Subʿ*, not specifically named by Ṭabarī, is certainly the Ṭayy, a powerful tribe of Yemen. The fact that it must have been the Ṭayy is evident from numerous references to it spread over hundreds of pages which Ṭabarī devotes to the events in Kūfa until the time of Muʿāwiya. The Ṭayy converted to Islam in 9/630, and when in 11/632 all other distant tribes apostatized, the Ṭayy remained steadfast in Islam. They joined Muthannā b. al-Ḥāritha in the wars of Iraq at the conquest of Al-Ḥīra, and then took part in the

battle of Al-Qādisīya. We then hear of Ṭayy as one of the strongest supporters of ʿAlī at Al-Jamal and Ṣiffīn.[26] Again we come across ʿAdī b. Ḥatim, the chief of Ṭayy, among the supporters of Ḥasan, urging the people of Kūfa to respond to the call of "their Imam, the son of the daughter of their Prophet".[27] It seems, however, that the number and strength of Ṭayy gradually declined in Kūfa itself and most of them went and joined their tribesmen in the stronghold of the mountains between Baṣra and Kūfa.[28] Thus we hear of Ṭirimmāḥ b. ʿAdī at-Ṭāʾī, who met Ḥusayn on his way to Kūfa and made a strong appeal to him to abandon his plan of going there and, instead, to come with the former to the safety of the invincible Ṭayy mountains.[29]

The city of Kūfa was thus organized into seven tribal contingents (*muqātila*) divided into seven military districts which became the gathering points for mobilization and the administration of stipends and booty. Each group was given its own *jabbāna*: open places for the grazing of cattle and for graveyards. These *jabbānas* were of great importance in the later development and expansion of the city, because they provided enough space for those who came to Kūfa later and joined their respective clansmen.

This grouping of the tribes continued for nineteen years until it underwent another change in 36/656, when ʿAlī came to Kūfa. As will be seen later, during the previous twenty-odd years the power structure within each of the seven groups had drastically changed: certain clans in the various groups had acquired an undue dominating position over the other component parts of the group. Also in this period, some tribes were joined by a large number of newcomers of their tribesmen and became exceedingly numerous, thus upsetting the power balance in the group. ʿAlī, therefore, while retaining the number of groups as seven, made some significant changes in the composition and external make-up of these seven groups by way of reshuffling or shifting certain tribes from one group to the other. According to Massignon's analysis, ʿAlī rearranged the tribes as follows:

1: Hamdān and Ḥimyar (Yemenis);
2: Madhḥij, Ashʿar, and Ṭayy (Yemenis);
3: Kinda, Ḥaḍramawt, Quḍāʿa, and Mahar (Yemenis);

4: Azd, Bajīla, Khathʿam, and Anṣār (Yemenis);
5: All the Nizārī branches of Qays, ʿAbs, Dhubya, and the ʿAbd al-Qays of Bahrayn;
6: Bakr, Taghlib, and all the branches of the Rabīʿa (Nizārīs);
7: Quraysh, Kināna, Asad, Tamīm, Ḍabba, Ribāb (Nizārīs).[30]

Three important points must particularly be noticed in this new grouping. First, there are a few clan names, such as Ashʿar, Mahar, and Ḍabba, which did not appear in the grouping of Saʿd. This probably means that these clans were numerically negligible at the time of Saʿd in 17/638; by 36/658, however, they had become numerous enough to require an individual identity. Secondly, in Saʿd's organization there were three Yemeni groups and four Nizārī. In ʿAlī's reorganization the number of Yemeni groups was raised to four and the Nizārīs' reduced to three. It will be pointed out below that from the very beginning the Yemenis were greater in number than the Nizārīs (12,000 and 8,000 respectively). ʿAlī seems to have taken into consideration the population strength of the two branches of the Arabs and reorganized the groups according to their numbers, thus giving the Yemenis their due importance in Kūfa. Finally, ʿAlī did not change the tribal basis of genealogies on which Saʿd had organized the population.

The fourth and last change in Kūfan administration took place fourteen years later, when Ziyād b. Abī Sufyān took charge of the city as governor in 50/670. He totally abolished the tribal organization into seven groups and re-organized the entire population into four administrative blocks (*arbāʿ*) as follows:

1: Ahl al-ʿĀliya;
2: Tamīm and Hamdān;
3: Rabīʿa (Bakr) and Kinda;
4: Madhḥij and Asad.[31]

There are many important points to be observed in Ziyād's reorganization. Firstly, he was governor not only of Kūfa but also of Baṣra, where, from the very beginning, the entire population was divided into four administrative blocks (*arbāʿ*). This division had proved so successful in controlling the people of Baṣra that Ziyād decided to apply the same administration system in Kūfa as well. Secondly, he completely disregarded the recognized Arabian principle of genealogies and alliances in forming tribal groupings. Instead, he mixed the Nizārīs and the Yemenis together, except for the first group, the *Ahl al-ʿĀliya.* Thirdly, again excepting the first group, he picked out the six most powerful tribes and merged all the other smaller clans or tribes with them.

The first group, the Ahl al-ʿĀliya, consisted of the branches of the Meccans and Quraysh which he did not disturb because they had been the natural allies of the Qurayshī governors from Saʿd onwards. Moreover, this was the smallest allied group of the population in Kūfa, and Ziyād had nothing to fear from them. In the second block (*rubʿ*) he combined the Tamīm (Nizārī) and Kinda (Yemeni). In the third were Bakr (Nizārī) and Kinda (Yemeni), and in the fourth, Asad (Nizārī) and Madhḥij (Yemeni). Over each block he appointed a chief or supervisor of his own choice,[32] among whose duties must have been the maintenance of a firm control over the component parts of their respective groups. Finally, one cannot fail to observe that Ziyād's reorganization of the Kūfan *asbāʿ* into *arbāʿ* was based neither on genealogies nor on alliances, but totally on political considerations intended to consolidate Umayyad power in the city.

The exact number of the first settlers in Kūfa is difficult to ascertain; nevertheless, from the various reports given by the sources we can make a fairly clear estimate of this. Ṭabarī gives a detailed account of the Arab forces who fought at the battle of Al-Qādisīya, and says there were about 30,000 Arabs in this battle.[33] This figure might be an exaggerated one, and in any case not all of the Al-Qādisīya veterans stayed at Kūfa. According to one report given by Yāqūt, ʿUmar ordered Sa'd to plan the mosque of Kūfa so that it could accommodate the 40,000 troops who were to be stationed there.[34] A more moderate and perhaps more reliable report is given by Balādhurī, who reports on the authority of Ash-Shaʿbī that the total number of the first Arab settlers at Kūfa was 20,000: 12,000 Yemenis and 8,000 Nizārīs. To this Balādhurī adds 4,000 Daylamites (al-Ḥamrā'), who were certainly among the first settlers alongside the Arabs.[35] It seems that the total of 24,000, being a moderate estimate compared to other inflated figures, was the number of settlers with which the city of

Kūfa started its history. Of these first settlers or early comers, as they are often described, special mention must be made of a sizeable body of 370 Companions of the Prophet, from among both the Muhājirūn and the Anṣār, who were domiciled at Kūfa soon after its foundation[36]. Among them were such important personalities as ʿAbd Allāh b. Masʿūd, ʿAmmār b. Yāsir, Ḥudhayfa b. al-Yamān, Al-Barāʿa b. ʿĀzib, Salmān al-Farisī, Zayd b. al-Arqam, and Abū Mūsa al-Ashʿarī. Ibn Saʿd counts 70 of them as among those who fought for Islam in the first encounter with the Meccans at Badr in 2/623, and 300 as among those who renewed their pledge of loyalty to the Prophet at the occasion of the treaty of al-Ḥudaybīya in 7/628.[37] This pledge is known as the *Bayʿat al-Riḍwān,* and was later considered a source of great Islamic prestige and honour for those who had demonstrated their unshaken belief in Muḥammad at that moment of trial.

The heterogeneous nature of the Kūfan population, with the absence of any one single tribe as a dominating group, prompted ʿUmar to take a special interest in the new city. He thought that the very agglomeration of so many clans and tribes, never experienced before in the Arabian social system, and the presence of so many companions of high standing to infuse Islamic spirit in them, would shape Kūfa into a genuinely Islamic cosmopolitan city. So great was ʿUmar's interest in Kūfa that he described it as "tower of Islam" (*qubbat al-Islām*) and "the head of the people of Islam" (*rās ahl al-Islām*). Similarly, in describing the settlers of Kūfa he said, "They are the lance of God, the treasure of faith, the cranium of the Arabs, who protect their own frontier forts and reinforce other Arabs."[38] It is important to note that these epithets of honour and distinction were not accorded to any other city, such as Damascus or Baṣra. ʿUmar was certainly opposed to the tribal supremacies so predominant in Arabian socio-political system. The heterogeneous character of the Kūfan population provided him with a suitable ground for establishing an Islamic socio-political system in which tribal hegemony might be submerged under Islamic hegemony. This in effect meant that predominance and leadership must be exercised only by those who possessed Islamic priority (*sābiqa*), and that tribal authority must be submerged under Islamic authority. The selection of ʿAmmār b. Yāsir, of no tribal prominence, but one of the earliest converts and a man most devoted to the cause of Islam, as the governor of Kūfa, and ʿAbd Allāh b. Masʿūd as deputy governor, was a clear manifestation of his policy.[39] At the time of their appointments ʿUmar wrote to the people of Kūfa:

> "I am sending you ʿAmmār as the governor and ʿAbd Allāh as your teacher [in Islam] and the deputy [to ʿAmmār]. Both of them are from among the most illustrious and distinguished (*nujabāʾ*) companions of the Prophet. Listen to them and follow them. I preferred you over my own self [otherwise I would have liked to keep them with me]."[40]

The emphasis put on the qualifications and distinctions of ʿAmmār and Ibn Masʿud as being among the most illustrious Companions of the Prophet and therefore chosen for the leadership of Kūfa reveals ʿUmar's intention to replace tribal claims with Islamic claims, and in this way to maintain the political hegemony of Medina.

When in 20/641 ʿUmar organized the system of distribution of stipends (*dīwān*) his sole criterion was the principle of Islamic priority. He divided the settlers of Kūfa into three groups: the various groups of the Muhājirūn and the Anṣār; people who took part in operations against the apostasy and rebellion or, say, prior to Yarmūk and Al-Qādisīya, and then took part in these battles and were known as *ahl al-ayyām wa'l Qādisīya*; and the *rawādif,* people who came to Kūfa after Yarmūk and Al-Qādisīya, or the second and third waves of migrants, who were graded depending on the time when they first participated in the conquests.[41] Accordingly, their stipends were fixed at the rates of 5,000 to 3,000, 3,000 to 2,000, and ranging from 1,500 to 200 dirhams per annum respectively. The most important point for our purpose here is that for the distribution of the stipends each category was divided into smaller groups or units, and a person from each group was appointed as the supervisor of distribution. These groups were known as *ʿirāfa* and the person in charge as the *ʿarīf* (pl. *ʿurafāʾ*). In most cases *ʿirāfas* were probably composed of people from the same clan, but essentially or coincidentally a group of people with identical standing in Islam,[42] since usually it was a clan as a whole or a group of related people who converted, rather than one individual. These *ʿurafāʾ* of

Kūfa must have had some dominating position in the political affairs of the city. The term *ashrāf al-qabāʾil* in the descriptions of Kūfan affairs is generally understood to be only the tribal leaders, but the numbers of these leaders cannot be as high as the impression one gets from the sources. It is, therefore, highly possible that these *ʿurafāʾ* might have assumed the role of leading their respective groups or *ʿirāfas* in the troubled days of ʿUthmān, ʿAlī, and later. It seems rather difficult to identify and apply the term *ashrāf,* as it is so commonly and widely used by the historians, if the body of Kūfan *ʿurāfāʾ* is not included in it.

The Muslim empire was expanding at an amazing rate during the caliphate of ʿUmar, and so grew also the population of Kūfa. Two important new influxes must immediately be recognized. First, there were waves of the Arab newcomers called the *rawādif,* who, after the completion of the conquests of Syria, Egypt and the Jezira by 20/641, seeing no more chances for booty on these western fronts, anticipated a renewal of the offensive into the Persian Empire and thought this would bring them fresh opportunities for booty and gain. This caused a new Arab influx into Kūfa. When the Muslim forces from Kūfa were mobilized for the battle of Nihāwand in 21/642, these newcomers were naturally the most enthusiastic to make their services available, and in the encounters with the Persians these were the people who demonstrated extraordinary valour. ʿUmar was so impressed by them that he made some modifications in the policy of his *dīwān,* and raised the stipend of these newcomers to the level of the first settlers, the *ahl al-Qādisīya.*[43] This gave a further incentive to others to flock into Kūfa, thus increasing the city's Arab population, in most cases adding to the number of the existing tribes and clans. The second influx into Kūfa was that of the new waves of Persians. There were many reasons (which will be elaborated shortly) for their flocking into Kūfa in greater numbers than in any other city.

As a result of these new influxes, however, the population of Kūfa in a few years' time, even before the close of ʿUmar's caliphate, had risen considerably. We are told that soon after ʿUmar's death, when ʿUthmān appointed Al-Walīd b. ʿUqba as governor of Kūfa in 24/645 or 25/646, the number of fighting men (*muqātila*) alone was 40,000.[44] Taking into consideration many of those early comers of Al-Qādisīya, who were no longer capable of bearing arms but made Kūfa their permanent home, and a great number of slaves and family members of these 40,000 troops, the population in a decade must have risen to well over 100,000. To this figure we must add a good number of those who gradually occupied the *Sawād* of Kūfa—the rich agricultural land of Iraq—, which 'Umar had ruled should not be divided among the conquerors of Al-Qādisīya, but must be left for those who would come to the region later. The original inhabitants of the *Sawād* were to be allowed to cultivate the land as people under protection (*dhimma*), and were to pay taxes to be used for the stipends of the Kūfans.[45] On the other hand, the lands belonging to the Sassanian kings and the royal families (known as *ṣawāfī*) were reserved by 'Umar for the exclusive use of the conquerors of Al-Qādisīya. They were allowed to divide it among themselves, settling on it if they so wished, or to put in charge of it administrators of their own choosing. The result was that in a short period of time the city of Kūfa was surrounded by densely populated villages inhabited by, besides the original cultivators, those who went there to work on the newly acquired estates. This was possible because of the increased number of slaves and labourer classes who were now assembled in the Kūfan territories. Moreover, with the expansion of economic life in Kūfa, as in other newly founded garrison cities, a great number of tradesmen, craftsmen, and domestics thronged into the towns and settled there permanently.

With this brief outline of the foundation and early development of Kūfa, we must now turn to our main purpose of examining the general structure, characteristics, and features of the population which influenced their religio-political tendencies and aspirations. This is not an easy task, however. There were many complex factors—geographical, historical, ethnic, racial, and economic—mixed together, and these made the city and its people most difficult to analyse. What must be noted first of all is that the population of the city almost since its very foundation was composed of two distinctly unique groups: the Arabs and the Persians. We may call the Arab group the "founding element" and the Persians the "second basic element".

The Arab element in Kūfa was extremely complex in its composition—more so than in any other Arab city. Looking at the list of the seven groups of the tribes enumerated earlier and the subsequent waves of the Arab early comers, one immediately notices that the "Arab element" was extraordinarily heterogeneous in origin and background. It was, in the first place, sharply divided into two groups, the Nizārīs and the Yemenis, among which we may further distinguish:

1 A small number of the Quraysh from the Ḥijāz, with their long-standing reputation for sedentary living, nobility, and *sharaf*;
2 Elements that were strongly nomadic, such as Muḍar groupings, especially the Tamīm and some of their Yemenite neighbours from among the Ṭayy;
3 Semi-nomadic elements such as Rabīʿa, Asad, Bakr, belonging to or coming from the north, northwest, east, and southeast of Arabia, and ʿAbd al-Qays from Al-Ḥajar;
4 Truly south Arabian elements coming from further afield, from Ḥaḍramawt and Yemen, some of whom had been living a semi-sedentary life there, such as Kinda and Bajīla, and others who had lived in true and very ancient settlements, such as Madhḥij, Ḥimyar, and Hamdān;[46]
5 Yet another section of the Arabs who settled down in Kūfa at the time of its foundation were some of the Christian tribes such as Taghlib, Nimr, Iyād and even some Christians from Najrān.[47] These Christian tribes had been accorded special terms and privileges by the Prophet, which were maintained by Abū Bakr and ʿUmar.
6 Still another section from among the Arabs counted above must necessarily be recognized: this consisted of the outstanding noble families known as the *buyūtāt al-ʿArab*. Ibn Saʿd particularly notes this point and says that all the noble houses of the Arabs were represented in Kūfa, whereas this was not the case in Baṣra.[48]

The second basic element of the Kūfan population in shaping the character of the city was that of the Persians. There were many factors which account for their great influx, particularly into Kūfa rather than into any other city. Three of these are conspicuous. First, the Arab conquests of Al-Madāʾin, Al-Qādisīya, and ultimately the great victory at the battle of Nihāwand resulted in a large number of Persian captives falling into the hands of the conquerors as slaves and being brought to the city of Kūfa. Most of them soon embraced Islam and earned their freedom from their Arab masters, but remained their allies or clients. Secondly, the geographical affinity of Kūfa, being on the border of Sassanian Iraq, made the city the most suitable place for migration for those of the Persians who had lost much of their means of livelihood in the Persian Empire. To them Kūfa promised fresh opportunities. Similarly, a large number of peasants, with the collapse of the Sassanian feudal system and the freedom provided by Muslim rule, found the land no longer profitable and moved to the growing cities for alternative occupations. Kūfa was the most attractive place for them. Thirdly, the presence of those 4,000 Persians known as the Daylamites, who had settled down in Kūfa from its very foundation, and the addition of a sizable number of Nihāwand prisoners of war, provided a congenial social atmosphere for other uprooted Persians to join their countrymen there. Moreover, among the prisoners of war there was a considerable number of women who had fallen to the lot of their Arab conquerors. These women became the lawful wives of their Arab captors and bore them children. The result was that in less than twenty years' time, by the time ʿAlī came to Kūfa, there was a youthful new generation of Kūfan Arabs who had Persian mothers. Thus, for example, the mother of the famous scholar of Kūfa of this period, Ash-Shaʿbī, was a woman captured at the battle of Jalula.[49] It is important to note here that the Persians in Kūfa were not granted equal status by their Arab co-citizens in the social system of the city. They were called *mawālī* (sing. *mawlā*), or clients, a term to indicate inferior social standing. Since the *mawālī* played an important role in Kūfan religio-political history, especially in Shīʿī movements, it would be helpful to know a little more about them. Though the term *mawālī* was originally meant for freed slaves, after the Muslim conquest it was extended to a variety of non-Arab peoples. In Kūfa, the *mawālī* can be divided into five groups:

1 The non-Arab soldiers who adopted Islam and joined the Arab armies. These were mostly the Persian soldiers, who accepted Islam and fought alongside the Arab forces, such as

the Hamrā', or the Daylamites. They were used by the Kūfan governors as the police force, and received fair treatment from the Arabs. In most cases they had to join an Arab clan or associate themselves with an Arab chief as their patron, as did the Daylamites when they accepted the leader of the tribe of Tamīm as their patron.

2 The peasants (mainly Persians) whose towns and villages were destroyed during the Muslim conquests and who left their cultivable land and moved to Kūfa in search of other work. The collapse of the Sassanian feudal system and the freedom given by the Muslim rulers allowed the peasants to abandon their land, which was no longer profitable. Due to this fact, the treasury began to lose land taxes and, as a result, the administration increased taxation on those who were still working on their land. This led to many more peasants leaving their land to avoid increased taxation and coming to Kūfa for more lucrative employment. These peasants, however, made up a group of *mawālī* who were not associated with any tribal group. They were under the direct jurisdiction of the governor, who had extensive powers over them and in return was responsible for their protection. In case of an unintentional homicide committed by any of them, the treasury had to pay the blood-wit.[50]

3 The vast groups of Persians and others who converted to Islam, many of them coming to Kūfa as traders and craftsmen. Their lands were conquered by the Muslims, yet they were not enslaved. They embraced Islam on their own, and in order to improve their economic conditions they moved to Kūfa and worked as traders and craftsmen. In terms of numbers they probably formed the largest *mawālī* group in Kūfa; and with the economic development of the city their numbers were constantly increasing. They were almost independent members of the tribes with which they were associated for administrative purposes.

4 Freed slaves. This group consisted of those who were taken by the Arabs as prisoners of war, converted to Islam, and earned their freedom, but were bound to be associated with the family of which they had been the slaves. In the technical or rather the original meaning of the term, they were the real *mawālī* and, in Kūfa, their numbers were second only to the third category mentioned above.

Persians and other converts to Islam who belonged to noble families. They were exempted from the poll-tax (*jizya*), which they regarded as degrading, but they had to pay on their own lands (*kharāj*). They seem to have been treated by the Arabs somewhat differently from the other groups of the *mawālī*, since they were the nobles of their own people, even though defeated. They were free to change their *wala* if they so desired from one tribe to another. Nevertheless, their status remained that of *mawālī*, or second-class citizens, and therefore of subservient positions in the tribe. In many cases, however, their interest in Kūfa coincided with that of the Arab tribal leaders.[51]

The total number of all classes of *mawālī*, however, increased to the extent that within only a few decades they almost outnumbered their Arab counterparts. In the battle of Jamājim, the *mawālī* forces which came to fight for Ibn al-Ashʿath are reported to have been 100,000.[52] With all their numbers and strength, on the whole they were treated by the Arabs as second-class citizens. The Arabs maintained against them not only the idea that they were the conquerors, but also a superior racial attitude. This naturally led to an ever-growing feeling of discontent among the *mawālī* in Kūfa.

To this population structure three observations must be added. Firstly, from its very beginning Kūfa was not a purely Arabian city such as Mecca, Medina, or even Damascus. Secondly, the majority of the first settlers in Kūfa, whether Arabs or Persians, were the military contingents who, in most cases, came without their families and for quite some time lived as a standing army ready for action. It seems natural that their militant character should persist even though ultimately they settled down as civilians and were joined by other sophisticated groups from among both the Arabs and the Persians. This, along with many other factors, explains their restlessness, their resentful and often rebellious behaviour. Finally, and perhaps most important, Kūfa had no tradition of its own which could have absorbed or influenced the people. After the great outward thrust from the Peninsula, those of the Arabs who migrated to the cities of Syria, Egypt, and Persia came under the direct impact of and were influenced by the existing traditions of those cities. Kūfa, on the other hand, was founded as a garrison on a virgin plain lying between the Arabian Desert and the old city of the Lakhmid kingdom of Al-Ḥīra, which had been under the suzerainty and cultural influence of Persia. The newly founded city had to evolve its own character, which was not so easy in such an agglomeration of people, where the Arabs of the North and the South, or the Nizārīs and Yemenis, the nomads and the sedentaries, the old aristocracies of the famous noble houses (*buyūtāt al-ʿArab*) and the commoners, and the Persians of various classes came to live together. Yet there was one factor to dominate the trend of the majority of the people. Among the Arab element of the population, the Yemenis, or South Arabians, were more numerous (12,000) than the Nizārīs, or the North Arabians (8,000). It has been discussed in detail in Chapter 1 that the South Arabians, due to their long and deep-rooted tradition of the priest-king with hereditary sanctity and therefore hereditary succession, were more prone toward what we called the Shīʿī ideal of leadership of the community. In this they were joined by the Persian element of the population, which had an almost similar tradition of religio-political leadership. Thus, the Yemenis and the Persians together, making more than two-thirds of the population, set the trend of the city well on the road toward Shīʿī inclinations and moods of thinking. This does not, however, mean that all the Yemenis residing in Kūfa were Shīʿīs, or that none of the Nizārīs of the northern Arabs sided with the Shīʿī school of thought. In such a complex situation a clear-cut categorisation would not be correct. What is suggested reflects general tendencies of the major groups based on certain backgrounds which might be easily suppressed should there arise politico-economic considerations.

The first serious tension in Kūfa, however, appeared on the surface as a clash of interests between the two power groups, which we may term the newly emerging "religious or Islamic hierarchy" and the "traditional tribal aristocracy". The first group consisted of those Companions of the Prophet whose claim to the leadership of Kūfa rested on their early conversion, their services to the cause of Islam, and above all the esteem in which they were held by the Prophet himself. As has been said earlier, ʿUmar wanted to govern Kūfa through those who possessed Islamic priority and thereby to undermine and suppress tribal authority. He did not, therefore, allow anyone from among the *ridda* leaders to have any position of command, no matter how powerful they were. The other power group consisted of tribal leaders whose claims, according to the old Arabian tradition, were based on their wealth and the status, strength, and prestige of the tribes they led. Naturally, it was difficult for them to tolerate for long the supremacy and leadership of those who had no tribal authority or who belonged to no ruling family.

As long as ʿUmar lived, the tribal leaders could not do much to exert their power. With the death of ʿUmar and the succession of the weak ʿUthmān in 23/643, things started to change drastically and the struggle for power, so far suppressed, came into the open. The appointment of Al-Walīd b. ʿUqba, ʿUthmān's half brother and an aristocrat himself, as the governor of Kūfa greatly helped the tribal leaders to restore their power and authority. Thus we find that not only the strong tribal leaders but even the *ridda* leaders emerged with full vigour and were soon at the helm of affairs in the province.[53] For example, Al-Ashʿath b. Qays al-Kindī, a famous leader of the apostates, was entrusted with sole command of Ardabīl, and a large number of people dispatched there to form a permanent settled force were put under his command.[54] This was done at the expense of those Kinda leaders, such as Ḥujr b. ʿAdī al-Kindī, who had more Islamic prestige than tribal. Another glaring example was the appointment of Saʿīd b. Qays al-Hamdānī to Rayy,[55] where Yazīd b. Qays al-Arḥabī had been in charge since 22/643.[56] The former belonged to one of the most influential families of Hamdān, but had no Islamic priority, whereas the latter possessed status mainly as an Islamic leader, though in Hamdānī tribal hierarchy he had hardly any significant place. That a leader such as Al-Ashʿath, with his *ridda* background, and Saʿīd b. Qays, with no standing in Islamic terms, should receive high offices, was clearly a major departure from the existing order. This suddenly changed the power structure and resulted in the displacement of those early comers whose social status and power base was Islamic rather than tribal. In the long list of such displaced leaders, of particular interest are Mālik b. Ashtar an-Nakhaʿī, Musayyab b. Najaba al-Fazārī, Yazīd b. Qays al-Arḥabī, ʿAdī b. Ḥātim al-Ṭāʿī, and Ṣaʿṣaʿa b. Ṣuḥan al-ʿAbdī. Unseated from their positions, these notables of Kūfa, also described by the sources as among the leading *qurrāʾ* of Kūfa,[57] were among the strongest opponents of Al-Walīd b. ʿUqba and his successor, Saʿīd b. al-ʿĀs, another aristocrat of Mecca, and consequently of ʿUthmān, who allowed himself to be dominated by the old aristocracy. Not long afterward, the opposition grew both in strength and dimension and was joined by a large number of people who came to Medina. The rebellion resulted in the murder of ʿUthmān. The mode of the city was thus set, dividing the population into two groups:

1: The strong and influential tribes and clan leaders along with their followings, especially from among the early comers. These leaders are generally described as the *ashrāf al-qabāʾil*;
2: People less influential in terms of tribal or clan leadership, who nevertheless had been in privileged positions during the time of ʿUmar due to their Islamic priority, and who were now deprived of their power. They included most of the late comers, a large number of the *qurrāʾ* or religious intelligentsia of different affiliations and backgrounds, a number of splinter clan groups, and a great majority of hodge-podge people from among both the early comers and the late settlers. The Persian element, or the *mawālī*, of the city naturally had to throw in their lot with this second category.

It is against this background that the third and most critical phase of Kūfan history began. The first phase had seen the city's foundation in 17/638 and extended until the death of ʿUmar in 24/644; the second ended with the death of ʿUthmān in 35/655; this ushered in the third phase, which was dominated by the rise of ʿAlī to the caliphate in the same year. As has been discussed in Chapter 4, ʿAlī was installed as the caliph mainly by the popular vote of the Anṣār of Medina and the rebel contingents who came from the provinces. The Kūfan contingent was the first to pay homage to ʿAlī under the leadership of Mālik al-Ashtar.[58] Naturally, the overwhelming support of these elements for ʿAlī's election to the supreme authority was taken as a serious threat not only by the Umayyad aristocracy, which during twelve years of ʿUthmān's rule had appropriated all positions of power and advantage for themselves, but also by Quraysh in general. In opposition to ʿAlī, therefore, besides the Umayyads in Syria, there emerged at Mecca a body of Quraysh, many of them Companions and Muhājirūn, who, while being opposed to Umayyad domination, in fact under their mask as Muhājirūn favoured overall domination by Quraysh.[59] Military power was now divided into two rival military camps, Kūfa and Baṣra, with large territories under their influence, whereas Syria was wholly under the firm control of the Umayyads. Taking advantage of the rivalry between Baṣra and Kūfa, the Meccans moved to Baṣra to mobilize tribal support from there. ʿAlī was thus left with no choice but to leave Medina for Iraq and count on the support of the Kūfans, who had shown their inclinations towards him. He arrived in the neighbourhood of Kūfa with about 1,000 men who accompanied him from Medina, and was readily joined by about 12,000 Kūfans.[60] They formed the main part of his army at the battle of Al-Jamal. The Meccan-Baṣran alliance was defeated, and ʿAlī was able to bring Baṣra well under his control and appointed ʿAbd Allāh b. ʿAbbās as his governor. ʿAlī then entered Kūfa, not to make it his capital, but only to mobilize further support and organize the Kūfans for another much more serious encounter with Muʿāwiya.

What should be noted here, however, is that at the battle of Al-Jamal, while a large section of the Kūfans supported ʿAlī, the clan and tribal leaders who had entrenched themselves during the caliphate of ʿUthmān did not wish to side with him, or at least they remained uncommitted. These tribal leaders, such as Al-Ashʿath b. Qays, Jarīr b. ʿAbd Allāh, and Saʿd b. Qays, undoubtedly felt the same fears of ʿAlī as did the Meccans and the Umayyads. In order to consolidate his power in Kūfa, ʿAlī had to establish a purely Islamic socio-political system, which meant that the old Islamic leadership in Kūfa had to be restored at the expense of traditional tribal aristocracy that had emerged during the caliphate of ʿUthmān. As has been said earlier, the population of Kūfa was organized in seven tribal groups according to either genealogies or alliances. It was in that tribal grouping that the new leadership had established its roots. The first step ʿAlī took to weaken this leadership was to make some drastic changes in the external composition of these seven groups by reshuffling and reorganizing the tribes from one group to the other. In this way he tried to restore to power those erstwhile leaders whose claims were based on Islamic priority. We see that men such as Mālik b. Ḥārith al-Ashtar, Ḥujr b. ʿAdī al-Kindī, and ʿAdī b. Ḥātim al-Ṭāʾī, eclipsed by the strong tribal leaders, re-emerged once again. For example, Al-Ashʿath b. Qays was replaced by Ḥujr b. ʿAdī, and in the battle of Ṣiffīn Ḥujr was given the leadership of Kinda.[61] Al-Ashtar became the leader of a new clan group consisting of Madhḥij, Nakhāʿī, and some other sub-clans. His position was further strengthened when he was appointed by ʿAlī as the governor of the Jazira.[62] Similarly, another early leader, ʿAdī b. Ḥātim, was supported by ʿAlī to become the sole leader of the Ṭayy, even though there was considerable opposition from other branches of the tribe.[63]

Leaders such as Al-Ashtar, Ḥujr, and ʿAdī, together with their following, especially from the newcomers of their tribes, formed the backbone of ʿAlī's supporters and were the nucleus of the Shīʿī of Kūfa. On the other hand, the strongest clan leaders, who had built themselves up on the strength of their tribes, did not show much interest in ʿAlī. The sharp contrast between these two groups is clearly illustrated by the fact that since ʿAlī's arrival in Kūfa, Al-Ashtar, Ḥujr, ʿAdī and other Shīʿī leaders consistently urged ʿAlī to attack Muʿāwiya without delay and without entering into correspondence with him, while most of the strong tribal leaders advised him not to take any early action.[64] When, however, the armies of ʿAlī and Muʿāwiya came to meet at Ṣiffīn, these tribal leaders of Kūfa saw their position as precarious. They could not remain completely aloof from ʿAlī and had to appear with him on the battlefield; yet they remained half-hearted and lukewarm. In fact, they saw their interests best served by a deadlock between ʿAlī and Muʿāwiya. They were in a dilemma, in that ʿAlī's success would mean a loss of their tribal power, but on the other hand, Muʿāwiya's victory would mean the loss of the Iraqi independence upon which their power depended. In short, "from the time of ʿAlī's arrival in Kūfa, through the time of the confrontation at Ṣiffīn and subsequent developments in Iraq, and until the time of his death, the position of these two alignments remained consistent. The Shīʿī leaders urged ʿAlī to fight Muʿāwiya, they were opposed to the arbitration proposal, and they pledged themselves to ʿAlī unconditionally. Most of the clan leaders, on the other hand, showed no inclination to fight Muʿāwiya, went to Ṣiffīn in a spirit of indifference, and accepted with alacrity the peace offered by the arbitration proposal."[65]

It is generally suggested that the *qurrā'* forced ʿAlī to submit to arbitration, but it seems that the tribal leaders and their following were in fact responsible, for they had nothing to gain from fighting and much to gain from a stalemate. Similarly, it is also stated that it was the *qurrā'* group which compelled ʿAlī to accept Abū Mūsā al-Ashʿarī as his arbitrator, though Abū Mūsā's record indicated that he had been in favour of the Meccans and of overall domination by Quraysh, and therefore must have been the choice of the tribal leaders.

The word *qurrā'* as used in the accounts of Ṣiffīn must be approached with some caution. The early *qurrā'* of Kūfa who led the revolt against ʿUthmān had as their leaders such men as Mālik, Ḥujr, and ʿAdī, and were the die-hard supporters of ʿAlī. Besides these original *qurrā'* of Kūfa, at Ṣiffīn we meet a great number of people who are described by the sources, rather conveniently, as *qurrā'*. Some of them came from Baṣra, others from far-off outposts of both territories. They must have been, therefore, tribesmen who were trying to advance their claims through Islamic priority. And these were the people who, misled by the tribal leaders, at first supported arbitration and then revolted against it. They became the *Khawārij,* and in the events that followed Ṣiffīn they further weakened ʿAlī's position both at home and against Muʿāwiya.

The main reason for the resentful attitude of the *ashrāf al-qabā'il* of Kūfa was perhaps ʿAlī's egalitarian policy. In the first place, in the distribution of stipends he abolished the distinction made between early and latecomers to Kūfa and instead made his criterion not only Islamic priority, but also adherence to Islamic values and standards. This is so very clear from the numerous addresses he delivered in this period, as preserved in the *Nahj al-Balāgha.*[66] When ʿAlī came to Kūfa, there was another influx of newcomers to the city, those who came with ʿAlī himself, and he treated them with equality irrespective of their early domicile. This was a serious threat to the tribal leaders who had been enjoying a larger share of the Kūfan treasury, which had already been shrinking in its resources due to the lull in the conquests. In the second place, ʿAlī observed equality in the allotment of stipends to Arabs and non-Arabs. This was especially offensive to the *ashrāf al-qabāʾil* since, besides financial considerations, they believed that the non-Arab *mawālī*, as conquered people, should not and could not be treated equally with their conquerors.[67]

It was beyond any doubt clear to the tribal leaders and their clansmen that under ʿAlī's rule they stood to lose whatever they had managed to gain due to their tribal strength under ʿUthmān. It was, however, still not possible or advisable for them, in the conditions in Kūfa at the time, to come out in open revolt against ʿAlī. Nevertheless, after the inconclusive results of Ṣiffīn and the unfavourable outcome of the arbitration that followed, the tribal leaders hitherto wavering between indifference and treachery became more pronounced in their resentful attitude toward ʿAlī. They did remain in the rank and file of his army, which he was mobilizing for a final and decisive encounter with Muʿāwiya, yet totally ignored his call to go out to fight the Syrians. Instead they insisted on dealing with the *Khawārij* who had gathered at Nahrawān.[68] What they were concerned with was the maintenance of their own position as Kūfan tribal leaders: the *Khawārij* were a threat to that, Muʿāwiya was not. After the *Khawārij* were defeated at Nahrawān and ʿAlī then called upon them to move against Muʿāwiya, Al-Ashʿath and other strong tribal leaders refused, ostensibly on lame excuses, and ʿAlī was thus obliged to return to Kūfa.[69] ʿAlī's position was further weakened since the battle of Nahrawān had earned him many enemies among the relatives and kinsmen of the slain *Khawārij*; additionally, the tribal leaders took further advantage of his increasing unpopularity among the large number of tribes. Moreover, since the arbitration Muʿāwiya had been in constant touch with these tribal leaders, trying to win them over through offers of power and wealth. They were thus deliberating on what could best serve their purposes.

The attitude of these Kūfans is best indicated by ʿAlī himself in a number of speeches which he delivered in this period. In one of his speeches shortly before he was assassinated, he addressed the people and said:

"Behold, I have called upon you day and night, secretly and openly, to fight these people [the Syrians]. I have said to you: 'Fight them before they fight you, for, by God, never do a people fight within their own territory without being dishonoured.' But you tarried and vacillated until you have been attacked repeatedly and your territory has been lost to you . . . How strange indeed—a strangeness in which God makes the hearts dead and brings grief—is the gathering of these people [Muʿāwiya's supporters] in their falsehood and your standing aloof from your right. Woe unto you, and fire upon you, for you have become a target which is shot at; you are raided and you raid not; you are attacked and you do not fight back; and God is disobeyed and you are content to see that.

"When I order you to march toward them during the summer season, you say: 'This is the season of intense heat; grant us respite until the heat has abated from us.' And when I command you to proceed toward them in winter, you say: 'This is the season of intense cold; give us time until the cold is dispelled from us.' With all this fleeing from heat and cold, by God, you will flee even more readily from the sword.

"O you who look like men but are not men, having the intellect of children and the wits of women, I wish I had never seen or known you, for acquaintance with you has drawn regret and brought in its wake grief and sorrow. May God destroy you. You have filled my heart with pus and have lined my breast with anger. You have made me drink draughts of anxiety one after the other and have corrupted my judgment by your disobedience and desertion, so that Quraysh say that the son of Abū Ṭālib is a brave man but had no knowledge of warfare. For God be their father! Is any one of them more experienced in warfare or does any of them occupy a place in it higher than mine? I started fighting when I was not yet twenty years of age, and here I am the same fighter when I have passed the age of sixty. But there could be no judgment for him who is not obeyed."[70]

ʿAlī thus left behind the people of Kūfa divided into two groups of conflicting interest which could now be more easily defined and categorised than when he arrived at Kūfa five years earlier. There was, firstly, a group of his faithful followers, both from the early and the late comers, who were not only committed to his person, but also believed that the leadership of the Muslims must remain in the house of the Prophet. In this, indeed, there appear to have been some considerations of a socio-economic nature, but these were only concomitant with the idea of justice and religious values which, they thought, could be realized only through a divinely inspired leader. Among them there were people, however small in number, to whom religious and spiritual considerations were the only driving force: economic factors, even though these seem to have been the cause of certain incidents, had nothing to do with their adherence to ʿAlī. For others, economic factors were just as important as religion; they felt that an appropriate combination of the two could be realized only through ʿAlī. Whatever the degree of emphasis on one aspect or the other, the conviction of both sections of ʿAlī's firm supporters was the same: the leadership of the Muslim community must come from the family of the Prophet.

Secondly, there was a group consisting of clan and tribal leaders, along with those whose interests were dependent on these leaders. They were basically interested in preserving and maintaining their political positions and economic monopolies, which would be seriously threatened should ʿAlī succeed in firmly establishing his rule in Kūfa. They were, therefore, indifferent to ʿAlī and were inclined towards Muʿāwiya, in whom they saw security for their privileged positions and vested interests. But at the same time, they were hesitant to openly submit to Muʿāwiya and thereby lose their bargaining position. It was for this reason that outwardly they remained in the rank and file of ʿAlī's army while putting pressure on Muʿāwiya for the guaranteeing of their privileges. They thus pretended to be the supporters of the Shīʿī cause. These were the people who composed the political supporters of ʿAlī, as discussed in Chapter 4.

To these two groups of opposite interest we must add a third, consisting of the vast masses of Kūfa, mostly the Yemenis and the non-Arab *mawāli,* who theoretically were inclined to the Shīʿī ideal of leadership but were hopelessly devoid of resolve in the face of any danger which might befall them. Emotionally, whenever they saw any hope of success of someone from the *Ahl al-Bayt,* they swarmed around him; practically, they deserted him as soon as they saw the hope of success dwindling away. They lacked the necessary courage or the firmness of character to withstand a moment of trial.

The events described in the following two chapters will explain the behaviour and attitude of these three groups.

Here it remains to note that after the death of ʿAlī and the abdication of his son Ḥasan, when Muʿāwiya took control of Kūfa, the strong tribal and clan leaders were made to serve as the intermediaries in the power structure of the province. The central authority in Damascus was concerned with exercising power both over and through them. The old style tribalism was reinforced and governmental power was grounded on a tribal organization in which tribal leaders supported and in turn were supported by the government. At the time of ʿAlī's death, the tribal leaders were on one side of the scale, the committed *Shīʿat ʿAlī* on the other, while the great masses were wavering between the two. The following years were to prove decisive in resolving this basic contradiction of interests.

Notes to Chapter 5

[1] Balādhurī, *Futūḥ al-Buldān,* trans. Philip K. Hitti, *The Origins of the Islamic State* (Beirut, 1966), p. 434; Yāqūt, *Muʿjam al-Buldān* (Tehran, 1965), IV, p. 323; Ṭabarī, I, p. 2485; Khalīfa b. Khayyāt, *Taʾrīkh,* ed. Zakkār (Cairo, 1967), I, p. 129

[2] See sources cited in note 1 above

[3] Muḥammad Ḥusayn al-Zubaydī, *Al-Ḥayāt al-ijtimāʿīya waʾl iqtiṣādīya fiʾl-Kūfa* (Cairo, 1970), p. 25; Yūsuf Khalif, *Ḥayāt al-Shiʿr fiʾl-Kūfa* (Cairo, 1968), p. 23

[4] Ṭabarī, I, p. 2360; Yāqūt, *Muʿjam al-Buldān,* IV, p. 322

[5] Balādhurī, *Origins,* p. 434

[6] M. Hind, "Kūfan Political Alignments in the Mid-7th Century AD", *International Journal of Middle East Studies,* (October, 1971), p. 351

[7] Balādhurī, *Origins,* pp. 435 f.; Yāqūt, *Muʿjam al-Buldān,* IV, p. 323

[8] Ṭabari, I, p. 2495

[9] ibid.

[10] For Kināna see ʿUmar Riḍā Kaḥḥāla, *Muʿjam Qabāʾil al-ʿArab* (Damascus, 1949), p. 996; *ʿIqd,* III, pp. 339, 359; for Jadīla of Qays ʿAylān see Kaḥḥāla, p. 173; *ʿIqd,* III, p. 350

[11] For the details of these Yemeni tribes, see Kaḥḥāla, pp. 957, 844 f., 63 ff., 131 f., 998 ff., 282, 15 ff. respectively; *ʿIqd,* III, pp. 371, 382, 388, 391 f., 403, 375, 385 respectively

[12] Kaḥḥāla, p. 64; *ʿIqd,* III, p. 388

[13] He led the delegation of Kinda to Medina in 9/630 to accept Islam. See Kaḥḥāla, p. 999

[14] From Madhḥij there were many important sub-tribes, such as Nakhkhāʾ and Ṭayy. See Kaḥḥāla, p. 1062; *ʿIqd,* III, p. 393

[15] Kaḥḥāla, pp. 305 f.; *ʿIqd,* III, p. 369

[16] Kaḥḥāla, p. 1225; *ʿIqd,* III, pp. 389 f.

[17] Kaḥḥāla, p. 1225; *ʿIqd,* III, p. 389

[18] Kaḥḥāla, pp. 126 ff., 315, 1231 respectively; *ʿIqd,* III, pp. 344 ff., 343 f., 353 ff.

[19] Kaḥḥāla, pp. 21 ff., 888, 1042, 1192, 664, 120 ff. respectively; *ʿIqd,* III, pp. 340 ff., 351, 319, 358, 356, 359

[20] Kaḥḥāla, pp. 52 ff.

[21] Of uncertain origin. Some said they belonged to the Qaḥṭānīs, others describe them as ʿAdnānīs from al-Dayth b. ʿAdnān. See Kaḥḥāla, pp. 802 f.

[22] Kaḥḥāla, pp. 726 f.; *ʿIqd*, III, p. 357
[23] Kaḥḥāla, p. 726
[24] Balādhurī, *Origins*, pp. 440 f.; *EI*[2] article "Daylam"
[25] Kaḥḥāla, p. 726
[26] Kaḥḥāla, p. 691
[27] *Maqātil*, p. 61; *Sharḥ*, XVI, p. 38. See p. 142 below
[28] Kaḥḥāla, p. 689
[29] Ṭabari, II, pp. 304 ff. See p. 200 ff. below
[30] Massignon, *Khiṭaṭ*, p. 11. Cf. Ṭabari, I, p. 3174; Khalīf, *Ḥayāt ash-Shiʿr fīʾl Kūfa*, p. 29
[31] Massignon, *Khiṭaṭ*, pp. 15 f. Cf. Ṭabari, II, p. 131; Khalif, op. cit., pp. 30 f.
[32] Ṭabarī, II, p. 131
[33] Ṭabarī, I, pp. 2221 f.
[34] *Muʿjam al-Buldān*, IV, p. 324
[35] Balādhurī, *Origins*, pp. 436, 440; Yāqūt, *Muʿjam al-Buldān*, IV, p. 323
[36] Ibn Saʿd, VI, p. 9
[37] ibid, VI, p. 12-66
[38] Ibn Saʿd, VI, p. 7; Balādhurī, *Origins*, p. 448
[39] Ibn Saʿd, VI, pp. 13 f.; Ṭabarī, I, p. 2645
[40] Ibn Saʿd, VI, p. 7
[41] Ṭabarī, I, pp. 2414 f.
[42] Ṭabarī, I, p. 2496. For the institution of the *ʿarīf* see *EI*[2] article "ʿArīf"
[43] Ṭabarī, I, p. 2633
[44] Ṭabarī, I, p. 2805
[45] Ṭabarī, I, p. 2418
[46] Massignon, *Khiṭaṭ*, p. 13; Ṭabarī, I, p. 2418
[47] Ṭabarī, I, pp. 2418 f.
[48] Ibn Saʿd, VI, p. 11
[49] Ṭabarī, I. p. 2464
[50] S.A.Al-ʿAlī, *Al-Tanẓīmāt al-ijtimāʿīya waʾl-iqtiṣādīya fīʾl-Baṣra*, 2nd ed. (Beirut, 1969), pp. 88 ff.
[51] ibid, p. 82
[52] Ṭabarī, II, p. 1072
[53] Ṭabarī, I, p. 2668
[54] Ṭabarī, I, p. 2927
[55] ibid.
[56] Ṭabarī, I, p. 2651
[57] Balādhurī, *Ansāb*, V, p. 46
[58] Ṭabarī, I, pp. 3075 ff.; *Al-Imāma waʾl-siyāsa*, I, p. 47
[59] Hind, op. cit., p. 361
[60] Ṭabarī, I, p. 3174
[61] Naṣr, *Waqʿat Ṣiffīn*, p. 105

[62] Ibn Aʿtham, II, p. 350; Naṣr, *Waqʿat Ṣiffīn,* p. 12

[63] Ṭabarī, I, p. 3279

[64] Ṭabarī, I, p. 3256

[65] Hind, op. cit., p. 363

[66] e.g., *Khuṭābāt* nos. 21, 23, 24, 42, to cite but a few

[67] For ʿAlī's fiscal policies and egalitarian attitude, see Ṭabarī, I, p. 3227

[68] Masʿūdī, *Murūj,* II, p. 404

[69] ibid., p. 407

[70] *Nahj al-Balāgha,* I, pp. 76–79; Mubarrad, *Kāmil,* I, pp. 20 f., with slightly different readings in some cases. I have followed the *Nahj al- Balāgha's* text.

Chapter 6

The Abdication of Ḥasan

During the last year of ʿAlī's caliphate, Muʿāwiya b. Abī Sufyān, the governor of Syria and the main challenger of ʿAlī, managed to bring a large part of the Muslim empire under his control. He also had the authority vested in him, though under doubtful and ambiguous circumstances, by ʿAmr b. al-ʿĀṣ at the arbitration of Aḍrūḥ after the battle of Ṣiffīn. Nevertheless, he could not claim for himself the title of *Amīr al-Muʾminīn* while ʿAlī was yet alive. ʿAlī was still the legitimate caliph chosen by the community at large in Medina; this was not publicly repudiated by the community as a whole, nor was the declaration of Abū Mūsā al-Ashʿarī deposing ʿAlī and that of ʿAmr b. al-ʿĀṣ installing Muʿāwiya accepted by the Muhājirūn and the Anṣār. Thus, despite all his military and political successes, Muʿāwiya could do no more than style himself only as *Amīr.*[1] With ʿAlī's assassination, the road was finally cleared for the realization of the ultimate goal of Muʿāwiya's ambitions. The very favourable circumstances that prevailed in the form of the impotence of Medina and the remnant of the pious section of the community and the vacillating nature of the Iraqi supporters of ʿAlī's successor Ḥasan, coupled with the characteristic shrewdness of Muʿāwiya, made it easier for him to complete the task he had initiated after the death of ʿUthmān: the seizure of the caliphate for himself and his clan.

Ḥasan, the elder son of ʿAlī and Fāṭima, was acclaimed as caliph by forty thousand people in Kūfa immediately after the death of his father.[2] We are told that at the battle of Ṣiffīn (Ṣafar 37/July 657), less than three years before his death, ʿAlī had in his army seventy Companions who fought for the

Prophet at Badr, seven hundred of those who renewed their allegiance to Muḥammad (*bayʿat ar-riḍwān*) at the time of the treaty of Hudaybīya, and another four hundred from other Muhājirūn and Anṣār.[3] Many of them were still residing in Kūfa with ʿAlī as he prepared for a final encounter with Muʿāwiya. They must have participated in the election of Ḥasan and must have accepted him as the new caliph, otherwise our sources would have recorded their opposition to his succession. To this there is no testimony at all. The people of Medina and Mecca seem to have received the news with satisfaction, or at least with acquiescence. This is evident from the fact that not a single voice of protest or opposition from these cities against Ḥasan's accession can be located in the sources.

Two major reasons can be advanced for this attitude. First, at the time of ʿAlī's death almost all the distinguished Companions of the Prophet from among the Muhājirūn were dead. Of the six members of the *Shūrā* appointed by ʿUmar, only Saʿd b. Abī Waqqāṣ was still alive; the other members of the leading élite of the community had also died. Among the younger nobility such as ʿAbd Allāh b. al-ʿAbbās, ʿAbd Allāh b. az-Zubayr, Muḥammad b. Ṭalḥa, and ʿAbd Allāh b. ʿUmar, none could match Ḥasan, the elder and dearest grandson of the prophet. The people of Medina still remembered that ardent love and affection which the Prophet had showered upon his grandsons: that he interrupted his sermon and descended from the pulpit to pick up Ḥasan, who had stumbled over his long tunic and fallen down while entering the mosque;[4] that he allowed his grandchildren to climb on his back while he was prostrating himself in prayer.[5] There are numerous accounts describing extraordinary favours being bestowed by Muḥammad on his grandsons; these are preserved not only by the Shīʿī sources, but are overwhelmingly transmitted by the Sunnī works as well.[6] Ḥasan is also unanimously reported to have resembled the Prophet in appearance.[7] Secondly, the people of Mecca and Medina naturally could not be expected to be pleased to see Muʿāwiya, the son of Abū Sufyān, the representative of the clan of Umayya, become their leader. It was Abū Sufyān who had organized the opposition to Muḥammad and had led all the campaigns against him. The Umayyads in general, and the

Sufyānids in particular, did not acknowledge Muḥammad until the fall of Mecca; their Islam was therefore considered to be of convenience rather than conviction. Muʿāwiya, for his part, depended on the support of the Syrians, whom he had consolidated behind himself, and to whom he had been attached for close to twenty years as governor of the province, and on the support of his large and powerful clan and their clients and allies who swarmed around him. It was therefore natural, under the circumstances, that the inhabitants of the holy cities, who formed the nucleus of the Islamic *Umma,* would not oppose Ḥasan's caliphate, especially since the alternative was the son of Abū Sufyān and Hind.

As for the people of Iraq, the eldest son of ʿAlī was the only logical choice, though not all of his supporters were motivated by the same feelings or attachment to the same cause. To a great number of them Ḥasan's succession meant the continuation of ʿAlī's policy against the rule of Muʿāwiya and against the domination of Syria over Iraq. To some others, Ḥasan was now the only person worthy of leading the community on religious grounds. Whether motivated by merely political or by religious considerations, however, it cannot be denied that the Iraqis acclaimed Ḥasan as caliph on the grounds that he was the grandson of the Prophet through ʿAlī and Fāṭima. Ḥasan's spontaneous selection after the death of ʿAlī also indicated Iraqi inclinations, though in vague terms, towards the legitimate succession to the leadership of the community in the line of ʿAlī. It seems that the people of Iraq, even at that early period, were quite clear in distinguishing the line of the Prophet through Fāṭima from other members of the Hāshimite clan, otherwise they would have chosen, for example, ʿAbd Allāh b. al-ʿAbbās, who was a cousin of the Prophet, was senior in age to Ḥasan and was experienced in affairs of state, having been ʿAlī's governor in Baṣra.[8] Ḥasan's close relationship to the Prophet is frequently referred to as the reason for the special consideration of the people for him.

Following the custom established by Abū Bakr, Ḥasan made a speech on the occasion of his accession to the caliphate. In this speech, reported in many sources with varying lengths and wordings, Ḥasan praised the merits of his family and the special rights and unmatched qualities of his father. He emphasized his own intimate relations with the Prophet, described his own merits and claims, and quoted the verses of the *Qur'ān* which exalt the special position of the *Ahl al-Bayt.*[9] Qays b. Sa'd b. 'Ubāda al-Anṣārī, an ardent supporter of 'Alī and a trusted commander of his army, was the first to pay homage to him. The forty thousand troops of Iraq who had sworn allegiance to 'Alī on the condition to die for him (*'ala'l-mawt*) readily hailed Ḥasan as their new caliph.[10] Apparently expressing his own sentiments as well as those of the Iraqi army, Qays tried to impose the condition that the *bay'a* should be based, not only on the *Qur'ān* and the *Sunna* of the Prophet, but also on the condition of the war (*qitāl*) against those who declared licit (*ḥalāl*) that which is illicit (*ḥarām*). Ḥasan, however, succeeded in avoiding this commitment by saying that the last condition was implicitly included in the first two. The more militant among the Iraqis, eager to fight against Mu'āwiya, were not in favour of exclusion of the third condition from the terms of the *bay'a*, but they nevertheless paid their allegiance to him.[11] Later events would demonstrate that Ḥasan was perhaps from the very beginning quite apprehensive of the fickle-mindedness of the Iraqis and their lack of resolution in time of trials; and thus he wanted to avoid commitment to an extreme stand which might lead to complete disaster. He was moreover a peace-loving man of mild temper who hated to see the shedding of Muslim blood.[12] However, according to the majority of the sources, the oath of allegiance taken by those present stipulated that: "They should make war on those who were at war with Ḥasan, and should live in peace with those who were at peace with Ḥasan."[13]

Ḥasan's acclamation as caliph by the Iraqis, and a tacit approval, at least an absence of protest or opposition, from the Hijaz, Yemen, and Persia, were a great cause of alarm to Mu'āwiya, who had been working for the office since the death of 'Uthmān and who, after five years of ceaseless struggle, at last saw a clear path to undisputed authority since 'Alī was no longer alive. He lost no time in taking action. First of all, as soon as the news of Ḥasan's selection reached Mu'āwiya, he denounced the appointment, and both in speeches and in letters announced his firm decision not to recognize Ḥasan as caliph.[14] Secondly, he dispatched many of his agents and spies to arouse the people against Ḥasan. Such agents had already been quite active in the provinces of Yemen, Persia, and the Hijaz, which were still within ʿAlī's domain though not fully under his control at the time he was killed. These agents were active even in the heart of Iraq and Kūfa, ʿAlī's only solid possession. Of this activity there is no doubt at all. This already organized espionage network was now intensified by Muʿāwiya and expanded to a much larger scale. There are numerous exchanges of letters on the subject of these spies between Ḥasan and Muʿāwiya and between ʿAbd Allāh b. al-ʿAbbās and Muʿāwiya.[15] Muʿāwiya did not even deny these subversive activities. Finally, he began preparations for war and summoned all the commanders of his forces in Syria, Palestine, and Transjordan to join him. Not long after, the Syrian leader marched against Ḥasan with an army of sixty thousand men,[16] taking the usual military route through Mesopotamia to Maskin, on the Tigris boundary of Mosul towards the Sawād. When Muʿāwiya's warlike intentions became clear, Ḥasan had to prepare for war and was compelled to take the field before he had time either to strengthen himself in his position or to reorganize the administration that had been thrown into chaos by the death of his father.

The purpose of this prompt action by Muʿāwiya was twofold: first, by his demonstration of arms and strength, he hoped to force Ḥasan to come to terms; and secondly, if that course of action failed, he would attack the Iraqi forces before they had time to consolidate their position. It was for the first reason that Muʿāwiya intentionally moved towards Iraq at a very slow pace, while sending letter after letter to Ḥasan asking him not to try to fight and urging him to come to terms. If Ḥasan was defeated on the battlefield, this would give Muʿāwiya only power and authority; but if Ḥasan abdicated, this would provide Muʿāwiya with a legal base and legitimize his authority as well. This was what Muʿāwiya was trying to achieve. Moreover, Ḥasan defeated, or even killed, still represented a serious threat unless he resigned his rights; another member of the Hāshimite house could simply claim to be his successor. Should he resign in favour of Muʿāwiya, such claims would have no validity and the Umayyad position would be secured. This strategy proved correct, as will be seen below. Even after the death of Ḥasan, ten years later, when the people of Iraq approached his younger brother Ḥusayn concerning an uprising, the latter advised them to wait as long as Muʿāwiya was alive because of Ḥasan's treaty with him.

The correspondence between Ḥasan and Muʿāwiya, which continued throughout this period, makes interesting reading and provides some useful information. Both referred to the old question of the caliphate with polemical arguments. In one of his long letters to Muʿāwiya, Ḥasan argued his rights to the caliphate on the grounds that the authority of the caliphate stems from the Prophet of God, who was the most excellent and the best of men on earth and through whose guidance the Arabs found light while they were deep in darkness and attained honour and glory while they were disgraced, and that Ḥasan was the nearest to the Prophet in blood and relationship. Ḥasan then used his father's argument, which the latter had advanced against Abū Bakr after the death of Muḥammad, that if Quraysh could claim the leadership over the Anṣār on the grounds that the Prophet belonged to Quraysh, then the members of his family, who were the nearest to him in every respect, were better qualified for the leadership of the community. In the last part of his letter Ḥasan wrote:

> "We were shocked to see that some people snatched away our right from us even though they were men of excellence, virtues, and merits, and were the forerunners in Islam [reference to the first three caliphs]. But now what a great astonishment and shock it is to see that you, O Muʿāwiya, are attempting to accede to a thing which you do not deserve. You do not possess any known merit in religion (*dīn*), nor have you any trace (*āthār*) in Islam which has ever been praised. On the contrary, you are the son of the leader of the opposition party from among the parties (*ḥizb min al-aḥzāb*) [a reference to the "confederacy" which under Muʿāwiya's father, Abū Sufyān, made the last united effort to crush Medina]; and you are the son of the greatest enemy of the Prophet from among Quraysh . . . so give up your persistence in falsehood (*bāṭil*) and enter into my homage as other people have done, for you are certainly aware of the fact that I am far more entitled to the caliphate than you in the eyes of God and all worthy people. Fear God, restrain yourself from rebellion and from shedding the blood of the Muslims; for, by God, there

would be no good for you to meet your Lord with the responsibility of the blood of the Muslims."[17]

Muʿāwiya's detailed reply to Ḥasan is even more interesting, especially since he used the argument used by ʿUmar b. al-Khaṭṭāb against ʿAlī. Writing to Ḥasan, Muʿāwiya argued:

"Whatever you said about the excellence and merits of the Prophet, he was indeed the most excellent among all men before and after him, past or present, young or old. Indeed God had chosen Muḥammad for His message, and through him we received guidance, were saved from destruction, and came out from darkness and error.

"You have mentioned the death of the Prophet and the dispute which took place among the Muslims at that time. In this you are clearly making accusations against Abū Bakr, ʿUmar, and Abū ʿUbayda, and against those virtuous men among the Muhājirūn and Anṣār. I hate this accusation against the people whose actions, according to us and other people, were beyond doubt and reproach.

"When this community had some disagreements after the Prophet concerning the leadership, it was not ignorant of your family's merits, your priority, and your close relationship to the Prophet; and the community was also not unaware of your exalted place in Islam and your qualifications in it. But the community saw that this thing [the caliphate] would be better placed among Quraysh in general and they therefore selected Abū Bakr. This is what the people thought best in the interest of the community. You are asking me to settle the matter peacefully and surrender, but the situation concerning you and me today is like the one between you [your family] and Abū Bakr after the death of the Prophet. Had I believed that you had a better grasp over the subject people than I do, that you could protect the community better than I, and you were stronger in safeguarding the properties of the Muslims and in outwitting the enemy than I, then I would have done what you have asked me. But I have a longer period of reign [probably referring to his governorship], and am more experienced, better in policies, and older in age than you. It would therefore be better for you not to insist on what you have asked me; if you enter into obedience to me now, you will accede to the caliphate after me."[18]

Muʿāwiya's letter is significant in that it gives a clear idea of the direction Muslim polity was henceforth opting to adopt openly. Muʿāwiya's arguments for his claims to the caliphate manifest those guidelines and the principles by which the question of the caliphate had been previously decided in the case of the first three caliphs, and he claimed that the same considerations must remain the deciding factors now and in the future. To him it was the interest of the state and the profane aspects of the community which must decide the question of the leadership. Muʿāwiya did not deny Ḥasan's exalted position in relation to the Prophet and his superior place in Islam, but claimed that this was not the criterion for the leadership of the community. The qualifications for the office, according to Muʿāwiya's arguments, were personal power and strength, ability in political affairs and administration, expansion of the empire, and ability to defend the Muslims and rule the subject effectively. In this way, Muʿāwiya made explicit what had been so far implicit: the separation between political and religious principles, which was henceforth permanently established. Thus, in due course, the majority of the Muslims placed the religious leadership in the totality of the community (*Jamāʿa*), represented by the *ʿulamāʾ*, as the custodian of religion and the exponent of the *Qurʾān* and the *Sunna* of the Prophet, while accepting state authority as binding. They came to be known as the Sunnīs. A minority of the Muslims, on the other hand, could not find satisfaction for their religious aspirations except in the charismatic leadership from among the people of the house of the Prophet, the *Ahl al-Bayt,* as the sole exponents of the *Qurʾān* and the Prophetic *Sunna,* although this minority too had to accept the state's authority. This group was called the Shīʿa.

Before proceeding further in an attempt to reconstruct the events which ultimately led to the abdication of Ḥasan, a word seems necessary regarding the sources of our information on the subject. The struggle between Ḥasan and Muʿāwiya has not yet been thoroughly and critically studied and remains one of the most obscure chapters of early Islamic history. Wellhausen, giving only a short and sketchy account of Ḥasan's abdication,[19] complains that the events are recorded with confusion and fragmentation and that it is, therefore, difficult to place certain critical details of the episode in precise chronological order. Indeed, chronology is always a serious problem in early Muslim histories. But in his brief description of the subject it seems that Wellhausen depended solely on Yaʿqūbī,[20] Dīnawarī,[21] and Ṭabarī.[22] Both Yaʿqūbī and Dīnawarī usually gloss over details in their short and compact histories, and it would therefore be futile to expect from them a comprehensive account of the abdication of Ḥasan. Ṭabarī provides more information than the first two but does not cover the subject with his usual thoroughness and he leaves the reader unsatisfied on many important questions. Moreover, all three of these sources suffer from a common weakness in that their renderings lack the exact sequence of events, a problem which makes it difficult to determine whether Ḥasan abdicated of his own free will or was forced by the circumstances to do so.

There are, however, three other early and important sources which were not used by or were unavailable to Wellhausen. These works, already referred to above, were authored by Ibn Aʿtham al-Kūfī[23] (died ca. 314/926), Abū'l-Faraj al-Iṣfahānī[24] (died 356/967), and Ibn Abī'l-Ḥadīd[25] (died 655/1257). Abū'l-Faraj records the whole event from Abū Mikhnaf with verifications and additions from five other chains of transmitters, commenting that "these narratives are mixed one with the other, but are near in meaning to each other." Ibn Abī'l-Ḥadīd, though a late author, is one of the best informed. He takes his material primarily from the famous early historian Madā'inī and completes the account from Abū Mikhnaf. The second part of Ibn Abī'l-Ḥadīd's account thus is similar to the corresponding portion of Abū'l-Faraj; the fact that both Abū Mikhnaf and Madā'inī wrote on the subject is confirmed by the lists of their works recorded by Ibn Nadīm.[26]

Abū Muḥammad Aḥmad b. Aʿtham al-Kūfī al-Kindī must be given a place of special importance, for his *Kitāb al-Futūḥ* is perhaps one of the earliest comprehensive and systematic works on the early conquests of Islam and the civil strife in the community. According to Doctor Shaʿbān,[27] a modern scholar, this work was composed in 204/819; this means his date of death must be placed some time in the middle of the 3rd/9th century and not in 314/926 as has so far been assumed. In any case, his history has proved to be a major source for the early history of the Arabs, particularly for events in Iraq. Ibn Aʿtham was fortunate enough to have access to the works of

Zuhrī, Abū Mikhnaf, Ibn al-Kalbī, and some other lesser traditionists in their original and unadulterated forms. According to his methodology, as is evident in the *Futūḥ,* he combines the traditions of these early writers into a connected and coherent historical narrative without interruptions and without citing his sources for each individual tradition. Nevertheless, whenever he records some significant tradition, he does mention the name of his source; in this respect Madā'inī is the most frequently cited authority. According to Shaʿbān, Ibn Aʿtham, being a contemporary of Madā'inī, had the pronounced advantage of quoting this great master in his lifetime.[28] Comparison of the narratives of Ibn Aʿtham with the tradition of Madā'inī recorded by Ṭabarī show that Ibn Aʿtham not only provides a useful check for the material recorded by Ṭabarī, but also adds important details which Ṭabarī has ignored and which are preserved in the *Kitāb al-Futūḥ.* In the episode of Ḥasan it is through Ibn Aʿtham that the complete narrative of Madā'inī has come down to us. This is confirmed by a comparison of Ibn Aʿtham's account with that of Ibn Abī'l-Ḥadīd, who cites Madā'inī as well; the latter gives only an abridged version of Ḥasan's abdication, but Ibn Aʿtham has recorded a complete description of the course of events from Madā'inī.

From these three sources we receive the complete texts of the lengthy correspondence between Ḥasan and Muʿāwiya, of which only two letters have been quoted above. There seems to be no reason for doubting the authenticity of these texts. There is a rich literature of correspondence exchanged between important personalities during the classical period of Islam, and this material is frequently quoted in the Arabic sources.[29] The correspondence between Ḥasan and Muʿāwiya must be considered in this light and must be given its due importance. Together with the other sources mentioned above, such literature enables us to form a clearer picture of the episode than has so far been available.

Ṭabarī narrates the events in two independent versions from Zuhrī and ʿAwāna. Zuhrī's account seems somewhat to favour the case of Muʿāwiya at the expense of Ḥasan,[30] or at least glosses over those details which might weaken the position of the founder of the Umayyad caliphate. This is understandable, for Zuhrī was closely attached to the

Umayyad court and was writing under the successors of Muʿāwiya. His account is an unclear isolated report not recorded by other authorities; and in contrast to this, ʿAwāna's account[31] appears to have been more balanced in describing the circumstances under which Ḥasan abdicated. Unlike Zuhrī's version, ʿAwāna's bears considerable historical merit in that it very largely conforms with the accounts reported by other authorities such as Yaʿqūbī and Dīnawarī.

According to Zuhrī, Ḥasan was from the very beginning inclined to hand over the caliphate to Muʿāwiya in return for the most favourable terms he could secure for himself from his rival. Before his death ʿAlī had entrusted the leadership of his forty-thousand-man Iraqi army to Qays b. Saʿd, one of his trusted and zealous supporters, for the campaign against Muʿāwiya. Qays was a great enemy of Muʿāwiya and the Syrians, and had sworn allegiance to ʿAlī to the death. Ḥasan knew that Qays would never agree to his plans for abdicating in favour of Muʿāwiya, and therefore he deposed Qays from the command of the army and appointed ʿAbd Allāh b. al-ʿAbbās in his place. The Kūfans were already suspicious of Ḥasan's intentions because he had not clearly committed himself to fight against Muʿāwiya at the time when homage was paid to the former. Soon they came to the conclusion that Ḥasan was not the person to lead them against their Syrian enemies, and they became increasingly restless. Not long after Ḥasan came to be aware of their ill-feelings towards him, he was attacked by a Kūfan and sustained a lance wound in his thigh. Unlike all the other accounts, Zuhrī specifies neither the place nor the timing of this attack on Ḥasan, which renders the whole account still more ambiguous and unclear.

After having been attacked, Ḥasan hastily wrote to Muʿāwiya that he was renouncing the caliphate on the condition of receiving from him a certain sum of money. As Ḥasan sent his envoy to Muʿāwiya with his letter, the latter simultaneously dispatched his own envoy to Ḥasan with a blank sheet of paper, signed and sealed by Muʿāwiya, on which Ḥasan was to inscribe whatever terms for abdication he wanted. The letters crossed. When Muʿāwiya received Ḥasan's letter he was overjoyed to see that the latter had decided to abdicate without much difficulty; he kept Ḥasan's letter as evidence of this and informed him that he had accepted Ḥasan's terms. When Ḥasan received Muʿāwiya's *carte blanche* letter, he added further financial demands on it. Upon meeting Muʿāwiya, perhaps on the occasion of the official transfer of power, he asked the Syrian leader to discard his previous letter and replace it with the *carte blanche* on which Ḥasan had written new terms regarding financial arrangements. Muʿāwiya now refused to grant anything further, saying: "Everything you first requested I agreed to and granted to you; my open offer to you cannot any more be binding on me since you have already committed yourself." Ḥasan therefore could get nothing more from Muʿāwiya and was sorry for his hasty action in writing his terms of abdication.[32]

Zuhrī also tells us that as soon as ʿAbd Allāh b. al-ʿAbbās noticed that Ḥasan was negotiating terms of abdication with Muʿāwiya, he himself secretly began treating with Muʿāwiya for safe conduct and a grant of money for himself. Muʿāwiya readily agreed to Ibn ʿAbbās' terms, whereupon the latter abandoned the army and moved to Muʿāwiya's camp in the darkness of night.[33] Ḥasan's army, finding itself without a leader, again chose Qays as commander on the condition that he carry on the war until the adherents of ʿAlī were granted amnesty and security for their lives and property. Qays easily gained these concessions from Muʿāwiya, who himself was quite willing to grant such concessions if it would enable him to reach a peaceful settlement and avoid a confrontation with Qays' strong army. He made direct offers to Qays himself, but the latter refused the money that was offered to him by Muʿāwiya and, without making any deal for himself, he gave up resistance on condition of amnesty and security for the Iraqi army.[34]

Zuhrī's pragmatism in reporting the events of the abdication of Ḥasan raises more questions than it answers. This account, which clearly shows minimal resistance on the part of Ḥasan, must have been circulated by the Umayyads themselves, who, in the absence of the three principles of *ijmāʿ*, *naṣṣ*, and *shūrā* by which the previous four caliphs had been nominated, were anxious to find a legal basis for their rule. Ḥasan's voluntary abdication in favour of Muʿāwiya, as Zuhrī would have us believe, provides such a legal ground. It was natural that Zuhrī, in the environment of Umayyad Damascus, should adopt the tradition which must have been most popular and in widest circulation in that city. The events that led to Ḥasan's abdication do not seem, however, to have been as simple as Zuhrī describes.

ʿAwāna's account in Ṭabarī[35] and in the other sources named above gives a somewhat different impression of the events and stands in sharp contrast to that of Zuhrī. According to ʿAwāna, Qays did not have command of the whole army during the lifetime of ʿAlī, but rather only of the vanguard of 12,000 men, over which he continued to retain command when Ḥasan succeeded his father. At the news of Muʿāwiya's advance towards Iraq, Ḥasan sent Qays with his 12,000 troops as an advance guard to check the enemy until Ḥasan himself could follow with the main force.[36] According to Yaʿqūbī, Abū'l-Faraj, and Ibn Abī'l-Ḥadīd, the vanguard of 12,000 men was sent by Ḥasan under the command of ʿUbayd Allāh b. al-ʿAbbās, and along with him were sent Qays b. Saʿd and Saʿīd b. Qays as advisors by whose counsel ʿUbayd Allāh was to be guided.[37] The reason for Ḥasan's delay in departure seems to have been some lack of enthusiasm on the part of his supporters. This is evident from a report that when he appealed to the Kūfans to march with him against Muʿāwiya, there was a poor response. It was only when ʿAdī b. Ḥātim, an old and devoted follower of ʿAlī and the chief of the tribe of Ṭayyi, addressed the Iraqis, urging them to respond to the call of "their Imam, the son of the daughter of their Prophet",[38] that they came out to participate in the war.

Soon after, Ḥasan left Kūfa with his main army and reached Al-Madā'in, where he encamped in the outskirts of the city. Qays and his vanguard had already reached Maskin, facing Muʿāwiya's army. The Syrian governor tried to bribe Qays by offering him a million dirhams if he would defect from the ranks of Ḥasan and join him. Qays rejected the offer with contempt, saying: "You want to deceive me in my religion."[39] Muʿāwiya then made a similar offer to ʿUbayd Allāh b. al-ʿAbbās (or his elder brother ʿAbd Allāh, as Zuhrī reports), who accepted it and went over to him with 8,000 men. Qays was thus left with 4,000 soldiers, waiting for the arrival of Ḥasan.[40] We may note here in passing that though ʿUbayd Allāh did go over to Muʿāwiya before Ḥasan announced his abdication, the timing of ʿUbayd Allāh's defection as given by Ya'qūbī does not seem correct. 'Ubayd Allāh's defection must have occurred only shortly before Ḥasan's abdication, as will be discussed below.

However, while Ḥasan's vanguard was waiting for his arrival at Maskin, Ḥasan himself was facing a serious situation at Al-Madā'in. Some of his troops rebelled against him, plundered his tent, and fell upon him. Five different versions of this rebellion are given in the sources. According to ʿAwāna,[41] someone suddenly spread the news in the army of Ḥasan that Qays had been defeated and slain and that the troops should flee. Ḥasan's tent was then plundered, and he himself was attacked. If this version is correct, the spreading of the rumour must have been a well-calculated ruse and an act of espionage by the spies of Muʿāwiya, who had, without any doubt, infiltrated the rank and file of Ḥasan's army. A second version is given by Yaʿqūbī,[42] who reports that as soon as Ḥasan reached Al-Madā'in, Muʿāwiya sent Al-Mughīra b. Shuʿba, ʿAbd Allāh b. ʿĀmir, and ʿAbd ar-Raḥmān b. Umm al-Ḥakam to Ḥasan as his mediators. After they talked to Ḥasan confidentially, and while leaving his camp, they spread the news that Ḥasan had agreed to abdicate in favour of Muʿāwiya, whereupon Ḥasan's soldiers fell upon him and plundered his tent. Yaʿqūbī also records that Muʿāwiya sent his men to Ḥasan's camp to spread the news that Qays had made peace with Muʿāwiya and had come over to his side, while simultaneously he spread the word in the army of Qays that Ḥasan had made peace with Muʿāwiya.[43] In this case, again, Muʿāwiya's machinations are responsible for the mutiny in Ḥasan's army.

The third version is given by Dīnawarī. According to his report, Ḥasan left Kūfa for Al-Madā'in, and by the time he reached Sabāṭ, in the outskirts of Al-Madā'in, he had discerned that some of his troops were showing fickleness, lack of purpose, and an indifferent or withdrawn attitude to the war.[44] Ḥasan therefore halted at Sabāṭ, encamped his army there, and made a speech, saying:

> "O people, I do not entertain any feeling of rancour against a Muslim. I am as much an overseer over yourselves [of your interests] as I am over my own self. Now, I am considering a plan; do not oppose me in it. Reconciliation, disliked by some of you, is better [under the circumstances] than the split that some

of you prefer, especially when I see that most of you are shrinking from the war and are hesitant to fight. I do not, therefore, consider it wise to impose upon you something which you do not like."[45]

When his people heard this, they looked at each other, reflecting their suspicions. Those among them who were of Khārijite persuasion said: "Ḥasan has become an infidel (*Kāfir*) as had become his father before him." They suddenly rushed upon him, pulled the carpet from under his feet, and tore his clothes from his shoulder. He called for help from among his faithful followers from the tribes of Rabīʿa and Hamdān, who rushed to his assistance and pushed the assailants away from him.[46]

The fourth version is given by Madāʾinī in Ibn Abīʾl-Ḥadīd,[47] who says that while Ḥasan was on his way to Al-Madāʾin he was wounded by a lance at Sabāṭ and his belongings were looted. When word of this reached Muʿāwiya, he spread the news far and wide, whereupon the nobles and leaders from among the 12,000-man vanguard of Ḥasan began defecting to Muʿāwiya. ʿAbd Allāh b. al-ʿAbbās informed Ḥasan of the grave situation, and it was at this point that Ḥasan called the Iraqi leaders of his main army and, with great disappointment, told them of his intention to terminate the struggle and abdicate. Before proceeding to the fifth version, it would be appropriate to point out here in passing that according to all four of these versions, Ḥasan's decision to abdicate was forced upon him by the circumstances and was not of his own free desire.

The fifth version is given by Ibn Aʿtham and Abūʾl-Faraj,[48] whose sources are not clear. Ibn Aʿtham, as noted above, does not often cite his source. At the beginning of his narrative Abūʾl-Faraj quotes Abū Mikhnaf along with five other informants; thus it is not clear whether this particular account is taken from Abū Mikhnaf himself or from any one of the other five narrators. According to this version, when Ḥasan arrived at Al-Madāʾin he suddenly halted his army there and made a speech in which he declared his intention to abdicate. Wordings of the speech, with few variations, are almost the same as that quoted above from Dīnawarī. After hearing Ḥasan's speech some of his troops fell upon him, plundered his tent, and tore his clothes. This version, unlike the other four described above, gives no reason for Ḥasan's decision to deliver his speech at that particular moment at Al-Madāʾin and thus renders it rather ambiguous. It also presents serious contradictions and raises many unsolved questions. One would ask, for example, why did Ḥasan encourage the people and make speeches asking them to join his army for the war against Muʿāwiya, as has been quoted earlier from Abūʾl-Faraj himself. Why would he go all the way from Kūfa to Al-Madāʾin with all the necessary preparations for battle, and yet suddenly change his mind and make a declaration of peace at Al-Madāʾin? We should therefore accept one of the four previous explanations, of which the most probable is Dīnawarī's: that Ḥasan's speech and his announcement of his resignation from the office were prompted by the Iraqis' treacherous attitude and finalized by Muʿāwiya's successful use of espionage and diplomacy.

After such treatment at the hands of his own troops, the disheartened and shaken Ḥasan found it impossible to stay in the army camp; he took to his horse and, escorted by his close associates and faithful followers, rode to the safety of the White Castle of Al-Madāʾin, the residence of his governor. It was on this road, just before reaching the castle, that a die-hard Khārijite, Al-Jarrāḥ b. Sinān al-Asadī, managed to ambush Ḥasan and wounded him in the thigh with a dagger, shouting: "You have become an infidel (*kāfir*) like your father before you."[49] Al-Jarrāḥ was overpowered and killed; Ḥasan, bleeding profusely, was carried to the castle, where he was cared for by his governor, Saʿd b. Masʿūd ath-Thaqafī. The news of the attack on Ḥasan, having been spread by Muʿāwiya, was soon in wide circulation. This further demoralized the already disheartened troops of Ḥasan and led to large-scale desertion from his army.[50]

After describing this, Yaʿqūbī, Dīnawarī, and Ṭabarī fail to give a detailed account of further events and hurriedly describe Ḥasan's abdication, although the first two sources do contain a few fragmentary sentences in passing which are of limited value. Keeping in view their method and style, this brevity is understandable. Ibn Aʿtham and Abūʾl-Faraj, however, record for us in detail the events which took place between the incident of the attack on Ḥasan and his abdication. The accounts of these two, however, vary in certain points and must be treated separately.

According to Ibn Aʿtham, at the time when Ḥasan was having these difficulties at Al-Madā'in, Qays b. Saʿd with his 12,000-man vanguard was already at Maskin, facing Muʿāwiya's army and awaiting Ḥasan's arrival. When he heard of the attack on Ḥasan, Qays thought it wise to engage his army in battle with the Syrians so that they should not have a chance to brood over the situation and become further demoralized. An encounter between the two armies took place, resulting in some losses on both sides. Muʿāwiya's envoys then came forward and addressed Qays, saying: "For what [cause] are you now fighting with us and killing yourself? We have received unquestionable word that your leader has been deserted by his people and has been stabbed with a dagger and is on the verge of death. You should therefore refrain from fighting until you get the exact information about the situation." Qays was thus forced to stop fighting and had to wait for the official news about the incident from Ḥasan himself. But by this time troops had begun defecting to Muʿāwiya in large numbers. When Qays noticed this large-scale desertion, he wrote to Ḥasan about the gravity of the situation.[51]

After receiving Qays' letter, Ḥasan lost heart and immediately called in the Iraqi leaders and nobles and addressed them in dejection and disgust:

> "O people of Iraq, what should I do with your people who are with me? Here is the letter of Qays b. Saʿd informing me that even the nobles (*ashrāf*) from among you have gone over to Muʿāwiya. By God, what shocking and abominable behaviour on your part! You were the people who forced my father to accept arbitration at Ṣiffīn; and when the arbitration to which he yielded [because of your demand] took place, you turned against him. And when he called upon you to fight Muʿāwiya once again, then you showed your slackness and lassitude. After the death of my father, you yourself came to me and paid me homage out of your own desire and wish. I accepted your homage and came out against Muʿāwiya; only God knows how much I meant to do [i.e. how full of zeal and spirit I was in facing Muʿāwiya's challenge]. Now you are behaving in the same manner as before [with my father]. O People of Iraq, it would be enough for me from you if you would not defame me in my religion, because now I am going to hand over this affair [the caliphate] to Muʿāwiya."[52]

Yaʿqūbī gives the same reason for Ḥasan's decision, though, as mentioned above, he covers the matter very briefly.

If this statement is accepted, it sufficiently explains the whole situation and the circumstances which made Ḥasan decide in favour of abdication. The statement clearly reflects that Ḥasan, from the very beginning, even from the time of Ṣiffīn, was suspicious of the unreliable character of the Iraqis. In his judgement they were impulsive people who talked with emotion, but when the time came for action and trial they never stood firm. This fact is not directly mentioned by the sources for the event of Ḥasan's abdication, but it appears at the time when his brother Ḥusayn was going to Iraq in response to the Kūfan appeal to lead them in rebellion. All those who advised Ḥusayn against responding positively to the Kūfan appeal clearly reminded him how the Iraqis had deserted (*khadhalū*) his father and brother at the critical moment.[53] Ḥasan's feelings are an echo of ʿAlī's attitude towards the majority of his Iraqi supporters, a sentiment which he expressed time and again in his speeches preserved in the *Nahj al-Balāgha* and in many other early sources.

After his speech before the leaders of the Iraqis, Ḥasan immediately sent word to Muʿāwiya informing him of his readiness to abdicate. When the news of Ḥasan's decision reached Qays, he told his associates: "Now you must choose between the two, either to fight without a leader (*Imām*) or to pay homage to the misled (*ḍalāl*) [Muʿāwiya]." They replied: "Paying homage is easier for us than bloodshed." Thus Qays, along with those who were still with him, left the battlefield at Maskin for Kūfa. Surprisingly enough, the name of ʿUbayd Allāh b. al-ʿAbbās does not appear at all in this account.

Turning to Abū'l-Faraj, we are told, as has already been quoted above from Yaʿqūbī, that the leader of the 12,000-man vanguard was ʿUbayd Allāh b. al-ʿAbbās and not Qays b. Saʿd. Both Muʿāwiya and ʿUbayd Allāh reached Maskin with their armies on the evening of the same day that Ḥasan reached Al-Madā'in. On the second day, after the morning prayer, while Ḥasan was confronted with the mutiny of his troops and was wounded, there was at Maskin a brief encounter between Muʿāwiya and ʿUbayd Allāh. When night fell, Muʿāwiya sent a message to ʿUbayd Allāh, saying:

> "Ḥasan has informed me of his decision to make peace and hand over the caliphate to me. If you come under my authority at once, you will be treated as a leader (*matbūʿ*); otherwise I will penetrate [into your forces] and then you will be made only a subject (*tābiʿ*). If you join me now I will pay you one million dirhams, half of which will be paid immediately, and the second half when I enter Kūfa."[54]

During the night, ʿUbayd Allāh secretly slipped through to Muʿāwiya's side. In the morning the people assembled, waiting for him to come and lead them in the morning prayer. When, after a search, he was not found, Qays came forward, led the prayer, and then made a fiery speech attacking ʿUbayd Allāh, his father ʿAbbās, and his brother ʿAbd Allāh for their wavering character and time-serving policies. Hearing Qays' words, people shouted: "Thanks be to God that he [ʿUbayd Allāh] has left our ranks; now we will rise and pounce on our enemy," and set off to make an attack. Busr b. Abī Arṭāṭ, a confidant of Muʿāwiya, came forward with 20,000 troops and shouted: "Here is your leader [ʿUbayd Allāh], who has already paid homage [to Muʿāwiya], and Ḥasan has also agreed to make peace. For what, then, are you killing yourselves?" Qays then addressed his people again and asked: "Choose one of the two, either fighting without an *Imām* or pay a strayed and misled homage [to Muʿāwiya]." The people said that they would continue to fight even without an *Imām,* made a brief attack on the Syrians, and then returned to their bases. When, however, it became clear that Ḥasan had agreed to abdicate, they returned to Kūfa.[55]

Abū'l-Faraj's rendering of the events between the attack on Ḥasan and his abdication is important in that it gives a more logical and understandable timing of the defection of ʿUbayd Allāh, which was confusingly recorded by other sources. From his account it also becomes clear that of the two brothers, the one who defected was ʿUbayd Allāh and not his elder brother ʿAbd Allāh, whose name appears only in Zuhrī's account. However, Abū'l-Faraj's report that the Iraqis replied to Qays that they would continue to fight even without an *Imām* must be rejected on the simple grounds that it is contrary to all other sources, who unanimously report that the troops replied in favour of accepting Muʿāwiya.

The terms and conditions on which Ḥasan abdicated are

reported by the sources not only with major variations, but also with confusion and ambiguity. Yaʿqūbī and Masʿūdī do not mention the terms of peace at all. Ṭabarī mentions three conditions directly, and the fourth indirectly in a different context. The first three conditions were:

1: that Ḥasan would retain the five million dirhams then in the treasury of Kūfa;
2: that Ḥasan would be allowed the annual revenue from the Persian district of Darabjird;
3: that ʿAlī would not be reviled and cursed, as had been the practice of Muʿāwiya since the beginning of ʿAlī's caliphate—at least not in Ḥasan's presence.[56]

The first condition, that Ḥasan would retain five million dirhams from the treasury of Kūfa, makes no sense for two obvious reasons. Firstly, Ḥasan, until his abdication, was the sole caliph in Kūfa, and thus the treasury was already in his possession. Secondly, our sources agree that it was ʿAlī's strict practice to empty the treasury at the end of every week. It is thus difficult to believe that within a few months of Ḥasan's accession,[57] especially considering the heavy expenditure for war and the unorganized state of the administration (and therefore of tax collection as well) due to ʿAlī's sudden death, the treasury of Kūfa had become gorged with five million dirhams. It is interesting to note that after a long gap in which Ṭabarī describes the brutalities of Busr b. Abī Arṭāṭ in administering Baṣra, he mentions a fourth condition of abdication. This tells us that "Ḥasan made peace with Muʿāwiya on the condition that all the friends and followers of ʿAlī, wherever they might be, would be given amnesty and safe conduct."[58] As will be seen below, this condition is recorded by other sources in its appropriate place.

In his account of the abdication, Dīnawarī records for us the following conditions:

1: that no one from among the people of Iraq will be treated with contempt, and that every one of them will be guaranteed peace and safety no matter what charge or offences might be pending against them;
2: that Ḥasan will be entitled to the annual revenue of the district of Ahwāz (instead of Ṭabarī's Darabjird);

3: that preference should be given to the Hāshimites (the ʿAlids and the ʿAbbāsids) over the Banū ʿAbd Shams (Umayyads) in the granting of pensions (*ʿaṭā*) and awards.[59]

Ibn ʿAbd al-Barr and Ibn al-Athīr, two judicious writers on the lives of the Companions of the Prophet, and some other sources, record yet another two conditions:

1: that no one from among the people of Medina, the Hijaz, and Iraq will be deprived or dispossessed of anything which they possessed during the caliphate of ʿAlī;
2: that the caliphate would be restored to Ḥasan after the death of Muʿāwiya.[60]

Abū'l-Faraj, like others, does not seem to be interested in recording the conditions in detail. According to him, Muʿāwiya sent ʿAbd Allāh b. ʿĀmir and ʿAbd ar-Raḥmān b. Samra as his envoys to Ḥasan to discuss the terms of peace. On behalf of Muʿāwiya, "they granted the terms of peace to Ḥasan to which Muʿāwiya had agreed: that no one from among the *Shīʿat ʿAlī* would be molested, that the name of ʿAlī would not be mentioned except in good terms, and some other things which Ḥasan wanted."[61]

The most comprehensive account, however, is given by Ibn Aʿtham,[62] which must have been taken from Madā'inī, since Ibn Abī'l-Ḥadīd[63] describes almost the same conditions, quoting Madā'inī as his authority. According to Ibn Aʿtham, after the incidents at Al-Madā'in and after the statement which Ḥasan made before the nobles of Iraq, as quoted above, he sent ʿAbd Allāh b. Nawfal b. al-Ḥārith to Muʿāwiya to inform him of Ḥasan's willingness to abdicate and to discuss the terms of abdication with the Syrian leader on his behalf. The only condition which Ḥasan stipulated to ʿAbd Allāh was a general amnesty for the people. ʿAbd Allāh reached Maskin and told Muʿāwiya that Ḥasan had authorised him to negotiate the conditions of peace on his behalf, laying down the following terms:

1: that the caliphate will be restored to Ḥasan after the death of Muʿāwiya;
2: that Ḥasan will receive five million dirhams annually from the state treasury;

3: that Ḥasan will receive the annual revenue of Darabjird;
4: that the people will be guaranteed peace with one another.[64]

Hearing this, Muʿāwiya took a blank sheet of paper, affixed his signature and seal, and said to ʿAbd Allāh: "Take this *carte blanche* to Ḥasan and ask him to write on it whatever he wants." Muʿāwiya asked his associates around him to stand witness to his signature and promise. ʿAbd Allāh, with the *carte blanche* and accompanied by some of the nobles of Quraysh, among them ʿAbd Allāh b. ʿĀmir, ʿAbd ar-Raḥmān b. Samra, along with some other nobles from among the Syrians, returned to Ḥasan and told him: "Mu'āwiya has agreed to all the conditions I have asked of him for you and which you yourself can write on this blank paper." Ḥasan replied: "As far as the caliphate is concerned, I am no more interested in it; had I wanted it I would not hand it over to Muʿāwiya. As for the money, Muʿāwiya cannot make it a condition for me when the [real] issue in question is a matter of concern for the Muslim [community]." Ḥasan then called his secretary and asked him to write: "These are the terms on which Ḥasan b. ʿAlī b. ʿAbī Ṭālib is making peace with Muʿāwiya b. Abī Sufyān and handing over to him the state or government of *Amīr al-Mu'minīn* ʿAlī:

1: that Muʿāwiya should rule according to the Book of God, the *Sunna* of the Prophet, and the conduct of the righteous caliphs;
2: that Muʿāwiya will not appoint or nominate anyone to the caliphate after him, but the choice will be left to the *shūrā* of the Muslims;
3: that the people will be left in peace wherever they are in the land of God;
4: that the companions and the followers of ʿAlī, their lives, properties, their women, and their children, will be guaranteed safe conduct and peace. This is a solemn agreement and covenant in the name of God, binding Muʿāwiya b. Abī Sufyān to keep it and fulfil it;
5: that no harm or dangerous act, secretly or openly, will be done to Ḥasan b. ʿAlī, his brother Ḥusayn, or to anyone from the family of the Prophet (*Ahl Bayt an-Nabī*); this agreement is witnessed by ʿAbd Allāh b. Nawfal, ʿUmar b. Abī Salama, and so and so."[65]

Ibn Aʿtham's rendering of the terms of peace as dictated by Ḥasan solves many problems and explains the different ambiguous accounts of other sources. The timing of the *carte blanche* sent by Muʿāwiya to Ḥasan was confusing in Ṭabarī, whereas Ibn Aʿtham's timing of it makes it understandable. Ṭabarī, Abu'l-Faraj, and some other sources cite the names of ʿAbd Allāh b. ʿĀmir and ʿAbd ar-Raḥmān b. Samra as being sent by Muʿāwiya as his envoys to Ḥasan to discuss the terms of peace; Ibn Aʿtham, while confirming this report, gives the proper and logical occasion of their commission. Ibn Aʿtham records the conditions in two parts: one laid down by Ḥasan's envoy ʿAbd Allāh b. Nawfal, and the other dictated by Ḥasan himself, as enumerated above. If both sets of conditions are combined together, these, with the exception of the first two conditions mentioned immediately above, are the same as those found scattered in an unorganized way in other sources. The first of these conditions, that Muʿāwiya should rule according to the *Qur'ān,* prophetic *Sunna,* and the conduct of the righteous caliphs, strongly reflects the tendency and spirit of the epoch which was still predominant in the function and character of the office of the caliphate. In all probability, the immediate successor of ʿAlī and the *Rāshidūn* caliphs would not have handed over the office without expressing this traditional condition, at least outwardly, if we must be so sceptical in accepting such reports. It should be noted, however, that from the time of the *Shūrā,* ʿAlī, his house, and his supporters always emphasized following only the *Sunna* of the Prophet and refusing to acknowledge the validity of the *Sunna* of the first three caliphs. It therefore seems likely that reference to the conduct of the righteous caliphs was added later on in an attempt at reconciliation of the *Jamāʿa* as has been seen above. Naturally Ḥasan could not contradict his own father's stand at the *Shūrā,* where the latter refused to accept the *Sunna* of Abū Bakr and ʿUmar.

The second condition—that Muʿāwiya would not nominate anyone to the caliphate and would leave the choice to the *Shūrā* of the Muslims—should not be difficult for us to accept. The precedent of nominating the successor, only to be endorsed by a few leading personalities, had already been set by Abū Bakr when he appointed ʿUmar as his successor. The decision of Abū Bakr was, however, dominated by his sincere concern for the interests of the Muslim community in general, and he did not appoint his son or even a relative to public office. It was not to be so with Muʿāwiya and the Umayyads. Thus the imposition of this condition on Muʿāwiya by Ḥasan was a natural corollary of the situation. The condition that the caliphate be restored to Ḥasan after Muʿāwiya's death, reported by many sources, must have been at least discussed. From the letter of Muʿāwiya quoted above, we may safely deduce that Muʿāwiya referred to Ḥasan's succession after himself as a strong possibility, but without giving any clear undertaking on his own part. Some time later, the Shīʿa, gathering together, showed their disapproval of the fact that Ḥasan had not asked for sufficient guarantees and had not secured an undertaking in writing from Muʿāwiya that the latter would leave him the caliphate after his death.[66]

Finally, the most interesting point seems to be Muʿāwiya's acceptance of the complete amnesty to all the followers and companions of ʿAlī. The acceptance of this particular term proves the falseness of Muʿāwiya's stated reason for fighting, which was to avenge the blood of ʿUthmān and punish those responsible for his murder. Among the *Shīʿat ʿAlī* who were given complete amnesty by Muʿāwiya in the terms with Ḥasan there were men such as ʿAmr b. al-Ḥāmiq al-Khuzāʿī, who was said to have been involved in the murder, and Mālik b. al-Ashtar, who was the leader of the rebel contingent of Kūfa. It becomes therefore clear that the reason for the revenge of the blood of ʿUthmān was, as has been pointed out elsewhere, a pretext which Muʿāwiya used to realize his ambition to seize the caliphate for himself.

The agreement having been concluded, Ḥasan returned to Kūfa, where Qays joined him. Soon afterwards, Muʿāwiya entered the city with the full force of his army. A general assembly was held, and different groups of people, one after the other, paid him homage. Our sources give a detailed description of the mixed feelings of the people in accepting Muʿāwiya as their new ruler. Many of them adopted a time-serving attitude to safeguard their interests; others could not hide their dislike, and even hatred, for the Umayyad ruler, but nevertheless had to reconcile themselves with the situation.[67] The heated remarks, bitter speeches, and resentful dialogues exchanged among the antagonists from both sides make interesting and informative reading which cannot be dealt with in detail here. The speech of Ḥasan delivered at the insistence of ʿAmr b. al-ʿĀṣ and Muʿāwiya is worth noting, however. Though quoted by all the sources, the speech is recorded with different wordings and content. The shortest version is given by Ṭabarī from Zuhrī and reads: "O people, God has guided you through our elders [Muḥammad and ʿAlī] and spared you from the bloodshed through those who followed [referring to himself]. Indeed this [the caliphate] is nothing but an ephemeral thing; these worldly possessions keep shifting and changing hands. God said to His Prophet: 'And I do not know if this may be a trial for you and a grant of [worldly] livelihood to you for a [limited] time.'" (*Qur'ān,* XXI, 111).

At this point, Muʿāwiya became alarmed and asked Ḥasan to sit down, reproachfully asking ʿAmr b. al-ʿĀṣ: "Is this what you advised me?"[68]

Madā'inī, quoted by Ibn Abī'l-Ḥadīd, gives a much longer version of the speech, in which Ḥasan explains the reasons for his abdication as, besides Muʿāwiya's ambitions and rebellion, the unreliable and treacherous attitude of his supporters. Ḥasan even referred to the time of ʿAlī and how the people failed him then.[69] Another source, Abū'l-Faraj, quotes only one sentence from Ḥasan's speech, which reads: "The *khalīfa* [successor of the Prophet] is one who dedicates himself to the way of God and the *Sunna* of His Prophet, and not the one who is an oppressor and aggressor; the latter is only a king (*malik*) who rules a kingdom (*mulk*), whose enjoyment is little, and whose pleasure is short-lived, leaving behind only a trace of it. I do not know if this is a trial for you and a grant of [worldly] livelihood to you for a [limited] period."[70] It is interesting to note that if this quotation is historically correct, it might be the origin of the use of the word *mulk* (king) instead of *khilāfa* (caliph) for Muʿāwiya and his successors, used by Muslim historians from the earliest times. However, there are numerous instances where Muʿāwiya is recorded as saying, in reference to himself, "I am the first king in Islam."[71]

The historical accounts of the circumstances facing Ḥasan from the beginning of his caliphate indicate that his abdication was not motivated by the lure of a life of ease and luxury, as some modern writers would have us believe. The sources specify the causes of Ḥasan's abdication as love of peace, distaste for politics and its dissensions, and the desire to avoid widespread bloodshed among the Muslims. Moreover, he realistically assessed the situation and was fully aware of the disastrous consequences for himself, his family, and his handful of trustworthy followers should he insist on settling the issue by force of arms.[72] He thus accepted the political realities then prevailing while gaining time for the Shīʿī trend of thinking to consolidate its own following on ideological grounds. This is evident from any one of the versions of his speech quoted above on the occasion of the transfer of the caliphate to Muʿāwiya.

In spite of his abdication of the caliphate, Ḥasan continued to be regarded as the leader, or *Imām,* of the Shīʿa after the death of ʿAlī. Even those of the Shīʿa who criticized his action of abdication never ceased to affirm that he had been designated by his father to succeed him as the Commander of the Faithful. The details of the theory of the imamate were no doubt worked out later on, but the fact remains that as long as Ḥasan was alive he was considered by both the Shīʿa and by all the family members as the head of the house of ʿAlī and of the Prophet, and that was enough for the Shīʿa throughout its history to consider him as the second Imām after ʿAlī.

Ḥasan's abdication was extremely distasteful to those of the Iraqis who had supported him and his father before him, mainly because of their hatred of Syrian domination. It was equally disturbing to those of the Khārijites who had gathered around Ḥasan in order to fight against Muʿāwiya; it was a Khārijite who furiously attacked Ḥasan when he heard of his intention to abdicate. There was yet another group, represented by men like Ḥujr b. ʿAdī al-Kindī, which was perturbed by Ḥasan's decision, but for other reasons. It was this last group that represented the true *Shīʿat ʿAlī* at this stage. They were the people who believed that ʿAlī and his house were entitled to the caliphate on religious grounds, as opposed to those who supported the cause of ʿAlī and then of Ḥasan for political or economic considerations. Thus the *Shīʿat ʿAlī,* from the time of the Umayyad domination of the provinces under ʿUthmān, must be divided into two distinct groups, political and religious. In the civil war between ʿAlī and Muʿāwiya, these two groups temporarily found themselves united against a common enemy. But when Muʿāwiya's overwhelming political and military power put the outcome of the conflict beyond doubt, the political group of Ḥasan's supporters crumbled and scattered, defecting in swarms to Muʿāwiya's side, while the religious supporters remained firm in their belief. They were disappointed by Ḥasan's action of abdication, but they still remained persistent in their ideals regarding the leadership of the community. They did not lose their identity as an opposition group to the rivals of the house of the Prophet, even after political support for the family of Muḥammad had collapsed; and they refused to accept[73] what the majority had willingly or unwillingly accepted, as will be seen below.

Later on, when the early events of Islam were committed to systematic writing, both Sunnī and Shīʿī historians and traditionists explained Ḥasan's action in terms of a "meritorious deed" by which he reconciled the opposing parties. The year of his abdication became known as the *ʿĀm al-Jamāʿa,* the year of the community, and a tradition attributed to the Prophet was reported as saying: "This son of mine is a lord (*sayyid*), and he will unite two branches of the Muslims."[74] This tradition reflects the efforts of the second half of the first and early second centuries when a "central body", or *Jamāʿa,* was emerging from a confused situation and thus clearly reflects the tendency by which this "central body" was being formed. The Shīʿīs thus defended Ḥasan's action against those extremists who were blaming him for abdication; on the other hand, the Sunnīs accepted such an explanation as it conformed to their needs for a reconciliation between the two opposing groups: the party of ʿUthmān, now represented by Muʿāwiya, and that of ʿAlī, now led by his son Ḥasan. This "central body" later on received the title of the *Jamāʿa* (commonly rendered in English as the "orthodox" branch) in Islam, leaving behind and branding as sectarian a body of those who could not and did not agree to reconcile themselves to this synthesis.

Though Ḥasan prevented a bloody military solution of the conflict by abdicating in favour of Muʿāwiya, he did not thereby heal the split in the community. In fact, his abdication had far-reaching consequences for the later development of

Shīʿism. Previously he had been, at least nominally, the head of the central body of believers. But now events were developing in the opposite direction, and the ʿUthmānīya branch, with Muʿāwiya at its head, became the central body, while the *Shīʿat ʿAlī* was reduced to the role of a small opposition party and thus was thrust into a sectarian position. The spokesman for this opposition, however, was not Ḥasan himself, but rather Ḥujr b. ʿAdī al-Kindī and his party. Supported by a number of diehard Shīʿīs of Kūfa, he never ceased to protest against Muʿāwiya and the official cursing of ʿAlī from the pulpits—a policy imposed by Muʿāwiya as a propaganda measure.

The nine-year period between Ḥasan's abdication in 41/660 and his death in 49/669 is one in which Shīʿī feelings and tendencies were passing through a stage of, so to speak, fire underground, with no conspicuous activities visible above the surface. An historical survey of this period for the development of Shīʿī ideals is very difficult, as our sources are almost silent. Nevertheless, it is not totally free from the occasional voices raised here and there in support of the house of the Prophet and against the rule of Muʿāwiya. Now and then we hear of individuals or small groups, mainly from Kūfa, visiting Ḥasan and Ḥusayn and asking them to rise in rebellion—a request to which they declined to respond.[75] The silence of the Shīʿīs during this period might have been due to two factors. Firstly, the tight grip which Muʿāwiya maintained over the empire through his trained and loyal Syrian forces was too strong to allow any rising; and secondly, the Shīʿī movement was yet not organized enough to take action against such a formidable power. But it was passing through a natural process of evolution until it could register a widespread support and then translate itself into action. Muʿāwiya was, however, fully aware of strong Shīʿī sentiments among certain parts of the population of Kūfa, and he took various measures to prevent insurrections. Soon after taking control of Kūfa, he transferred some of the tribes that were devoted to the house of ʿAlī from the city, replaced them with others from Syria, Baṣra, and Al-Jazīra who were loyal to him.[76]

After his abdication, Ḥasan left Kūfa and settled in Medina, leading a quiet retired life without engaging in politics. His attitude could be understood from the fact that during the journey back to Medina, at Al-Qādisīya, he received a letter from Muʿāwiya asking him to take part in a campaign against a Khārijite revolt which had just erupted. Ḥasan replied that he had given up fighting against Muʿāwiya in order to bring peace to the people, and that he would not take part in a campaign at his side.[77] This passive and withdrawn attitude towards Muʿāwiya he maintained while pacifying those of the Shīʿīs who occasionally visited him and expressed their bitter feelings against the Umayyad ruler.

Ḥasan did not live long, however. He died in 49/669, long before his rival. Muʿāwiya took the caliphate from Ḥasan at the age of 58 and died in 60/680 at the age of 77, while Ḥasan at the time of his abdication was only 38 and died at the age of 45 or 46. This difference in age is very important to note, especially when we read of Muʿāwiya's ambitious plans to perpetuate the caliphate in his own house and nominate his son Yazīd as his heir-apparent. This was not possible, because of the terms on which Ḥasan had abdicated to Muʿāwiya; nor, considering the vast difference in age, could Muʿāwiya have hoped that Ḥasan would die before him. To carry out his plan and fulfil his desire, Muʿāwiya had to remove Ḥasan from the scene. The majority of our sources, both Sunnī and Shīʿī, historians and traditionists, report that the cause of Ḥasan's death was poison administered by one of his wives, Juʿda bint al-Ashʿath.[78] Muʿāwiya is reported to have suborned her with the promise of a large sum of money and of marrying her to his son Yazīd. After she had completed the task, Muʿāwiya paid her the promised sum of money but refused to marry her to Yazīd, saying that he valued the life of his son.[79] The overwhelming historical testimony, Muʿāwiya's desire to nominate his son as his successor, which he did immediately after Ḥasan's death, combined with many other clues found in the sources, make it likely that Muʿāwiya must have been the instigator of the poisoning, though this will probably never be clearly established. Nevertheless, the fact that the cause of Ḥasan's death was poison, administered by his wife Juʿda, is beyond any doubt an historical truth. According to Ḥasan's own statement, this was the third time he had been poisoned, and this time it proved fatal. Our sources also tell us that upon receiving the news of Ḥasan's death, Muʿāwiya could not hide his feelings of relief and even joy and passed taunting remarks to Ibn ʿAbbās.[80] Another fact which the sources unanimously record is that soon after Ḥasan's death, Muʿāwiya initiated the process of nominating Yazīd as his successor,[81] as will be seen below.

While Muʿāwiya took the opportunity of Ḥasan's death to go ahead with his plans to secure Yazīd's nomination to the caliphate, the Shīʿīs of Kūfa, on the other hand, found the occasion appropriate for making another bid to restore the caliphate to the house of ʿAlī. As soon as the Shīʿīs of Kūfa heard the news of Ḥasan's death, they held a meeting in the house of Sulaymān b. Ṣurad al-Khuzāʿī and wrote a long letter to Ḥusayn. In it, after expressing their grief and condolences on the death of "the son of the *Waṣī,* the son of the daughter of the Prophet, and the banner of the guidance", they invited Ḥusayn to rise against Muʿāwiya and assured him that they would be ready to sacrifice their lives in his cause. Ḥusayn, however, honouring his brother's treaty with Muʿāwiya, refused to respond and advised them to refrain from agitation and to stay calm in their houses as long as Muʿāwiya was alive.[82]

The most enthusiastic among the Shīʿīs, however, could no longer remain idle. Ḥujr b. ʿAdī al-Kindī and his associates, who had never compromised their Shīʿī ideals, now came out in open revolt against Muʿāwiya and his lieutenant Ziyād b. Abī Sufyān, who governed both Kūfa and Baṣra after the death of the governor of Kūfa, Al-Mughīra b. Shuʿba, in 51/671. The revolt is reported in great detail by the early sources and demonstrates the strong Shīʿī feelings of the movement as it re-emerged at this stage. Even though it was of hardly any consequence or significance militarily, the fact that many early works devote long chapters to Ḥujr[83] indicates that the episode was of not insignificant proportions in the revolutionary events of early Islam.

We are told that these die-hard Shīʿīs had been consistently protesting not only against the cursing of ʿAlī, but also against the rule of Muʿāwiya, whom they considered a usurper of the rights of the house of ʿAlī to the caliphate. Their slogan was that "the caliphate is not valid and permissible except in the family of Abū Turāb."[84] While Ziyād himself was in Baṣra, and Kūfa was being administered by his deputy ʿAmr

b. Ḥurayth, they repeatedly went to the mosque and publicly denounced Muʿāwiya and Ziyād. When ʿAmr tried to warn them, during one of the Friday sermons, of the consequences of this open rebellion, they stoned him and forced him to take refuge in the governor's palace.[85] The numerical strength of those who thus demonstrated their support for the Shīʿī cause can be judged from the report that "they used to occupy half of the mosque of Kūfa." [86] It may be noted that the mosque of Kūfa had the capacity of accommodating as many as 40,000 people.

Informed by his deputy of the alarming situation, Ziyād rushed back to Kūfa. The governor first sent some Yemeni tribal leaders of Shīʿī inclination, with whom he had managed to establish a *modus vivendi*, to warn Ḥujr of the dangerous path he was following. The sources bear enough testimony that from the time Ziyād took over the governorship of Kūfa in 51/671 he tried his best to win over Ḥujr. Ziyād had already offered him a seat in his administrative council and was willing to enhance Ḥujr's position in the tribe of Kinda. Nothing could change the latter's attitude, however. Indeed, if the problem is regarded as one of a political nature, then it must be pointed out that almost all political concessions and material rewards had already been offered by the governor to satisfy Ḥujr. Furthermore, his refusal to accept any of the concessions which the governor was rather generously offering him could not possibly have involved an aspiration for further personal power on Ḥujr's part. He was simply too old. Even if he had succeeded in bringing the Shīʿa to power by making Ḥusayn caliph, his position would not have been any better than it had been during ʿAlī's time. Such personal gains had already been offered to him by Ziyād, but he totally refused them. In the final analysis, we are left with no choice but to accept that Ḥujr's only motive was his religious conviction and his unshakable faith in the leadership of the *Ahl al-Bayt*. The tribal leaders, some of them old friends of Ḥujr, who were sent to him to mediate and seek a compromise, failed in their efforts, but nevertheless asked the governor to treat him leniently.[87] This indicates the deep respect and high regard in which Ḥujr was held by them. One could hardly expect tribal leaders to defend a power-thirsty politically motivated self-seeker and troublemaker who might challenge or undermine their own leadership. They would, on the other hand, defend a man whose deeper religious convictions agreed with their own and who had greater moral courage to stand by his principles.

Ziyād, however, refused to listen to their pleas for Ḥujr and sent out his police to arrest him, but Ḥujr's active supporters were numerous enough to repulse them. Realizing the seriousness of the situation, Ziyād immediately summoned the nobles and leaders, especially those of the Yemeni tribes, and addressed them, saying that it was their people who were helping Ḥujr, and if they did not withdraw their support from him Ziyād would call in the Syrian forces for a complete crackdown. A phrase of Ziyād's address quoted by the sources is most illustrative of the character and attitude of these tribal leaders of Kūfa. According to Ṭabarī, Ziyād said: "Your bodies are with me, but your affection and passions are with Ḥujr."[88] Abū'l-Faraj quotes a rather elaborate statement which reads: "Your bodies are with me, but your passions are with this foolish man surrounded by flies [i.e., by people who, like flies, gather around any object]; you are with me, but your brothers, sons, and your clansmen are with Ḥujr."[89] Afraid of losing their positions, the tribal leaders of Kūfa once again demonstrated their characteristic weakness and persuaded their respective clansmen not to expose themselves to Syrian arms. While the majority of those who had gathered around Ḥujr finally deserted him, there was still a sizeable group who refused to leave and resisted Ḥujr's arrest. Ziyād had to call in the regular army, specifically choosing troops from the Yemeni contingent in Kūfa, to deal with the situation.

The task was not so easy, however, not only because of the personal prestige and the widespread support Ḥujr enjoyed among the Kūfan masses, but also because of the fear of tribal complications. A skilled politician with extraordinary abilities in dealing with rebellions, Ziyād tactfully managed to involve in the operations the Yemeni tribes to whom Ḥujr himself belonged. In this way Ziyād avoided the greater danger of a serious conflict between the Nizārī and the Yemeni groups of the tribes. Among the Yemeni tribes themselves, he played one off against the other and terrorized the members and nobles of Kinda, Ḥujr's own tribe, threatening them with death and the destruction of their property if they did not hand over Ḥujr to him. The lengthy account of the episode given by Abū Mikhnaf and other early authorities, as recorded by Ṭabarī and Abū'l-Faraj, is interesting in many ways. It reveals how the personal interests of the tribal leaders were exploited to make them act against their own religious aspirations, how tribal rivalries were played off against each other, how the supporters of Ḥujr were coerced, and how ultimately Ziyād succeeded in arresting one of the most respected leaders of the Shīʿīs of Kūfa and in suppressing a deep-rooted movement.

Besides Ḥujr, thirteen other prominent Shīʿīs were rounded up and arrested.[90] The tribal affiliations of the fourteen men arrested break down as follows: Kinda, two; Ḥaḍramawt, one; ʿAbs, two; Khathʿam, one; Bajīla, two; Rabīʿa, one; Hamdān, one; Tamīm, three; and Hawāzin, one. It is interesting to note that of these fourteen, eight were from various Yemeni tribes—Kinda, Ḥaḍramawt, Khathʿam, Bajīla, and Hamdān—and six were from the Nizārī tribes of the North—ʿAbs, Rabīʿa, Tamīm, and Hawāzin. This shows the dimension of the movement and indicates that the Shīʿī feelings in Kūfa were not strictly confined to the Yemenis.

Ziyād decided to dispatch his captives to Syria to be dealt with by Muʿāwiya. Along with them he had to send an indictment duly attested to by the people. He therefore called in the four heads of the four administrative divisions of the Kūfan population.[91] These leaders spelled out the charges against Ḥujr as follows:

1: "Ḥujr gathers the crowds around himself and openly reviles and curses the caliph;
2: He exhorts people to fight against the *Amīr al-Muʾminīn*;
3: He caused disturbances in the city and ousted the caliph's governor;
4: He believes in and propagates the claim that the caliphate is not valid except in the family of Abū Ṭālib;
5: He preaches that Abū Turāb (ʿAlī) was completely free of all blame, he praises him, and he urges people to love and respect him;
6: He calls for secession from and denunciation of the enemies of ʿAlī and all those who fought against him;

7: And those of the persons who are with him are the leaders of his followers and are of a similar opinion."[92]

The charges spelled out in this document against Ḥujr by the four chiefs of Kūfa were no doubt accurate and representative of the thinking, feelings, and activities of Ḥujr and his associates. This document, which appears to have been preserved without any attempts to falsify or suppress its content, gives us perhaps the clearest picture of the Shīʿī religious position at the time of Ḥujr, their feelings and aspirations, their love for the house of ʿAlī, and their resentment against Muʿāwiya as a usurper.

Ziyād did not like the indictment, however. The reason, so clearly recorded by the sources, is very important to note as it sheds light on the real situation. As Ziyād said after examining the document: "I do not think this indictment is conclusive enough; I want the attestations of more witnesses than just these four chieftains to be affixed to it."[93] The charges laid down in the original document dealt almost exclusively with Ḥujr's Shīʿī cause and his love for the house of ʿAlī. Ziyād considered that not very many Yemenis, whom he particularly wanted to bear witness to the charges, would be willing to sign, on the grounds of Ḥujr's activities in the cause of Shīʿī ideals. Most of the Yemenis were of Shīʿī inclination, with of course varying degrees of practical commitment. Moreover, it seems, Ziyād was hesitant to inform Muʿāwiya officially that Shīʿī feelings and activities were so strong and were being so openly demonstrated in Kūfa while Ziyād was the governor of the province. It was indeed a unique privilege for him to hold the governorships of both Kūfa and Baṣra simultaneously, an honour no official had ever before enjoyed.

Consequently, another indictment was prepared, laying down the following charges:

1: "Ḥujr b. ʿAdī has cast off his allegiance to the Caliph;
2: He has caused a schism in the community;
3: He curses the Caliph;
4: He calls for war and has created discord;
5: He gathers the people around him and exhorts them to break off allegiance to the *Amīr al-Muʾminīn* and remove him from office;
6: He disbelieves in God."[94]

The marked difference between the two documents is clear enough. While the charges laid down in the first indictment centred on Ḥujr's activities and open rebellion for the Shīʿī cause, the second stressed his rebellion against the state and the authority of Muʿāwiya, with no reference to the Shīʿī movement. The first document places much emphasis on Ḥujr's unshakable love for ʿAlī and devotion to his family on religious grounds; the second replaces this charge with an accusation that Ḥujr disbelieved in God, which according to the precedent set by Abū Bakr provided firm grounds for execution. All the evidence at our disposal leaves us in no doubt that the charges listed in the first document are authentic, whereas the second indictment is a revision fabricated for the reasons elaborated above. This explains the reports that Muʿāwiya was hesitant to accept the indictment and reluctant to take drastic action against Ḥujr. Moreover, as will be seen below, the only condition given by Muʿāwiya for the Shīʿī leaders to save their lives was that they must curse and denounce ʿAlī. This also indicates that their main offence was their pro-Shīʿī activity and not crimes against the state and Caliph as presented in the second indictment.

It hardly need be said that Ḥujr was unmistakably held by the Kūfans as a die-hard and uncompromising Shīʿī leader. He was also considered an extremely pious Muslim. To this fact even those who did not share his Shīʿī views bore testimony. The *qāḍī* Shurayḥ b. Ḥārith wrote to Muʿāwiya, saying: "I bear witness that Ḥujr is a pious Muslim, steadfast in prayer; he gives alms, observes the fast in the month of Ramaḍān, and always performs the *ḥajj* and *ʿumra* . . . and he indeed commands a high place in Islam."[95]

Nevertheless, Ziyād called the people to attest to the authenticity of the indictment. Seventy people, of whose names forty-five are specifically recorded, are reported to have signed the document.[96] Some of these signatures were certainly forged, as is commonly indicated by the sources listing these names. Qāḍī Shurayḥ protested in his letter to Muʿāwiya that he never signed the document and that his name had been added without his knowledge. Some others apologized later for signing, indicating that Ziyād had put pressure on them to attest to the charges.[97]

When the prisoners reached Muʿāwiya, there was strong

pressure on him from the various tribes to release their respective clansmen. Seven of the fourteen prisoners were freed through the efforts and influence of their relatives. Ḥujr and the other six were given a chance to save their lives if they would publicly curse and denounce ʿAlī. Muʿāwiya's executioners told them: "We are commanded to give you a chance to save yourselves by denouncing ʿAlī and cursing him; if you refuse to do this we will kill you." Ḥujr and the other six with him steadfastly replied: "By God, we will never do this." They were thereupon beheaded.[98]

That these men would sacrifice their lives rather than denounce ʿAlī is a matter that cannot be taken lightly: there must have been a meaning to it much deeper than the level of political interests. The history of religion is full of men who have died rather than compromise their faith, and the history of man cannot be explained only in political and economic terms. To read history only in material terms is indeed a regrettable phenomenon of modern historiography. On the other hand, to accept religious consciousness in one case and deny it in another, though the circumstances are similar, is an equally regrettable example of prejudice. No doubt, in most cases popular movements in human society are dominated by political or economic factors, yet there is no dearth of instances where individual conscience has gone far beyond these considerations. Ḥujr was certainly one of these examples. Not only was he given the opportunity to save his life, but he was also offered by Ziyād both political power and economic advantages. He refused. To him, achieving these through denouncing and cursing ʿAlī meant the denunciation of the faith itself. There are political implications to this episode only insofar as political considerations were ancillary to religious objectives. Thus Ḥujr's concern with who should be the caliph was not a political or economic question: he believed in and was prepared to die for, as he did, the idea of special qualities being granted by God to the family of the Prophet, making them specially suited to rule.

Ḥujr and his companions must therefore be considered as representative of those first Shīʿīs who voiced their religious opinion in support of ʿAlī immediately after the death of the Prophet, and they were the forerunners of a progressively developing movement soon to be crystallized as a full-fledged section of the Muslim community. He was a distinguished companion of the Prophet, widely respected for his piety and devotion to religious practices, even though a great partisan of ʿAlī. His tragic fate sent a wave of grief and shock through the holy cities. Even the Prophet's widow ʿĀ'isha and ʿAbd Allāh b. ʿUmar vehemently protested against his execution.[99] It is interesting to note that the tragedy of Ḥujr initiated the martyrology of the Shīʿa, and his death was lamented in numerous elegies that developed into a rich literature in Shīʿī Islam. Naturally, the tragedy affected the Kūfans most. Their sentiments were stirred up with a deep sense of calamity and produced serious reactions. They sent a delegation to Ḥusayn at Medina and urged him to lead an armed revolt against Muʿāwiya. Ḥusayn turned down the request with the same advice as before.[100] Muʿāwiya was not unaware of these overtures to Ḥusayn and was alarmed by such activities, especially when he received a letter from his governor in Medina, Marwān b. al-Ḥakam, warning that the delegation sent from Kūfa was staying in Medina and having frequent meetings with Ḥusayn. The Caliph wrote a threatening letter to Ḥusayn as a warning, but the latter maintained in his reply the same indifferent attitude towards the existing order and assured Muʿāwiya that he would continue to honour the treaty of his brother.[101]

Except for the revolt of Ḥujr, suppressed by rather severe measures, the period between the deaths of Ḥasan and of Muʿāwiya is again a quiet and subdued one in the history of the Shīʿī movement. The general impression which we get from the sources is of an atmosphere of fear and caution on both sides. Muʿāwiya's apprehensive attitude towards the potential of a Shīʿī uprising is demonstrated by his extreme measures against Ḥujr and his limited, but quite serious, revolt. The fact that Muʿāwiya, well known for his shrewd diplomacy in achieving his goals, should act in such a violent manner against Ḥujr indicates his uncompromising attitude towards Shīʿī sympathies, an attitude perhaps resulting from fear of the deep-rooted Shīʿī movement, especially in Kūfa where the group was strongest. On the other hand, Ḥusayn's repeated refusal to lead the Kūfan enthusiasts in open revolt reveals his own cautious attitude and desire to avoid giving Muʿāwiya any excuse to completely annihilate the supporters of the house of ʿAlī. Throughout this period, Muʿāwiya seems to have been trying to destroy, at the slightest pretext, those of ʿAlī's followers who could not be bought or intimidated into submission; until this could be accomplished, the Umayyad hold on the caliphate would remain insecure.

It is not unlikely that one of the reasons for the imposition of cursing ʿAlī from the pulpits was to provoke the Shīʿī sympathizers into open revolt and thus subject them to attack and destruction at the hands of the Umayyad forces. When Al-Mughīra b. Shuʿba was appointed governor of Kūfa in 41/661, one of the duties specified to him by Muʿāwiya was that he should vigorously carry out the cursing of ʿAlī, propagandize against him and his followers, increase the intensity of the campaign to disgrace, dishonour, and impugn the character of ʿAlī and his followers, and finally popularize and propagate the virtues of ʿUthmān and his supporters. The same instructions were given to Ziyād b. Abī Sufyān when he was entrusted with the governorship of Kūfa after the death of Mughīra in 50/670.[102] Both of these governors carried out these duties to the satisfaction of Muʿāwiya. Ḥujr and a few others could not tolerate this continuous provocation and fell into the trap, while others remained cautious and careful. Ḥusayn, on his part, fully understanding the situation, wisely avoided any provocation against Muʿāwiya and waited for an appropriate opportunity to move into action. In this way, he saved himself and his party from severe repression on the one hand, and honoured his brother's treaty, which indirectly involved Ḥusayn as well, on the other.

Perhaps the most important event in the history of the development of the Shīʿī "Passion" was Muʿāwiya's nomination of his son Yazīd to succeed him. The Caliph could not act in this direction as long as Ḥasan lived, and it is significant that immediately after the news of Ḥasan's death, Muʿāwiya began actively working on the project that would fulfil his desire of perpetuating the rule of his family. This was no easy task, and the Caliph had to move with great caution and use all those devices characteristic of his rule: diplomacy, generous gifts, bribes, and finally threats and oppression. It is not our intention here to go into the details of how Muʿāwiya succeeded in buying off the leaders of the tribes and silencing the more resolute with severe repression. These details are preserved in the sources with hardly any serious differences. It will suffice for our purpose here to note that after careful arrangements through his governors, Muʿāwiya managed to bring together from most of the provinces deputations which, as planned, declared their allegiance to Yazīd as heir-apparent.[103] It was different with the Hijaz, where there lived the élite of Islamic nobility and the sons of the most prominent Companions of the Prophet, most important among them being Ḥusayn b. ʿAlī, ʿAbd Allāh b. ʿUmar, ʿAbd Allāh b. az-Zubayr, and ʿAbd ar-Raḥmān b. Abī Bakr. Any delegation from Medina without them would have been meaningless, thus their refusal to co-operate was of the utmost gravity. Muʿāwiya therefore went to Medina in person with 1,000 selected horsemen to deal with the recalcitrants.

According to one version, Muʿāwiya, reaching Medina and calling these four to meet him in the outskirts, treated them in such a harsh manner that they fled to Mecca. This worked as planned, and in their absence Muʿāwiya declared the nomination of Yazīd; this was approved by his supporters, while others had not the courage to resist. The problem of Medina solved, Muʿāwiya proceeded to Mecca. There he changed his attitude and first tried to win over these four by treating them with exceptional friendliness. After spending quite some time with them and showing his great affection and regard for them, just before he was about to set out on his return home, he expressed his desire for their support for Yazīd. He explained that he was not demanding much from them, that Yazīd would be ruler only in name, and that, under Yazīd's name, it would in fact be they who would have real control of the government. After a spell of silence, Ibn az-Zubayr spoke and, in the name of all, he rejected the Caliph's suggestion. The enraged Muʿāwiya said: "On other occasions, when I speak in the pulpit, I allow anyone to object to my speech if he so wishes; but he who contradicts me today, a sword will silence him." Then he entered the mosque of Mecca, taking his four opponents with him, and declared: "These four men, without whom no decision concerning the succession can be made, have agreed to Yazīd's nomination; so now none of you people should have any difficulty in doing the same." Thereupon people did homage to Yazīd, while the four remained silent out of fear.[104] Even if this version is cautiously regarded as a later elaboration, Muʿāwiya's going to the Hijaz for the purpose of trying to compel these persons not to oppose Yazīd cannot be denied.[105]

Notes to Chapter 6

[1] Ṭabarī, II, p. 5

[2] Ṭabarī, II, pp. 1 ff.; Masʿūdī, *Murūj*, II, p. 426; *Tanbīh*, p. 300; *ʿIqd*, IV, p. 361; Yaʿqūbī, II, pp. 214 f.; Dīnawarī, pp. 216 f.; *Istīʿāb*, I, p. 385; *Usd al-ghāba*, II, p. 14

[3] Yaʿqūbī, II, p. 188. According to Ibn Saʿd, VI, pp. 4, 370 early Ṣaḥāba immediately moved into Kūfa and settled there as soon as ʿUmar b. al-Khaṭṭāb founded the garrison city.

[4] *Usd al-ghāba*, II, p. 12; Tirmidhī, II, p. 306; *Musnad*, V, p. 354; Ḥadīd, *Sharḥ*, XVI, p. 27

[5] *Musnad*, II, p. 513

[6] The standard works of tradition usually devote a separate chapter to the special merits of Ḥasan and Ḥusayn (*Bāb Manāqib al-Ḥasan wa'l-Ḥusayn*).

[7] Ibn Ḥabīb, *Muḥabbar*, p. 46; Bukhārī, *Ṣaḥīḥ*, II, pp. 175, 198; *Usd al-ghāba*, II, p. 13

[8] According to Abū'l-Faraj al-Iṣfahānī, *Maqātil aṭ-Ṭālibiyīn*, p. 52, ʿAbd Allāh b. al-ʿAbbās himself was the first to advance Ḥasan's nomination and invite the people to pay homage to him as the caliph after the death of ʿAlī. See also Ḥadīd, *Sharḥ*, XVI, pp. 31 f.

[9] Dīnawarī, p. 216; *Maqātil*, p. 52; Ḥadīd, *Sharḥ*, XVI, p. 30

[10] Ṭabarī, II, p. 1; *Usd al-ghāba*, II, p. 14; Ḥadīd, loc. cit.; *Istīʿāb*, I, p. 383

[12] ibid.

[13] Ibn Aʿtham, IV, p. 148; Ṭabarī, II, p. 5; Ḥadīd, *Sharḥ*, XVI, p. 22

[14] *Maqātil*, pp. 52 f.; Ḥadīd, *Sharḥ*, XVI, pp. 25 f.

[15] *Aghānī*, XXI, p. 26; *Maqātil*, loc.cit.; Yaʿqūbī, II, p. 214; Ḥadīd, *Sharḥ*, XVI, p. 31

[16] Ibn Aʿtham, IV, p. 153; Ḥadīd, *Sharḥ*, XVI, p. 26

[17] *Maqātil*, p. 56 (from Abū Mikhnaf); Ibn Aʿtham, IV, p. 151; Ḥadīd, *Sharḥ*, XVI, p. 24 (from Madā'inī), p. 33 (from Abū Mikhnaf with slight variations)

[18] *Maqātil*, p. 57 (from Abū Mikhnaf); Ibn Aʿtham, IV, p. 152; Ḥadīd, *Sharḥ*, XVI, p. 25 (from Madā'inī), p. 35 (from Abū Mikhnaf with slight variations)

[19] *Arab Kingdom*, pp. 104-7

[20] *Ta'rīkh*, II, pp. 214 f.

[21] *Akhbār*, pp. 217 ff.

[22] *Taʾrīkh,* II, pp. 1-8

[23] *Kitāb al-futūh,* IV, pp. 148-67

[24] *Maqātil,* pp. 46–77

[25] *Sharḥ,* XVI, pp. 9–52

[26] *Fihrist,* pp. 93, 101 f., respectively. The importance of these two authors in early Muslim historiography has been discussed in Chapter 2.

[27] M. A. Shabān, *EI²* article "Ibn Aʿtham"

[28] Shabān, op. cit. Cf. Yāqūt, *Irshād al-Arīb ilā maʿrifat al-Adīb,* ed. D.S. Margoliouth, (Leiden, 1907–31), I, p. 379; C.A. Storey, *Persian Literature: a Bio-bibliographical Survey* (London, 1927), I, ii, p. 1260

[29] See Aḥmad Zakī Ṣafwat, *Jamharat Rasāʾil al-ʿArab fī ʿuṣūr al-ʿArabīyat az-Zāhira* (Cairo, 1937), a four-volume work in which all the letters from the time of the Prophet until the end of the ʿAbbāsid period have been collected with documentation.

[30] Ṭabarī, II, pp. 1 f., 5–8. See Wellhausen, *Arab Kingdom,* p. 107

[31] Ṭabarī, II, pp. 2–5

[32] Ṭabarī, II, pp. 1, 5 ff.

[33] Ṭabarī, II, pp. 2, 7

[34] Ṭabarī, II, pp. 7–8

[35] Ṭabarī, II, pp. 2–4

[36] Ṭabarī, II, p. 2

[37] Yaʿqūbī, II, p. 214; *Maqātil,* p. 62; *Sharḥ,* XVI, p. 40

[38] *Maqātil,* p. 61; *Sharḥ,* XVI, p. 38

[39] Yaʿqūbī, II, p. 214

[40] ibid.

[41] Ṭabarī, II, p. 2

[42] Yaʿqūbī, II, p. 115

[43] ibid.

[44] The Arabic phrase reads: *fa lamma intahā ilā Sabāṭ rāyā min aṣḥābihi fashl wa tawākul ʿan al-ḥarb.*

[45] Dīnawarī, p. 216

[46] ibid.

[47] *Sharḥ,* XVI, p. 22

[48] *Futūh,* IV, p. 154; *Maqātil,* p. 63

[49] Dīnawarī, p. 217; Ibn Aʿtham, IV, p. 155; Yaʿqūbī, II, p. 215; *Maqātil,* p. 64

[50] Dīnawarī, loc. cit.; Ibn Aʿtham, loc. cit.; Yaʿqūbī, loc. cit.; *Maqātil,* loc. cit.

[51] Ibn Aʿtham, IV, pp. 156 f.

[52] ibid., p. 157

[53] Ṭabarī, II, pp. 220, 223, 274; Dīnawarī, pp. 243, 299; *ʿIqd,* IV, p. 376

[54] *Maqātil,* pp. 64 f.

[55] *Maqātil*, pp. 65 ff.

[56] Ṭabarī, II, pp. 3–4

[57] The shortest period given for his caliphate is three months, the longest is seven months.

[58] Ṭabarī, II, p. 13

[59] Dīnawarī, p. 218

[60] *Istīʿāb*, I, pp. 355 f. *Usd al-ghāba*, II, p. 14, adds: "and some other conditions like this." See also Ibn Ḥajar al-Haythamī, *Ṣawāʾiq al-muḥriqa*, p. 134; *Al-Imāma waʾs-siyāsa*, I, p. 140

[61] *Maqātil*, pp. 66 f.; *Sharḥ*, XVI, pp. 43 f.

[62] Ibn Aʿtham, IV, pp. 158 f.

[63] *Sharḥ*, XVI, pp. 22 f.

[64] Ibn Aʿtham, IV, p. 158

[65] Ibn Aʿtham, IV, pp. 159 f.; *Sharḥ*, XVI, pp. 22 f.

[66] Ibn Aʿtham, IV, p. 165

[67] See Ibn Aʿtham, IV, pp. 161–7; *Maqātil*, pp. 68–73; Ṭabarī, II, pp. 6–9; Ya'qūbī, II, pp. 216 f.

[68] Ṭabarī, II, p. 6; Ya'qūbī, II, p. 215

[69] Ḥadīd, *Sharḥ*, XVI, p. 28

[70] *Maqātil*, pp. 72 f.

[71] *Istīʿāb*, III, p. 1420; Ibn Kathīr, *al-Bidāya Waʾn-Nihāya*, VIII, p. 135

[72] See, for example, his reply to Ḥujr that he abdicated to save the lives of his handful of true followers, in Dīnawarī, p. 220

[73] Ibn Aʿtham, IV, pp. 164 ff.; *Maqātil*, pp. 67 ff.; Yaʿqūbī, II, pp. 216 f.; Dīnawarī, pp. 220 f.; *Istīʿāb*, I, pp. 387 f.

[74] *Usd al-ghāba*, II, pp. 13 f.; *Istīʿāb*, I, p. 384; Bukhārī, *Saḥīḥ*, II, p. 198; Ṭabarī, II, p. 199; Jāḥiẓ, *Rasāʾil*, "Risāla fī Banī Umayya," p. 65; ʿĀmilī, *Aʿyān*, IV, p. 54

[75] Dīnawarī, pp. 220 f.

[76] Ṭabarī, I, p. 1920

[77] Balādhurī, *Ansāb*, IVA, p. 138; Ḥadīd, *Sharḥ*, XVI, p. 14. Also see Vaglieri, *EI*² article "Ḥasan"

[78] Masʿūdī, *Murūj*, II, pp. 426 f.; *Maqātil*, pp. 73 f.; Ḥadīd, *Sharḥ*, XVI, pp. 10 f., 17; *Istīʿāb*, I, pp. 389 f.; *Usd al-ghāba*, II, p. 14; Yaʿqūbī, II, p. 225; Ibn Khallikān, *Wafayāt*, II, p. 66

[79] Masʿūdī, *Murūj*, II, p. 427; *Maqātil*, p. 73; Ḥadīd, *Sharḥ*, XVI, p. 11

[80] Dīnawarī, *Akhbār*, p. 222; Yaʿqūbī, II, p. 225; ʿ*Iqd*, IV, p. 361; Masʿūdī, loc. cit.

[81] Ibn Aʿtham, IV, pp. 206, 224 f.; *Maqātil*, p. 73; Yaʿqūbī, II, p. 228; *Istīʿāb*, I, p. 391

[82] Yaʿqūbī, II, p. 228; Dīnawarī, p. 221

[83] See Ṭabarī, II, pp. 111–55; Balādhurī, IVA, pp. 211–36; *Aghānī*, XVII, pp. 78–96; Dīnawarī, pp. 223–5; *Istīʿāb*, I, pp. 329–33

[84] Ṭabarī, II, p. 131; Dīnawarī, pp. 223 f.; *Aghānī*, XVII, pp. 79 f.

[85] *Aghānī*, XVII, p. 81; Balādhurī, IVA, p. 214

[86] *Aghānī*, XVII, p. 81; Balādhurī, IVA, p. 214

[87] Ibn Saʿd, VI, p. 219

[88] Ṭabarī, II, p. 117; Balādhurī, IVA, p. 214

[89] *Aghānī*, XVII, p. 82

[90] See Ṭabarī, II, pp. 117 ff.; 136

[91] After assuming control of Kūfa, Ziyād regrouped the entire population into four administrative quarters and appointed a head of his own choosing in charge of each quarter. This has been discussed in Chapter 5 in connection with the general assessment of the situation in Kūfa.

[92] Ṭabarī, II, p. 131; *Aghānī*, XVII, p. 89

[93] Ṭabarī, loc. cit.; *Aghānī*, loc. cit.

[94] Ṭabarī, II, p. 132; *Aghānī*, loc. cit.; Balādhurī, IVA, p. 221

[95] Balādhurī, IVA, pp. 222 f.; Ṭabarī, II, p. 137

[96] Ṭabarī, II, pp. 133 ff.; also, with some variations, Balādhurī, IVA, pp. 221 ff.; *Aghānī*, XVII, pp. 89 ff.

[97] See sources cited in note 95 above

[98] Ṭabarī, II, p. 140; *Aghānī*, XVII, pp. 92 f.; Balādhurī, IVA, p. 224

[99] Ṭabarī, II, p. 145; *Istīʿāb*, I, p. 229 f.; Balādhurī, IVA, pp. 22, 228, 229 ff.

[100] Dīnawarī, p. 224

[101] ibid.

[102] Ṭabarī, II, pp. 111 f.; Balādhurī, IVA, pp. 211 f.

[103] For details, see Ṭabarī under the years 56 to 60; also Masʿūdī, *Murūj*, III, pp. 27 f.

[104] For details see Ibn Aʿtham, IV, pp. 235–49; Ibn Athīr, *Al-Kāmil fi'l-Ta'rīkh*, (Beirut, 1965) III, pp. 508–11

[105] See references quoted above in notes 103 and 104 and also Ṭabarī, II, pp. 175 f.

Chapter 7

The Martyrdom of Ḥusayn

On Muʿāwiya's death, his son Yazīd assumed the caliphate in accordance with the former's unprecedented testament in Rajab 60/March 680. A true representative of the way of life common among the pre-Islamic youth of the Umayyad aristocracy, Yazīd commanded no respect in the community. His anti-Islamic behaviour and openly irreligious practices were well known throughout the Muslim world and earned for him contempt and disfavour, especially among those who cared for religion. Even those few writers who attempt to hush up some of the information unfavourable to the Umayyad house could not refrain from reporting that Yazīd was the first among the caliphs to drink wine in public and that he sought out the worst company, spending much of his time in the pleasures of music and singing and amusing himself with apes and hunting-hounds. He himself had no use for religion, nor had he any regard for the religious sentiments of others. Addicted to wine-bibbing, attracted to singing-girls, and exposed to all sorts of vices, Yazīd has never been presented in good terms by any Muslim writer of any period or by any school of thought.[1] His open and persistent violations of Islamic norms were still more shocking to the community because of his close proximity to the Prophet and the *Rāshidūn* caliphs, of whom he claimed to be the successor and from whose authority he derived his title. Nevertheless, Muʿāwiya's meticulous arrangements, coupled with his formidable military grip on the Muslim world, ensured the smooth succession of his son. Yazīd was thus hailed as the "Commander of the Faithful" by all the tribes and the provinces; yet his title was not secure until he could receive homage from the four most notable personalities of Islam, whom Muʿāwiya, in spite of his utmost efforts, could neither buy nor coerce as he had done with all other men of prominence and the chiefs of the tribes.

With the death of Muʿāwiya, the last of the first generation who could claim for himself at least some political importance, the caliphate had to pass on to the second generation (*tābiʿūn*) after the Prophet. The grandees of this generation, as has been described in the preceding chapter, were Ḥusayn b. ʿAlī, ʿAbd Allāh b. az-Zubayr, ʿAbd Allāh b. ʿUmar, and ʿAbd ar-Raḥmān b. Abī Bakr, the sons of the most prominent Companions of the Prophet who were held in great respect by the community; Ḥusayn, also being the only surviving grandson of the Prophet, enjoyed greater regard than the other three. It was therefore obvious that without their recognition Yazīd's authority could not be firmly consolidated. Muʿāwiya was fully aware of the importance of these four, and having failed to secure their agreement to Yazīd's succession, he warned his son of the danger before he breathed his last. On his deathbed Muʿāwiya advised Yazīd:

> "O my son, I have arranged everything for you, and I have made all the Arabs agree to obey you. No one will now oppose you in your title to the caliphate, but I am very much afraid of Ḥusayn b. ʿAlī, ʿAbd Allāh b. ʿUmar, ʿAbd ar-Raḥmān b. Abī Bakr, and ʿAbd Allāh b. az-Zubayr. Among them Ḥusayn b. ʿAlī commands great love and respect because of his superior rights and close relationship to the Prophet. I do not think that the people of Iraq will abandon him until they have risen in rebellion for him against you. As far as is possible, try to deal with him gently. But the man who will attack you with full force, like a lion attacks his prey, and who will pounce upon you, like a fox when it finds an opportunity to pounce, is ʿAbd Allāh b. az-Zubayr. Whenever you get a chance, cut him into pieces."[2]

Muʿāwiya's advice, commonly reported by many sources, confirms the reports that Muʿāwiya's efforts to secure the approval of these grandees of Islam for Yazīd's succession had not been successful.

In order to secure undisputed possession of the caliphate, the first task Yazīd undertook was to order the governor of Medina, Al-Walīd b. ʿUtba, to exact homage from the refractory, especially from Ḥusayn and Ibn az-Zubayr. In his letter to the governor, he gave strict orders that they should not be allowed to delay, and if they refused, that Walīd should behead them at once. Some sources include the name of Ibn ʿUmar as also having been specifically mentioned in this letter.[3] Walīd b. ʿUtba accordingly sent for Ḥusayn and Ibn az-Zubayr at an unusual hour of the night to oblige them to pay homage to the new caliph. Both of them realized that Muʿāwiya was dead, and both had decided to stand by their refusal to pay homage to Yazīd. Ibn az-Zubayr did not go to the palace and fled to Mecca the following night. Ḥusayn went to see the governor, but was accompanied by a strong band of his supporters in case of a serious confrontation. Leaving his supporters at the gate, Ḥusayn went into the palace alone. Walīd read to him Yazīd's letter and asked for immediate recognition of the new caliph. Ḥusayn replied uncommittedly that the *bayʿa*, in order to be valid, must be made in public and that the governor should arrange a public gathering in the mosque where he would also be present. With this reply, when Ḥusayn rose to leave the palace, Marwān b. al-Ḥakam, who was present there as well, rebuked the governor, saying: "By God, if you allow Ḥusayn to leave without paying the homage now, you will never be able to get it from him; so arrest him and do not free him until he pays the homage, or behead him." In fact, Marwān had already advised Walīd to call these two for the *bayʿa*, and if they refused, to kill them at once before the news of Muʿāwiya's death became known to the people. Walīd, however, did not accept this advice: as Ḥusayn left the palace, the former retorted to Marwān's harsh attitude, saying:

> "Do not reproach me for this, O Marwān. You have advised me to do something in which there lies complete destruction and the ruin of my religion. By God, if the entire wealth and treasures of the whole world were given to me I would not kill Ḥusayn. Should I kill him only because he refuses to pay homage, I would suffer total destruction on the Day of Judgement, for in the sight of God there cannot be anything more accountable than the blood of Ḥusayn."[4]

The reply of Walīd to Marwān, so commonly recorded by the sources, reflects that particular regard and respect with which the grandson of the Prophet was held not only by his followers, but by a great number of Muslims in general.

Ḥusayn, however, succeeded in avoiding the demand for the *bayʿa* for two days and finally escaped at night with his family and most of the Hāshimites to Mecca. Walīd b. ʿUtba paid for his lenient attitude towards the grandson of the Prophet: he was shortly thereafter dismissed from his post as governor of Medina.

Ibn az-Zubayr, who reached Mecca before Ḥusayn, had gathered people around him against Yazīd, and he is reported to have been harbouring secret ambitions for the caliphate himself. But as soon as Ḥusayn arrived in the city, the people abandoned Ibn az-Zubayr and gathered around Ḥusayn. This was only natural, for our sources clearly state that "Ḥusayn was much dearer and far more respected by the people of the Hijaz than Ibn az-Zubayr, who knew that the people there would never follow him as long as Ḥusayn was in Mecca."[5] So great were the inclinations of the people to Ḥusayn that after his arrival there people prayed with him, performed the *ṭawāf* of the Kaʿba with him, and preferred to stay around him most of the time.

Ḥusayn, like his brother Ḥasan, combined in his person the right of descent both from the Prophet and from ʿAlī; and now after the death of Ḥasan he was the only candidate from the Prophet's family. But in the preceding years he had done very little to support his rights, restricting himself to a negative attitude towards Yazīd's nomination. Nor, due to Ḥasan's treaty with Muʿāwiya, was it possible for him to act as long as Muʿāwiya was alive. This he explained to the Shīʿīs of Kūfa whenever they approached him concerning an uprising. The death of Muʿāwiya changed the situation. On the one hand, Ḥusayn was now free from the treaty obligations of his brother and, on the other, the demand for active guidance and leadership from the Shīʿīs of Kūfa became increasingly pressing. As soon as this group received word of Muʿāwiya's death, they held a series of meetings expressing their renewed and enthusiastic support for Ḥusayn. They sent out numerous letters and a succession of messengers urging Ḥusayn to come to Kūfa to take their leadership, as they had no *Imām* other than him. The first letter Ḥusayn received on 10 Ramaḍān 60/15 June 680; it was signed by Sulaymān b. Ṣurad al-Khuzāʿī, Al-Musayyab b. Najaba, Rifāʿa b. Shaddād, Ḥabīb b. al-Muẓāhir, and Muslim

b. Awsaja in the name of the Shīʿīs and Muslims of Kūfa, and read:

"We thank God for casting down the tyrannical rule of your enemy, who had usurped the power to rule this community without any right, allowed the possession of God to pass into the hands of the powerful and the rich, and killed the best men [an allusion to Ḥujr b. ʿAdī and his supporters] while allowing the worst of the people to remain alive. We invite you to come to Kūfa, as we have no Imām to guide us; and we hope that through you God will unite us on the path of truth. We do not go to Friday congregational prayers to pray with Nuʿmān b. Bashīr, the governor of Kūfa, nor do we assemble with him at the occasion of the *ʿĪd*. If we hear that you are coming to us, we will oust the governor from our city. Peace and mercy of God be upon you."[6]

This letter, signed by the men named above, must have served as a major incentive to Ḥusayn, for the signatories had been trusted followers of his house from the very beginning and had proven their loyalty at the battles of Al-Jamal and Ṣiffīn with ʿAlī. Though they had been extremely perturbed and disappointed by Ḥasan's abdication in favour of Muʿāwiya, they nevertheless remained loyal to the former and hostile to the latter. Apart from these early Shīʿīs, a great number of other Kūfans also wrote letters to Ḥusayn, each signed by numerous individuals for the same purpose.[7] Similar letters urging Ḥusayn to assume active leadership were also sent by the Shīʿīs of Baṣra. Not all of them, however, had the same degree of religious motivation: some had political aspirations, hoping to throw off the yoke of Syrian domination.

The actions of Ḥusayn, however, show that from beginning to end his strategy was aimed at a much higher goal than simply accession to the caliphate. There is no evidence that he tried, while at Mecca, to enlist active supporters from among the people who gathered around him or to propagate his cause among the great numbers of people who were coming to Mecca for the *Ḥajj*; there is also no evidence that he attempted to send his emissaries to stir up any rebellion in provinces such as Yemen and Persia, which were sympathetic to his house, even though advised by some of his family members to do so. And above all, had he acted promptly on the invitation of the Kūfans, while the governorship of the city was in the hands of the weak Nuʿmān b. Bashīr, he might have had a fair chance of success. His speedy arrival would not only have forestalled any effective action on the part of the Umayyad government, but would also have stirred real enthusiasm among the Kūfans. This was emphasized by the leaders of the movement when they wrote:

> "In the name of God, the Merciful, the Compassionate; to al-Ḥusayn b. ʿAlī, from his *shīʿa*, the faithful Muslims: Further make haste, for the people are awaiting you, as they have no Imām other than you! So haste, and again haste! Peace."[8]

This last letter was signed by a number of people and was sent with a delegation consisting of Hānī b. Hānī as-Sabiʿī and Saʿīd b. ʿAbd Allāh al-Ḥanafī, the two most trusted Shīʿīs of Kūfa. In response to all these approaches, however, Ḥusayn sent only one letter in reply through this last delegation. The content of this letter is worthy of note; it reads:

> "From Ḥusayn b. ʿAlī to the believers and the Muslims [note that the word *Shīʿa* is not used]. Hānī and Saʿīd came to me with your letters, they being the last among your messengers and delegations to come to me. I have understood what you said and that you have invited me to come to you because you have no Imām to guide you, and that you hope my arrival there will unite you in the right path and in the truth. I am sending my cousin and the trusted one from my family [Muslim b. ʿAqīl] to report to me about your affairs. If his report conforms with what you have written, I will soon come. But you must be clear about the fact that the Imām is only one who follows the Book of God, makes justice and honesty his conduct and behaviour, judges with truth, and devotes himself to the service of God. Peace."[9]

The last sentence of the letter, explaining the duties of an *Imām* and the nature of the Imamate, helps us to understand Ḥusayn's approach and attitude towards the whole problem.

Abū Mikhnaf has also preserved for us Ḥusayn's letter to the Shīʿīs of Baṣra, which is equally worthy of quotation here. It reads:

> "God has chosen Muḥammad from among his people, graced him with His Prophethood and selected him for His message. After he admonished the people and conveyed His message to them God took him back unto Himself. We, being his family (*ahl*), his close associates endowed with the quality of guardianship (*awlīyā'*), his trustees and vice regent (*awṣīyā'*), and his heir and

legatee (*wārith*), are the most deserving among all the people to take his place. But the people preferred themselves over us for this [privilege]. We became contented, disliking dissension and anxious to preserve the peace and well-being [of the community], though we were fully aware that we were more entitled to this [leadership] than those who had taken it for themselves . . . I have sent my messenger to you and I call you to the Book of God, and the *Sunna* of his Prophet, the *Sunna* which has become obliterated and innovations have become active and energetic. If you listen to me and obey my orders I will guide you to the right path. May the Peace and the Mercy of God be upon you."[10]

The content of this letter is a complete statement of the Shīʿī doctrine of the Imamate even at this early stage. That the historical sources have recorded little of what we may call Shīʿī religio-political theory is due to the fact that their main interest has been in events, not in the underlying principles behind those events. Yet in narrating the events the sources have preserved certain documents such as letters or speeches which give us a glimpse of those ideals which underly the events. We have quoted one of Ḥasan's letters in the previous chapter and pointed out the thinking of the *Ahl al-Bayt*. Now in the time of Ḥusayn, twenty years after, Ḥusayn's letters give exactly the same vein of thinking. In these letters Ḥusayn adequately explains the concept of *walāya*, which means that God has bestowed upon the family of the Prophet special honour and qualities, thereby making them the ideal rulers, and that through their presence on earth His grace is disseminated. The other two terms of doctrinal importance are *wiṣāya*, trusteeship or custodianship, and *wārith*, heir and legatee, which are used by Ḥusayn. We have seen in Chapter 4 that at the time of ʿAlī's election for the caliphate, he was hailed in these terms by his closest associates. Now after thirty-five years the same terms are being used by Ḥusayn. Both these terms carry the idea of God's recommendation of the family of the Prophet to the people, that Muḥammad recommended ʿAlī, and that at his death ʿAlī recommended Ḥasan, who left the legacy of the House for Ḥusayn. It may, however, be too early for these concepts to have assumed the full flowering of their doctrinal content, yet one can see their presence in their embryonic form.

The other important part of Ḥusayn's letter is his

declaration that the right of ruling the community is the exclusive right of the family of the Prophet and they alone can guide the people in the right path; or in other words, they alone, by virtue of their special qualities, can combine temporal power and religious guidance together. Moreover, by this statement Ḥusayn made a judgement on the caliphates of Abū Bakr, ʿUmar and ʿUthmān. Then, in the last part of his letter, by calling people to the *Sunna* of the Prophet Ḥusayn implicitly rejected the interpretations of the first three caliphs who were not among the *Ahl al-Bayt*. The followers of the House of the Prophet would, therefore, go back directly to the *Sunna* of the Prophet and their Imāms, who are divinely inspired (*walāya*).

However, Ḥusayn decided to respond to the call. Two obvious factors inspired him to act. Firstly, being the grandson of the founder of Islam, he must have felt it his duty to respond to the repeated appeals of these Muslims; and secondly, Yazīd's pressing demand for homage was such that Ḥusayn's filial piety and pride could not allow him to accept. It was a difficult situation. Acceptance of the authority of Muʿāwiya as the head of the Muslim state was an entirely different matter from the acceptance of Yazīd. Muʿāwiya, in spite of his worldliness and indifferent attitude towards religion, did not totally violate the norms of Islam, at least not outwardly. Yazīd not only violated Qur'ānic norms and Prophetic *Sunna*, but also openly subjected them to contempt and ridicule, as has been the consensus of Muslim writers of all times. Even Muʿāwiya's own agents, in implementing the plan for Yazīd's nomination, were concerned about the latter's character. Thus when Muʿāwiya asked Ziyād to prepare the people of Baṣra and Kūfa to accept Yazīd's nomination, the governor advised Muʿāwiya to try to mend the ways of his son before asking people to swear allegiance to him.[11]

It would indeed be a great mistake to assess the case of Yazīd without taking into consideration the living impact of the Prophet and the first generation of Islam. The tense contradiction between this and the character of Yazīd ultimately provoked the tragedy of Karbalā, to which we must now turn. In order to maintain the continuity of our narrative, the sources of our information and their authenticity will be discussed at the end of the chapter.

In spite of repeated appeals and hundreds of letters sent by the Kūfans, Ḥusayn did not take a hasty decision, and as a precaution sent his cousin, Muslim b. ʿAqīl, to Kūfa as his emissary with instructions to ascertain the truth of these representations and report back on his findings. As soon as Muslim arrived at Kūfa there was held in the house of Sulaymān b. Ṣurad al-Khuzāʿī a meeting which, for the sake of secrecy at this stage, was attended only by the leaders of the movement. In response to Ḥusayn's letter, read before those present and quoted above, Shīʿī leaders such as ʿĀbis b. Abī Ḥabīb ash-Shākirī, Ḥabīb b. Muẓāhir, and Saʿīd b. ʿAbd Allāh al-Ḥanafī made passionate speeches and declared their wholehearted support for Ḥusayn until the last breath.[12] We shall see shortly that their pledges were not empty words: they remained loyal to the cause, fulfilled their promises, and ultimately gave their lives with Ḥusayn at Karbalā. Apart from these religiously devoted people supporting the cause of the *Ahl al-Bayt*, the political supporters of ʿAlī from among the people of Kūfa did not think it wise to lag behind in supporting a movement which they thought might be successful in throwing off Umayyad domination and raising new opportunities for them. Muslim b. ʿAqīl thus quickly gathered thousands of pledges of support. The number of people who registered their names and swore allegiance to Muslim in the name of Ḥusayn is variously given as 12,000 and 18,000, the majority of the sources recording the second figure.[13] Soon the movement became so widespread that Muslim b. ʿAqīl was able to preside over the public meetings from the pulpit in the mosque of Kūfa.

Confident of Kūfan support, Muslim consequently wrote to Ḥusayn to come to Kūfa and assume leadership of the people. The letter of Muslim was sent to Ḥusayn not by an ordinary messenger, but by ʿĀbis b. Ḥabīb ash-Shākirī, a trusted leader of the Shīʿīs of Kūfa.[14] Having been assured of the extent of Kūfan enthusiasm, Ḥusayn decided to go to Iraq. Already Ibn al-Ḥanafīya at Medina, and then ʿAbd Allāh b. ʿUmar and ʿAbd Allāh b. al-ʿAbbās, when they met Ḥusayn on the road between Medina and Mecca, had warned Ḥusayn against the dangers. Again at Mecca Ibn ʿAbbās, along with many other friends, reiterated their advice with greater insistence and tried to persuade him not to rely on

Kūfan promises, reminding him of their instability, their treacherous nature, and how they had betrayed, at the hour of trial, his father and brother.[15] On the other hand, ʿAbd Allāh b. az-Zubayr first hypocritically voiced his concern for the safety of Ḥusayn in the enterprise[16] but nevertheless urged him to go on with the plan, for he wanted to make a bid for power himself. While Ḥusayn was in the Hijaz this was impossible, as the people would never give Ibn az-Zubayr precedence over the grandson of the Prophet.[17] The former was thus pleased to see that Ḥusayn should leave the field free for him in Mecca. In spite of all the advice, however, Ḥusayn did not abandon his project, for he had in mind a definite plan and strategy, as will be discussed later.

Receiving word of Muslim's arrival in Kūfa and the support given to him by the people there, Yazīd, no longer trusting the mild-tempered and weak governor of the town, Nuʿmān b. Bashīr, appointed his strong man ʿUbayd Allāh b. Ziyād, the governor of Baṣra, to take charge of Kūfa as well and to go there at once. The immediate task to be carried out was to crush the Shīʿī movement by taking whatever measures were required for this purpose. The text of Yazīd's letter is preserved by various sources and gives a clear idea of his violent attitude towards the movement in support of Ḥusayn.[18] Fully aware of the insurrection in Kūfa in favour of Ḥusayn, Ibn Ziyād rode into the city in disguise, wearing a black turban, covering his face, and surrounding himself with a small squadron of horsemen. The Kūfans, who were expecting Ḥusayn, mistook Ibn Ziyād for the former, gathered all around his horse, greeted him enthusiastically, and shouted: "Hail to you, O son of the Prophet; we have been awaiting you."[19] Ibn Ziyād, quietly observing the people's enthusiasm for Ḥusayn, entered the mosque along with the crowds, mounted the pulpit, and then suddenly tore the veil from his face. He delivered a terrifying speech, declaring death and unprecedented punishment for the sympathizers of Ḥusayn, while making tempting promises for those who would prove their loyalty to the Caliph.[20] The Kūfans, known for their lack of resolution, were stricken by awe and fear, completely lost heart, and ultimately abandoned Muslim, who after attempting in vain to organize an immediate revolt, was captured and beheaded together with Hānī b. ʿUrwa, in whose house he had stayed.[21] This unreliable attitude of the political supporters of Ḥusayn, the so-called Shīʿīs of Kūfa in general, once again demonstrates the weakness of their character, as had been pointed out to Ḥusayn by those of the travellers coming from Kūfa who happened to meet him on his way. For example, at a place called Ṣifāḥ he met the poet Farazdaq and inquired about conditions in Kūfa. Farazdaq replied: "Their hearts are with you, but their swords are with your enemies."[22]

Ḥusayn left Mecca on 8 Dhū'l-Ḥijja/10 September 680, the same day Muslim b. ʿAqīl was beheaded in Kūfa. He had only about 50 men from among both his relatives and friends able to bear arms, besides women and children, accompanying him from Mecca on the fateful journey. Ḥusayn's sudden departure from Mecca, where he had been staying for the past five months and where a great number of people were arriving for the *Ḥajj*, only two days away, cannot have been without some serious cause. Ṭabarī and other sources, quoting Ḥusayn himself, report that the Umayyad government sent some soldiers disguised as pilgrims to arrest him or even assassinate him.[23] Though it is difficult to ascertain the authenticity of this sort of report, still we cannot rule out a possibility of this kind in view of what happened to the holy cities later at the hands of the army sent by Yazīd in connection with the rebellion of Ibn az-Zubayr.

While Ḥusayn was heading towards Iraq, Ibn Ziyād, after killing Muslim and Hānī, made Kūfa a scene of terror and horror. First, he applied severe economic pressure on the population through the *ʿarīfs*, whose function and importance as being responsible for distribution of stipends and the maintenance of law and order in their respective *ʿirāfas* has already been discussed in Chapter 5. He exploited these state functionaries and ordered them to write down the names of any strangers or rebellious or suspicious people in their *ʿirāfas*. He held the *ʿarīfs* responsible for any trouble that might occur in their *ʿirāfa* and threatened that the *ʿarīf* would be crucified and the entire *ʿirāfa* would be deprived of its stipend if anything was concealed from Ibn Ziyād. Secondly, he made a declaration that anyone suspected of supporting Ḥusayn would be hanged without trial, his house would be set on fire, and his property would be confiscated.[24] Kūfa was thus soon brought under full control. At the same time, Ibn Ziyād blockaded all the roads leading from the Hijaz to Kūfa and gave strict orders forbidding anyone from entering or leaving the territory of Kūfa. At Al-Qādisīya, which by the normal route links Kūfa with the Hijaz, he set up a strong military post with an army of 4,000 troops under the command of Ḥuṣayn b. an-Numayr at-Tamīmī. Similarly, other border areas like Quṭquṭāna, Laʿlaʿ, and Kaffān, which link Kūfa with Baṣra and other parts of Iraq, were being heavily patrolled by the Umayyad army;[25] and consequently it was almost impossible for anyone to enter or leave Kūfa. Ḥusayn learned of all these strict measures from the bedouins, but continued his journey undeterred. When he reached Ath-Thaʿlibīya he received word from some travellers of the execution of Muslim b. ʿAqīl and Hānī b. ʿUrwa at Kūfa; then at Zubāla he learned that his messenger Qays b. Mushīr aṣ-Ṣaydāwī, whom he had dispatched from Ḥājir, the fourth stage from Mecca, with a letter for the Kūfans informing them of his imminent arrival, had been captured at the checkpoint at Al-Qādisīya and that he had been brutally killed by Ibn Ziyād in Kūfa: he was thrown from the top of the governor's palace when he refused to curse Ḥusayn to save his own life.[26] Ḥusayn could not control his tears at the tragic fate of his trusted follower and, quoting a verse of the Qur'ān, said:

> "'Among the believers are men who have been true to their covenant with God. Some of them have completed their vow [i.e. have sacrificed their lives in fulfilling their vow], and some others are still waiting [to die]; but they have never changed [their determination] in the least.' (Qur'ān, XXXIII, 23). O God, make Paradise an abode for us [the surviving ones] and for them [the ones who have been killed], and unite both of us in a resting place under your mercy and make your reward our only object of desire and our treasure."[27]

This statement by Ḥusayn is clear enough to demonstrate that he was fully aware of what was going to happen to him and that he was fully prepared for it. Another expression of Ḥusayn's thinking is reflected by his proclamation to his companions which he made after receiving this news at Zubāla. He stood among those accompanying him and after informing them of the doleful news and of the obvious danger of death and complete destruction for which he was heading, he asked them to leave him and withdraw to safety. Those who had joined him during the journey with certain hopes of material gains did depart, and there remained with him only those who had followed him from the Hijaz.[28] These statements by Ḥusayn must be taken into consideration, for they are important for an understanding of his thinking, which will be discussed below.

Leaving Zubāla, Ḥusayn reached Baṭn ʿAqīq, a place a few stages from Kūfa; and upon learning in detail of the strong military force stationed at Al-Qādisīya, he changed his route to enter Kūfa from another direction. Ḥuṣayn b. Numayr, the commander at Al-Qādisīya, was informed of Ḥusayn's change of route and sent a detachment of 1,000 troops under the command of Ḥurr b. Yazīd at-Tamīmī al-Yarbūʿī to intercept him. When they appeared on the horizon, Ḥusayn ordered his people to pitch their tents at a nearby place called Dhū Ḥusm (or Ḥusam). The army of Ḥurr soon reached Ḥusayn. The day was hot and Ḥurr's army had run out of water; the grandson of the Prophet could not tolerate that even his enemies should suffer from thirst, and he ordered his men to give water to the Umayyad troops and to their horses. Ḥusayn himself took part in serving water to those badly affected by thirst and the heat.[29] Ḥurr had a certain regard for Ḥusayn, and at both prayers of the day he, along with his troops, prayed behind him. Even when four of the leading Shīʿīs of Kūfa who had managed to escape from the city joined Ḥusayn at this point, Ḥurr, though he protested, did not dare to use force.[30] After each of the two prayers, Ḥusayn explained to his adversaries the reasons which had caused him to set out:

> "O people of Kūfa! You sent to me your delegations and wrote me letters saying that you had no Imām and that I should come to unite you and lead you in the way of God ... You wrote that we, the *Ahl al-Bayt*, are more qualified to govern your affairs than those who claim things to which they have no right and who act unjustly and wrongfully.... But if you have changed your minds, have become ignorant of our rights, and have forgotten your delegations and repeated appeals to me to come for the sake of your religion ... I shall turn back."[31]

Then Ḥusayn showed Ḥurr two sacks full of the letters sent by the Kūfans to him, but Ḥurr said he knew nothing of these and that he had come with the orders of Ibn Ziyād to arrest him and his party as prisoners to be handed over to Ibn Ziyād. Ḥusayn refused to submit, but still Ḥurr did not use force against him. After some argument it was agreed that Ḥusayn should keep on travelling along the Euphrates in the opposite direction from Kūfa until fresh orders arrived from the governor, and that Ḥurr would follow Ḥusayn closely. When they reached the district of Nīnawa (or Naynawa) a horseman arrived from Kūfa. Without greeting Ḥusayn, he gave Ḥurr a letter from Ibn Ziyād ordering him not to allow the "rebels" to make a halt except in a desert place without fortifications or water.[32] Zuhayr b. al-Qayn, a companion of Ḥusayn, then suggested that he should attack Ḥurr's small detachment and occupy a fortified village called Al-ʿAqr, but Ḥusayn refused to be the one to initiate hostilities. Ḥusayn, however, managed to proceed only a little farther until they reached the plain of Karbalā and there pitched their tents. It was 2 Muḥarram 61/2 October 680.

On the third of Muḥarram the situation deteriorated as ʿUmar b. Saʿd arrived with the Umayyad army of 4,000 men and assumed overall command on the field. Upon reaching Karbalā Ibn Saʿd learned that Ḥusayn now intended to return to Medina; but Ibn Ziyād, on receiving word of this development, ordered that all the "rebels" should render homage to Yazīd. Meanwhile, they were to be prevented from reaching the river. ʿUmar b. Saʿd accordingly stationed a force of 500 cavalry on the road to the river, and for three days before the massacre on the tenth of Muḥarram Ḥusayn and party suffered terribly from thirst. A daring sortie led by ʿAbbās, Ḥusayn's brother, managed to reach the river but succeeded in filling only a few waterskins. Ibn Saʿd was still trying to persuade the governor to find some peaceful means to avoid shedding the blood of the grandson of the Prophet, but all in vain. Ibn Ziyād sent his final orders through Shamir b. Dhū'l-Jawshan (commonly written as Shimr) either to attack Ḥusayn immediately or to hand over the command of the army to Shamir, the bearer of the letter.[33] The orders also specified that when Ḥusayn fell in the fighting his body was to be trampled, because he was "a rebel, a seditious person, a brigand, an oppressor".[34] Ibn Sa'd had to act, as he was anxious to retain his appointment as the deputy of the governor of the province of Ray' and was well aware of the fact that Ḥusayn would never submit, for the latter "had a proud soul in him".

Soon after receiving these new orders on the evening of 9 Muḥarram, Ibn Sa'd advanced with his army towards the camp of Ḥusayn. Noticing this, Ḥusayn sent his brother 'Abbās, along with some followers, to ascertain the reason for their approach. 'Abbās was told of the orders of Ibn Ziyād, and when informed of this Ḥusayn sent 'Abbās back to request a respite of one night. This was granted. At this point Ḥusayn assembled his relatives and supporters and delivered a speech. This speech is unanimously reported in the events of the night of 'Āshūra by the sources through different authorities, and it is useful in understanding Ḥusayn's thinking. He said:

> "I give praise to God who has honoured us with the Prophethood, has taught us the Qur'ān, and favoured us with His religion . . . I know of no worthier companions than mine; may God reward you with all the best of His reward. I think tomorrow our end will come . . . I ask you all to leave me alone and to go away to safety. I free you from your responsibilities for me, and I do not hold you back. Night will provide you a cover; use it as a steed . . . You may take my children with you to save their lives."[35]

With only a few exceptions, his supporters, from among both friends and relatives, refused to leave or survive after him; through their speeches, to be discussed later, they showed an unshakable devotion to his cause. After some measures were taken for the safety of women and children and for defence by bringing the tents closer together, tying them to one another, digging ditches in the rear and on the flanks and filling them with wood, the rest of the night was spent in prayer, recitation of the Qur'ān, and worship and remembrance of God.[36]

The borrowed night ended, and the fateful morning of 10 Muḥarram brought with it the summons of death and the tragic end of the family of the Prophet and its handful of supporters. Ḥusayn drew up in front of the tents his small army of 72 men: 32 horsemen and 40 foot soldiers of varying ages ranging from the seventy-year-old Muslim b. ʿAwsaja to the fourteen-year-old Qāsim b. Ḥasan b. ʿAlī. The rear of the tents was protected by setting on fire the heaps of wood and reeds. Zuhayr b. al-Qayn was given command of the right wing, Ḥabīb b. Muẓāhir al-Asadī of the left, and ʿAbbās b. ʿAlī was entrusted with the standard of the Hāshimite house.

Ḥusayn, preparing himself for the fateful encounter, dressed himself in the cloak of the Prophet, perfumed himself with musk, and rode on horseback with the Qur'ān raised in his hand. Addressing his enemies and invoking God in a long and beautiful sermon, he said:

> "O God, you are my only Trust in every calamity; you are my only hope in every hardship; you are the only promise in the anxiety and distress in which hearts become weak and [human] action becomes slight, in which one is deserted and forsaken by his own friends, and in which the enemies take malicious pleasure and rejoice at his misfortunes. O God, I submit myself to You; my complaint is to You alone against my enemies, and to You alone is my desire and request. Who else other than you can relieve me from grief. You alone are the custodian of every blessing and the Master of every excellence and the last resort for every desire."[37]

The enemy replied to Ḥusayn's discourse with the most insulting and heinous remarks; among them, Shamir, seeing the fire burning by Ḥusayn's tents, said: "Ḥusayn, you are hastening for the fire in this world even before the Fire of the Day of Judgement." Ḥusayn's companion, Muslim b. ʿAwsaja, could not control himself at this heinous insult and asked his permission to reply with an arrow, but Ḥusayn stopped him, saying: "We will never start the fighting from our side."[38] As the situation grew hotter and an attack from the Umayyad army imminent, Ḥusayn once again came forward; after praising God and praying for His blessing on Muḥammad, he addressed his enemies:

> "O people! you are accusing me, but think who I am! Then search your hearts for what you are doing to me. Consider well if it be lawful for you to kill me and violate my sacrosanctity. Am I not the son of the daughter of your Prophet, the son of the Prophet's *waṣī* and cousin . . .? Did not the Prophet say of me and my brother that 'they are the lords of the youth of Paradise'? You

> cannot deny the truth of what I have said concerning the merits of the family of Muḥammad. Are all these not sufficient to prevent you from shedding my blood?"

And again:

> "If you search in the whole East and the West you will not find a grandson of the Prophet other than me."[39]

Ḥusayn's numerous speeches and repeated appeals in the name of the Prophet to his enemies' religious sentiments, which he made throughout the day and after each loss of life among his supporters, were all in vain. The only reply he received was that he must submit himself to Yazīd or be killed. To this demand Ḥusayn's reply was that he could never humiliate himself like a slave.

The day-long battle—sometimes in single combat, sometimes collectively—began in the morning and ended shortly before sunset. The phases of the battle can be followed fairly clearly. After Ḥusayn's first speech, the Umayyad army began firing arrows and duels took place. For most of the day there were series of single combats, with dialogues between the adversaries which are vividly recorded in the sources and which will be discussed in some detail later. It seems that two major assaults were made by the Umayyads before noon and were met with stiff resistance, but the Umayyad cavalry and 500 archers maintained steady pressure on Ḥusayn's small force. As the latter could be approached only from the front, Ibn Sa'd sent some men from the right and left towards the Ṭālibī's tents to destroy them, but the supporters of Ḥusayn, slipping among the tents, defended them energetically. Shamir, with a strong force under his command, approached the tent of Ḥusayn and his wives and would have set it on fire, but even his comrades reproached him for this and he went away ashamed.[40]

At noon Ḥusayn and his followers performed the prayer of the *Ẓuhr* according to the rite of the *Ṣalāt al-khawf* (the prayer prescribed for when one faces a disastrous situation and calamity). It was in the afternoon that the battle became fiercer, and Ḥusayn's supporters one after the other fell fighting in front of him. Until the last of them had perished not a single member of Ḥusayn's family came to harm,[41] but finally it was the turn of his relatives. The first to be killed was ʿAlī al-Akbar, the son of Ḥusayn, followed in quick succession by the son of Muslim b. ʿAqīl, the sons of ʿAqīl, three brothers of ʿAbbās b. ʿAlī from ʿAlī's wife Umm al-Banīn, then Qāsim, the son of Ḥasan, a young and beautiful boy whose body was trampled and mutilated and whose death is described in touching terms. Ḥusayn watched the fall of each of them and ran to the field to bring back their bodies and lay them in a row before his tent.[42] One by one all the Ṭālibīs gave their lives fighting the enemy, and eventually there remained only two: Ḥusayn and his half-brother ʿAbbās b. ʿAlī, the standard bearer of the vanquished army. Famous for his physical strength and bravery and known as "the moon of the Banū Hāshim" because of his extraordinary beauty, the latter was a great support to Ḥusayn throughout the period of torture and calamity. Now it was time for him to throw himself on to the swords of the bloodthirsty Umayyad army. With broken hearts, distressed and spattered with the blood of their dearest ones, both brothers went together and fell upon the enemy. The enraged ʿAbbās penetrated deep into the ranks of his foes, became separated from Ḥusayn, and was killed some distance away.[43] Alone and weary, Ḥusayn returned to the tents to console the terrified and grief-stricken women and children for what would befall them after his demise and to bid them farewell for the last time. Trying to calm his thirsty and crying infant child, Ḥusayn took him in his arms just as an arrow struck the baby. Ḥusayn lifted his hands with the dead child toward heaven and prayed to God for justice and rewards for his sufferings.[44]

Exhausted and weary, lonely and dejected, wounded and bleeding, Ḥusayn seated himself at the door of his tent. The Umayyad forces wavered for a moment, hesitant to kill the grandson of the Prophet. Finally it was Shamir who advanced with a small group of soldiers, but even he did not dare to deliver the final blow on Ḥusayn; there merely ensued an altercation between the two. At last the son of ʿAlī rose and threw himself on the Umayyads. Attacked from every side, he finally fell face-down on the ground just in front of his tent, while the women and children watched the dreadful scene. A boy of tender age, ʿAbd Allāh, the youngest son of Ḥasan b. ʿAlī, in a fit of horror and terror, could not be controlled by the women, rushed from the tent, and stretched his hands around his uncle to protect him. A sword fell upon him and cut off the hands of the young boy.[45] Finally, as Sinān b. Anas b. ʿAmr raised his sword again to make the final blow on Ḥusayn, the latter's sister Zaynab came out of the tent and cried, addressing Ibn Saʿd:

> "O ʿUmar b. Saʿd, will Abū ʿAbd Allāh [Ḥusayn's *kunyā*] be killed while you are standing by and watching?"[46]

Nothing could help. Sinān cut off the head of the grandson of the Prophet in front of the tent where the women and children were watching and crying. Khawalī b. Yazīd al-Aṣbaḥī took the head into his custody to be taken to Kūfa.[47]

The combat having thus ended, the soldiers turned to pillage and looting. They seized Ḥusayn's clothes, his sword, and whatever was on his body. They looted the tents and seized from the women their ornaments, their baggage, and even the mantles from their heads. The only surviving male of the line of Ḥusayn, his son ʿAlī, who because of serious illness did not take part in the fighting, was lying on a skin in one of the tents. The skin was pulled from under him and Shamir would have killed him, but he was saved when Zaynab covered him under her arms and Ibn Saʿd restrained Shamir from striking the boy.[48] The tragic day is known as *al-ʿĀshūra*, the tenth day of the month of Muḥarram.

The atrocities were not yet over. Ḥusayn's body, already torn by numerous wounds, was trampled by the horses of ten mounted soldiers who volunteered to inflict this final indignity on the grandson of the Apostle of God.[49] On the morning of 11 Muḥarram, bodies of the Umayyad troops who had fallen in the battle were collected together; and after the prescribed prayer for the dead led by Ibn Saʿd, they were buried. But the headless bodies of Ḥusayn and of those killed with him were even left uncovered. On 12 Muḥarram, however, when the Umayyad forces left Karbalā, the people of the tribe of Banī Asad from the nearby village of Ghāḍirīya came down and buried the bodies of Ḥusayn and his companions on the spot where the massacre had taken place.[50] It is of interest to note that those whose bodies were left in such a pitiful and contemptible manner not long before were so honoured and immortalized that their graves have become one of the most venerated sanctuaries, have been embellished with gold, and have been ornamented with splendid decoration; they soon became the centre of pilgrimage for a countless number of devotees. There is hardly any trace of the graves or of the memory of those who were the victors at Karbalā, whereas the tombs of Ḥusayn and his vanquished supporters with their lofty minarets have become landmarks and symbols of grace and hope for the destitute.

The morning of 12 Muḥarram saw a peculiar procession leaving Karbalā for Kūfa. Seventy-two heads were raised on the points of the lances, each of them held by one soldier, followed by the women of the Prophet's family on camels and the huge army of the Umayyads.[51] Abū Mikhnaf describes the scene of the departure of Zaynab and other women of the Prophet's family as captives from Karbalā. Their lamentations at the sight of the massacred bodies of their sons, brothers, and husbands which were lying uncovered in front of them, caused even their enemies to shed tears. Qurra' b. Qays at-Tamīmī, a member of the Umayyad army, is reported by Abū Mikhnaf as saying that he could never forget the scene when Ḥusayn's sister Zaynab passed by the mutilated body of her brother; she cried in hysterical fits, saying:

> "O Muḥammad! O Muḥammad! The angels of Heaven send blessings upon you, but this is your Ḥusayn, so humiliated and disgraced, covered with blood and cut into pieces; and, O, Muḥammad, your daughters are made captives, and your butchered family is left for the East Wind to cover with dust!"[52]

After reaching Kūfa the captives and the heads of the victims were presented to Ibn Ziyād, and the head of Ḥusayn was placed in a tray in front of him in a court ceremony crowded with nobles and spectators. Ibn Ziyād, having a cane in his hand, struck the lips of Ḥusayn again and again. Zayd b. Arqam, an old Companion of the Prophet present in the court, not aware of what had happened, recognized Ḥusayn's face, was stricken by shock and grief, and shouted to Ibn Ziyād:

> "Remove your cane from these lips! By God, on these lips have I seen the lips of the Prophet of God, kissing and sucking them."[53]

He left the court weeping; outside, people heard him saying:

> "O people of the Arabs, after this day you have made yourselves home-born slaves and cattle. You have killed the son of Fāṭima and made your ruler Ibn Marjāna [*kunyā* of Ibn Ziyād], who will now keep on killing your best men and force you to do the most hateful things. You must now be ready for the utmost disgrace."[54]

The head of Ḥusayn was erected for public display in Kūfa before it was sent to Yazīd in Damascus. How long the captives were detained in Kūfa in a dungeon is not quite clear, but it seems that before long the captives and the heads were dispatched to Damascus to be presented to the Caliph. When the head of Ḥusayn and the captive women and children were presented before Yazīd, in a court ceremony equally as lavish as that of Ibn Ziyād, Zaḥr b. Qays, who led the caravan as the representative of Ibn Ziyād, made a long speech of presentation describing how Ḥusayn and his companions had been massacred and how their bodies had been trampled and left for the eagles to eat.[55] The reaction of Yazīd is reported to have been different from that of Ibn Ziyād, and he regretted the haste with which his governor had acted. This seems to be contrary to all those reports which describe Yazīd's orders to his governor in Medina, and then to Ibn Ziyād, in which he clearly ordered them to either exact homage from Ḥusayn and his followers or behead them without delay. The conversation which took place between Yazīd and both Zaynab and ʿAlī b. al-Ḥusayn, in which the Caliph rebuked them and treated them harshly, also cast doubt on his alleged feelings of remorse. Moreover, as is pointed out by Ibn Kathīr, a Syrian pupil of Ibn Tamīya usually hostile to the Shīʿī cause, if Yazīd had really felt that his governor had committed a serious mistake in dealing with Ḥusayn he would have taken some action against him. But, says Ibn Kathīr, Yazīd did not dismiss Ibn Ziyād from his post, did not punish him in any way, or even write a letter of censure for exceeding his orders.[56] If Yazīd at all expressed his remorse it must have been due to the fear of reaction or revolt by some section of the Muslim community.

After some time, however, Yazīd released the captives and sent them back to Medina. Thus ended the most pathetic tragedy in the history of Islam. Edward Gibbon, with his limited sources of Islamic history and mainly depending on Ockley's narrative of Karbalā, could not help but comment:

"In a distant age and climate, the tragic scene of the death of Ḥusayn will awaken the sympathy of the coldest reader."[57] We have seen in the previous chapter how ardently and passionately the Prophet loved his grandsons Ḥasan and Ḥusayn, but only fifty years after the Prophet's death, as Dīnawarī points out,[58] while many of the Prophet's Companions who were well aware of this affection were still alive, one of these beloved grandsons was brutally murdered at the hands of those who claimed to be members of the *Umma* of Muḥammad.

With this brief summary of the lengthy accounts of the tragic end of Ḥusayn, it is intended firstly to analyse how it became so easy for the Umayyads to destroy him and crush the Shīʿī movement behind him; and secondly, to determine the elements of purely religious sentiment among those who readily sacrificed their lives with Ḥusayn and thus made another step forward towards the consolidation of Shīʿī thought in Islam.

It has already been pointed out that of those who invited Ḥusayn to Kūfa, and then those 18,000 who paid homage to his envoy, Muslim b. ʿAqīl, not all were Shīʿīs in the religious sense of the term, but were rather supporters of the house of ʿAlī for political reasons—a distinction which must be kept clearly in mind in order to understand the early history of Shīʿī Islam. They wrote to Ḥusayn hundreds of letters, each signed by groups, and when Muslim b. ʿAqīl reached Kūfa they gathered around him; but this was for most of them an expression of their desire to throw off Syrian domination, a goal which at that time they thought was possible through Ḥusayn. But as soon as Ibn Ziyād, well known in Islamic history for his high-handed policy, took over the governorship of Kūfa and after all those extreme and severe measures carried out by him to crush the movement, the Kūfans saw their hopes gone, and their characteristic lack of resolution in times of trial overcame their political aspirations. They thus submitted to the reality of circumstances rather than endanger themselves for the cause.

There was, however, a small group of the Kūfans who had invited the grandson of the Prophet and led the movement motivated purely by their religious feelings. Where were they when Ḥusayn was so helplessly killed at Karbalā? We have seen that after the execution of Muslim b. ʿAqīl and Hānī b. ʿUrwa, Kūfa was kept under firm control. Anyone suspected of sympathy for Ḥusayn was to be executed. Naturally all the sincere leaders of the movement adopted the stratagem of hiding to escape arrest and execution, not because they betrayed Ḥusayn and wanted to save their lives, but, as we shall see presently, because they wanted to make themselves directly available to Ḥusayn, then on his way to Kūfa. This may be seen by comparing the lists of names of those who gave their lives at Karbalā with Ḥusayn or later with the *Tawwābūn*, with those who wrote the first letters of invitation to him and who had been leading the movement in Kūfa. We have seen that four of these Shīʿī leaders of Kūfa managed to join Ḥusayn at Dhū Ḥusm in spite of Ḥurr's objection. As soon as they heard of Ḥusayn's arrival at Karbalā, those who could, in spite of all the obstacles, somehow manage to reach Karbalā did so; they laid down their lives before Ḥusayn or any one from among his family members were hurt. And of those who were not with Ḥusayn at Karbalā, some had already been arrested and some others, due to the heavy blockade of the roads, could not make their way to Karbalā until it was too late.

When Ḥusayn had left Mecca there were only 50 persons with him, 18 Ṭālibīs or close relatives, and 32 others. After the battle, however, 72 heads were taken to be presented before Ibn Ziyād, 18 of them Ṭālibīs and 54 Shīʿīs, though the real number of those who fell at Karbalā with Ḥusayn seems to have been more than 72. Samāwī and some other sources enumerate the non-Ṭālibīs and give the total number of victims as 92.[59] If this was the case, then it seems that the heads of those who had no tribal identity were not taken to Ibn Ziyād, thus resulting in the lower figure of 72 deaths. Ṭabarī and Dīnawarī list the names of the tribes and the numbers of heads carried by them to Kūfa as follows: Kinda, thirteen; Hawāzin, twenty; Tamīm, seventeen; Asad, six; Madhḥij, seven; Thaqīf, twelve; Azd, five; and another seven of unknown tribal affiliation.[60] There is a slight variation between the lists of Ṭabarī and Dīnawarī. While Ṭabarī mentions the Madhḥij as carrying seven heads and does not record Thaqīf's twelve, Dīnawarī omits Madhḥij's seven and mentions the Thaqīf as having carried twelve heads, in addition to mentioning five heads held by the Azd. Scrutiny of other sources confirms both: seven heads carried by Madhḥij and twelve by Thaqīf. This gives a total of 87 victims of the massacre whose heads were presented at the court of Ibn Ziyād.

Ṭabarī and other sources also tell us in detail how Ḥusayn's true followers managed to escape secretly from Kūfa and reach Karbalā.[61] In addition, we find a few names of those who came to Karbalā with the Umayyad army and, when they saw the sacrilegious treatment by the Umayyads of the grandson of the Prophet, could no longer resist their feelings for the house of the Prophet, defected from the Umayyad ranks, and cast their lot with Ḥusayn. Besides Ḥurr, whose defection is reported in great detail, it is also commonly recorded that on the morning of ʿĀshūra, just before the battle began, thirty nobles of Kūfa who were with the army of Ibn Saʿd defected from him over to Ḥusayn's side and fought for him.[62]

Furthermore, it should be noted again that the blockade of all the roads coming into Kūfa and its vicinity made it almost impossible for the majority of those Shīʿīs of Kūfa who were in hiding, and also for those residing in other cities like Baṣra, to come to the aid of Ḥusayn. Nevertheless, a few persons from Baṣra did reach Karbalā and shared the fate of Ḥusayn.[63] We have, therefore, good grounds for supposing that had there not been so many obstacles and had there been sufficient time and opportunity to mobilize their strength, quite a few of the *Tawwābūn* (penitents), to be discussed in the following chapter, who later on sacrificed their lives in the name of Ḥusayn, would have been with him at Karbalā. Circumstantial evidence allows us to suggest that those who gave their lives for the sake of the slain Ḥusayn would have gone at least as far for the living Ḥusayn. On the other hand, the aim of elaborating this fact is not to suggest that had there not been those unavoidable circumstances Ḥusayn's fate would have been any different. It would certainly have been the same in any case because of the well-organized and formidable military strength of the Umayyads and the characteristic fickleness of the majority of the Kūfans, coupled with the as yet weak and disorganized movement of the religiously motivated Shīʿīs. Our purpose is to suggest that under slightly better circumstances the defeat at Karbalā would not have occurred so helplessly and without there being any conspicuous resistance, and thus we would have a clearer picture of the physical strength of the Shī'ī movement at this stage. To support this hypothesis we can cite the successes achieved not long after Karbalā, but under better circumstances and with better opportunities, by Al-Mukhtār and Ibn az-Zubayr, both far less important than the grandson of the Prophet.

We will only point out here in passing that Al-Mukhtār b. Abī 'Ubayda ath-Thaqafī seized possession of Kūfa in 66/686–687 and captured Mesopotamia and some parts of the eastern provinces from the Umayyads mainly in the name of the blood of Ḥusayn. He, however, lost control of the situation and was killed in 67/687 or 68/688. 'Abd Allāh b. az-Zubayr proclaimed his caliphate in 61/680–681 and by 64/684 had established his power in Iraq, in southern Arabia, and in the greater part of Syria. He was killed in battle against Ḥajjāj in 73/692 after ruling for almost nine years.

An analysis of the sources describing the movement of and the support given to both Al-Mukhtār and Ibn az-Zubayr leaves us in hardly any doubt that some of the component parts of Ḥusayn's movement, later on frustrated and perverted, gave vent to their indignation against the Umayyads under the banners of these two adventurers. This comparison leads us to another important point. Al-Mukhtār and Ibn az-Zubayr achieved considerable political success in their enterprises, and both were able to rule certain parts of the Muslim world for quite a few years; but neither could leave any religious following behind him after he had fallen, though both were, in a sense, as much martyrs as Ḥusayn himself. There is no evidence at all that Ibn az-Zubayr left any sectarian following behind him; the name of Al-Mukhtār was kept alive for a very short time and was followed by a small group, but it soon afterwards lost its identity and was merged in a wider group.[64] The reason is both obvious and vital. Neither Al-Mukhtār, nor Ibn az-Zubayr, nor their supporters had any specific ideal or any particular view which could keep their memory alive in the annals of religious thought in Islam. Ḥusayn and his cause, on the other hand, though militarily a complete failure, were so conspicuously upheld by a sizable part of the Muslim community that his name became an emblem of the identity or entity of the second largest group in Islam. This was due to the fact that his movement was based on a particular view of the leadership of the community, which has been elaborated in the first two chapters above and which has also been pointed out in the letters written by Ḥasan to Muʿāwiya and by Ḥusayn to the Shīʿīs of Kūfa. The memory of Al-Mukhtār and Ibn az-Zubayr died with the lapse of time and could only find place in the annals of history. The memory of Ḥusayn remained alive in the hearts and minds of the Muslims and has become a recurrent theme for certain values. The section of the Muslim community which upheld the cause and memory of Ḥusayn at the expense of and in disregard for political realities, but still remaining an integral part of the religious entity of Islam, was thrust into a sectarian role by that majority which, though unwillingly, compromised with the political realities at the religious level.

Some Muslim historians writing directly under the influence of the ruling authorities of the time, and those theologians who by necessity tried to find a compromise position between the ruling authorities on the one hand and the Islamic community on the other, described Ḥusayn's action as an ambitious attempt to wrest political power and as a mistake of judgement. Western scholars of Islam, in their rather superficial attempts to study Ḥusayn's action, have subjected themselves to a certain mechanical methodology which they term a "scientific historical approach". The German school of orientalists, the first to enter the field of modern orientalism, though it indeed made valuable and solid contributions in certain branches of Arab-Islamic studies with admirable thoroughness and depth, was so committed to a particular historical methodology that it could never grasp the "feelings" and "necessary aptitude" so vitally important in understanding religious history and its development. The impact of the German school has been so strong that this trend has persisted, and the subsequent schools of the French and British scholars, with very few exceptions, have followed the same trend. It is thus rather regrettable that the tragedy of Karbalā has been regarded by these scholars with the same mechanical historicism: none of them has ever tried to study Ḥusayn's action in its meaning and purpose. It was therefore natural for these scholars to describe Ḥusayn as an ill-fated adventurer attempting to seize political power, his movement as a rebellion against the established order, and his action as a fatal miscalculation of Kūfan promises.[65]

We have already hinted in passing that Ḥusayn had been fully aware of the situation and the consequences. On the road from Medina to Mecca, then at the time when he was leaving the "House of God" for Kūfa, and finally throughout the journey from Mecca to Kūfa, he was warned by dozens of people about the danger and that "the hearts of the Iraqis were for him but that their swords were for the Umayyads." But Ḥusayn's replies to all of those who attempted to deflect him from his purpose were always more or less in the same vein:

> "God does as He wishes . . ., I leave it to God to choose what is best . . ., God is not hostile to him who proposes the just cause."[66]

From these replies it is clear that Ḥusayn was fully aware of the dangers he would encounter and that he had a certain strategy and plan in mind to bring about a revolution in the consciousness of the Muslim community. Furthermore, it is also very clear from the sources, as has been stated before, that Ḥusayn did not try to organize or mobilize military support, which he easily could have done in the Hijaz, nor did he even try to exploit whatever physical strength was available to him. Among many instances in this respect we will restrict ourselves to citing only one. At a place called ʿUzayb al-Hujaynāt, after having already learned about the Kūfan abandonment of his envoy Muslim b. ʿAqīl and his subsequent death, it was clear to Ḥusayn that he had no hope of support or even survival in Kūfa. Nevertheless, he totally refused an offer of safety, if not success, extended to him. Abū Mikhnaf and other sources relate that at this place four of the leading Shīʿīs of Kūfa managed to reach Ḥusayn with the help of Ṭirimmāḥ b. ʿAdi aṭ-Ṭāʾī, who acted as a guide (*dalīl*). Ṭirimmāḥ made a strong appeal to Ḥusayn, saying:

> "By God I have left Kūfa in such a condition that when you reach there you will not find a single person who could help you against your enemies. By God, if you go there, you and those who are travelling with you will be instantly butchered. For God's

sake, abandon your plan and come with me to the safety of our mountains here. By God, these mountains have been beyond the reach of the kings of Ghassān and Ḥimyar, from Nuʿmān b. al-Mundhir, and from any black and red [i.e., from any formidable power]. By God, if you decide to come with me no one can humiliate you or stop you from doing so [reference to Ḥurr]. Once you reach my villages on the mountains, we will send for men of [the tribes of] Baʿja and Salma of the Tayy'. Then, even ten days will not pass before the horsemen and the foot soldiers of Tayy' arrive to help you. You can stay with us as long as you wish, and if then you want to make an uprising from there, or if you are disturbed, I would lead a force of twenty thousand men of the Tayy' with you, who would strike [at your enemies] with their swords in front of you. By God, no one will ever be able to reach you, and the eyes of the people of Tayy' would remain guarding you."[67]

Ḥusayn's only reply to this extremely valuable and timely offer, when all hopes of support in Kūfa had already vanished, was:

"God bless you and your people, but I am committed to some people, and I cannot go back from my word, though I did not know what would happen between us and them. However, things are destined."[68]

One cannot help asking how it would be possible for a man making a bid for power to refuse to accept such a promising offer of support. Can anyone think that after knowing all of the latest developments in Kūfa Ḥusayn was still hoping to find any support or even the slightest chance of survival in Kūfa? Moreover, we have detailed descriptions of the fact that when at Zubāla Ḥusayn learned of the brutal execution of his envoy Qays b. Mushir, he gathered those accompanying him and asked them to leave him alone and go to safety. After Zubāla, Ḥusayn made this proclamation to his companions time and again, the last of these being on the night of ʿĀshūra. Is it conceivable that anyone striving for power would ask his supporters to abandon him, no matter how insignificant their number might have been? No one can answer these questions in the affirmative. What then did Ḥusayn have in mind? Why was he still heading for Kūfa?

It is rather disappointing to note that Western scholarship on Islam, given too much to historicism, has placed all its attention on the discrete external aspects of the event of Karbalā and has never tried to analyse the inner history and agonizing conflict in Ḥusayn's mind. Anatomy of the human body can give knowledge of the various parts and their composition, but cannot give us an understanding of man himself. In the case of Ḥusayn, a careful study and analysis of the events of Karbalā as a whole reveals the fact that from the very beginning Ḥusayn was planning for a complete revolution in the religious consciousness of the Muslims. All of his actions show that he was aware of the fact that a victory achieved through military strength and might is always temporal, because another stronger power can in course of time bring it down in ruins. But a victory achieved through suffering and sacrifice is everlasting and leaves permanent imprints on man's consciousness. Ḥusayn was brought up in the lap of the Founder of Islam and had inherited the love and devotion to the Islamic way of life from his father. As time went on, he noticed the great changes which were rapidly taking place in the community in regard to religious feelings and morality. The natural process of conflict and struggle between *action* and *reaction* was now at work. That is, Muḥammad's progressive Islamic *action* had succeeded in suppressing Arab conservatism, embodied in heathen pre-Islamic practices and ways of thinking. But in less than thirty years' time this Arab conservatism revitalized itself as a forceful *reaction* to challenge Muḥammad's *action* once again. The forces of this *reaction* had already moved into motion with the rise of Muʿāwiya, but the succession of Yazīd was a clear sign that the reactionary forces had mobilized themselves and had now re-emerged with full vigour. The strength of this *reaction*, embodied in Yazīd's character, was powerful enough to suppress or at least deface Muḥammad's *action*. Islam was now, in the thinking of Ḥusayn, in dire need of reactivation of Muḥammad's *action* against the old Arabian *reaction* and thus required a complete shake-up. Such a shake-up would not have been so effective at the time of Ḥasan, for his rival Muʿāwiya, though he had little regard for religion, at least outwardly tried to veil his reactionary attitude of the old Arabism. Yazīd did not care even for this; he exposed these pretensions and his conduct amounted to open ridicule of Muḥammad's *Sunna* and Qur'ānic norms. Now, through

Yazīd, *reaction* of the old Arabism was in direct confrontation against the Islamic *action* of Muḥammad. This could be seen by such instances as when Yazīd, during his father's reign, once came to Medina in the season of the *Ḥajj* and became badly intoxicated from wine-drinking. Ibn ʿAbbās and Ḥusayn happened to pass by him, whereupon Yazīd called his servant and ordered him to serve wine to Ḥusayn, insisting that the latter take it. When Ḥusayn angrily refused and rose to leave, Yazīd, in his drunken stupor, sang:

> "O my friend, how strange it is that I have invited you, but you do not accept,
> To women singers, pleasures, wine, and music,
> And to a brimming full jar of wine on the lip of which sits the master of the Arabs.
> And among them [the singing girls] there is one who has captured your heart, and she did not repent by doing this."

Ḥusayn stood up and said:

> "But your heart, O son of Muʿāwiya."[69]

Now this same Yazīd was the Caliph of Islam and was asking Ḥusayn to accept his authority. Ḥusayn's acceptance of Yazīd, with the latter's openly reactionary attitude against Islamic norms, would not have meant merely a political arrangement, as had been the case with Ḥasan and Muʿāwiya, but an endorsement of Yazīd's character and way of life as well. This was unthinkable to the grandson of the Prophet, now the head of Muḥammad's family and the embodiment of his *Sunna*.

In order to counteract this *reaction* against Islamic *action*, Ḥusayn prepared his strategy. In his opinion he had the right, by virtue of his family and his own position therein, to guide the people and receive their respect. However, if this right were challenged, he was willing to sacrifice and die for his cause. He realized that mere force of arms would not have saved Islamic *action* and consciousness. To him it needed a shaking and jolting of hearts and feelings. This, he decided, could only be achieved through sacrifice and sufferings. This should not be difficult to understand, especially for those who fully appreciate the heroic deeds and sacrifices of, for example, Socrates and Joan of Arc, both of whom embraced death for their ideals, and above all of the great sacrifice of Jesus Christ for the redemption of mankir.d.

It is in this light that we should read Ḥusayn's replies to those well-wishers who advised him not to go to Iraq. It also explains why Ḥusayn took with him his women and children, though advised by Ibn ʿAbbās that should he insist on his project, at least he should not take his family with him. Aware of the extent of the brutal nature of the reactionary forces, Ḥusayn knew that after killing him the Umayyads would make his women and children captives and take them all the way from Kūfa to Damascus. This caravan of captives of Muḥammad's immediate family would publicize Ḥusayn's message and would force the Muslims' hearts to ponder on the tragedy. It would make the Muslims think of the whole affair and would awaken their consciousness. This is exactly what happened. Ḥusayn succeeded in his purpose. It is difficult today to evaluate exactly the impact of Ḥusayn's action on Islamic morality and way of thinking, because it prevailed. Had Ḥusayn not shaken and awakened Muslim consciousness by this method, who knows whether Yazīd's way of life would have become standard behaviour in the Muslim community, endorsed and accepted by the grandson of the Prophet. No doubt, even after Yazīd kingship did prevail in Islam, and the character and behaviour in the personal lives of these kings was not very different from that of Yazīd, but the change in thinking which prevailed after the sacrifice of Ḥusayn always served as a line of distinction between Islamic norms and the personal character of the rulers.

Except for a few mediaeval writers committed to certain interests, Muslim historians and authors have always paid their utmost tribute in praising Ḥusayn's heroic action. It is indeed encouraging that in modern times more and more Muslim scholars of all schools of thought have been contributing independent works to explain Ḥusayn's philosophy of sacrifice and martyrdom. Among the numerous books published in the past few decades, coinciding with the reawakening of the Muslim world, we would refer our readers to only two. One is by the famous Egyptian author ʿAbbās Maḥmūd al-ʿAqqād and entitled *Abū ash-shuhadāʾ, al-Ḥusayn b. ʿAlī*[70] (Father of Martyrs, Ḥusayn b. ʿAlī). The other is by a great Lebanese scholar and shaykh, ʿAbd Allāh al-ʿAlā'ilī, and is entitled *Al-Imām al-Ḥusayn, sumū'l-maʿna fī sumū'dh-dhāt*[71] (The Imam Ḥusayn, Loftiness of Purpose in a Lofty Personality), a comprehensive study of Ḥusayn's life, times, and martyrdom. Both writers, the former a secular scholar of history and philosophy, the latter a religious scholar of very high standing and scholarship, have discussed thoroughly the meaning, purpose, philosophy and the highest ideal of Ḥusayn's deed.

Now we must turn to examine the second inference to be drawn from the outline of the episode of Karbalā given above: to determine the religious feelings of those who willingly gave their lives with Ḥusayn. In describing the tragedy our sources do not fail to provide ample material on those doctrinal feelings which compelled the supporters of Ḥusayn to choose to die with him rather than to live in peace and comfort, a choice which remained open to them even up to the last moment. This can be elucidated by examining those speeches and pledges of loyalty made by these persons on several occasions. It is also illustrated by that war poetry in *rajaz* (verbal duels) which was exchanged between the combatants of both sides. In Arabian warfare it was customary that when two combatants came to fight each other, each would declare his tribe, its deeds and status, and the stand for which he was going to fight. Only a few examples, however, from each of these three categories will be cited here to show that there was a particular doctrinal stand for which the followers of Ḥusayn stood and died.

1 We have seen that Ḥusayn's messenger Qays b. Mushir, whom he had sent from Ḥājir to inform the Kūfans of his arrival, was arrested at al-Qādisīya and sent to Ibn Ziyād for trial. The governor ordered him to go to the top of the palace and curse Ḥusayn if he wanted to save his life. Qays used this opportunity to propagate his cause; he addressed the people, saying:

> "O people of Kūfa. I am Ḥusayn's messenger, and I declare before you that Ḥusayn, the grandson of the Prophet, is the best man of his time among the men of God on earth and has better claims upon you than anyone else. It is therefore your duty to respond to him."

Qays then called for the curse of God upon Ibn Ziyād and God's blessing for ʿAlī.[72] He was thereupon thrown to his death. If we compare Qays' attitude with that of Ḥujr b. ʿAdī al-Kindī about twelve years earlier, mentioned in the preceding chapter, we find a consistent way of thinking which links them in an unbroken chain of Shīʿī thought. Qays' introduction of Ḥusayn with special reference to his relationship with the Prophet and stating that he was the best man of God of his time on earth goes back to the ideas promulgated from the very beginning by the supporters of ʿAlī.

2 As mentioned above, on the eve of ʿĀshūra (9 Muḥarram) Ibn Saʿd ordered his forces to advance towards Ḥusayn's camp after receiving Ibn Ziyād's orders for an immediate attack. Ḥusayn sent his brother ʿAbbās along with some leading followers to ask for a night's respite. After some argument this was granted, and ʿAbbās returned to inform Ḥusayn; but Ḥabīb b. Muẓāhir and Zuhayr b. al-Qayn, who had come along with ʿAbbās, remained behind to try to convince the Umayyad army of their wrongdoings. There are some useful dialogues recorded between these two men and their opponents. Ḥabīb b. Muẓāhir spoke first to the enemy:

> "By God, how evil and wretched those people will be when they appear before God after killing the family and the *Ahl al-Bayt* of their own Prophet. The people of this sacred family are those who are the best worshippers of God and who spend their mornings striving in the devotion to God, devoting themselves to the best of His remembrance."

Azra b. Qays from the Umayyad side tauntingly replied: "You go ahead with the purification of your soul as much as you like" (implying: "but do not try to convince us"). To this Zuhayr b. al-Qayn responded:

> "O Azra! God has indeed purified our souls and has guided us. So fear God, O Azra, because I am one of your sincerest advisors. May God make you think, O Azra. Would you like to be one of those who have fixed for themselves the path of error by killing these sacred and purified souls [Ḥusayn and other members of the *Ahl al-Bayt*]?"

Azra b. Qays again retorted:

"O Zuhayr, you were not among the Shīʿīs of ʿAlī, but were known to be an ʿUthmānī."

Zuhayr replied:

"But now being with Ḥusayn you must recognize that I am a Shīʿī of ʿAlī."[73]

3 After this respite of only one night, and with all hopes gone, it was certain that the following morning would bring the summons of death for Ḥusayn and his supporters. He gathered his companions and asked them to leave him alone as the enemy wanted nothing but his head. All the prominent companions and relatives of Ḥusayn, in reply to his address, refused to leave him until all of them were killed. Perhaps we should avoid considering the pledges made on this occasion by the relatives of Ḥusayn, like ʿAbbās, his half-brother and others,[74] which may be interpreted as the clannish loyalty to the head of the clan. We would, therefore, record here the pledges of those who had no blood, clan, or even tribal relationship with Ḥusayn, but only ties of religious or doctrinal loyalty.

From among the followers of Ḥusayn the aged Muslim b. ʿAwsaja stood up and exclaimed:

"How can we leave you? What excuse then will we have before God in discharging our duty towards you? No, by God, we will not depart from you. I will fight with you until my last breath and until I die with you."[75]

Then Saʿd b. ʿAbd Allāh al-Ḥanafī addressed Ḥusayn, saying:

"By God, we will not depart from you until by sacrificing our lives we have proven to God that we have faithfully fulfilled the duty we owe to the Prophet concerning you. By God, if I knew that I would be killed and then again be given a new life, and that then my body would be burned alive, all this being repeated seventy times, I would still not leave you until I died in front of you. And why should I not do that when I know that I can only be killed once, leading to an everlasting honour and privilege. [The last sentence in *Bidāya* reads:] By God, if I knew that I would be killed before you a thousand times, and by this your life and the lives of the other *Ahl al-Bayt* would be saved, I would love to be killed a thousand times; but this is only to be killed once, leading to an everlasting honour."[76]

After quoting a similar speech by Zuhayr b. al-Qayn, our sources say that all the companions of Ḥusayn pronounced more or less in the same vein and declared their complete loyalties to Ḥusayn, saying:

> "By God, we will never leave you alone until all of us are killed and our bodies are torn to pieces. By this we will have fulfilled our duties to you."[77]

The contents of all these statements and pledges provide very useful points with which to emphasize that religious urge which made the companions of Ḥusayn so firm and enthusiastic, even at that moment of calamity. The points prevailing in these pledges are: 1: emphasis on Ḥusayn's close and direct relationship with the Prophet, and not specifically with ʿAlī; 2: that to betray Ḥusayn is to betray the Prophet, or similarly, that loyalty to Ḥusayn is loyalty to Muḥammad, the Prophet of God; 3: that to give up Ḥusayn is to denounce Islam, which was revealed by his grandfather, the Prophet; 4: that betrayal of Ḥusayn this day would cause them to perish on the Day of Judgement and would deprive them of the intercession of the Prophet. The essence of all these aspects, however, is that in their thinking there was an Imām or central authority who was the focal point for the love normally directed to the person of the Prophet himself.[78]

4 On the day of ʿĀshūra, shortly before the fateful battle began, Ḥurr b. Yazīd, a respected commander of the Umayyad army, the first who confronted Ḥusayn and forced him to halt at Karbalā as mentioned above, was himself now confronted by his own conscience and feelings. A great conflict arose in his mind: he was forced to choose between either wetting his hands in the sacred blood of the grandson of the Prophet or giving up his rank, power, and a bright career lying before him. His feelings ultimately won him over and he chose the latter. He suddenly spurred his horse towards Ḥusayn's camp, threw himself at Ḥusayn's feet, and exclaimed:

> "O son of the Prophet! Here is the man who did you great injustice in detaining you at this place and causing you so much trouble. Is it possible for you to forgive a sinner like me? By God, I never imagined that these people would go so far as to shed the blood of the grandson of their Prophet. I only thought that they would accept one of these three options you offered; and thus

some sort of reconciliation would ultimately prevail, and in this way I would be able to retain my rank and position. But now, when all hopes for peace are gone, I cannot buy Hell for this worldly gain. Forgive my mistake and allow me to sacrifice myself for you. Only by doing this can I redeem myself in the eyes of God for my sin against you."[79]

Ḥusayn embraced Ḥurr and said: "You are as free-born and noble (*ḥurr*) as your mother named you." Ḥurr then at once went before the Umayyad army and addressed his fellow men in a long speech in favour of Ḥusayn. Condemning their sacrilegious actions against the grandson of the Prophet, he put them to shame and reminded them of the Day of Judgement.[80] Consequently, Ḥurr was among the first to give his life for Ḥusayn. The defection of Ḥurr to Ḥusayn shortly before the battle began and his being killed by the Umayyad army is as historical as the event of Karbalā itself; to his defection all the sources bear unanimous testimony.

The physical defection of Ḥurr from the established order was, however, not of much importance. It was the principle on which Ḥurr defected from the Umayyad army which should be considered seriously. This was, perhaps, the greatest visible victory for the Shīʿī point of view, for which the companions of Ḥusayn were fighting to the death. The working of Ḥurr's mind at this last moment, as expressed in his statements mentioned above, was exactly the same as that of the companions of Ḥusayn. This again supports the view that there was a particular way of thinking directed to the Shīʿī doctrine.

5 Not of least importance in this connection are those *rajaz* verses exchanged between Ḥusayn's companions and their opponents. Among the most illuminating are the following:

1: The same Ḥurr, when engaged in battle, proclaimed:

"I will strike my sword on your heads in the cause of that *Imām* who is the best among all the inhabitants of Mecca."[81]

2: Nāfiʿ b. Hilāl al-Jamalī, of Ḥusayn's camp, came forward and asked for his combatant, proclaiming:

"I am from the tribe of Banū Jamal, and I am of the religion of ʿAlī (*dīn ʿAlī*)."

From the opposite side one Muzāḥim b. Ḥurayth came forward, saying:

"I will fight with you; I am of the religion of ʿUthmān (*dīn ʿUthmān*)."

Nāfiʿ retorted:

"No, you are of the religion of Satan."[82]

3: When Zuhayr b. al-Qayn came to fight he said:

"I am Zuhayr, and I am the son of Qayn; I will defend and protect Ḥusayn with my sword."

Turning to Ḥusayn he said:

"I will proceed leading to a rightly guided path the day when I meet your grandfather, the Prophet, [and the day] when I will meet Ḥasan and ʿAlī al-Murtaḍā and the one of the two wings [reference to Jaʿfar aṭ-Ṭayyār]."[83]

The war poetry in *rajaz* pronounced by the combatants of both sides, which has come down to us from reliable sources to be examined later, makes useful reading and provides important points. We have quoted only three of them for the sake of brevity. These pronouncements, however, sufficiently indicate that the Shīʿī trend of thinking was fully active among those who chose to die with Ḥusayn. The statement of Ḥurr that Ḥusayn was an *Imām*, the best of all the residents of Mecca, and Nāfiʿ and Zuhayr's declarations that they were of the religion of ʿAlī and on the rightly guided path, are complete explanations in themselves and require no further comment. Yet the pronouncement of Ḥusayn's followers that they were of the religion of ʿAlī does not fail to suggest that they meant this term in a strictly religious sense, in contrast to those who had also called themselves by the same name at Al-Jamal, at Ṣiffīn, and on other occasions with ʿAlī, but on political grounds, and who with the changing circumstances assimilated with the ruling majority who were now going to kill the son of ʿAlī. On the other hand, by looking at all these quotations referred to above we find that throughout the incident of Karbalā there had been a persistent and continuous doctrinal tendency among the followers of Ḥusayn, based on their declaration of being of the religion of ʿAlī. This very tendency in course of time, as we shall see later, was translated into a more elaborate form of Shīʿī tenets and developed its own theological doctrine (*kalām*) and legal system (*fiqh*) in opposition to the rest of the Jamāʿa.

Commenting on the tragedy of Karbalā, even a scholar like Philip Hitti lets himself write that "Shīʿīsm was born on the tenth of Muḥarram."[84] All the information derived from our sources and all the evidence given above totally reject this view. Instead, a careful study of the material handed down to us from the sources of different schools of thought confirm the fact that the Shīʿī doctrinal stand had been in evidence right from the time of the death of the Prophet, and the death of Ḥusayn only "set the seal of an official Shīʾism."[85] For that purpose we have gone into the detail of citing from those speeches, pledges, and war poetry pronounced *before* the death of Ḥusayn, all of which clearly demonstrates the nature of the existing tendencies prevailing *before* the tragedy occurred. What is really true to say, however, is that the tragedy did play an immensely important role, not in the creation of Shīʿism, but in the consolidation of the Shīʿī identity. The fate of Ḥusayn was destined to become the most effective agent in the propagation and comparatively rapid spread of Shīʿism. It is also undoubtedly true that the tragedy added to Shīʿī Islam an element of "passion", which renders human psychology more receptive to doctrine than anything else. Henceforth we find that this element of "passion" becomes a characteristic feature of the Shīʿīs. The tragedy of Karbalā in its immediate and far-reaching consequences created three thousand *Tawwābūn* (penitents) who let themselves die as a way of repenting for their inability to fulfil their commitments to the grandson of the Prophet. It provided a ground from which Mukhtār was able to launch his movement. It provided an effective slogan to the ʿAbbāsids for overthrowing the Umayyad regime. And ultimately, the name and memory of Ḥusayn became an inseparable part of Shīʿī moral and religious fervour.[86]

A brief comment on the authenticity of the sources of our information for the whole account of Karbalā, including the speeches, pledges, and *rajaz* material pronounced by the supporters of Ḥusayn, is in order. The main source of our knowledge of the tragedy is Abū Mikhnaf Lūṭ b. Yaḥyā (died 157/774), the first to produce a comprehensive account of

Karbalā. This work was entitled *Maqtal al-Ḥusayn,* and in the list of Abū Mikhnaf's numerous works this one is unanimously mentioned by all bibliographers.[87]

Abū Mikhnaf, one of the earliest and best Arab historians, has been thoroughly and critically studied by scholars such as Wellhausen[88] and others, and recently by Ursula Sezgin in an admirable work entitled *Abū Mikhnaf.*[89] All have found him generally the most reliable and authentic writer on the annals of Kūfa and Iraq under the Umayyads. It is now established that, as a rule, he does not take his material from predecessors or far-distant sources, but rather collects it himself by enquiring in the most diverse directions from all possible people who could have first-hand information or who had been present to see and hear for themselves. The chain of transmitters with him is a reality and not merely a literary form, and it is always very short. Writing shortly after the events he describes, Abū Mikhnaf often relates from an eyewitness account with only one intermediary between himself and his source.[90] Gibb suggests that Abū Mikhnaf presents an Iraqi or Kūfan, rather than purely Shīʿī, point of view in his narratives.[91] In this his sympathies are no doubt on the side of Iraq against Syria; for ʿAlī, against the Umayyads. Yet in the opinion of Wellhausen there is not much of a bias noticeable, at least not so much as to positively falsify fact.[92]

The *Maqtal* of Abū Mikhnaf has come to us through numerous sources. It is, however, Ṭabarī who used this work in full for the first time and thus becomes our main source of the text. In most cases Ṭabarī quotes Abū Mikhnaf directly, but quite a few traditions he quotes from Hishām b. Muḥammad al-Kalbī, most of these, no doubt, going back to Abū Mikhnaf himself. Ṭabarī sometimes begins his narrative by saying: "Abū Mikhnaf said from so-and-so . . ."; and other times by saying: "Hishām (b. al-Kalbī) said from Abū Mikhnaf from so-and-so . . ." This indicates that in the former case Ṭabarī is quoting directly from Abū Mikhnaf's work, while in the latter he quotes Abū Mikhnaf in the recension of Ibn al-Kalbī. Besides Abū Mikhnaf and Ibn al-Kalbī, Ṭabarī also quotes quite a few traditions transmitted from other traditionists, which add a few variants to the preceding ones and in most cases confirm Abū Mikhnaf.

Another source for Abū Mikhnaf is Balādhurī (died 279/892-893), whose *Ansāb al-ashrāf* pertaining to Ḥusayn has not yet been published, but has been used by Veccia Vaglieri in her long and thorough article on Ḥusayn in the new edition of the *Encyclopaedia of Islam.* Vaglieri finds that "Al-Balādhurī almost always used the same sources as Aṭ-Ṭabarī, but often made résumés of them, introducing them by *qālū* (they said), and he provides some additional verses." Our own examination of the manuscript leads us to agree with her findings, thus detailed references to the *Ansāb* manuscript seem unnecessary.[93]

Besides these two, who have used Abū Mikhnaf in full, we have also referred to Ibn Kathīr (died 774/1372–1373), a pupil of Ibn Taymiyya and a committed Sunnī of the Syrian school, often very critical of the Shīʿī, whom he often refers to as the *Rawāfiḍ.* Ibn Kathīr, often selective, naturally ignores those parts of Abū Mikhnaf which are directly against his interests, such as the references to ʿUthmān, etc.; otherwise he accepts most of the material of Abū Mikhnaf. On the other hand, early Shīʿī writers, like Shaykh al-Mufīd (born 336/947, died 413/1022) in his *Irshād,* and others, relate the tragedy of Karbalā, apart from Abū Mikhnaf from their own sources, often going back to ʿAlī b. al-Ḥusayn. This son of Ḥusayn, twenty-three years old when he was present at Karbalā, could not take part in the battle due to his illness and was thus saved from the general massacre. This makes him a major narrator of the tragedy. It is indeed very interesting and useful to note that in general outline and in all the major events, the renderings of Shaykh al-Mufīd, a very committed die-hard Shīʿī, are closely paralleled by those of the Syrian Ibn Kathīr.

In examining Abū Mikhnaf's *Maqtal al-Ḥusayn* one must particularly take into consideration the time factor to the author's advantage. We do not know precisely the date of his birth, but at the rising of Ibn Ashʿath against Ḥajjāj in 80–82/699–701,[94] Abū Mikhnaf had already reached manhood.[95] The tragedy of Karbalā took place in 61/680. This means that Abū Mikhnaf must have been born about the year of the tragedy, and at the time of Ibn al-Ashʿath's revolt he must have been somewhere between the ages of eighteen and twenty-two. It is certain that many of those who took active part in the battle of Karbalā on the Umayyad side were still living, and thus the author had the opportunity of meeting and interviewing personally those who had witnessed the event themselves. For this reason, in the *Maqtal*, Abū Mikhnaf cites his authority with the clear observation *wa kāna qad shahida qatl al-Ḥusayn* (and he witnessed the murder of Ḥusayn). Without exception, throughout his narrative he uses the verb *ḥaddathanī* (he told me); and if his report is not directly from an eyewitness, he cites only one or two intermediaries who had received the account from the eyewitness himself. Thus in our quotations above concerning the statements of loyalty, pledges, and *rajaz*, the *isnād* runs:

1: Abū Mikhnaf—Muḥammad b. Qays (eyewitness).
2: Abū Mikhnaf—Ḥārith b. Ḥaṣira and ʿAbd Allāh b. Sharīk al-ʿĀmirī (eyewitnesses).
3: Abū Mikhnaf—ʿAbd Allāh b. ʿĀṣim and Ḍaḥḥāk b. ʿAbd Allāh (eyewitnesses).
4: Abū Mikhnaf—Abū Janāb al-Kalbī and ʿAdī b. Ḥurmula (eyewitnesses).
5: Abū Mikhnaf—Muḥammad b. Qays (eyewitness).[96]

Often he further strengthens his *isnād* by citing more than one eyewitness, for instance in 2, 3, and 4 above. Reporting the pledges of the supporters of Ḥusayn on the night of ʿĀshūra, he says that ʿAlī b. al-Ḥusayn said: "I was lying sick in my bed and heard my father's speech and the replies of his supporters thereto."

The *Maqtal al-Ḥusayn* of Abū Mikhnaf must have soon received widespread popularity, and numerous copies must have been made and circulated. This is evident from an examination of the *isnāds* and reference to sources in which the work is used by other authors. Ṭabarī's source was no doubt mainly Hishām b. al-Kalbī directly. But Mufīd, Abū'l-Faraj (*Maqātil al-Ṭālibiyīn*), Ibn Kathīr, and many others give different sources and names through whom the work reached them. For example, Mufīd often begins his narrative with the prefatory comment: "What is reported by Al-Kalbī, Al-Madā'inī, and others than these two from among the biographers (*aṣḥāb as-Siyar*)."[97] Similarly, Abū'l-Faraj quotes Abū Mikhnaf from Ibn al-Kalbī and Madā'inī, and additionally from sources such as Ḥusayn b. Naṣr, the son of the famous Naṣr b. Muzāḥim al-Minqarī, the author of *Waqʿat*

Ṣiffīn, and ʿAwāna, the famous historian. Abū'l-Faraj alone uses about five different *isnāds* going back to Abū Mikhnaf, and quite a few other independent *isnāds* going back to ʿAlī b. al-Ḥusayn, and then as usual summarises the accounts of all of them together. Basically, however, Abū'l-Faraj's source for Abū Mikhnaf is Madā'inī.[98] Likewise still other authorities and different sources are given by Ibn Kathīr, through whom he was able to use Abū Mikhnaf.[99]

Mention must finally be made of the four manuscripts of the *Maqtal,* located at Gotha (No. 1836), Berlin (Sprenger, Nos. 159–160), Leiden (No. 792), and St. Petersburg (Am No. 78). It was from the first two that Ferdinand Wüstenfeld made a German translation of the work entitled *Der Tod des Ḥusein Ben ʿAlī und die Rache* (Göttingen, 1883). Wüstenfeld, while convinced of the early origin of these manuscripts, doubts that the author was Abū Mikhnaf.[100] The foremost argument he puts forward is that it contains some miraculous and supernatural types of stories, such as terrible manifestations of grief in natural phenomena: reddening skies, bleeding sands, and so forth. Ursula Sezgin questions Wüstenfeld's criticism at several points and suggests that while the existing manuscripts may be the recensions or rewritings made by some later unknown writers, the fact remains that Ṭabarī's main source of Abū Mikhnaf was Ibn al-Kalbī.[101]

However, some of these miraculous stories or fantasies have found a place even in Ṭabarī, which suggests that these might have been originally written by Abū Mikhnaf himself or may have been incorporated by Ibn al-Kalbī when he rewrote his master's work. But to cast doubts on Abū Mikhnaf's authorship of the *Maqtal* only on the grounds that some supernatural and miraculous events are recorded, as Wüstenfeld is inclined to suggest, would mean to ignore certain tendencies of the age. It would perhaps be a grave error to expect that a book written in the early eighth century about a great religious personality would not accept supernatural occurrences as a matter of course, especially when the main event itself is so charged with emotion and suffering. The Near East has produced an enormous number of books on the miracles of saints and holy men, and it would be strange indeed if Islam had not followed in the footsteps of its predecessors in glorifying the deeds of its Prophet and his family, even at the expense of their human greatness. Moreover, as explained in the first chapter, the Arabs always believed in certain supernatural powers endowed on some sacerdotal families. Similarly, certain reactions of natural elements in certain conditions were also a commonplace factor in the system of Arab beliefs. After the Arabs' conversion to Islam, the miraculous stories were growing in narration right from the time of the Prophet, to which the *Sīra* of Ibn Hishām bears testimony.

The most extraordinary circumstances of Ḥusayn's death, immediately followed by the *Tawwābūn* Movement highly charged with passion and remorse, and the propaganda carried out by the *Tawwābūn* and by Al-Mukhtār naturally produced some supernatural stories alongside the accounts of the tragedy. We can, therefore, conclude that even if a few popular legends and supernatural events related to the tragedy are described in the *Maqtal,* this does not mean that the work is not of Abū Mikhnaf's authorship, nor that the whole account is unreliable. The inclusion of such stories does not eclipse the fact that the *Maqtal* also contains and comprises the efforts of a prominent Arab historian to collect and preserve the most reliable and the most contemporary historical accounts of Ḥusayn's martyrdom available to scholarship at a time when many participants in the events were still alive and able to contribute their knowledge to Abū Mikhnaf's research.

Notes to Chapter 7

[1] For the character and conduct of Yazīd, see Jāḥiẓ, *Rasā'il*, "Risāla fī Banī Umayya", pp. 294 ff.; Balādhurī, IVB, pp. 1–11; *Aghānī*, XV, p. 232; Mas'ūdī, *Murūj*, III, p. 67; Damīrī, *Ḥayāt al-Ḥayawān*, pp. 261 ff.; Ya'qūbī, II, p. 228. It is indeed surprising to note that Henri Lammens, in his *Le califat de Yazīd*, contrary to the unanimous reports of Muslim writers of all times, has taken great pains to depict Yazīd as an ideal character. Lammens' unusual regard for the Umayyad house often led him to read the Arabic text to suit his own purposes.

[2] Balādhurī, IVB, pp. 122 f.; *'Iqd*, IV, p. 226; Ṭabarī, II, pp. 196 f.; Dīnawarī, p. 226

[3] Balādhurī, IVB, p. 12; Ya'qūbī, II, p. 241; Ṭabarī, II, p. 216; *'Iqd*, IV, p. 227; *Bidāya*, VIII, pp. 146 f.

[4] Ṭabarī, II, p. 219; Balādhurī, IVB, p. 15; Dīnawarī, p. 228; *Bidāya*, VIII, p. 147

[5] See Ṭabarī, II, pp. 233, 276; Balādhurī, IVB, p. 13; Dīnawarī, p. 229; Mas'ūdī, *Murūj*, III, p. 55; *Bidāya*, VIII, p. 151

[6] Ṭabarī, II, pp. 233 f.; *Maqātil*, p. 96

[7] Ṭabarī, II, p. 234; Dīnawarī, p. 229; *Bidāya*, VIII, pp. 151 f.

[8] Ṭabarī, II, pp. 234 f.; Ya'qūbī, II, p. 242

[9] Ṭabarī, II, p. 235; Mufīd, *Irshād*, II, pp. 35 f.

[10] Ṭabarī, II, p. 240

[11] See details in Ṭabarī, II, pp. 174 f.

[12] Ṭabarī, II, pp. 237 f.; Mufīd, *Irshād*, II, p. 36; *Bidāya*, VIII, p. 152

[13] Ṭabarī, II, p. 264; Mas'ūdī, *Murūj*, III, p. 54; Dīnawarī, p. 235; Balādhurī, II, p. 80; Mufīd, *Irshād*, II, p. 38; Bidāya, VIII, p. 152. Ibn 'Abd Rabbih gives the figure as more than 30,000 in *'Iqd*, IV, p. 378

[14] This letter of Muslim was sent to Ḥusayn on 12 Dhū'l-Qa'da 60/15 August 680, 27 days before the murder of Muslim; see Ṭabarī, II, pp. 264, 271; Mufīd, *Irshād*, II, pp. 67, 72

[15] Ṭabarī, II, pp. 220 f.; 223, 274 f.; Dīnawarī, pp. 229, 243 f.; *'Iqd*, IV, p. 376; *Maqātil*, p. 109; *Bidāya*, VIII, pp. 159 f.; 160 ff.

[16] Ṭabarī, II, pp. 274–76; *Bidāya*, VIII, p. 166

[17] Ṭabarī, *loc. cit.*; Balādhurī, IVB, p. 14; Dīnawarī, p. 229; *Maqātil*, p. 109; *Bidāya*, VIII, pp. 160, 163

[18] See the text of Yazīd's order in Ṭabarī, II, pp. 228, 240. A still more detailed version is given by Jahshiyārī, *Al-Wuzarā' wa'l-*

Kuttāb, ed. Saqqa, Ibyarī, and Shiblī (Cairo, 1938), p. 31; Dīnawarī, pp. 231, 242; *Bidāya*, VIII, p. 152; Mufīd *Irshād*, II, p. 40

[19] Ṭabarī, II, pp. 229, 241; Dīnawarī, p. 232; Masʿūdī, *Murūj*, III, p. 57; *Maqātil*, p. 96; *Bidāya*, VIII, p. 153; Mufīd, *Irshād*, II, p. 41

[20] Ṭabarī, II, p. 242; Dīnawarī, p. 232; *Maqātil*, p. 97; *Bidāya*, VIII, p. 154; Mufīd, *Irshād*, II, p. 41

[21] See Ṭabarī, II, p. 267; Masʿūdī, *Murūj*, III, pp. 59 f.; Dīnawarī, p. 240; *Maqātil*, pp. 100–8; *Bidāya*, VIII, pp. 153–7; Mufīd, *Irshād*, II, pp. 42–67

[22] Ṭabarī, II, pp. 242, 277; Dīnawarī, p. 245; *Bidāya*, VIII, p. 166

[23] Ṭabarī, II, p. 278; Yaʿqūbī, II, p. 249; *Bidāya*, VIII, p. 167. Shīʿī sources state that Yazīd sent some soldiers disguised as pilgrims to assassinate Ḥusayn amidst the crowds assembled for the Ḥajj; see Mufīd, *Irshād*, II, p. 69

[24] Ṭabarī, II, p. 242

[25] Ṭabarī, II, pp. 285, 288 f.; Dīnawarī, p. 243; Mufīd, *Irshād*, II, p. 71

[26] Ṭabarī, II, pp. 289 ff.; 293, 303; Dīnawarī, pp. 247 f.; *Bidāya*, VIII, pp. 268, 274; Mufīd, *Irshād*, II, p. 72

[27] Ṭabarī, II, p. 303; *Bidāya*, loc. cit.

[28] Ṭabarī, II, p. 294; Dīnawarī, p. 248; *Bidāya*, VIII, p. 169; Mufīd, *Irshad*, II, p. 77

[29] Ṭabarī, II, pp. 296 f.; Dīnawarī, p. 249; *Bidāya*, VIII, p. 172; Mufīd, *Irshād*, II, pp. 78 ff.

[30] Ṭabarī, loc. cit.; Dīnawarī, loc. cit.; *Bidāya*, loc. cit.; Mufīd, loc. cit.

[31] Ṭabarī, II, pp. 298 f. See also Dīnawarī, p. 249; *Bidāya*, VIII, p. 172; Mufīd, *Irshād*, II, p. 81

[32] Ṭabarī, II, pp. 299–307; Dīnawarī, pp. 249–51; *Bidāya*, VIII, pp. 172–5; Mufīd, *Irshād*, II, p. 84

[33] For details see Ṭabarī, II, pp. 308–16; Dīnawarī, pp. 253–5; *Bidāya*, VIII, pp. 175 f.; Mufīd, *Irshād*, II, pp. 85–91

[34] Ṭabarī, II, p. 316; Dīnawarī, p. 255; *Bidāya*, VIII, p. 175

[35] Ṭabarī, II, pp. 319 ff.; *Bidāya*, VIII, p. 176; *Maqātil*, p. 112; Mufīd, *Irshad*, II, pp. 93 f.

[36] Ṭabarī, II, pp. 324 f.; *Bidāya*, VIII, p. 177; Dīnawarī, p. 256; Mufīd, *Irshād*, II, p. 97

[37] Ṭabarī, II, p. 227; *Bidāya*, VIII, pp. 169, 178; Mufīd, *Irshād*, II, p. 99

[38] Ṭabarī, II, p. 328; Mufīd, loc. cit.

[39] Ṭabarī, II, p. 329; *Bidāya*, VIII, p. 179; Mufīd, *Irshād*, II, p. 100

[40] See Ṭabarī, II, pp. 335 ff., 337 ff., 344, 346; *Bidāya*, VIII, pp. 181 ff.

[41] Ṭabarī, II, pp. 347, 351 ff., 355 f.; *Bidāya*, VIII, pp. 184 f.; Mufīd, *Irshād*, II, p. 109; Dīnawarī, pp. 256 f.

[42] Ṭabarī, II, pp. 356–9; Dīnawarī, loc. cit.; *Bidāya*, VIII, pp.185–9; Mufīd *Irshād*, II, pp. 110–14; *Maqātil*, pp. 80–113

[43] Ṭabarī, II, p. 386; Dīnawarī, pp. 257 f.; *Maqātil*, p. 84; Mufīd, *Irshād*, II, p. 113

[44] Ṭabarī, II, p. 360; Dīnawarī, p. 258; Mufīd, *Irshād*, II, p. 112; Yaʿqūbī, II, p. 240; Maqātil, p. 115

[45] Ṭabarī, II, pp. 361, 363; *Bidāya*, VIII, p. 187; Mufīd, *Irshād*, II, p. 114

[46] Ṭabarī, II, p. 365; *Bidāya*, loc. cit.; Mufīd, *Irshād*, II, p. 116

[47] Ṭabarī, II, p. 366; *Bidāya*, VIII, p. 188; Dīnawarī, p. 258; Mufīd, *Irshād*, II, p. 117

[48] For the details of these cruel acts, see Ṭabarī, II, p. 367; *Bidāya*, loc. cit.; Dīnawarī, p. 258; Mufīd, *Irshād*, II, pp. 117 f.; *Maqātil*, pp. 117 ff.

[49] Ṭabarī, II, pp. 368 f.; *Maqātil*, p. 119; Mufīd, loc. cit.

[50] Ṭabarī, loc. cit.; Dīnawarī, p. 260; *Bidāya*, VIII, p. 189

[51] Ṭabarī, II, p. 369; Dīnawarī, p. 259; *Bidāya*, VIII, p. 190; Mufīd, *Irshād*, II, pp. 118 f.

[52] Ṭabarī, II, p. 370; *Bidāya*, VIII, p. 193

[53] Ṭabarī, II, p. 371; Dīnawarī, pp. 259 f.; *Bidāya*, VIII, p. 190

[54] See sources cited in note 53

[55] Ṭabarī, II, p. 375; *Bidāya*, VIII, p. 191; Mufīd, *Irshād*, II, p. 123

[56] *Bidāya*, VIII, p. 203. For Yazīd's reported remorse see *Bidāya*, VIII, pp. 191 ff.; Ṭabarī, II, pp. 376 ff.

[57] *History of the Decline and Fall of the Roman Empire*, ed. J.B. Bury, 2nd ed. (London, 1901), V, p. 391

[58] *Akhbār*, p. 259

[59] *Ibṣār al-ʿayn fī aḥwāl al-anṣār al-Ḥusayn* (Najaf, 1341 AH), pp. 47 ff.

[60] Ṭabarī, II, p. 386; *Akhbār*, p. 259

[61] See Ṭabarī, II, pp. 303, 335

[62] *Bidāya*, VIII, p. 170; ʿIqd, IV, p. 380

[63] Ṭabarī, II, p. 236

[64] See B. Lewis, *Origins of Ismāʿīlism* (Cambridge, 1940), p. 27; also Nawbakhtī, *Firaq ash-Shīʿa*, p. 45

[65] The best example of this, among many others, is Henri Lammens' *Le califat de Yazīd* and his *EI*[1] article "Ḥusayn". Also see Wellhausen, *Arab Kingdom*, pp. 145–7

[66] Ṭabarī, II, pp. 216–95; also note 14 above

[67] Ṭabarī, II, pp. 304 f.

[68] ibid.

[69] *Aghānī*, XV, p. 233

[70] 2nd ed. (Cairo, n.d.)

[71] 2nd ed. (Beirut, 1972)

[72] Ṭabarī, II, pp. 288, 303; *Bidāya*, VIII, pp. 168, 174

[73] Ṭabarī, II, pp. 318 f.; *Bidāya*, VIII, p. 176, gives only a summary of the address of Habīb b. Muẓāhir;

[74] For their pledges see Ṭabarī, II, p. 322; Mufīd, *Irshād*, II, p. 94; *Bidāya*, VIII, p. 176; *Maqātil*, p. 112

[75] Ṭabarī, loc. cit.; *Bidāya*, VIII, p. 177. Mufīd, *Irshād*, II, p. 95, gives a longer and more forceful version.

[76] Ṭabarī, II, p. 322; *Bidāya*, VIII, p. 177; Mufīd, *Irshād*, II, p. 95

[77] ibid.

[78] A. A. A. Fyzee, "Shī'ī Legal Theories," *Law in the Middle East*, ed. Majid Khadduri and H. J. Lesbesny (Washington, 1955), p. 113

[79] Ṭabarī, II, pp. 333 f.; Mufīd, *Irshād*, II, pp. 103 f. *Bidāya*, VIII, p. 180, only summarises the statement of Ḥurr.

[80] See Ṭabarī, loc. cit.; Mufīd, loc. cit. *Bidāya*, VIII, pp. 180 f., gives here the full text of Ḥurr's speech as in Ṭabarī.

[81] Ṭabarī, II, p. 350; *Bidāya*, VIII, p. 183

[82] Ṭabarī, II, pp. 342, 350; Mufīd, *Irshād*, II, pp. 106 f. *Bidāya* naturally does not mention this final retort of Nāfi'.

[83] Ṭabarī, II, p. 350; *Bidāya*, VIII, p. 183

[84] *History of the Arabs*, p. 191

[85] Fyzee, op. cit., p. 113

[86] cf. Hodgson, "How Did the Early Shī'a become Sectarian?" p. 3

[87] Ibn Nadīm, *Fihrist*, p. 93; Ṭūsī, *Fihrist*, Nos. 155, 585; Najāshī, *Rijāl*, p. 245; Ahlwardt, Nos. 9028–9, 9031–8; Ursula Sezgin, *Abū Mikhnaf, Ein Beitrag zur Historiographie der Umaiyadischen Zeit* (Leiden, 1971), pp. 116–23, a discussion of the *Maqtal* itself. On Ṭūsī and his *Fihrist*, see Sprenger's preface to his edition of this work in the *Bibliotheca Indica* (Calcutta, 1853), and Brown's discussion of biographical authorities in *A Literary History of Persia* (Cambridge, 1902–4), IV, pp. 355–8. On Najāshī also see Brown, loc. cit.

[88] See his preface to *The Arab Kingdom and its Fall*

[89] See above, note 87

[90] Wellhausen, loc. cit.

[91] *EI*² article "Abū Mikhnaf"

[92] Wellhausen, loc. cit.

[93] In the Istanbul Ms. of the *Ansāb*, Ḥusayn is discussed in Ms. 597, ff. 219a–251b

[94] For his revolt see Veccia Vaglieri, *EI*² article "Ibn al-Ash'ath", and sources cited therein.

95 Wellhausen, op. cit., p. vii
96 See Ṭabarī, index
97 e.g. Mufīd, *Irshād,* II, p. 29
98 See *Maqātil,* p. 95
99 See *Bidāya,* VIII, pp. 60, 61
100 See *Der Tod des Husein,* Wüstenfeld's preface
101 Sezgin, *Abū Mikhnaf,* pp. 190 ff.

Chapter 8

The Reaction after Karbalā

The martyrdom of Ḥusayn was of great religious significance and had a deep heart-searching after-effect upon the Shīʿīs, giving a new turn to the mode and nature of the Shīʿī movement. The tragic fate of the grandson of the Prophet stirred religious and moral sentiments, particularly among those of the Kūfan followers of the House of the Prophet who had so zealously asked Ḥusayn to come to Iraq to guide them on what they considered to be the path of God. But when Ḥusayn came to Iraq they did not or could not stand with him in the hour of trial. Soon afterwards, however, they realized that their inability, or rather weakness, had been the cause of the tragedy. A deep sense of repentance set in, provoking their religious conscience; and in order to expiate their negligence and obtain God's forgiveness, they thought they must make similar sacrifices. They believed that they could only prove their real repentance by exposing themselves to death while seeking vengeance for the blood of Ḥusayn. Hence they named themselves the *Tawwābūn* (penitents) and are known in Islamic history by this self-imposed title.[1] This movement, as will be seen below, proved to be an important step forward in the consolidation of Shīʿī Islam.

The movement began under the leadership of five of the oldest and most trusted associates of ʿAlī, with a following of a hundred diehard and devoted Shīʿīs of Kūfa, none of whom was below sixty years of age.[2] This age factor should particularly be noted, as it indicates the maturity of their religious thinking and behaviour. The five leaders of the movement, Sulaymān b. Ṣurad al-Khuzāʿī, Al-Musayyab b. Najaba al-Fazārī, ʿAbd Allāh b. Saʿd b. Nufayl al-Azdī, ʿAbd

Allāh b. Wālin at-Taymī, and Rifāʿa b. Shaddād al-Bajalī, had always been in the forefront of all Shīʿī activities in Kūfa, and were highly respected by the Shīʿa for their sincerity of purpose and unshaken devotion to the cause of the *Ahl al-Bayt.* Similarly, the other hundred who joined these leaders of the movement are described as "the most select from among the followers of ʿAlī".[3] Towards the end of 61/680 they held their first meeting in the house of Sulaymān b. Ṣurad.[4] This was the first opportunity for them to come out from their hiding places and meet together, since the state of martial law imposed on Kūfa before the massacre at Karbalā had now been relaxed.

Detailed accounts of this first meeting and the passionate speeches made by these five leaders are preserved for us by the sources. The first to speak was Al-Musayyab b. Najaba al-Fazārī. He said:

> "We invited the son of the daughter of our Prophet to come to Kūfa to guide us on the right path, but when he responded to our call we became greedy for our own lives until he was killed in our midst. What excuse would we have before our Lord, and before our Prophet when we meet him on the Day of Resurrection, while his most beloved son, family, and progeny were massacred in our midst. By God, there is no other way for us to expiate ourselves for the sin except to kill all his murderers and their associates or be killed. Perhaps by doing so our Lord may forgive our sin. You must, therefore, now select someone from among you as your leader, who can organize and mobilize you under his command and proceed with the plan of seeking God's forgiveness by taking the action which has been proposed."[5]

Rifāʿa b. Shaddād al-Bajalī, another senior member of the five leaders, then spoke, appealing passionately to the religious sentiments of those present. After emphasizing further what Al-Musayyab had said, he proposed:

> "Let us give command of our affairs to *Shaykh ash-Shīʿa,* the companion of the Prophet, possessor of priority in Islam, Sulaymān b. Ṣurad, the one praised for his intrepidity and for his religion and the one who has been dependable and reliable in his judiciousness and prudence (*ḥazm*)."[6]

The other three leaders named above spoke in the same vein and seconded the proposal to chooose Sulaymān as their leader on the same grounds as mentioned by Rifāʿa. It is important to note that the qualifications for the leadership of the movement, which was indeed dedicated to the Shīʿī cause, were companionship with the Prophet and priority or precedence in Islam (*sābiqa*). This, like many other instances, means that the main emphasis of the Shīʿīs was to enforce the Islamic ideal, which they thought could only be achieved through the *Ahl al-Bayt,* the people nearest to the Prophet.

Sulaymān b. Ṣurad, accepting the responsibility of leading the movement, made a forceful speech in which he laid down the severest standards required of those who wanted to participate and emphasized that they should be ready to sacrifice their lives for the noblest task ahead of them.[7] The response from all those present was equally enthusiastic. They pledged to seek God's pardon by fighting to the death the killers of the grandson of the Prophet. In order to prove the purity of their intentions many of them willed all of their properties and possessions, except for arms, as *ṣadaqāt* for the Muslims. Sulaymān appointed ʿAbd Allāh b. Wālin at-Taymī as the treasurer to collect the contributions made by the Shīʿa and to use the money for the preparation of the mission.[8] With no loss of time Sulaymān undertook the organization of the movement. He entered into correspondence with Shīʿī leaders in other cities, namely with Saʿd b. Ḥudhayfa al-Yamān in Al-Madā'in and Al-Muthannā b. Mukharriba al-ʿAbdī in Baṣra. The movement, however, went on secretly for about three years, increasing in numbers and strength and waiting for an appropriate time and opportunity.

Circumstances took a sudden turn in favour of the movement with the unexpected death of Yazīd in 64/683, encouraging the *Tawwābūn* to come out in the open. Some of the leading members urged Sulaymān to rise publicly, oust ʿAmr b. Ḥurayth, deputy of ʿAbd Allāh b. Ziyād, from the city, pursue those responsible for the blood of Ḥusayn, and call the people to support the *Ahl al-Bayt.* Sulaymān, however, opted for a more restrained policy, pointing out that the murderers of Ḥusayn were in fact the *ashrāf al-qabā'il* of Kūfa, who would have to pay for his blood. If the action were immediately directed against them, they would become very oppressive; and a revolt against them at this stage would achieve nothing but disaster or even the complete destruction of the Shīʿīs themselves. The purpose of avenging the blood of Ḥusayn would be lost. It would therefore be advisable, at this stage, to intensify their propaganda campaign only among their own Shīʿīs and among others throughout Kūfa, enlisting as much support as possible. He added that since Yazīd was now dead the people would join them more readily and quickly.[9] Sulaymān's suggestion prevailed and the movement, so far a secret organization, came into the open with an intensified campaign on a large scale. A number of emissaries began ceaselessly working to invite people to join the movement.

Abū Mikhnaf has preserved for us a speech of one of these emissaries, ʿUbayd Allāh al-Murrī. It is reported from a man of Muzayna, who said he heard it so many times that he learned it by heart. The narrator further comments that he had never seen anyone in his time more eloquent than Al-Murrī, and that the latter would never miss an opportunity to preach if he happened to see a group of people. He would begin by praising God and praying for His messenger. Then he would say:

> "God chose Muḥammad from among all His creatures for His Prophethood; He singled him out for all of His bounties. God strengthened you by making you his followers and honoured you with having faith in him; through Muḥammad, God saved you from the shedding of blood, and through him He made your dangerous paths safe and peaceful. 'You were on the brink of the pit of Fire and God saved you from it. Thus God makes His signs clear to you. Perhaps you may be guided.' (*Qur'ān,* III, 103). Has God created anyone from the first to the last with greater right over this *Umma* than its Prophet? Has the offspring of anyone from among the Prophets or the Messengers or anyone else greater right over this *Umma* than the offspring of its own Prophet? No, by God, this has never been the case, nor will it ever be. [O you people], you belong to God. Don't you see, don't you understand what a crime you have committed against the son of the daughter of your Prophet? Don't you see the people's violation of his sanctity, their slackness towards him while he was lonely and helpless, and their staining him with blood? They were pulling him violently on the ground, not thinking of God in regard of him nor his relationship to the Prophet. Eyes have never before seen the like of this. By God, Ḥusayn b. ʿAlī, what a betrayal of truth, forbearance, trust, nobility, and resolution: the

> son of the first Muslim in Islam and the son of the daughter of the Messenger of the Lord of the Worlds. Around him his defenders were few, and his attackers were in multitudes. His enemies killed him while his friends deserted him. Woe to the killers and reproaches to the deserters! God will accept no excuse from those who killed him, nor any argument from those who deserted him except that the latter should sincerely repent before God and fight against the killers and repudiate and eliminate the unjust and the corrupt. Only then, perhaps, God may accept our repentance and remove our guilt. We invite you to the Book of God and the *Sunna* of his Prophet, to vengeance for the blood of his [Prophet's] family and to war on the heretics and deviators from the true religion. If we are killed, there is nothing better for the pious than to be with their God; if we are successful, we will restore power to the *Ahl al-Bayt* of our Prophet."[10]

In all the preceding chapters dealing with the developments from the time of the death of the Prophet till the death of Ḥusayn, the Shīʿī doctrinal stand and their religio-political aspirations have repeatedly been pointed out. If we recall the arguments put forward by the supporters of ʿAlī on the occasions of the Saqīfa and the *Shūrā,* the contents of the letters written by Ḥasan to Muʿāwiya and that of Ḥusayn to the Shīʿīs of Kūfa and Baṣra, the pledges and statements made by the supporters of Ḥusayn at Karbalā, and the speeches delivered by the leaders of the *Tawwābūn* in their first meeting, Al-Murrī's exhortations can be seen as nothing other than an echoing of the same ideals. It would suffice to say that throughout Al-Murrī's speech the main emphasis is laid on Ḥusayn's relationship with the Prophet through Fāṭima. The name of ʿAlī appears only twice: the first time in Ḥusayn's name as "Ḥusayn b. ʿAlī", which was a usual way of describing anyone, and the second when Ḥusayn is mentioned as "the son of the first Muslim", but even in this his position as "the son of the daughter of our Prophet" is immediately referred to. (Even at the time of the Saqīfa and the *Shūrā* the main emphasis was on ʿAlī's nearness and close association and relationship with the Prophet.) Thus the *Tawwābūn* put far more emphasis on the idea of succession to the Prophet by blood than to ʿAlī by blood. The main part of the speech, that to kill the murderers of Ḥusayn in order to avenge his blood or be killed in order to expiate their failure in supporting

Ḥusayn, and thus to seek God's forgiveness, was a new dimension necessitated by the tragedy of Karbalā. Finally, a call to the Book of God and the *Sunna* of the Prophet, as has been pointed out earlier, was an implicit rejection of the precedent of the first three caliphs and thereby gave ʿAlī and other Imams of the family of the Prophet exclusive authority to interpret or reinterpret the Prophetic *Sunna.*

The campaign of the *Tawwābūn,* however, succeeded in gaining the support of 16,000 Kūfans,[11] since the situation in Kūfa was much more conducive to success now than ever before. The sudden death of Yazīd greatly weakened Umayyad control of the province. The sickly son of Yazīd, Muʿāwiya II, succeeded his father only six months before his own death, and the old Marwān b. al-Ḥakam managed to become the new Umayyad caliph. In Syria this led to a bloody conflict between the two rival tribal groups of Kalb and Qays, leaving the Umayyad capital in chaos and unable to maintain its firm control over neighbouring Iraq. In the Hijaz, ʿAbd Allāh b. az-Zubayr, who had already put forward his own claims to the caliphate and was taking advantage of Yazīd's death and of Syrian confusion and weakness, organized and consolidated his power afresh and assumed the title of *Amīr al-Muʾminīn.* The Umayyad governor and the strong man, ʿUbayd Allāh b. Ziyād, who resided in Baṣra as the governor of both Kūfa and Baṣra, was expelled by a rebellion of the inhabitants of the latter city and fled to Marwān in Syria. The Kūfans, on their part, ousted ʿAmr b. al-Ḥurayth, the deputy of Ibn Ziyād in Kūfa.[12] In the power vacuum, the *ashrāf* of Kūfa promptly wrote to ʿAbd Allāh b. az-Zubayr to take advantage of the situation and appoint his governor. With the Shīʿī groups emerging and the Syrian domination weakening, the tribal and clan leaders of Kūfa found it in their interest to align themselves with Ibn az-Zubayr, who represented the old Meccan-Qurayshite hegemony. Ibn az-Zubayr immediately sent to Kūfa ʿAbd Allāh b. Yazīd al-Anṣārī as his governor in charge of military affairs, and Ibrāhīm b. Muḥammad b. Ṭalḥa in charge of the *kharāj.*[13]

Now with the obstacles removed, Sulaymān b. Ṣurad started final preparations for action. He wrote to the Shīʿī leaders in Al-Madāʾin and Baṣra, calling them to be ready to rise to avenge the blood of Ḥusayn and to put right the affairs which had gone wrong and had become unjust. He asked them to meet at Nukhayla, outside Kūfa, on the first of Rabīʿ II of the next year, 65/684. The Shīʿī leader in Al-Madā'in, Saʿd b. Ḥudhayfa b. al-Yamān, called in the Shīʿa of that region and read the letter to them and received an enthusiastic response. The Shīʿī leader in Baṣra, Al-Muthannā b. Mukharriba al-ʿAbdī, also accepted the call and mobilized the Shīʿīs of that city. The long texts of these letters,[14] which Abū Mikhnaf has meticulously preserved for us, make extremely useful and revealing reading for an understanding of the religious sentiments and feelings and the doctrinal stand of the Shīʿa of this period. In essence these are much the same as the speeches of the *Tawwābūn* and that of Al-Murrī.

At this stage, Al-Mukhtār b. Abī ʿUbayda ath-Thaqafī, also a devoted follower of the *Ahl al-Bayt,* appeared in Kūfa. His mission was the same as that of the *Tawwābūn* insofar as the revenge for the blood of Ḥusayn and establishing the rights of the *Ahl al-Bayt* were concerned, but differed in that he wanted to achieve political authority through a more organized military power. Mukhtār, therefore, tried to persuade the *Tawwābūn* not to take any hasty action and to join him for a better chance of success. The *Tawwābūn* refused to join Mukhtār, as they had no wish to participate in any doubtful adventure or to deviate from their main purpose of atonement through sacrifice. They said that they would follow only *Shaykh ash-Shīʿa* Sulaymān b. Ṣurad.[15] Two points in Mukhtār's arguments with the *Tawwābūn* are worth noting here, since they reveal fundamental differences between them. Mukhtār said that firstly Sulaymān did not know how to organize the military for warfare, nor did he have any knowledge of diplomacy or politics; secondly, Mukhtār had been appointed by the Mahdī, Muḥammad b. al-Ḥanafīya, as his deputy, confidant, and minister to avenge the blood of Ḥusayn.[16] (Muḥammad b. al-Ḥanafīya was ʿAlī's third son from a Ḥanafite woman, and was not a descendant of the Prophet.) The refusal of the *Tawwābūn* to support Mukhtār on these grounds indicates that they were interested neither in purely military ventures nor in political affairs; nor were they ready to accept even the eldest surviving son of ʿAlī as their Imam, as he was not the direct descendant of the Prophet through Fāṭima. Thus the disagreement over strategy or tactics was secondary to the disagreement over the Imam.

Though the *Tawwābūn* did not openly proclaim any particular member of the *Ahl al-Bayt* as their Imam, there are strong indications that they believed that the rightful Imam was now Ḥusayn's surviving son ʿAlī, later known as Zayn al-ʿĀbidīn. There are many factors that support this view. Firstly, the very idea of the leadership based in the hereditary sanctity, which attracted the Arabs of Shīʿī tendency, was still confined to the progeny of Muḥammad through Fāṭima; it had been transferred from Ḥasan to Ḥusayn and not to any other member of the Hashimite clan. It has repeatedly been pointed out in what we have discussed so far that only rarely are Ḥasan and Ḥusayn described as the sons of ʿAlī; they were much more frequently referred to as "the son of the daughter of our Prophet". Secondly, the name of Muḥammad b. al-Ḥanafīya had not been cited at the time when the *Tawwābūn* first held their meeting soon after Karbalā in 61/680; Mukhtār arrived in Kūfa after the death of Yazīd in 64/684 and began his campaign in the name of Ibn al-Ḥanafīya. Thus the name of Ibn al-Ḥanafīya appeared for the first time four years later, when the *Tawwābūn* were almost ready for action. Thirdly, even Mukhtār, who was the main progenitor of Ibn al-Ḥanafīya's leadership, first approached ʿAlī b. al-Ḥusayn, as will be seen later, and only when the latter refused to involve himself in any public movement did Mukhtār turn to Ibn al-Ḥanafīya and ingratiate himself with his name.

Since ʿAlī b. al-Ḥusayn himself refused to make any public claims or to allow any claims to be made on his behalf, the *Tawwābūn* refrained from mentioning his name. Nevertheless, since certain vague references made by the *Tawwābūn* during their campaign, such as the verses composed by their poet, ʿAbd Allāh b. al-Aḥmar, in which he speaks of "a caller who invited them to salvation",[17] obviously refer to an Imam, and since the name of Ibn al-Ḥanafīya would not be associated with the imamate for another three years, the reference must have been to ʿAlī b. al-Ḥusayn. This is based on the fact that the Shīʿa of Kūfa had already established a precedent when they proclaimed Ḥasan b. ʿAlī, and not any other member of the Hashimite house, as the successor of his father. It seems also that the *Tawwābūn,* after their sad experience vis-à-vis Ḥusayn, decided not to put forward ʿAlī b. al-Ḥusayn's name for the leadership until they had been successful in throwing off Umayyad rule in Kūfa or else sacrificing themselves in active repentance for their failure in carrying out their duties with regard to Ḥusayn.

The main body of the *Tawwābūn,* however, refused to join Mukhtār, though at least 2,000 of these who had registered their names with Sulaymān did switch over to him, obviously in the hope of better political prospects.

As the time for action was approaching, Sulaymān b. Ṣurad and other leaders of the movement were putting more and more emphasis on disavowing any intention of political conquest and discouraged those who might have joined them for material benefits or worldly gains. According to their plan, in the beginning of Rabīʿ II, 65/November, 684, they raised their call for "revenge for the blood of Ḥusayn (*yā latha'rāt al-Ḥusayn*)" and set out on their mission. They gathered at Nukhayla, a suburb of Kūfa, from where they had to march against the forces of ʿUbayd Allāh b. Ziyād, the Umayyad governor who had been responsible for the massacre at Karbalā. The rigorous standards set by Sulaymān b. Ṣurad, however, proved to be too much for the majority of the volunteers: of the 16,000 who had registered themselves, only 4,000 came to the rendezvous at Nukhayla. The governor of Ibn al-Zubayr, ʿAbd Allāh b. Yazīd, tried to dissuade them from carrying out their plans and suggested to Sulaymān that he wait until the former could prepare an army to join them. They refused to change their plan or to accept his help,[18] as it would have compromised their whole position. Their intention was to avenge the blood of Ḥusayn, to establish the Shīʿī imamate or to die. They were prepared to die rather than to have ʿAbd Allāh b. Yazīd's non-Shīʿī support. If they had accepted it they would have merely been joining one political faction, the supporters of Ibn az-Zubayr, against another, the Umayyads. Now, with the *Tawwābūn* volunteers reduced from 16,000 to 4,000, they could hardly hope for any success except in fighting to the death and seeking atonement and repentance. They were determined to carry out their pledges to themselves.

They spent three days in prayer and remembrance of God

at Nukhayla. The Shī'a from Al-Madā'in and Baṣra had not yet arrived, and some of those at Nukhayla wanted to await their arrival, but Sulaymān insisted that they should proceed without further delay. He told them:

> "There are two kinds of people. There are those who want the benefits of the hereafter, who hurry towards it and do not seek any worldly reward; and there are those whose acts are motivated by worldly gains. You are going for the benefits of the life hereafter: remember God in abundance in any situation and you will soon attain nearness to God and receive His best reward by fighting in His way and being patient in all calamities. Let us then proceed to our goal."[19]

According to Balādhurī the people responded from all sides, "We are not seeking the world and we have not come out for it."[20] But in the morning another 1,000 were missing from his army. Sulaymān was not discouraged and merely said that it was better that such people should go.

From Nukhayla the *Tawwābūn* first went to Karbalā to the grave of Ḥusayn, where they gave themselves up to wild and unprecedented expressions of grief, weeping and wailing for the suffering and tragic death of the grandson of the Prophet.[21] Wellhausen points out that this was the first incidence of the glorification of the grave of Ḥusayn and was purely Arabian in its character and nature since the Arabs were used to glorifying the Black Stone fixed in the Ka'ba.[22] After spending a day and night in mourning they left the grave of Ḥusayn.

When they reached the village of Qarqisīya, the fifth stage from Karbalā on the road to the Syrian border, they were generously entertained by the chief of the village, Zufar b. al-Ḥārith, who informed them that 'Ubayd Allāh b. Ziyād, with a 30,000-man Syrian army, had reached 'Ayn al-Warda. The chieftain provided Sulaymān with plenty of provisions and advised him further about 'Ubayd Allāh's army and gave him the names of other leaders who were with him. Zufar also told Sulaymān that he, along with his people, would fight the Syrians if the *Tawwābūn* would stay with him and use Qarqisīya as a base. But Sulaymān did not agree.

The *Tawwābūn* ultimately reached 'Ayn al-Warda and engaged the Syrians fiercely, shouting, "Paradise! Paradise for the Turābites!"[23] The battle lasted for three days, and the *Tawwābūn* fought with unprecedented resolution, determination, and zeal. Even though greatly outnumbered, on the first day they inflicted heavy losses on the Syrians. On the second day, however, their own losses began to tell and their leaders fell one after the other. The first to be killed was Sulaymān b. Ṣurad himself, followed by Al-Musayyab b. Najaba, ʿAbd Allāh b. Saʿd b. Nufayl, and then ʿAbd Allāh b. Wālin at-Taymī, each taking the leadership and the *Tawwābūn* standard in succession one after the other. By the end of the third day the majority of the *Tawwābūn* had fulfilled their pledge to sacrifice their lives in the name of Ḥusayn. The only surviving leader, Rifāʿa b. Shaddād, advised the handful of survivors to return, and while on their way back they were met by the Shīʿis of Al-Madā'in and Baṣra, who had been coming to join them, but now turned back to Qarqisīya.[24]

In an attempt to analyse the *Tawwābūn* movement, a few points are conspicuous. Firstly, all the 3,000 *Tawwābūn* who fought in the battle were Arabs: there were no *mawālī* among them.[25] It was Mukhtār who first mobilized the Persian *mawālī* in active participation, thus giving the Shīʿī movement a wider appeal. Secondly, among these 3,000 *Tawwābūn,* though the majority were from South Arabian or Yemeni tribes, the northern and central Arabian tribes of Muḍar and Rabīʿa were by no means under-represented. In fact, the second in command, Al-Musayyab b. Najaba, was from Muḍar. Looking at the names of some of the *Tawwābūn* as given by the sources,[26] one finds that many of the chief tribes of the Arabs of both Yemenis and Nizārīs were well represented. Thus Shīʿī feelings were not confined to any single group of the Arabs. Thirdly, the penitent army included a very large number of the original *qurrā'* of Kūfa,[27] all the five leaders being among them.

All of these facts, however, indicate two fundamental points. Firstly, the Shīʿī movement till the time of the *Tawwābūn* (65/684) was still purely Arabian in character and totally untouched by non-Arab elements, doctrinal or otherwise. And secondly, the movement of the *Tawwābūn* was totally a religious affair. Ḥusayn himself, when he met Yazīd's army, was fully aware of his dignity as the grandson of the Prophet, as well as the son of ʿAlī, and the *Tawwābūn* by their action were certainly combining loyalty to ʿAlī with loyalty to Muḥammad himself, and thus were taking the matter strictly as a religious issue. Finally, if we compare the feeling and the expressions of those of the Shīʿa who gave up their lives with Ḥusayn at Karbalā, as explained in the previous chapter, with the speeches and expressions made by the *Tawwābūn,* recorded earlier in this chapter, we find that the arguments and sentiments of both groups were based on the same religious principles.

But there is a great difference between the two, however. At Karbalā the presence of Ḥusayn himself was a great personal obligation on the Shīʿa who fought and were killed with him. In the case of the *Tawwābūn* there was no personal binding force which could keep them zealous enough to make them die except a strong feeling of duty and a deep sense of religious obligation. Thus the *Tawwābūn* pushed Shīʿism another step forward towards an independent and self-sustaining existence.

Notes to Chapter 8

[1] Balādhurī, V, pp. 204 ff.; Ṭabarī, II, p. 497; Masʿūdī, *Murūj*, III, p. 93; Wellhausen, *Die religiös-politischen Oppositionsparteien im alten Islam*, trans. ʿAbd ar-Raḥmān Badawī, *Aḥzāb al-muʿāraḍa as-siyāsīya al-dīnīya fī ṣadr al-Islām* (Cairo, 1968), p. 189

[2] Ṭabarī, II, p. 498; Wellhausen, loc. cit.

[3] Ṭabarī, II, p. 498; Balādhurī, V, pp. 204 f.

[4] Ṭabarī, II, p. 497; Balādhurī, loc. cit.

[5] Ṭabarī, II, p. 498; Balādhurī, V, p. 205

[6] Ṭabarī, II, p. 499; Balādhurī, loc. cit.

[7] Ṭabarī, II, pp. 499 f.; Balādhurī, V, pp. 205 f.

[8] Ṭabarī, loc. cit.; Balādhurī, loc. cit.

[9] Ṭabarī, II, pp. 506–7

[10] Ṭabarī, II, pp. 507–8

[11] Balādhurī, V, p. 208

[12] Balādhurī, V. p. 207

[13] Balādhurī, V, p. 207; Ṭabarī, II, p. 509

[14] Ṭabarī, II, pp. 502–5

[15] Balādhurī, V, p. 207; Ṭabarī, II, p. 509

[16] Balādhurī, loc. cit.; Ṭabarī, loc. cit.

[17] Masʿūdī, *Murūj*, III, p. 93

[18] Ṭabarī, II, pp. 543 f.; Balādhurī, V, p. 209

[19] Ṭabarī, II, p. 545

[20] Balādhurī, V, p. 209

[21] Balādhurī, loc. cit.; Ṭabarī, II, p. 546; Wellhausen, *Aḥzāb*, p. 194

[22] *Aḥzāb*, p. 194. Cf. Ṭabarī, II, p. 546; Balādhurī, V, p. 209

[23] Masʿūdī, *Murūj*, III, p. 94. "Turābites": reference to Abū Turāb, ʿAlī's *kunyā*

[24] See the detailed account of ʿAyn al-Warda in Balādhurī, V, pp. 210 f.; Ṭabarī, II, pp. 558 ff; Masʿūdī, *Muruj*, III, p. 94

[25] Wellhausen, *Aḥzab*, p. 194

[26] See Ṭabarī, II, pp. 497, 559, 566, 599, 601; Balādhurī, V, pp. 207 ff.; Wellhausen, loc. cit.

[27] Wellhausen, loc. cit.

Chapter 9

The Struggle for Legitimacy

What has so far been said completes the first and fundamental phase in the history of the development of Shīʿī Islam. In this phase a rather specific direction, a well-defined trend of thought, an ideal of polity, and an underlying principle of religious adherence were established which can easily be distinguished as the Shīʿī interpretation of Islam. Perhaps even at this early stage one can discern the basic difference between the Shīʿa and the rest of the community, for while the former preferred to accept the leadership of only those who derived their authority directly from the person of the Prophet and in this way enjoyed divine sanction, the latter vested the authority for the leadership in the community as a whole, which was thus entitled to choose the leader.

With the death of Ḥusayn, however, Shīʿism entered the second phase of its history. While the basic principle remained the same, disagreements arose over the specific criteria for deciding who the divinely inspired leader was, and this led to the internal division of Shīʿī Islam. A study of the history of religions would show that a common phenomenon of world religions and their factions has been that they always split over certain details when they enter the second phase of their development. Islam too, and within it both the major groups of Shīʿīs and Sunnīs, could not escape this fate.

We have seen in the previous chapter that shortly before the *Tawwābūn* marched against the Syrians, Mukhtār arrived in Kūfa and tried to gain the support of Sulaymān b. Ṣurad and his followers for his own plan to rise against the Umayyads. The *Tawwābūn,* however, refused to join him. The personality and character of Mukhtār have been subjected to a great controversy in early Shīʿī history. Some sources present him as an ambitious adventurer seeking political authority for himself in the name of the *Ahl al-Bayt*. Others give him the benefit of the doubt and accept that his actions were in reality motivated by his love for the family of the Prophet, though his approach and tactics were different from those of the *Tawwābūn*.

An exhaustive scrutiny of the sources may well prove that he was a devoted follower of the House of ʿAlī and a sincere supporter of their cause, but whatever the case may be, the fact remains that he has generally been treated rather unsympathetically by the sources of different schools for different reasons. The Twelver Shīʿī sources present him in an unfavourable light since it was he who for the first time began propaganda for the Imamate of Muḥammad b. al-Ḥanafīya, thus deviating from the line of Fāṭima. The non-Shīʿī sources, on the other hand, seem to have been influenced by the anti-Mukhtār propaganda launched by both the sympathizers of Ibn az-Zubayr and those of the Umayyads. No serious study has so far been done on Mukhtār, and the sketchy accounts given by some of the modern scholars[1] are generally influenced, without a critical assessment, by the sources usually hostile to him. Recently, however, Hodgson has hinted that the blackening of Mukhtār's reputation and the attempt to discredit him began from the time of his death.[2]

The fact, however, remains that Mukhtār, in all probability due to the quiescent policy of Zayn al-ʿĀbidīn, to be discussed below, was responsible for shifting the Imamate from the descendants of the Prophet through Fāṭima to another son of ʿAlī, Muḥammad b. al-Ḥanafīya, thus creating the first deviation from the *legitimist* body of the Shīʿa. The word *legitimist* may not be a good expression, but it is perhaps the nearest English approximation to the idea of a *central body* of the Shīʿa, where the Imamate remained strictly restricted in the line of ʿAlī and Fāṭima, coming from Ḥasan to Ḥusayn and then through explicit nomination from father to son, usually to the eldest surviving son, until it ended with the twelfth Imam. Our intention in the following chapters is, therefore, to restrict our attention to the survey of this *legitimist* or *central body* of the Shīʿa, which was reduced to an almost insignificant number after the death of Ḥusayn by the newly emerging revolutionary or Messianic branches of the Shīʿa. The use of the term *legitimist* and *central body* may seem at this stage arbitrary and a premature description of a later development; nevertheless, the fact remains that it was this legitimist faction which ultimately re-emerged as the largest and thus the central body of the Shīʿa, and was eventually to be known as the *Imāmīya* or *Ithnā-ʿasharīya* (Twelver) Shīʿa. The movement of Mukhtār and the idea of the *Mahdī* attached to the person of Muḥammad b. al-Ḥanafīya, with its extremist and esoteric doctrines, or other ramifications of the Shīʿa, are therefore beyond the scope of this study.

It may, however, be pointed out here for future reference that from this time of the confusion in the leadership which followed the death of Ḥusayn, this study has to address itself to two different questions: first, how legitimist Shīʿism maintained its separate identity without being absorbed into the emerging Sunnī synthesis; and second, how it maintained its own character distinct from the revolutionary and extremist branches within Shīʿism itself. To resist the latter form of absorption was indeed more difficult, since extremist and revolutionary ideas are often more appealing than moderate ones.

As long as Ḥusayn was alive the Shīʿīs remained united, considering him the only head and Imam of the House of the Prophet. But his sudden death and the quiescent attitude of his only surviving son ʿAlī, more commonly known as Zayn al-ʿĀbidīn, left the Shīʿa in confusion and created a vacuum in the active leadership of the followers of the *Ahl al-Bayt*. Thus the period following Ḥusayn's death marks the first conflict over the leadership of the followers of ʿAlī, resulting in the division of the Shīʿa into various groups.

ʿAlī Zayn al-ʿĀbidīn was the only one of the sons of Ḥusayn whose life was spared during the massacre at Karbalā, since he did not take part in the fighting due to illness. He was at that time twenty-three years old.[3] After his return from Karbalā, Zayn al-ʿĀbidīn lived in Medina for most of his life, avoiding any political involvement as much as he could. The tragedy of Karbalā left a deep mark on him and it was only too natural that he bore a deep grudge against the Umayyads, holding them responsible for the massacre of his father and all other family members. In spite of this feeling, however, he refrained from expressing any hostile attitude towards them. As a result, the Umayyads also tried to maintain good relations with him; in particular, Marwān b. al-Ḥakam and his son ʿAbd al-Malik even showed a certain respect and affection for him.[4]

When the Medinese rose against Yazīd b. Muʿāwiya in the year 62/681, Zayn al-ʿĀbidīn, in order to emphasize his neutrality in the political struggle in the community, left Medina and went to stay on his estate outside the city.[5] When Marwān, the governor of Medina, was compelled by the Medinese to leave the city, he took his wife to Zayn al-ʿĀbidīn and asked him to protect her. Zayn al-ʿĀbidīn demonstrated his magnanimity by accepting this responsibility; he sent her to Ṭā'if escorted by his son ʿAbd Allāh.[6] When Yazīd's army, led by Muslim b. ʿUqba, however, defeated the Medinese in the battle of Ḥarra, and sacked and looted the city, Zayn al-ʿĀbidīn and his family were left unmolested. Moreover, while all the Medinese were obliged to take a humiliating oath of allegiance, declaring themselves slaves of the Caliph Yazīd, Zayn al-ʿĀbidīn was exempted.[7] If this information, so widely reported by the sources, on the one hand illustrates the neutral policy of Zayn al-ʿĀbidīn, on the other hand it also indicated that the Umayyads, after killing Ḥusayn, began to realize the respect and regard which the progeny of the Prophet commanded among the majority of the Muslims.

In the conflict between the Umayyads and ʿAbd Allāh b. az-Zubayr, Zayn al-ʿĀbidīn remained neutral. Ibn az-Zubayr did him no harm, but held him in Mecca under his supervision. Still another important factor in Zayn al-ʿĀbidīn's policy was his reserved attitude towards Mukhtār, who tried his best to gain his explicit support. Besides many approaches to Zayn al-ʿĀbidīn, which Mukhtār made while he was in the Hijaz, he even wrote a letter to Zayn al-ʿĀbidīn from Kūfa, offering his allegiance.[8] In avenging the blood of Ḥusayn, Mukhtār beheaded most of those responsible for the tragedy. The head of ʿUbayd Allāh b. Ziyād, the chief architect of the massacre at Karbalā, was sent by Mukhtār to Zayn al-ʿĀbidīn, not to Ibn al-Ḥanafīya, and was delivered in a most dramatic manner.[9] The son of Ḥusayn is reported to have been seen so happy at that occasion that people said that they had never noticed him so elated since that tragedy at Karbalā. Nevertheless, he continued his reserved and withdrawn attitude towards Mukhtār. The sources even report Zayn al-ʿĀbidīn as publicly denouncing Mukhtār in violent terms which seem to warrant serious examination.[10] If these reports are correct, however, the reason for Zayn al-ʿĀbidīn's resentful attitude towards Mukhtār seems to have been the latter's proclamation of Ibn al-Ḥanafīya's imamate, which Zayn al-ʿĀbidīn considered as the usurpation of his own rights.

Shīʿī sources record a number of traditions stating that Ḥusayn expressly appointed Zayn al-ʿĀbidīn as his successor. The most commonly reported tradition in this connection is that Ḥusayn, before leaving for Iraq, entrusted Umm Salima, the widow of the Prophet, with his will and letters, enjoining her to hand them over to the eldest of his male offspring in case he himself did not return. Zayn al-ʿĀbidīn was the only son who came back and so he was given his father's will and became his nominee.[11] Another tradition states that Ḥusayn nominated Zayn al-ʿĀbidīn as his successor and the next Imam of the House of the Prophet just before he went out to meet the Umayyad forces for the last encounter at Karbalā.[12] There is no criterion for an historian either to accept or to reject this sort of tradition. Perhaps the only guiding principle which may be used is the general tendency of the epoch and the common practice of the people of that period. Judging from this angle, we may recall our earlier comment in Chapter 7 that Ḥusayn, by virtue of his family and his own position therein as the grandson of the Prophet, thought that it was his right to be the Imam of the community. It would therefore be natural to think that he bequeathed his heritage to his son to maintain his family's tradition of leadership coming down from the Prophet. Nevertheless, the fact remains unchallenged that after Ḥusayn's death the majority of the Shīʿīs followed Muḥammad b. al-Ḥanafīya and not Zayn al-ʿĀbidīn, though the *Tawwābūn,* as we have seen, thought of the latter as their prospective Imam. Even the remnants of the *Tawwābūn* who survived the battle of ʿAyn al-Warda were attracted by Mukhtār to the side of Ibn al-Ḥanafīya.[13] The reason was obvious. The Shīʿīs in Kūfa, especially the *mawālī* among them, wanted an active movement which could relieve them from the oppressive rule of the Syrians. They found an outlet only under the banner of Mukhtār, and saw a ray of hope in the Messianic role propagated by him for Ibn al-Ḥanafīya.

On his part, Ibn al-Ḥanafīya did not repudiate Mukhtār's propaganda for his Imamate and Messianic role; he nevertheless maintained a carefully non-committal attitude and never openly raised his claims to the heritage of Ḥusayn.[14] It is indeed difficult to say whether Ibn al-Ḥanafīya's policy of not publicly laying claims to the leadership of the Shīʿīs was because of the serious risk such a claim would have entailed or because he was aware of the fact that he was not the descendant of the Prophet. We have repeatedly pointed out throughout this work, from the event of Saqīfa till the movement of the *Tawwābūn,* that the main emphasis of the Shīʿīs regarding the leadership of the community has been focused upon the direct relationship to the Prophet. With reference to Ḥasan and Ḥusayn, we always find far more emphasis on the idea of succession to the Prophet by blood than to ʿAlī by blood. If all these overwhelming reports have any historic merit, then it seems very strange indeed that immediately after Ḥusayn's death the emphasis has so suddenly changed from the lineage of the Prophet to that of ʿAlī. It is, therefore, most probable that, besides political danger, Ibn al-Ḥanafīya, not being the descendant of the Prophet, was hesitant to claim the Imamate for himself. This also explains why Mukhtār was first so anxious to gain the support of Zayn al-ʿĀbidīn; and when he lost all hopes of winning the son of Ḥusayn, only then did he turn to Ibn al-Ḥanafīya. As for the other part of the problem, that is, how the Shīʿīs of Kūfa so readily changed their attitude and accepted as their Imam a son of ʿAlī who was not the descendant of the Prophet, whereas Zayn al-ʿĀbidīn was, some explanation must be sought. Perhaps the only answer to the riddle may be found in the fact that most of the original and main body of the Shīʿa, with a clear doctrinal stand regarding the idea of the leadership, had been much reduced in number, first in the Karbalā massacre with Ḥusayn, and then in the battle of ʿAyn al-Warda under the command of Sulaymān b. Ṣurad al-Khuzāʿī. They were not only the hard core and well grounded in their Shīʿī ideals, but also provided intellectual and religious leadership and guidance to the masses of the Shīʿa of Kūfa. After Karbalā and ʿAyn al-Warda, what remained in Kūfa in the name of the Shīʿa were mostly the wavering commoners of the Arabs and the *mawālī*, who in that desperate situation could not make the delicate doctrinal distinction between merely a son of ʿAlī and a son of ʿAlī from Fāṭima. To them, ʿAlī was, after all, the cousin of the Prophet and also a member of the priestly clan of Hāshim. That the sanctity of the Banū Hāshim was confined to Muḥammad after the Prophethood had been bestowed on him, to the exclusion of other members of the family of Hāshim, as understood by the original body of the Shīʿa, was lost among these commoners. They were thus easily carried away by the talented eloquence of Mukhtār and his successful propaganda for Ibn al-Ḥanafīya as the deliverer (Mahdī) from the tyranny and injustice inflicted upon them by the Umayyads. It was, therefore, not so much the rights and personality of Ibn al-Ḥanafīya which made the masses of the Shīʿīs of Kūfa accept him as Mahdī-Imam as it was their desperate yearning for a deliverer from Umayyad domination and oppressive rule. A careful examination of Mukhtār's propaganda for Ibn al-Ḥanafīya would show that the overriding emphasis in introducing him was on his role as Mahdī and not so much on his being the Imam. This may prove to have been the main factor which attracted people to him.

Once, however, the idea was implanted it found its way and swept away most of the unstable Shīʿī masses. Once it became a popular movement with certain hopes pinned to it, even some of the remnants of the original Shīʿa were also carried away. It is indeed difficult to resist what we may call a popular appeal and, especially in the situation prevalent in Iraq at that time, even some of the firm believers in the leadership of the descendant of the Prophet could not remain unaffected. Thus the Mahdism of Ibn al-Ḥanafīya soon became the order of the day among the Shīʿīs of Kūfa. And, in course of time, the idea was popularly spread and accepted by the people and developed its own doctrines and dogma, legends and beliefs. It produced its own poets, such as Kuthayyir and Sayyid al-Ḥimyarī and others. The majority of the Shīʿa thus in that particular period became the followers of the Mahdī-Imam (and not of the Imam only) attached to the person of Ibn al-Ḥanafīya, and eclipsed, though only for a short period of time, the Imams from the line of Ḥusayn.

Being the son of Ḥusayn and the eldest surviving descendant of the Prophet, Zayn al-ʿĀbidīn could not tolerate this situation for long. Though he maintained his quiescent policy of not getting involved in any politico-religious movement, he nevertheless resisted the acceptance of Muḥammad b. al-Ḥanafīya as the Imam, and the latter's own silence, which to Zayn al-ʿĀbidīn seemed to imply Ibn al-Ḥanafīya's tacit approval of Mukhtār's propaganda. The traditions recorded in this connection by Shīʿī traditionists[15] may or may not be authentic in their details, but it does seem that he did make known to the people his own claims to the heritage of the House of the Prophet against those made on behalf of his uncle. This is deduced from the fact that some of those of the prominent Shīʿīs who had become followers of Ibn al-Ḥanafīya, such as Abū Khālid al-Kābulī,[16] Qāsim b. ʿAwf,[17] and a few others, abandoned Ibn al-Ḥanafīya and went over to Zayn al-ʿĀbidīn's side. The nucleus of his following, though, was not formed before 73/692, the year which marks the death of Ibn az-Zubayr and a complete collapse of the political aspirations of the peoples of the Hijaz and Iraq. The majority of the Shīʿīs, however, continued to recognize the Imamate of Ibn al-Ḥanafīya and later on his son Abū-Hāshim ʿAbd Allāh.

Towards the end of his life Zayn al-ʿĀbidīn seems to have succeeded in gathering round himself a small group of his adherents, some of them quite prominent figures of the erstwhile followers of the *Ahl al-Bayt.* Among them, apart from Yaḥyā b. Umm aṭ-Ṭiwāl[18] and Muḥammad b. Jubayr b. Muṭʿim[19] was also Jābir b. ʿAbd Allāh al-Anṣārī,[20] a respected Companion of the Prophet and a devoted supporter of ʿAlī b. Abī Ṭālib. On account of his prestige as one of the most devoted Companions of the Prophet who took part in the pledge of Al-ʿAqaba and in the *Bayʿat ar-Riḍwān,* Jābir's recognition of Zayn al-ʿĀbidīn was of great significance for the latter. Another important figure was the Kūfan Saʿīd b. al-Jubayr,[21] a *mawlā* of Banū Asad and a warm-hearted and brave man who even refused to hide his partisanship and support for the House of the Prophet. A well-known traditionist, Sa'īd was Zayn al-'Ābidīn's main spokesman and gained for the son of Ḥusayn many sympathizers among the ranks of his fellow traditionists, especially from the old companions of 'Alī b. Abī Ṭālib. The group of Zayn al-'Ābidīn's active supporters also included two young but energetic Kūfans: Abū Hamza Thābit b. Dīnār,[22] an Arab from the tribe of Azd, and Furāt b. Aḥnaf al-'Abdī.[23] Their attachment to the family of Ḥusayn remained strong, and both were later close companions of Zayn al-'Ābidīn's son and successor Muḥammad al-Bāqir. That these people became the followers of Ḥusaynid Imams and were in the close circles of Zayn al-'Ābidīn and then of Muḥammad al-Bāqir is further indicated by the fact that a great number of Shī'ī traditions from the above-mentioned Imams are frequently transmitted on their authority.[24] Obviously the Twelver Shī'ī traditionists would not have accepted them in their *isnāds* had they not been the followers of these Imams. Thus there seems to be no serious reason to doubt the reports that these people formed a nucleus of the followers of Zayn al-'Ābidīn.

Perhaps the most important role in enhancing Zayn al-'Ābidīn's prestige was played by Farazdaq, a renowned poet of the time. He composed numerous verses to propagate the cause of Zayn al-'Ābidīn, the most famous of which was his *qaṣīda* (ode) in praise of the Imam, which celebrates the occasion when the Caliph Hishām b. 'Abd al-Malik was overshadowed by the respect the people demonstrated for the great-grandson of the Prophet. It was at the time of the *Ḥajj* when both of them were trying to reach the Black Stone in the crowded Ka'ba. The people gave way to Zayn al-'Ābidīn while the Caliph was struggling to reach the relic. This deeply offended Hishām, and in a sarcastic manner he inquired who was the person to whom the people gave preference. Farazdaq, present at the scene, upon hearing this remark, spontaneously composed the *qaṣīda* and recited it, addressing Hishām. A few lines from this famous *qaṣīda,* which is also considered as one of the masterpieces of Farazdaq and of Arabic literature, are worth quoting:

> It is one whose footsteps are well known to every spot
> and it is he who is known to the *Bayt* [Ka'ba], in Mecca,
> the most frequented sanctuary.

It is he who is the son of the best of all
men of God [reference to the Prophet],
and it is he who is the most pious and devout,
pure and unstained, chaste and righteous
and a symbol [of Islam].
This is ʿAlī [b. al-Ḥusayn], whose father is the Prophet,
and it was through the light of his [the Prophet's] guidance
that the darkened road changed into the straight path.
This is the son of Fāṭima, if you are ignorant of him;
and with his great-grandfather the Prophethood
came to an end
and Muḥammad became the seal of the Prophets.
Whosoever recognizes his God knows also
the primacy and superiority of this man [ʿAlī b. al-Ḥusayn],
because religion reached the nations
through his house.[25]

The authenticity of this famous *qaṣīda* of Farazdaq, and also the occasion at which it was composed and recited, has never been questioned by anyone. It must therefore be taken as a most reliable and useful contemporary document describing Zayn al-ʿĀbidīn, with particular emphasis on his noble birth as a descendant of the Prophet as distinct from Muḥammad b. al-Ḥanafīya. One may note with interest that the poet, in praising Zayn al-ʿĀbidīn, describes him with emphasis on his being the grandson of Fāṭima and the great-grandson of Muḥammad, while he does not refer to his being the grandson of ʿAlī b. Abī Ṭālib.

Farazdaq, however, had to pay for his praise of the Imam, and was imprisoned by the order of Hishām. When Zayn al-ʿĀbidīn heard about the misfortune of the poet, he sent him a gift of 12,000 dirhams, but Farazdaq refused to accept it, saying that he had composed the poem purely from his religious zeal. Farazdaq remained in prison and then began to satirize Hishām. Fearing the poet's biting tongue, the prince released him.[26]

All these reports of Zayn al-ʿĀbidīn's adherents suggest that the Ḥusaynid line had never ceased to be a focus of devotion and special regard, though in this period by a small minority of the Shīʿīs, and that Zayn al-ʿĀbidīn gathered around himself a committed following who looked upon him as the legitimist Imam of the House of the Prophet. Yet it cannot be denied that in the period between the death of

Ḥusayn in 61/680 and the death of Ibn az-Zubayr in 73/692, Zayn al-ʿĀbidīn was left without any active following. Indeed, the *Tawwābūn* did consider, it seems, that Zayn al-ʿĀbidīn was their Imam, but they never declared it publicly; and the small number of them who survived the battle of ʿAyn al-Warda went over to Mukhtār and thus accepted Ibn al-Ḥanafīya as their Imam. This is confirmed even by Muḥammad al-Bāqir in one of his traditions quoted by Kashshī, which must be accepted as genuine. Muḥammad al-Bāqir said: "After the death of Ḥusayn all the people apostatised except three—Abū Khālid al-Kābulī, Yaḥyā b. Umm aṭ-Ṭiwāl, and Jubayr b. Muṭʿim—and only later did others join them and their numbers increased."[27] Moreover, that Zayn al-ʿĀbidīn was not of much significance as an Imam or leader of any visible group until the year 73/692 is further evident from the fact that among the ʿAlids, including Ibn al-Ḥanafīya, whom Ibn az-Zubayr held in the prison of ʿĀrim, the name of Zayn al-ʿĀbidīn is nowhere mentioned. This means that he was of no potential danger to Ibn az-Zubayr and that until that time he remained quiet and did not make his claims to the Imamate publicly. Silence does not, however imply the complete absence of an idea, the expression of which often depends on the prevailing circumstances and opportunities.

Apart from the small number of followers, mentioned above, who looked upon Zayn al-ʿĀbidīn with special regard as their Imam and the only religious authority of the time, he was also held in great respect and high esteem by the learned circles in Medina in general. This was the period when there was a growing sympathy and regard for the descendants of the Prophet among the people, though it was indeed altogether different from that of the Shīʿīs. This was also the period of growing interest in Medina in Prophetic traditions, especially those dealing with legal matters. This was the "epoch of the seven lawyers of Medina" whom we have mentioned in the second chapter of this book. In this setting of Medina we find that Zayn al-ʿĀbidīn was considered an eminent traditionist in the Medinese circle of scholars. The greatest Medinese lawyer of this time, Saʿīd b. al-Musayyab, regarded the Imam with the highest esteem.[28] The Shīʿī sources assert that Saʿīd was a follower of the Imam, which cannot be true. In fact, though Saʿīd respected Zayn al-ʿĀbidīn and was also a close friend of his, he did not have common views in legal matters with him. However, at that time the schools of legal thought were still in their embryonic state, and therefore there might not have been many serious differences of opinion between Zayn al-ʿĀbidīn and Saʿīd. Yet it is possible that the former, as well as his uncle, Muḥammad b. al-Ḥanafīya, adhered only to the traditions related on the authority of ʿAlī b. Abī Ṭālib.

Another great jurist and traditionist of the period, Az-Zuhrī, was also a great friend and admirer of the Imam. The honorific name *Zayn al-ʿĀbidīn* (the ornament of the pious), due to his excessive prayers, was given to him by Az-Zuhrī;[29] from the overwhelming reports recorded by both the Shīʿī and the Sunnī authorities,[30] it seems, however, that Zayn al-ʿĀbidīn was widely respected by the community in general for his extraordinary qualities, such as the long duration of his prayers, his piety, and his generosity. His piety must have been of a high degree, for he was not inclined to making a show of his virtues. When travelling with people who did not know him, he remained incognito so as not to take advantage of the fact that the Prophet was his ancestor.[31]

Zayn al-Ābidīn died in the year 94/712–713, and was buried in the cemetery of Al-Baqīʿ. He lived thirty-four years after the death of Ḥusayn, a period long enough to establish himself as the trustee of the heritage of his father, and to leave an imprint of his personality on his followers and associates.

According to the unanimous Shīʿī traditions, before his death Zayn al-ʿĀbidīn nominated Muḥammad al-Bāqir, his eldest son, as his *waṣī* and successor to his heritage.[32] One may doubt the existence of any explicit will of Ḥusayn for the nomination of Zayn al-ʿĀbidīn as his successor, but we should accept the tradition that Zayn al-ʿĀbidīn, before his death, must have explicitly nominated his son Al-Bāqir, at least in the circle of his adherents. The obvious factor in support of the credibility of this tradition is that during Zayn al-ʿĀbidīn's time the majority of the Shīʿīs abandoned the Ḥusaynid line and went over to Ibn al-Ḥanafīya, and then accepted the Imamate of the latter's son, Abū Hāshim; Zayn al-ʿĀbidīn thought this a usurpation of his rights and, not without much difficulty, succeeded in winning over a group of followers on the principle of legitimate succession through Fāṭima in the line of Ḥusayn. It is then only natural that he would have entrusted his eldest son to continue the task on the same ground he had established.

Zayn al-ʿĀbidīn, by raising claims to the heritage of Ḥusayn and by collecting around himself a number of followers, had only laid the foundation of the legitimist group of the Shīʿa; it was the task of Muḥammad al-Bāqir to evolve the principles of legitimacy in the concept of succession. Some scholars[33] have cast doubts on whether Muḥammad al-Bāqir really achieved any degree of success in his lifetime, or even whether he claimed the Imamate for himself. There is indeed a possibility that many traditions attributed to Al-Bāqir in this connection might have been produced by some of his followers who survived him. Yet, there being no decisive criterion for either admission or rejection of these traditions, we must, as far as circumstantial evidence allows, accept them in the form in which they are found in the earliest Shīʿī collection of *Ḥadīth, Al-Uṣūl al-Kāfī*. Moreover, the testimony of the following Imams of the same line, and their own rejection of many a tradition forged by some of the fanatical followers of the House, makes stronger the case in favour of the surviving traditions.

Though Muḥammad al-Bāqir inherited his father's following, he had to face many more serious problems than did his father. Zayn al-ʿĀbidīn had only to counteract the propaganda of Mukhtār for the Imamate of Ibn al-Ḥanafīya, which he could easily do on the grounds that he was the descendant of the Prophet as well as of ʿAlī. After the death of Zayn al-ʿĀbidīn many descendants of Fāṭima too, either motivated by ambitions or discontented with the idea of the Imam being merely a spiritual guide, as adopted by Zayn al-ʿĀbidīn, raised their own claims to the heritage of the Prophet. Thus the immediate problem facing Al-Bāqir was not from outside, but from within the family circle. The movements of his two most potential rivals, ʿAbd Allāh al-Maḥḍ, who worked for his son Muḥammad an-Nafs az-Zakīya, and Al-Bāqir's half-brother Zayd b. ʿAlī Zayn al-ʿĀbidīn, will be discussed in detail in the following chapter. Here it would suffice to point out in passing that Zayd b. Zayn al-ʿĀbidīn's energies appealed to many Shīʿīs and were a serious challenge to the Imamate of Al-Bāqir. In these rivalries, however, Al-Bāqir and his followers were markedly overshadowed by Zayd and led the former to put increasing emphasis on legitimism within the Shīʿī movement. Thus, against the claims of his half-brother, Al-Bāqir resorted to the principle of nomination by an explicit "text" (*Naṣṣ*)—a fundamental legitimist principle which will be discussed in detail in Chapter 11. He claimed that Zayn al-ʿĀbidīn had appointed him to the succession in the presence of his brothers and had entrusted him with a casket containing secret religious scrolls and the weapons of the Prophet.[34] A number of traditions are recorded by the Shīʿī traditionists[35] in which Al-Bāqir explains the nature and function of an Imam, who possesses certain special qualities which come down to him through the *naṣṣ* of the preceding Imam. In this way Al-Bāqir introduced certain ideas which were to be fully elaborated by his son Jaʿfar aṣ-Ṣādiq. The traditions of Al-Bāqir, however, make it abundantly clear that he tried to establish his position as an Imam, declaring himself the representative of God on earth and the divinely inspired interpreter of His Word.

Now the most vital question with which we are concerned here is how far Al-Bāqir succeeded in establishing the principle of legitimacy in the concept of the Imamate, and thereby whether he could really achieve any success of religious consequence in his lifetime. A close scrutiny of the biographical literature from both Sunnī and Shīʿī sources will help us to find an answer to this question. In this attempt, it is immensely useful to note that the names of the followers of Al-Bāqir, which have been recorded with full biographical details by the Imamite writers, were never disputed by the Sunnī compilers of biographical dictionaries (*Kutub ar-Rijāl*). Instead, whenever Sunnī writers mention the names of the adherents of the legitimist Imams, they immediately remark that he was a *rāfiḍī,* or a *ghālī,* or a Shīʿī. Besides biographical dictionaries, the heresiographical works such as Al-Baghdādī's *Al-Farq bayn al-Firaq,* Ibn Ḥazm's *Al-Faṣl,* and Ash-Shahrastānī's *Al-Milal wa'l-Nihal* also describe these names with often derogatory remarks. Finally, it should be noted that the Imamite writers themselves specifically remark that such-and-such a person changed his affiliation at such-and-such a time to Zayd or An-Nafs az-Zakīya, whatever the case may have been. Furthermore, the writers of the Zaydīya and

Ismāʿīlīya sects, which produced a considerable religious literature of their own, do not claim adherents of Al-Bāqir as among their numbers. There was, indeed, a considerable shift from one ʿAlid claimant to another by some, such as Bayān b. Simʿān and Al-Mughīra b. Saʿīd al-ʿIjlī, but they are vocally repudiated by the Imamite writers. All these facts, however, support the view that the list of Al-Bāqir's followers, which we are going to enumerate here as the legitimist faction, is not a mere fiction. No matter how much "the biographies of these men have been touched up by Shīʿite [Imamite] writers in the attempt to show that all along they [the Ḥusaynid Imams] claimed to be Imams and acted as such,"[36] these reports must have been based on certain facts. Indeed, Zayn al-ʿĀbidīn, Al-Bāqir, and Jaʿfar were unimportant politically and as a matter of policy they avoided involvement in any political adventures, but this does not mean that they did not claim a strictly religious "function" as Imams for themselves. In fact the very policy of quiescence caused them to be overshadowed by other activist members of the family; at the same time, through this very policy, they in the long run survived as the Imams and emerged as the recognized leaders of the future majority group of the Shīʿa.

It is no doubt true, however, that immediately after the death of Zayn al-ʿĀbidīn a struggle for the leadership began between Al-Bāqir and his half-brother Zayd, and that a great number from among the Shīʿīs preferred the latter because of his activist policy and his bold attitude. Yet, in the course of time Al-Bāqir succeeded in winning back some of those who had gone over to Zayd, as well as in attracting some new followers. The most important of them were Zurāra b. Aʿyān, his brother Ḥumrān, and Ḥamza b. Muḥammad b. ʿAbd Allāh aṭ-Ṭayyār. Zurāra in particular was a very important acquisition, for he became the most eminent theologian and traditionist of his time, with a wide circle of disciples in Kūfa.[37] His brother Ḥumrān was formerly a close associate of Zayn al-ʿĀbidīn and later made himself known as an extremely devoted supporter of Al-Bāqir, who promised him Paradise and declared that "Ḥumrān would be from our Shīʿa in this world and the next."[38] Ḥamza b. aṭ-Ṭayyār, although for a time opposed to Al-Bāqir, after hesitating between various claimants, finally chose to follow him.[39]

Apart from Zurāra, other important adherents of Al-Bāqir, who became the main authorities on Twelver *fiqh* when their Shīʿī legal school was formulated later on, were Maʿrūf b. Kharrabūdh,[40] Abū Baṣīr al-Asadī,[41] Burayd b. Muʿāwiya,[42] Muḥammad b. Muslim b. Riyāḥ aṭ-Ṭā'ifī,[43] and Al-Fuḍayl b. Yasār.[44] The prominent figure among them was Muḥammad b. Muslim b. Riyāḥ, a Kūfan *mawlā* of the Thaqīf, a miller by trade, known also as Al-Aʿwar (the one-eyed). Described as the "most trustworthy of all men", he was well known as a great jurist in Kūfan circles and a contemporary fellow-lawyer of Ibn Abī Layla, Abū Ḥanīfa, and Sharīk al-Qāḍī. He seems to have been a counterpart of Zurāra, for while the latter was a traditionist as well as a speculative theologian, and the originator of the Shīʿī school of *kalām*, Muḥammad b. Muslim combined knowledge of the science of Tradition with the work of a practical lawyer, and was renowned for quick and drastic solutions. He was also a well-known ascetic.

Among these followers of Al-Bāqir, Abū Baṣīr Layth al-Bakhtarī al-Murādī also attained fame and reputation as a great Shīʿī *faqīh* and traditionist. Abū Baṣīr, a *mawlā* of Banū Asad, became the favourite companion of Al-Bāqir and later of Jaʿfar aṣ-Ṣādiq. Jaʿfar is reported to have said that Abū Baṣīr, Burayd, Zurāra, and Muḥammad b. Muslim were the "tent pegs of the world", and that without them the Prophetic traditions would have been lost.[45] They were the fastest runners and the closest associates of the Imams. Another striking figure was Abū Ḥamza ath-Thumālī, who occupied a high place among Al-Bāqir's associates, and to him may be traced many traditions of an extremist tendency, especially those relating to miracles.[46]

Al-Kumayt b. Zayd al-Asadī,[47] a renowned poet of his time, was another great and very important supporter of Al-Bāqir. He served the cause of the Imam more than any other follower through his poetic genius. His devotion, which found expression in his talented poetry, took the name and fame of Al-Bāqir far and wide. But his collection of poetry, devoted to the praise of the *Ahl al-Bayt,* the "al-Hāshimīyāt", caused him some serious trouble. The anti-ʿAlid viceroy of Iraq, Yūsuf b. ʿUmar, brought this work to the attention of the Caliph ʿAbd al-Malik.[48] Kumayt, however, managed to extricate himself from danger, and in order to please the Caliph he even wrote some poems in praise of the Umayyads.[49] Nevertheless, the poet remained a great favourite of the legitimist line of the Ḥusaynid Imams, and Jaʿfar aṣ-Ṣādiq said of him: "Kumayt has not ceased to be aided by the Holy Spirit."[50]

Though the city of Baṣra was generally anti-Shīʿī, Al-Bāqir succeeded in gaining several followers there too, such as Muḥammad b. Marwān al-Baṣrī[51] and Mālik b. Aʿyān.[52] In Mecca also, Al-Bāqir earned quite a few staunch followers.

However, the popularity of the movement of Zayd b. Zayn al-ʿĀbidīn overshadowed Al-Bāqir's efforts to establish the legitimist Imamate, yet Al-Bāqir restricted himself to attacking only the friends and followers of Zayd. Nevertheless, when an opportunity presented itself, he did not hesitate to contest Zayd's rights quite sharply. Thus when Saʿīd b. al-Manṣūr, one of the leaders of the Zaydīya circle, asked him: "What is your opinion about *nabīdh,* for I have seen Zayd drinking it?" Al-Bāqir replied: "I do not believe that Zayd would drink it, but even if he did, he is neither a Prophet nor a Trustee of a Prophet, only an ordinary person from the Family of Muḥammad, and he is sometimes right and sometimes may commit an error."[53] This was both an open denial of Zayd's rights to the Imamate, and an indirect assertion of his own position as the Prophetic *Waṣī.* Muḥammad al-Bāqir was the son of Fāṭima, the daughter of Al-Ḥasan,[54] and so, being the descendant of the Prophet and of ʿAlī on both sides, he had a great advantage over Zayd, whose mother was a slave-woman from Sind,[55] but the former never showed any inclination to organize an active movement and maintained the pacific policy of his father. On the other hand, Zayd, a close associate of Wāṣil b. ʿAṭā', the Muʿtazilite, was strongly impressed by the latter's ideas and laid emphasis on the principle of "ordering good and prohibiting evil", if necessary, by force. Accordingly, he believed that if an Imam wanted to be recognized, he had to claim his right, sword in hand.[56] Al-Bāqir and Zayd quarrelled over this point, for when the latter asserted that an Imam must rise against the oppressors, the former remarked: "So you deny that your own father was an Imam, for he never contested the issue."[57] When Abū Bakr b. Muḥammad al-Ḥaḍramī and his brother ʿAlqama, two Kūfan Shīʿīs, asked Zayd whether ʿAlī was an

Imam before he resorted to the sword, he refused to answer the question, which made them break their allegiance with Zayd and go over to Al-Bāqir.[58]

A crucial question was that of the rights of Abū-Bakr and ʿUmar. Zayd, agreeing with the Muʿtazilites, held that the first two caliphs had been legally elected Imams, though ʿAlī was the preferable candidate, and this greatly impressed the traditionist circles. At the same time he rejected the Muʿtazilite doctrine of the "intermediate state", but did not object to the opinion of Wāṣil, that in the conflict between "ʿAlī and his adversaries" one of the opposing sides was certainly wrong though Wāṣil was not sure which,[59] whereas Zayd regarded the virtues of ʿAlī as of such a high order that the idea of his not being in the right was inadmissible.

However, Zayd's special emphasis on accepting the caliphates of Abū Bakr and ʿUmar and his popularity on this ground among moderate circles show, on the one hand, that the question of the caliphates of the first two caliphs had already been under serious discussion in some Shīʿī circles at that time, and on the other hand, that Zayd's success by adopting this stand created an embarrassing and complicated situation for Al-Bāqir. Zayn al-ʿĀbidīn himself never spoke against the first two caliphs, but during Al-Bāqir's lifetime some of the extremists who sided themselves with him started asking this question among the legitimist section of the Shīʿa. Al-Bāqir was thus asked time and again what he thought of Abū Bakr and ʿUmar, but he did not publicly discredit them and rather confirmed that they were caliphs.[60] Yet certain Shīʿīs of Kūfa asserted that he disavowed the first two caliphs and only concealed his real opinion by resorting to the principle of dissimulation.[61] This propaganda on the part of some of the Kūfan followers of Al-Bāqir no doubt earned him the sympathy of many extremist and semi-extremist circles, but on the other hand it discouraged those who wanted an active and more practical movement to bring the *Ahl al-Bayt* to power, and were already disappointed with Al-Bāqir's quiescent policy. These moderates therefore preferred to range themselves on the side of Zayd,[62] who in order to secure certain advantages became more emphatic in his acceptance of the first two caliphs, at the same time rejecting the principle of *Taqīya*. Al-Bāqir was infuriated by the attitude of these Kūfan Shīʿīs and said, "Even if the Butrites formed one battle-line from east to west, God would not grant glory to the world through them."[63]

Among these Kūfan Shīʿīs was Al-Ḥakam b. ʿUtayba al-Kindī, one of the most eminent lawyers of his city.[64] He put ʿAlī b. Abī Ṭālib above Abū Bakr, but nevertheless remained mild in his Shīʿī partisanship, which made him highly popular among the followers of Zayd. As the judge of Kūfa, he exercised a strong influence among his fellow-citizens, thus greatly helping the cause of Zayd.[65] Naturally Al-Bāqir, who considered that he possessed better rights to the Imamate than his younger half-brother, and also objected to the generally compromising attitude of Zayd and his partisans, spoke of them in a bitter way, giving expression to his displeasure thus: "Ḥakam b. ʿUtayba and other associates of Zayd led astray many people. They say, 'We believe in God and the Last Day,' but they are not believers."[66] The successor of Al-Bāqir, Jaʿfar aṣ-Ṣādiq, upheld the same view and accused Ḥakam of blaspheming against Al-Bāqir,[67] and even called the Zaydites *an-Nuṣṣāb* (dissenters) who hated ʿAlī.[68]

The question of the first two caliphs at this stage draws our attention to another problem: that of religious practices. Al-Bāqir adhered to the traditions derived from ʿAlī and his supporters. There were, however, certain disagreements even among the *Ahl al-Bayt,* for Zayd was inclined to accept the practice of the *Aṣḥāb al-Ḥadīth* of Kūfa, mainly based on the rulings of ʿUmar. Thus it was Al-Bāqir who established the beginnings of the *madhhab* (legal school) of the *Ahl al-Bayt.* Kashshī records for us a very important tradition which says:

> "Before the Imamate of Muḥammad al-Bāqir the Shīʿīs did not know what was lawful and what was unlawful, except what they learned from the [other] people; until Abū Jaʿfar [Al-Bāqir] became the Imām, and he taught them and explained to them the knowledge [of law], and they began to teach other people from whom they were previously learning."[69]

This tradition clearly indicates that until the time of Al-Bāqir there were hardly any differences in legal practices among the Shīʿīs and *Aṣḥāb al-Ḥadīth* of Medina, Kūfa, and elsewhere. Even later the differences in the sphere of legal matters (*furūʿ*) were in reality few,[70] such as while Al-Bāqir absolutely forbade all intoxicants, including *nabīdh* (fermented drinks)[71] the Kūfan jurists allowed *nabīdh*. Another problem was that of *mutʿa* (temporary marriage), over which the Shīʿī and Kūfan jurists differed, the former allowing it on the authority of ʿAlī, the latter forbidding it, referring to the decision of ʿUmar.[72] The argument was that if ʿUmar could revoke a permission granted by the Prophet, then ʿAlī could revoke a ruling of ʿUmar.

However, the above-mentioned accounts seem to make it highly probable that Muḥammad al-Bāqir did claim the Imamate as the inheritance of his father, and that the small nucleus established by Zayn al-ʿĀbidīn began to develop under him into a legitimist faction within the Shīʿī movement. If we reject this then we will have to reject many established historical facts, foremost among them being the rivalry and even the quarrel, overwhelmingly reported by the sources, between him and Zayd. Nevertheless, the dates of the deaths of the chief associates of Al-Bāqir indicate that these developments in his favour took place towards the end of his life, for most of the renowned traditionists and jurists of his circle survived him by at least a decade.

At the time of Al-Bāqir's death, the legitimist faction, though still limited in number, was to be found in all the main centres of the Ḥijāz and Iraq. It possessed the elements necessary for its future growth into a strong and popular discipline. It possessed a theoretical foundation, still only partly formulated and uncertain, and although it was not completely separated from the current ideas permeating the *Madhhab Aṣḥāb al-Ḥadīth,* it was nevertheless sufficiently individualized to be regarded as a doctrine in its own right. It had in Zurāra and his disciples its own school of speculative theology and an embryo for a school of jurisprudence. Finally, in Kumayt it was able to produce its own literature and gain widespread public exposure.

Much has been recorded about Muḥammad al-Bāqir's person and extraordinary qualities, many of which he inherited from his father. He was extremely generous, devoted to acts of piety, and peaceful by nature, never thinking to organize a revolt to assert his rights.[73] Instead he strove to impress people by his extensive knowledge in matters of religion, and in fact he came to be considered as one of the most erudite men of his time. Because of this learning, according to Yaʿqūbī, he was nicknamed Al-Bāqir, "the one who splits knowledge open": that is, he scrutinized it and examined the depths of it.[74] But according to Ibn Khallikān, he received the appellation Al-Bāqir, "the ample", because he collected an ample fund (*tabaqqar*) of knowledge.[75] Many jurists, attracted by the fame of his learning, used to visit him to discuss legal problems. Among them were Muḥammad b. Minkadir, Abu Ḥanīfa an-Nuʿmān, Qatāda b. Diʿāma, ʿAbd Allāh b. Muʿammar al-Laythī, and the Khārijite Nāfiʿ b. Azraq.[76]

It is not certain when Al-Bāqir died. The earliest date is given as 113/731–732,[77] the latest as 126/743–744.[78] The most acceptable however, seems to be 117/735, as given by Yaʿqūbī.[79] There can be no doubt that he was no longer alive when Zayd revolted in Kūfa, but he could not have been dead for many years then, as Jaʿfar aṣ-Ṣādiq's position was still not well established.

Shahrastānī tells us that some of Al-Bāqir's followers refused to believe that he had died and expected his *rajʿa* (return).[80] These people must have been former Kaysānites who abandoned Abū Hāshim and attached themselves to Al-Bāqir's following. If, however, this report has any truth in it, it is a further proof that Al-Bāqir in his lifetime was recognized by a group of people as their Imam. Nawbakhtī classifies his followers as Al-Bāqirīya,[81] which was replaced after his death by Al-Jaʿfarīya, derived from his son and successor.[82] These titles given by heresiographers, however, should not be taken literally, as they are used to mention the followers of certain persons, and not a sect.

Muḥammad al-Bāqir, by the time he died, had lived as an Imam for about nineteen years. He left his heritage to his son and successor Jaʿfar aṣ-Ṣādiq, to whom we now turn our attention.

Notes to Chapter 9

[1] Wellhausen, *Aḥzāb,* pp. 198–234; K. A. Fariq, *The Story of an Arab Diplomat* (New Dehli, 1967)

[2] Hodgson, "How Did the Early Shī'a Become Sectarian?", *JAOS* (1955), p. 3

[3] Ibn Sa'd, V, p. 212

[4] Ibn Sa'd, V, pp. 212, 220; Ṭabari, II, p. 209

[5] Ṭabarī, II, p. 220

[6] ibid.

[7] Mas'ūdī, *Murūj,* III, p. 70; Mubarrad, *Kāmil,* I, p. 260; Dīnawarī, p. 266

[8] Balādhurī, V, p. 272; Mas'ūdī, *Murūj,* III, 74

[9] Ya'qūbī, II, p. 259

[10] Balādhurī, V, p. 272; Ibn Sa'd, V, p. 213

[11] Muḥammad b. Ya'qūb al-Kulaynī, *Uṣūl al-Kāfī* (Karachi, 1965), I, p. 353; Majlisī, *Biḥār,* XI, p. 7; 'Āmilī, *Ā'yān,* IV, p. 332. Also see Mas'ūdī, *Murūj,* III, p. 225

[12] Kulaynī, loc. cit.

[13] Ibn Khaldūn, *'Ibar* (Cairo, 1867), III, p. 172

[14] Balādhurī, V, p. 218

[15] Kulaynī, *Kāfī,* pp. 352 f.

[16] Kashshī, *Ikhtiyār Ma'rifat ar-Rijāl* (Tehran, n.d.), p. 121

[17] ibid., p. 124

[18] ibid., p. 123

[19] ibid., p. 115

[20] ibid., p. 4; Ibn 'Imād, *Shadharāt adh-Dhahab* (Cairo, 1350 A.H.), I, p. 84

[21] Kashshī, *Rijāl,* p. 119

[22] ibid., pp. 201–3

[23] ibid., p. 124

[24] e.g., Kulaynī, *Kāfī, passim*

[25] Farazdaq, *Dīwān,* I, p. 847 f.; *Aghānī,* XXI, pp. 400 ff.; Ibn Khallikān, *Wafayāt,* VI, pp. 95f.; Bayhaqī, *Kitāb al-Maḥāsin wa'l-Masāwī,* ed. Schwally (Giessen, 1902), pp. 131 f.; Abū Nu'aym, *Ḥilyat al-Awlīya* (Cairo, 1938), III, p. 139; Kashshī, *Rijāl,* p. 130 ff.; Subkī, Abū Naṣr, *Ṭabaqāt ash-Shāfi'īya,* ed. Aḥmad b. 'Abd al-Karīm (Cairo, n.d.), I, pp. 153 ff.; Ibn Kathīr, *Bidāya,* IX, pp. 108 f.

[26] See the detailed account in the references cited in note 25 above.

[27] Kashshī, *Rijāl,* p. 123

[28] Ibn Saʿd, V, p. 216; Kashshī, *Rijāl* 155 ff.

[29] Ibn Saʿd, V, p. 216

[30] For Sunnī sources, see Ibn Saʿd, V, pp. 216–22; Ibn Khallikān, III, pp. 266 ff.; Mubarrad, *Kāmil,* I, p. 260; II, p. 138; III, pp. 120 f.; Ibn Kathīr, *Bidāya,* IX, pp. 103–15. For Shīʿī sources, see Yaʿqūbī, II, p. 247; Masʿūdī, *Murūj,* III, p. 160; Kulaynī, *Kāfī,* I, *Kitāb al-Ḥujja* and *passim;* Mufīd, *Irshād,* II, pp. 138–45; ʿĀmilī, *ʿĀʿyān,* IV, pp. 308–461

[31] Mubarrad, *Kāmil,* II, p. 138

[32] Kulaynī, *Kāfī,* I, pp. 354 f.; Majlisī, *Bihār,* XI, pp. 100 ff.; Qāḍī Nuʿmān, *Sharḥ,* fol. 32a

[33] Montgomery Watt, "Shīʿīsm under the Umayyads", pp. 168 f.; Hodgson, op. cit., p. 1

[34] See references cited in note 32 above

[35] See specifically Kulaynī, *Kāfī,* "Kitāb al-Ḥujja"

[36] Montgomery Watt, op. cit., p. 166

[37] Kashshī, *Rijāl,* pp. 133 ff.

[38] ibid., pp. 161, 176 ff.

[39] ibid., pp. 276, 347 ff.

[40] ibid., pp. 211, 238. See also Ḥāʾirī *Muntahā al-Maqāl* (Tehran, 1302 AH), pp. 304–5

[41] Kashshī, *Rijāl,* pp. 169, 238

[42] ibid., p. 238

[43] Kashshī, *Rijāl,* pp. 161, 238; Ḥāʾirī, *Muntahā,* p. 243

[44] Kashshī, *Rijāl,* pp. 213 f.; Ḥāʾirī, *Muntahā,* p. 243; Najāshī, *Rijāl,* p. 219

[45] Kashshī, *Rijāl,* p. 170; Ḥāʾirī, *Muntahā,* pp. 249–50

[46] Kashshī, *Rijāl,* pp. 201 ff.; Ḥāʾirī, *Muntahā,* p. 73

[47] See *Aghānī,* XVI, pp. 330 ff.; Jāḥiẓ, *Bayān,* I, p. 46

[48] *Aghānī,* XVI, p. 333

[49] Kashshī, *Rijāl,* pp. 206 f.; *Aghānī,* loc. cit.

[50] Kashshī, *Rijāl,* p. 206 f.

[51] Kashshī, *Rijāl,* p. 214; Ḥāʾirī, *Muntahā,* p. 293

[52] Kashshī, loc. cit.; Ḥāʾirī, loc. cit.

[53] Kashshī, *Rijāl,* p. 232

[54] Ibn Saʿd, V, pp. 211, 320, 325 f.

[55] Abūʾl-Faraj, *Maqātil,* p. 127; Ibn Saʿd, V, pp. 211, 325 f.

[56] Shahrastānī, *Milal,* I, pp. 154 f.

[57] ibid.

[58] Kashshī, *Rijāl,* pp. 416 f.

[59] Shahrastānī, *Milal,* I, p. 49

[60] Ibn Kathīr, *Bidāya,* IX, p. 311; Dhahabī, *Taʾrīkh,* IV, p. 300; Ibn al-Jawzī, *Ṣifat aṣ-Ṣafwa,* II, p. 61; Abū Nuʿaym, *Ḥilya,* III, p. 185

[61] Traditions referring to the poet Kumayt quote Al-Bāqir as very violently disavowing Abū Bakr and ʿUmar; see Kashshī, *Rijāl*, pp. 205 f. On the other hand Kumayt did not express himself openly against the first two caliphs; see his verse in *Hāshimīyāt*, p. 155

[62] Nawbakhtī, *Firaq*, pp. 52 ff.; Kashshī, *Rijāl*, p. 229

[63] Kashshī, *Rijāl*, p. 232. The Butrīya were those who drew no distinction between the claimants from the house of ʿAlī and supported any ʿAlid claimant who revolted, sword in hand.

[64] Dhahabī, *Taʾrīkh*, IV, p. 242; Ibn Ḥajar, *Tahdhīb*, II, pp. 434 ff.

[65] Ibn ʿImād, *Shadharāt*, I, p. 151

[66] Kashshī, *Rijāl*, p. 209

[67] Kashshī, *Rijāl*, p. 209; Ḥāʾirī, *Muntahā*, p. 263

[68] Kashshī, *Rijāl*, pp. 209, 229

[69] Kashshī, *Rijāl*, p. 289

[70] Schacht, *Origins*, pp. 262 ff.

[71] Kulaynī, *Furūʿ al-Kāfī*, II, p. 193. Also see Dhahabī, *Tadhkirat al-Ḥuffāz*, I, p. 160; Qāḍī Nuʿmān, *Sharḥ Al-Akhbār*, fol. 36a

[72] Schacht, *Origins*, pp. 266 ff.; Mālik b. Anas, *Muwaṭṭaʾ*, III, p. 23; Murtaḍā b. Dāiʿ, *Tadhkirat al-ʿAwāmm*, pp. 270–271

[73] Ibn Saʿd, V, p. 321; Kulaynī, *Kāfī*, pp. 299 ff.; Qāḍī Nuʿmān, *Sharḥ al-Akhbār*, fol. 32a ff.; ʿĀmilī, *Aʿyān*, IV, pp. 262 ff.; Ibn Khallikān, IV, p. 176; Majlisī, *Biḥār*, XI, pp. 100 ff

[74] Yaʿqūbī, II, p. 320; Bayhaqī, *Kitāb al-Maḥāsin waʾl-Masāwi*, III, pp. 298 ff.; Qāḍī Nuʿmān, *Sharḥ al-Akhbār*, fol. 33a

[75] Ibn Khallikān, IV, p. 176

[76] Qāḍī Nuʿmān, loc. cit.; ʿĀmilī, *Aʿyān*, pp. 490 ff.; Majlisī, *Biḥār*, XI, pp. 100 f.; Kulaynī, *Kāfī*, pp. 299 ff.; Bhahlanjī, *Nūr al-Ibṣār*, pp. 160 ff.

[77] See Ibn Saʿd, V, p. 324; Ibn Khallikān, IV, pp. 174; Abūʾl-Maḥāsin, *Nujūm*, I, pp. 273 f. The last source here says he died in AH 114.

[78] Masʿūdī, *Murūj*, III, p. 219

[79] Yaʿqūbī, II, p. 320. Also see Dhahabī, *Taʾrikh*, IV, p. 300

[80] Shahrastānī, *Milal*, I, p. 166

[81] *Firaq*, p. 25

[82] *Al-Jaʿfarīya* should not be confused with the name *Madhhab al-Jaʿfarī*, given very often to the present Twelver Shīʿa.

Chapter 10

The Imamate of Jaʿfar aṣ-Ṣādiq

The sixth Imam, Abū ʿAbd Allāh Jaʿfar, the eldest son of Muḥammad al-Bāqir, was born in Medina either in 80/699–700 or 83/703–704.[1] On his father's side Jaʿfar was of course a Ḥusaynid descendant of the Prophet, and like his father he had a doubly strong relationship to ʿAlī, since Muḥammad al-Bāqir was an ʿAlid on both his father's and his mother's sides.[2]

On his mother's side Jaʿfar was the great-great-grandson of Abū Bakr,[3] and thus he was the first among the *Ahl al-Bayt* who combined in his person descent from Abū Bakr as well as from ʿAlī. His mother Umm Farwa was the daughter of Al-Qāsim b. Muḥammad b. Abī Bakr.[4] Qāsim married the daughter of his uncle ʿAbd ar-Raḥmān b. Abī Bakr, and thus Umm Farwa was the great-granddaughter of Abū Bakr on both the father's and the mother's sides.

For the first fourteen years of his life Jaʿfar was brought up under the guardianship of his grandfather Zayn al-ʿĀbidīn. He observed the latter's acts of charity, his love for long series of prostrations and prayers, and his withdrawal from politics. At the same time, Jaʿfar noticed his grandfather's claims to the Imamate and his efforts, though meagre and limited, to collect around himself some devoted followers who resisted the popular appeal of the Imamate of Muḥammad b. al-Ḥanafīya and then the latter's son, Abū Hāshim. Jaʿfar also saw the respect with which Zayn al-ʿĀbidīn was held by the famous lawyers and scholars of Medina and elsewhere.[5] In his mother's house young Jaʿfar saw his maternal grandfather, Qāsim b. Muḥammad b. Abī Bakr, considered by the people of Medina as one of the most erudite and esteemed traditionists of his time.[6]

Outside the family the childhood of Jaʿfar coincided with a rapidly growing interest in Medina in the acquiring of knowledge of Prophetic traditions and of seeking explanations of the Qur'ānic verses. His boyhood also witnessed the culmination of Umayyad power, the final establishment of their administrative imperium, a period of peace and plenty, but hardly of religious fervour, as will be elaborated below. It seems probable that an environmental background of this kind in the life of a boy of fourteen may have influenced his thinking and personality, giving his future work a certain direction.

With the death of Zayn al-ʿĀbidīn, Jaʿfar entered his early manhood and spent about twenty-three years under his father Muḥammad al-Bāqir. In all these years not only did Jaʿfar see his father's efforts to establish himself as the Imam of the House of the Prophet, but as the eldest son he participated in these activities. When Al-Bāqir died, Jaʿfar was thirty-seven or thirty-four years old and was destined to live for a period of at least twenty-eight years as the head of the Shīʿa following the elder line of the Ḥusaynid Imams—a period longer than any other Imam of the House attained.[7]

Jaʿfar's fame for religious learning was great, greater than that of his father or of any other Twelver Imam except for ʿAlī b. Abī Ṭālib himself. Perhaps the earliest historical reference presenting Jaʿfar as one of the most respected and highly esteemed personalities of his epoch, and as having profound knowledge and learning, is Yaʿqūbī's statement that it was customary for scholars who related anything from him to say: "The Learned One informed us."[8] Even the famous jurist of Medina, the Imam Mālik b. Anas, is reported to have said, when quoting Jaʿfar's traditions: "The *Thiqa* (truthful) Jaʿfar b. Muḥammad himself told me that . . ."[9] Similar compliments for Jaʿfar are attributed to the Imam Abū Ḥanīfa,[10] who is also reported to have been his pupil. Shahrastānī said of Jaʿfar:

> "His knowledge was great in religion and culture, he was fully informed in philosophy, he attained great piety in the world, and he abstained entirely from lusts. He lived in Medina long enough to greatly profit the sect that followed him, and to give his friends the advantage of the hidden sciences. On his father's side he was

connected with the tree of prophecy, and on his mother's side with Abū Bakr."[11]

The Imamate of Ja'far aṣ-Ṣādiq saw the most crucial period of Islamic history, both in political and in doctrinal spheres. It coincided with many epoch-making events, violent movements, the natural results of various undercurrent activities and revolutionary attempts, and above all the compromising attitude between the *Ahl al-Ḥadīth* and the Murī'ites in their efforts to standardize a corpus of doctrine for the synthesis of the Muslim community, or *Jamā'a.* The very existence of this many-sided and complex situation facilitated the rise of Ja'far's Imamate to a prominence not previously attained by the Imamates of his father and grandfather. Thus the fundamental point to be investigated is how the Imamate of Ja'far attained so great a prominence, as attested to by the testimony of Shī'ī as well as Sunnī sources, after having been reduced to an insignificant following by the abandonment of the line of the quiescent Imams by the majority of the Shī'īs, who had been persuaded to join the extremist and revolutionary factions. The answer to this question, however, cannot be found without examining a series of events and their ultimate results—the results which appeared in the success of the 'Abbāsid house and the subsequent repudiation and frustration of the Shī'ī cause. As Moscati has observed, after their success the 'Abbāsids joined hands with the rest of the Muslims and pushed the Shī'īs, on whose strength they had risen to power, into the role of an opposition.[12] It is not possible, nor would it be desirable, to go into the details of all those events of far-reaching consequences which took place before and during the Imamate of Ja'far and, as we have tentatively assumed above, made it crucial. Nevertheless, a broad outline and brief survey is necessary.

When the Umayyad's autocratic rule and their libertine way of life frustrated the expectations of Muslims, especially after the massacre at Karbalā, many Muslims conceived the idea of *Al-Mahdī,* a leader they considered as directly guided by God. Though the use of the term Mahdī became the chief characteristic of the Shī'īs, it had a great appeal among non-Shī'īs as well. The first to be proclaimed as the Mahdī was 'Alī's third son Muḥammad,[13] born of a Ḥanafite woman.

The massacre of Ḥusayn,[14] the only surviving grandson of the Prophet, at Karbalā, the destruction of the Kaʿba, the siege of Medina and the misfortunes inflicted on the pro-ʿAlid Kūfans were sufficient grounds for a Mahdī uprising, though vengeance for "the blood of the Son of the Prophet" was the main cry.[15] The reluctance of Ḥusayn's surviving son Zayn al-ʿĀbidīn to involve himself in political adventures caused the restless Kūfan sympathizers of the House to seek the moral support of any other member of ʿAlid descent. Thus, in the beginning it was perhaps not the personality of Muḥammad b. al-Ḥanafīya which impressed the Kūfans, but rather the basic need for a figurehead in whose name the movement could be launched. In fact, even Muḥammad b. al-Ḥanafīya had always been reluctant to claim the role of the Mahdī for himself.[16]

Mukhtār understood the situation only too well and made full use of it. He gathered the Kūfan Shīʿīs in his house and declared:

> "Al-Mahdī Muḥammad b. ʿAlī, the son of the *Waṣī,* sent me to you as his trusted man, minister, and chosen supporter, and as his commander. He ordered me to fight against the blasphemers and claim vengeance for the blood of the people of his House, the excellent ones."[17]

It is interesting to note that the emphasis is placed not on Muḥammad b. al-Ḥanafīya, but on the "Mahdi" and on the "son of the *Waṣī*". Ibn al-Ḥanafīya in fact may have agreed to Mukhtār's suggestions, when the latter said, "Your silence is your agreement," but nevertheless maintained an uncommitted attitude. In any case, Mukhtār might have so understood Ibn al-Ḥanafīya's behaviour, as he interpreted it before the people of Kūfa.

Mukhtār's propaganda for Ibn al-Ḥanafīya's Mahdism gained the unqualified support of the great majority of the Shīʿīs, comprising both the Arabs and a large number of Persian *mawālī* living in Kūfa, who, as we have already seen, had by this time outnumbered the former. These *mawālī,* who formed the backbone of Mukhtār's movement, called themselves *Shīʿat al-Mahdī* (the party of Al-Mahdī), *Shīʿat Āl-Muḥammad* (the party of the Family of Muḥammad), or the *Shīʿat al-Ḥaqq* (the party of Truth).[18] Consequently, a sect in its own right, considerably well organized, active, and equipped with ideas of different extractions, emerged with the name of the Kaysānīya, named after either the *kunya* of Mukhtār himself or the highly controversial figure of Abū ʿAmra Kaysān, the *mawlā* of Mukhtār.[19]

Though Mukhtār's rule was soon ended by his being killed with the majority of his followers, Kaysānism, introduced by his followers to various provinces, became too widespread to be eradicated. These sectarians, some of whom lived as far away as Khurāsān, continued to recognize Ibn al-Ḥanafīya as their Imam-Mahdī and to revere him to an extravagant degree. After his death in 81/700–701,[20] the extremists of the sect believed in his concealment (*ghayba*) and return (*rajʿa*), while the majority accepted the eldest of his sons, Abū Hāshim ʿAbd Allāh, as the new Imam directly appointed by him.[21] The former group was represented by three notable poets, Abū 'l-Ṭufayl ʿĀmir b. Wā'ila, Kuthayyir, and Sayyid al-Ḥimyarī;[22] the last of these later became a follower of Jaʿfar aṣ-Ṣādiq.

Kashshī records an interesting story about two men from the entourage of Jaʿfar aṣ-Ṣādiq, Aṣ-Ṣarrāj and Ḥammād b. ʿĪsā, who were known to believe that Muḥammad b. al-Ḥanafīya was still alive. Jaʿfar reproached them and pointed out that Ibn al-Ḥanafīya was seen being buried, and his property had been divided and his widow had re-married.[23] Nevertheless, the doctrine of "return" from that time became one of the chief characteristics of most branches of the Shīʿīs.

The messianic expectations of the Kaysānites, however, influenced a great number of the Muslims, Shīʿīs as well as non-Shīʿīs. Mahdism in fact became a common vehicle for the expression of the general feelings of the epoch, and was used as an effective instrument for political adventures.

There was a widespread dissatisfaction of both a political and a social nature which had many causes. The Arabs of Iraq were opposed to the hegemony of the Syrians. The non-Arab *mawālī* resented the high-handed treatment meted out to them by the Arab ruling class, and the increasing number of Arabs entitled to the allowances must have added to the burdens imposed on the subject and conquered peoples. Because of the omnipresence of religion in every sphere of life, the social ferment and opposition against the existing regime were expressed in religious terms. General discontent, however, was not directed against the legal and religious foundations of the Islamic state as such.[24] The laws contained in the Qur'ān and the *Sunna* were the Word of God and the example of the Prophet under divine inspiration, and so they could not be wrong. But the rulers who applied these laws, and whose duty it was to maintain and administer justice, were responsible for distorting or neglecting the commands of God and the custom of the Prophet. Thus the hope for liberation and a change in the political and social system meant not the abolition of the existing legal basis and the introduction of another law, but the faithful application of the divine rules.[25]

Thus anti-Umayyad propaganda found expression mainly, and perhaps spontaneously, in religious terms. "The main concern of the Umayyads," as Schacht remarks, "was not with religion and religious law, but with political administration, and here they represented the organizing, centralising, and increasingly bureaucratic tendency of an orderly administration. They were interested in questions of religious policy and theology insofar as these had a bearing on loyalty to themselves."[26] To this another observation may be added. The close proximity in time of Umayyad rule with that of Muḥammad and the *Rāshidūn* caliphs and the vast difference between their respective ways of life made the Muslims watch with shock and concern the personal lives, conduct, and behaviour of the Umayyads, addicted to wine-bibbing and singing-girls. Thus, with emphasis placed on their impiety and ungodliness, the Umayyads were regarded as usurpers, who deprived the family of the Prophet of their rights and inflicted untold wrongs upon them.[27] The sack of Medina and the burning of the Kaʿba were also a black spot on the record of the dynasty.[28]

These observations by the Muslims led them to decry the Umayyads and depict their rule as an epoch of tyranny (*ẓulm*), at the same time placing before the eyes of the masses a hope for liberation. The victory of justice being understood as one of faith over impiety, it could be achieved only by divine sanction and under a God-inspired leader. Thus rather naturally the majority believed that this leader, Al-Mahdī, should be a man descended from the Prophet, or at least a member of his family, the *Ahl al-Bayt.* At the same time it should be particularly noted that the Messianic idea did not imply a mere passive waiting for salvation or spiritual guidance, a policy distinctly adopted by the legitimist line of the Imams: Jaʿfar and his predecessors. The concept of *Jihād,* which required every believer to expose his life and property in the cause of religion, did not allow for such a passive attitude.

The first ʿAlid of the Ḥusaynid line who rose against the tyranny of the Umayyads was Zayd, the second son of Zayn al-ʿĀbidīn. After the death of Zayn al-ʿĀbidīn, when his eldest son Al-Bāqir, who became the legitimate Imam of the house, strictly followed his father's quiescent policy and restricted himself to the claims of religious leadership, Zayd proclaimed the principle of establishing good and prohibiting evil by force if necessary. Zayd preached that if an Imam wanted to be recognized, he should claim his rights sword in hand. It was, in fact, an expression of the deeply felt feelings not only of the Shīʿīs of Kūfa, but also of the majority of Medinese, which Zayd understood only too well. Thus many followers of Zayn al-ʿĀbidīn left Al-Bāqir and went over to Zayd. They were joined by a considerable number of those of the Shīʿīs who had previously upheld the Imamate of Ibn al-Ḥanafīya and Abū Hāshim, but the moderate views of Zayd's followers could not be reconciled with the extremist doctrines of the Kaysānites. At the same time, Zayd, by adhering to Wāṣil b. ʿAṭā' and his doctrines, gained the whole-hearted support of the Muʿtazilites, and his acceptance of the legitimacy of the first two caliphs earned him the full sympathy of the traditionist circles. These combinations reveal two fundamental points. Firstly, Zayd and his close followers rejected the ideas prevailing among other Shīʿī groups. Zayd and his followers wanted no quiescent or hidden Imams, like Al-Bāqir and Ibn al-Ḥanafīya. The Imam, in their eyes, although he had to be a descendant of ʿAlī and Fāṭima, yet could not claim allegiance unless he asserted his Imamate publicly. Secondly, Zayd realized the fact that in order to run for the caliphate, he must have the main body of Muslim opinion behind him, and must, therefore, accept the main body of Islamic traditions. Thus he expressed this attitude by declaring his acceptance of Abū Bakr and ʿUmar as legally elected caliphs. At the same time, he maintained the Shīʿī belief that ʿAlī was superior; nevertheless, he accepted the "Imamate of the Inferior" (*Mafḍūl*), that is, of Abū Bakr and ʿUmar, as permissible in order to secure certain temporary advantages.[29]

After the death of Al-Bāqir, Jaʿfar maintained his father's policy towards Zayd and his movement and remained a rather passive spectator. Being the uncle of Jaʿfar, Zayd had the superior position and Jaʿfar could not dare to deny his merits outwardly. It does not mean, however, that Jaʿfar did not have a close group of his own followers whom he inherited from his father and who resisted the Zaydite viewpoint. Moreover, the concession to non-Shīʿīs given by Zayd, especially his emphasis on the rights of the first two caliphs, raised objections and ultimately caused many zealous Shīʿīs to abandon him. They revoked their oath and transferred their allegiance to Jaʿfar.[30]

According to one tradition Zayd said to the deserters: "You have abandoned me (*rafaḍtumūnī*)," and zealous Shīʿīs have since been called *Rāfiḍa*.[31] A party of Kūfan Shīʿīs went to Medina and informed Jaʿfar of Zayd's ideas and activities. Maintaining his regard for his uncle, Jaʿfar simply said, "Zayd was the best of us and our master."[32]

Zayd's revolt took place in Ṣafar 122/December 740 and was unsuccessful. He himself was killed, and many of his followers were massacred.[33] The Caliph Hishām then commanded that all eminent Ṭālibīs should publicly dissociate themselves from the insurrection and condemn its leader.[34] Among them were ʿAbd Allāh b. Muʿāwiya and ʿAbd Allāh al-Maḥḍ,[35] but the name of Jaʿfar aṣ-Ṣādiq is nowhere mentioned. It shows that Jaʿfar must have shown himself distinctly and categorically opposed to the movements of the activist members of the family. It also recalls the time of Jaʿfar's grandfather, Zayn al-ʿĀbidīn, in the reign of Yazīd, when, after the suppression of the Medinese revolt, all of Banū Hāshim were forced to swear allegiance and declare themselves slaves of the Caliph, while Zayn al-ʿĀbidīn was exempted.[36] Now Jaʿfar was spared in a similar situation, which indicates the continuity of the same policy in the legitimist line.

Zayd's son Yaḥyā, however, continued his father's activities and managed to reach Khurāsān in order to win the sympathies of the Kūfan Shī'īs, whom Al-Ḥajjāj and other Umayyad viceroys of Iraq had exiled to that distant province. But in 125/743, after three years' futile efforts, Yaḥyā met the same fate as his father.[37] Zayd's movement, in fact, was unable to captivate the hearts of the activist groups because he did not claim to be the Mahdī—an idea which had become so dear to the Shī'ī masses. Moreover, his moderate policy eventually deprived him of the popular support of the Shī'īs. Yet his revolt left a very deep mark upon the development of the whole Shī'ī movement. Numerous learned men of Kūfa, among them the great jurists Abū Ḥanīfa an-Nu'mān and Sufyān ath-Thawrī, the traditionist Al-A'mash, the Qāḍī of Madā'in Hilāl b. Hubāb, and others, along with other leaders from other cities, supported or at least sympathized with his cause.[38]

The movement of Zayd, however, though it ended in failure, paved the way for other claimants and offered ready ground for a more effective revolt. His and his son's deaths, which created a vacuum for active leadership, enhanced the prospects of two of their relatives and hitherto rivals: Ja'far aṣ-Ṣādiq and Muḥammad an-Nafs az-Zakīya. Since the former adhered to the quiescent policy of his father and grandfather, he was not inclined to make a bid for the leadership of an active movement with political implications.

Here we should note that the whole of Shī'īsm at this stage was divided into three doctrinal groups. Firstly, there were the extremist and messianic groups originating from the Kaysānites; secondly, there was the moderate group which emerged from the teachings of Zayd and was backed by the Mu'tazilites and the traditionists of Medina and Kūfa; and finally, the third group was under the personal influence of Ja'far aṣ-Ṣādiq, who had been quietly propounding and expressing his own views and theories about the Imam and his function, which had neither Messianic pretensions nor Zaydite conciliatory moderation, as we shall see later.

Thus there remained only Muḥammad an-Nafs az-Zakīya, from the House of the Prophet, who could attract both the Zaydites and the pro-Shī'ī Mu'tazilites as well as a number of extremists on account of his Messianic claims. Though the actual revolt of An-Nafs az-Zakīya took place long after, in the sequence of events it would be in order to note that his Messianic movement in fact originates at this point.

Muḥammad an-Nafs az-Zakīya was designated from his childhood for the role of Al-Mahdī by his father ʿAbd Allāh b. al-Ḥasan al-Muthannā b. al-Ḥasan b. ʿAlī b. Abī Ṭālib, known as Al-Maḥḍ. A grandson of Ḥasan b. ʿAlī b. Abī Ṭālib, Muḥammad b. ʿAbd Allāh was renowned as one of the most virtuous men of his time and was famous for his religious learning and eloquence.[39] When he reached manhood ʿAbd Allāh spared no efforts to extol the expected destiny of his son. A tradition from the Prophet on the authority of ʿAbd Allāh b. Masʿūd was circulated, in which the Prophet is reported to have said:

> "Even if there remains for the world but one single day, God will extend it until He sends a man from the people of my House, whose name will be the same as mine, and the name of his father will be that of my father. He will fill the earth with equity and justice, just as it now is filled with tyranny and oppression."[40]

As this tradition could also be applied to Muḥammad al-Mahdī, the son of Manṣūr,[41] another tradition was produced to assure the role of the Deliverer to An-Nafs az-Zakīya: "On the authority of Umm Salima, who reported; 'I heard the Apostle of God say, Al-Mahdī will be from the descent of Fāṭima.'"[42]

The candidature of An-Nafs az-Zakīya for the position of the Mahdī was supported not only by his close relatives, but also by the extremist Al-Mughīra b. Saʿīd al-ʿIjlī.[43] He had a reputation for being an extremist Shīʿī, and Jaʿfar aṣ-Ṣādiq repeatedly warned his followers not to accept Mughīra's traditions.[44]

Even after Al-Mughīra was executed, his followers remained faithful to An-Nafs az-Zakīya.[45] Besides, a number of moderate traditionists as well as the Muʿtazilites, led by ʿAmr b. 'Ubayd and Wāṣil b. ʿAṭā',[46] recognized the young ʿAlid as the most suitable person to take the place vacated by Zayd and Yaḥyā.[47]

After the death of Al-Walīd b. Yazīd, however, when the Umayyad dynasty was apparently disintegrating and the revolt of 'Abd' Allāh b. Muʿāwiya had gained a certain success in Khurāsān, ʿAbd Allāh al-Maḥḍ, along with other partisans of the 'Alid cause, decided to act.[48] During a pilgrimage to Mecca, 'Abd Allāh al-Maḥḍ invited his relatives and followers to take the oath of allegiance to his son. That was done first in the Ḥaram of Mecca and again at Al-Abwa, in the neighbourhood of Medina.[49] According to Abū'l-Faraj,[50] among those who took the oath were the three 'Abbāsid brothers Ibrāhīm al-Imām, Abū'l-Abbās as-Saffāḥ, and Abū Ja'far al-Manṣūr (b. Muḥammad b. 'Alī b. 'Abd Allāh b. al-'Abbās) as well as other members of the 'Abbāsid house. There is no confirmation of this report that all these 'Abbāsids took part in the ceremony at Al-Abwa. Only the name of Abū Ja'far al-Manṣūr is given by some other historians.[51] This latter report seems acceptable as Al-Manṣūr in his youth was a Mu'tazilite[52] and a companion of 'Amr b. 'Ubayd,[53] who probably induced him to pay homage to An-Nafs az-Zakīya. The only opposition from the Hāshimites to An-Nafs az-Zakīya at Al-Abwa is reported to have come from Ja'far aṣ-Ṣādiq's side,[54] for he considered himself the only rightful person for the function of the Imamate, and was against any military organization.

However, in spite of An-Nafs az-Zakīya's popularity, neither he nor his father acted with sufficient energy, and they allowed the 'Abbāsids to take the initiative. Both the father and the son were but passive spectators to the great upheaval and downfall of the Umayyad dynasty. Indeed, all the necessary elements for a successful revolution were present, and it was only a matter of strike and action. Whoever could strike first would gain the prize.

Ideas as to who should and who should not be regarded as the *Ahl al-Bayt* were no doubt much confused at this time. Every claimant in 'Alī's family and their supporters and followers spread different theories to justify their own claims. One group of the Shī'īs held that after 'Alī only the sons through Fāṭima had the right to the heritage of the Prophet as the "family of the Prophet", and among them, since Ḥusayn succeeded Ḥasan by the latter's expressed will, all rights were transferred to Ḥusayn and his posterity to the exclusion of the Ḥasanid branch. This group, which we are referring to as the legitimist faction of the Shī'a, though it never ceased to make its existence felt, was undoubtedly reduced to a small minority at this particular time, after the *Tawwābūn* movement. Others believed that any descendant of ʿAlī and Fāṭima, whether from the line of Ḥusayn or Ḥasan, was entitled to the leadership of the community. In this group come the followers of Zayd and An-Nafs az-Zakīya. The third and major group of the Shīʿa in this transitional period, the Kaysānites, included also ʿAlī's progeny by other women, in particular Muḥammad b. al-Ḥanafīya and after him his son Abū Hāshim. These distinctions were largely understood and observed by the more theoretical and legalistically-minded people in Medina and Kūfa. The mass of the people, however, full of hatred, discontent, and the feeling of being suppressed by the Umayyad aristocracy, were ready to swarm around any member of the revered clan of the Ṭālibīs who could liberate them from their sufferings.

Swayed by these feelings, therefore, a large part of the local population of Kūfa, especially of the lower classes, were prepared to range themselves with any anti-Umayyad movement. Such was the support given to the dubious claims of ʿAbd Allāh b. Muʿāwiya,[55] a great-grandson of ʿAlī's elder brother Jaʿfar b. Abī Ṭālib. Ṭabarī mentions that the majority of his supporters consisted of the slaves and commoners of Kūfa and the villagers of the *Sawād*.[56] After an unsuccessful rising in Kūfa, Ibn Muʿāwiya managed to reach Persia and controlled a large area there until he was assassinated, probably by Abū Muslim.[57] It might be accepted that Ibn Muʿāwiya attained success in Persia by connecting himself with the Kaysānīya through the claim that he was the emissary of Abū Hāshim. Ibn Muʿāwiya's propaganda in Khurāsān, however, made the task easier for a more vigorous leader to organize a successful revolt.

After all the preceding movements and revolts, the time was now ripe for a successful rising which was not, in fact, in favour of an ʿAlid, but rather for the ʿAbbāsids, who had for some time been plotting in the background and watching for their opportunity. ʿAlī b. ʿAbd Allāh b. al-ʿAbbās b. ʿAbd al-Muṭṭalib was the first person of the Abbāsid house to nourish political ambitions, but had nothing tangible to support him from a legal point of view. His grandfather Al-ʿAbbās, the uncle of the Prophet, had never claimed the caliphate for himself. Moreover, his being a late convert to Islam and his opportunistic policy[58] had marred his reputation among the

Muslims. ʿAbd Allāh b. ʿAbbās too, though renowned for his learning, had no political aspirations and always championed the cause of ʿAlī b. Abī Ṭālib.[59] He was ʿAlī's governor in Baṣra and also his personal representative attached to the arbiter Abū Mūsā al-Ashʿarī.[60] It is possible that ʿAlī b. ʿAbd Allāh might have been inspired by certain rights based on old tribal customs. The Meccan clan of Priest-Sayyids included all the descendants of ʿAbd al-Muṭṭalib, and so, from the viewpoint of legitimism, their claims were better than those of the Banū Umayya, which were based mainly on political factors. The Umayyads on their part endeavoured to prove that the whole clan of the Banū ʿAbd Manāf were the ruling house of the Quraysh.[61] Nevertheless, even if ʿAbbās, once the custodian of the Kaʿba, and his progeny had as strong a claim to supreme leadership as ʿAlī b. Abī Ṭālib, the ʿAbbāsids had neglected it for too long. Moreover, the fact that ʿAlī was one of the earliest converts to Islam, while ʿAbbās tarried until the conquest of Mecca, was detrimental to the position of the ʿAbbāsids within the Muslim community. Then, the Shīʿīs had accustomed themselves to the idea that the rights to the caliphate belonged to the ʿAlids. Obviously, therefore, it was not possible for the ʿAbbāsids to claim the caliphate directly.

ʿAlī b. ʿAbd Allāh saw an opportunity, in inducing Abū Hāshim, the son and successor of Ibn al-Ḥanafīya, who had no son and was a lonely person under the detention of the Umayyads in Damascus, to bequeath to the ʿAbbāsids his rights to the Imamate. He instructed his youthful son Muḥammad to gain the Imam's favour and confidence. After some time, the Caliph Sulaymān b. ʿAbd al-Malik allowed Abū Hāshim to return home. On his way to the Ḥijāz, it is said that he was poisoned, either at the instigation of the Caliph Sulaymān or by Muḥammad on his own account.[62] He died at Ḥumayma, the headquarters of the ʿAbbāsids, where he stayed as the latter's guest. Before his death he made Muḥammad b. ʿAlī his legatee and gave him letters addressed to Shīʿī circles in Khurāsān.[63] In this way Muḥammad became Imam and was recognized by the majority of the Hāshimīya sect, and thus "the ʿAbbāsids inherited the party and organization of Abū Hāshim, along with his claims."[64]

Though the ʿAbbāsid movement was first organized and

directed from Kūfa, it seems that the ʿAbbāsids were not very sure of the Kūfans, due to the latters' pro-ʿAlid sympathies, and so were afraid that the Iraqis would be unwilling to accept their claims to the Imamate. Although many of the Hāshimīya sectarians recognized the validity of the ʿAbbāsids' claims, some of them refused to accept the transfer of the Imamate from the ʿAlids to another branch of the Hāshimites. This was particularly characteristic of the attitude of the Kūfans, whose pro-ʿAlid sympathies were very strong. Some Shīʿīs believed that Abū Hāshim was not dead, but had concealed himself, and that he was Al-Mahdī. Others admitted that he had died, but had appointed his brother ʿAlī to the Imamate, which then passed from father to son in the same line.[65]

On the other hand, Khurāsān was still largely a virgin land insofar as sectarian conflicts were concerned. The majority of the so-called Shīʿīs in that distant country were not so much interested in the differences between the various branches of the *Ahl al-Bayt,* but they were ready to follow any leader from the House of the Prophet against the Umayyads.[66] Still, Abū Muslim, the chief organizer of the movement, though appointed by Ibrāhīm,[67] the head of the ʿAbbāsid family, claimed to be acting on behalf of an Imam from the *Ahl al-Bayt* who had not yet been chosen or designated. In this way he gained the support of many who would not have been ready to support him had they known that the Imam from the family of Hāshim would in fact be from the family of Al-ʿAbbās.[68] The support given by the followers of Al-Mukhtār may strengthen this assumption.

However, Ibrāhīm was arrested by the orders of the Caliph Marwān b. Muḥammad, brought to Damascus, and subsequently dispatched to Ḥarrān and imprisoned, where he died either of plague or—as the ʿAbbāsids assert—was put to death at the Caliph's command.[69] According to Ibrāhīm's instructions, his brother Abū'l-ʿAbbās, in the company of a third brother, Abū Jaʿfar ʿAbd Allāh, and fourteen other members of the family, left Al-Ḥumayma and reached Kūfa.[70] In Kūfa the local representative of the ʿAbbāsids was Abū Salama Ḥafṣ, a Kaysānite follower of Abū Hāshim. At this critical moment Abū Salama is reported to have thought of breaking his allegiance to the ʿAbbāsids since he felt bound by loyalty to Imam Ibrāhīm, but not to his brothers.[71] He lodged the 'Abbāsid fugitives in a house and tried to conceal their whereabouts from the Khurāsānian leaders in Kūfa.[72]

According to what Jahshiyārī and Ṭabarī report, when the news of the death of Ibrāhīm al-Imam reached Kūfa, Abū Salama "on the suggestion and advice of some other Shī'īs of Kūfa, intended to establish the Imamate of the 'Alids,"[73] and accordingly he wrote letters to Ja'far aṣ-Ṣādiq, 'Abd Allāh al-Mahḍ, and 'Umar b. 'Alī Zayn al-'Ābidīn, asking each one of them in turn to come to Kūfa in person and he would support their claims to the Imamate. The messenger was ordered first to contact Ja'far, and only if he refused, then to go to 'Abd Allāh, and in case of his refusal, to 'Umar b. 'Alī. When the messenger, however, presented the letter first to Ja'far, the latter called for a lamp, burned the letter, and said to the messenger, "Tell your master what you have seen."[74] Mas'ūdī tells the story in a different colour, saying: "When the 'Abbāsid leader Ibrāhīm al-Imam was killed by Marwān II, Abū Salama feared that this would mean the failure of their undertaking, and he attempted therefore to induce Ja'far aṣ-Ṣādiq, and in case he refused, then 'Abd Allāh and lastly 'Umar b. 'Alī, to come to him in person and to openly declare his claims to the Imamate."[75]

The same story asserts that 'Abd Allāh al-Maḥḍ accepted the offer and was only too delighted to receive the help of Abū Salama. Ja'far aṣ-Ṣādiq, in all the sources which have recorded this story, is reported to have severely warned 'Abd Allāh "not to indulge and endanger his and his son's life in this game of power and treachery, as Abū Salama is not our Shī'a and the Khurāsānians are not our followers." 'Abd Allāh bitingly retorted, "You are jealous of me and my son."[76] If this conversation is true it would throw light on Ja'far's extremely cautious policy of keeping entirely out of politics. As for Abū Salama, Moscati points out that in his wavering attitude "one can perhaps see a consequence of the deliberate ambiguity about the rights of the 'House of the Prophet', put into circulation by the revolutionary propaganda."[77]

The events in Kūfa moved quickly in favour of the 'Abbāsids. Their presence or concealment[78] in Kūfa was betrayed through one Abū Jahm to Abū Ḥumayd, who, with other Khurāsānian chiefs encamped in the vicinity of Kūfa, came and at once paid homage to Abū'l-ʿAbbās[79] as the Imam and Caliph, compelling Abū Salama to comply.[80]

Immediately after, Abū'l-ʿAbbās, together with his supporters, went to the mosque where he made his inaugural speech. In this speech he named himself as-Saffāḥ (the Bloodshedder) and identified the glory of God with his own interests and those of his house. He named "the Abbāsids as the *Ahl al-Bayt* from whom uncleanness was removed", and denied that the ʿAlids were more worthy of the caliphate.[81] As-Saffāḥ's address was followed by a speech from his uncle, Dā'ūd b. ʿAlī, who emphasized that the rights of the ʿAbbāsids were legally inherited and there were but two legal caliphs in Islam: ʿAlī b. Abī Ṭālib and As-Saffāḥ. He added that the caliphate would remain in the hands of the ʿAbbāsids until they passed it over to ʿĪsā b. Maryam (Jesus).[82]

The accession of Abū'l-ʿAbbās was followed immediately by the first breach with the extremist Shīʿīs. The testament of Abū Hāshim was of the utmost importance to the ʿAbbāsids, for at the onset of their propaganda it allowed them to take over the sectarian circles in Persia and so establish the nucleus of their own religio-political party. Once the aim was achieved, the ʿAbbāsids, on their own accession to the caliphate, justified their rights by different arguments, without even mentioning Abū Hāshim's name. Now they found it necessary to allow the memory of the bequest to pass into oblivion, for its connections with Shīʿī extremism were too strong and could be dangerous or embarrassing. The first task, therefore, before As-Saffāḥ was to break the alliance with the extremists and to remove those who supported the cause basically on that sectarian ground. Thus the first who had to pay with his life was Abū Salama, either on account of his strong connections with the extremist Shīʿīs or because of his alleged pro-ʿAlid leanings and his offer of support for their bid for the caliphate. The second reason cannot be completely ignored as an immediate cause of his assassination. There seems no difficulty in accepting that, at first, knowing nothing about Abū Salama's recent pro-ʿAlid activities, the ʿAbbāsids called him by the title *Wazīr Āl Rasūl Allāh*,[83] but as soon as As-Saffāḥ came to know about his fickleness he successfully arranged for his assassination. This is what both Ṭabarī and Masʿūdī clearly describe as the reason for Abū Salama's assassination.[84] Nevertheless, this immediate cause was coupled with As-Saffāḥ's policy to get rid of revolutionary sectarians, of whom Abū Salama was the most powerful leader.

As-Saffāḥ's rule lasted for four years, during which period the ʿAlids in Medina, "disorganized by the frustration of their hopes",[85] kept quiet and affairs remained stationary. But when Manṣūr assumed the caliphate in 136/753, the ʿAlids, embittered by the usurpation of their rights by the house of ʿAbbās, began to voice their complaints. On the other hand, except for the *Shīʿat Banī ʿAbbās,* who regarded As-Saffāḥ not only as Caliph and Imam but also as the Mahdī, the Shīʿī masses were also dissatisfied; and this popular dissatisfaction, which became manifest even during As-Saffāḥ's rule,[86] grew with the accession of Al-Manṣūr. They felt that the expected Kingdom of Righteousness had not materialised: one evil rule had been replaced by another.

Thus, at the accession of Manṣūr, Muḥammad an-Nafs az-Zakīya, who had long been coveting the role of Al-Mahdī, refused to take the oath of allegiance to him and started his Messianic propaganda. This angered Manṣūr, and in 140/758 he decided to compel An-Nafs az-Zakīya and his brother Ibrāhīm to pay him homage. He ordered the arrest of ʿAbd Allāh al-Maḥḍ and many other ʿAlids; of the thirteen arrested, some were cruelly scourged to try to force them to disclose the hiding place of the other fugitives, but in vain.[87] It is important to note that though An-Nafs az-Zakīya tried to gain support in many parts of the Muslim population,[88] it was chiefly the people of the Ḥijāz, rather than Kūfa, who enthusiastically responded to his appeal, and with few exceptions, swore the oath of allegiance to him.[89] The traditionist circles of Medina wholeheartedly supported and upheld his cause; Mālik b. Anas declared that the oath sworn to the ʿAbbāsids was no longer binding as it had been taken under compulsion.[90] The Zaydites and Muʿtazilites of Kūfa and Baṣra were also ready to help him.[91] In Ramaḍān 145/December 762, however, a fierce battle was engaged and resulted in the utter defeat of the Medinese and in the death of An-Nafs az-Zakīya while fighting the ʿAbbāsid army. The experience and death of An-Nafs az-Zakīya resulted in many traditions, some of them attributed to

Jaʿfar aṣ-Ṣādiq, who was said to have foreseen the fate of An-Nafs az-Zakīya.[92]

An-Nafs az-Zakīya's abortive uprising was followed by another by his brother Ibrāhīm in Baṣra, where he was collecting supporters for the former. The Zaydite and Muʿtazilite circles of Kūfa and Baṣra supported Ibrāhīm in a body.[93] The jurists of Kūfa—Abū Ḥanīfa, Sufyān al-Thawrī, Masʿūd b. Kudam, and many others—wrote letters to Ibrāhīm inviting him to their city or backed him by issuing legal decisions (*fatāwā*) favouring his cause.[94] With a force of 15,000 men Ibrāhīm left Baṣra for Kūfa to join his Kūfan sympathisers, but was encountered by the ʿAbbāsid army at Bakhamra, which resulted in Ibrāhīm's death.[95] This was the end of ʿAlid risings of any consequence and of Messianic hopes aspired to by them or placed in them. Some of An-Nafs az-Zakīya's followers then found an outlet for their hopes in certain supernatural ideas. They regarded him as the Mahdī and refused to accept the fact of his death, asserting that only a devil in human form had been killed in his stead, while he was concealed in a mountain in Najd.[96] The failure of Ibrāhīm's revolt also practically marked the end of the Medinese desire to establish a caliphate of their own choice. The long cherished hopes of the Shīʿīs, especially those of activists and extremists, were frustrated.

All these events and circumstances, however, form the background against which the Imamate of Jaʿfar happened to fall. But before we try to examine his position and his standpoint in this religio-political setting, there remains still another vital aspect to be elaborated.

We have seen that the great Hāshimite party of the Umayyad era was now split into ʿAlids and ʿAbbāsids. So the struggle assumed a new form. It was no longer a deadly struggle between "a usurping dynasty" and a legitimist opposition, but rather between the two factions of Banū Hāshim, each claiming legitimist rights for itself with the total exclusion of the other: the descendants of the Prophet's uncle and the descendants of the Prophet's cousin and daughter, ʿAlī and Fāṭima. And to further complicate the situation, the house of ʿAlī was itself divided into three factions: the line of Ḥusayn; the line of Ibn al-Ḥanafīya; and the line of Ḥasan, which emerged later. Thus the house of

'Abbās was on one side, and the house of 'Alī, divided into three groups, was on the other.

The first 'Abbāsid caliph, As-Saffāḥ, fully anticipated this situation and from the very first moment of his caliphate began the task of justifying the rights of his house on legitimist grounds, as is evident from his inaugural speech discussed above. In this way he laid down the foundation of his family's policy in the forthcoming struggle to repudiate the claims of the house of 'Alī. But, owing to the fact that during the short-lived reign of As-Saffāḥ the 'Alids themselves could not come out with any serious or visible opposition, things remained rather confused and stationary.

It was Manṣūr who had to face the most threatening opposition from the 'Alids to the newly established authority of his house. Thus in order to save, strengthen, and consolidate his caliphate, Manṣūr concentrated his efforts on two basic and fundamental objectives. The first was to justify the rights of his house on legal and religious grounds. This logically implied the repudiation of the claims of the 'Alids through legal argumentation. The second was to gain for his caliphate the acceptance of the Muslim *Jamā'a.* This required the severance of all relations and connections with all revolutionary and extremist groups and organizations. Manṣūr realised only too well that Kaysānite Shī'ism, Rawandite extremism,[97] revolutionaries of Abū Muslim's following (who held beliefs which comprised a mixture of Kaysānite Shī'ism and Mazdakism), or the Shī'at of 'Abbāsīya, could not serve as the religious basis for the 'Abbāsid caliphate. Repudiating all of the above groups, Manṣūr approached the traditionist circles (*Ahl al-Ḥadīth*), which he recognized as the representative section of the Muslim community and the exponents of the *Jamā'a.* It would be in order if we consider this aspect later and examine first his endeavour to vindicate the rights of his house to the caliphate.

The best and probably the most authentic and relevant documentary evidence in this connection is an exchange of letters between Manṣūr and his most serious 'Alid rival, Muḥammad an-Nafs az-Zakīya. In order to understand Manṣūr's method of argumentation and his approach to the problem it is necessary to first consider An-Nafs az-Zakīya's letter to him. It reads:

"Our father ʿAlī was the *Waṣī* and the *Imām*. How is it that you appropriate his inheritance while we are still alive? You know that there is no one among the Hāshimites who himself has points of excellence and honour comparable to our past and present, our descent and our cause ... We are the children of Fāṭima, the daughter of ʿAmr, at the time of paganism, whereas you are not; we are the children of the Prophet's daughter Fāṭima at the time of Islam, and you are not. And I happen to be the golden medium in the line of descent amongst Banū Hāshim, and the best of them all as regards parentage. No Persian did I have for a mother and no slave-girls were on the maternal side of my ancestors ...[98] I was twice-born from the loins of Muḥammad the Prophet ... amongst my grandfathers I have the highly esteemed in Paradise and the least tormented in Hell; I am therefore the son of the best of the excellent people.

"As for the amnesty you have given me, may I ask what kind of amnesty it is? Is it the same that you gave to Ibn Hubayra or to your uncle ʿAbd Allāh b. ʿAlī or the one that was given to Abū Muslim?"[99]

It is clear from this letter that first of all An-Nafs az-Zakīya claims his rights on the basis that his ancestor ʿAlī b. Abī Ṭālib was the *Waṣī* and the *Imām*, and then he strengthens this by emphasizing the circumstance of his birth from both his father's and his mother's sides: *sharaf* from the father's side and dignity from the mother's side. At the end he alludes to the treacherous nature of the ʿAbbāsids. It is particularly interesting to note that in spite of his reference to ʿAlī as the *Waṣī* and the *Imām*, and to Fatimid descent,[100] the Ḥijāz was unanimous in supporting the cause of An-Nafs az-Zakīya.

It would be most revealing to see how Manṣūr argued against the claims of his ʿAlid rival and how he justified his own rights to the supreme leadership of the community. Manṣūr replied to An-Nafs az-Zakīya in this way:

"I received your letter. You know that our greatest honour in the times of ignorance, namely the dispensing of water for the pilgrims and the guardianship of the well of Zamzam, became the privilege of ʿAbbās alone among all his brothers. Your father [ʿAlī] litigated concerning this privilege with us, but ʿUmar has given judgement in our favour so that we have never ceased to be in possession of this honour in the times of the *Jāhilīya* as well as in those of Islam ...

"Most of your pride is based on descent from the mother's

side,[101] which would only deceive the uncouth and the common. God has not made the women like uncles, fathers, fathers-in-law and the responsible relatives . . . As for your claim that you are the son of the Apostle of God, Almighty God has rejected such a claim when he said, 'Muḥammad is not the father of any of your men, but he is the Apostle of God and the Seal of the Prophets.' [102] But you are the children of the daughter. Verily it is a close relationship, but she is a woman who can inherit but cannot become an Imam. How on earth then could the Imamate be inherited through her? . . . You know that after the death of the Prophet no son of ʿAbd al-Muṭṭalib remained alive other than Al-ʿAbbās, and that ʿAbbās inherited his rights as the uncle of the Prophet. Then more than one of the Banū Hāshim sought the caliphate, but none attained it except the descendants of ʿAbbās, and so the *Siqāya* and the inheritance of the Prophet, as well as the caliphate, belong to him and his progeny, and will remain in their possession. For ʿAbbās was heir and legatee to every honour and virtue that ever existed in the times of the *Jāhilīya* and of Islam." [103]

This letter is a most important document for our understanding of the line of argument which Manṣūr adopted against his ʿAlid rivals. If we analyse the contents of the letter the following points will be evident. Firstly, he resorted to the customary law of the Arabs according to which when the father dies, the paternal uncle takes his place. Secondly, he placed special stress on ʿUmar's ruling in favour of ʿAbbās, thus emphasizing the second caliph's authority in the same way as the *Aṣḥāb al-Ḥadīth*. Thirdly, ʿAbbās, as the uncle, had better claims to the heritage of the Prophet than ʿAlī did as a cousin and son-in-law. Fourthly, he rejected any claim through Fāṭima, which was a great prerogative for commanding respect among the Shīʿīs in particular and among the Muslims in general. Finally, the ʿAlids, due to the weakness of their legal claim, coupled with their lack of energy, successively failed in their attempts to procure the caliphate for themselves, while the progeny of ʿAbbās attained it due to their better claims, coupled with competence and ability. It is also very important to note that both An-Nafs az-Zakīya and Manṣūr go back for their arguments of rights to the *Jāhilīya* period and consider the prerogative of that time honourable and applicable to the Islamic era.

It is, however, evident from the support given to the risings of An-Nafs az-Zakīya and his brother Ibrāhīm, which took place after this correspondence, by the *Ahl al-Ḥadīth* (whether of Murjite brand or otherwise) that they were not impressed by the arguments of Manṣūr for the alleged rights of ʿAbbās; they continued to assert that the only just candidates to the Imamate were the ʿAlids. We have pointed out that when An-Nafs az-Zakīya rose in rebellion, Mālik b. Anas declared that the oath of allegiance taken by the inhabitants of Medina to the ʿAbbāsids was unlawful, as it had been enforced under duress.[104] Similarly, during the revolt of Ibrāhīm b. ʿAbd Allāh, Abū Ḥanīfa, Sufyān ath-Thawrī, Al-Aʿmash and other Kūfan jurists and *Ahl al-Ḥadīth* gave their most emphatic support and encouragement to those who wished to participate in insurrection.[105]

After the reconquest of Medina and the suppression of the revolt of Ibrāhīm, Manṣūr ordered Mālik b. Anas to be flogged, and considered Abū Ḥanīfa as an enemy so dangerous that he imprisoned him until his death.[106] Apart from these few strong and rather irreconcilable personalities who actively opposed him and were to be severely punished, Manṣūr did not attack the traditionists as such. On the contrary, he regarded them as the basic element on which he could establish the foundation of a theocratic state, headed by the *Khalīfat Allāh*, the vice-regent of God, obedience to whom was an absolute religious duty (*farḍ*).[107] Thus, for example, when Manṣūr said in a sermon: "Only I am the authority of God upon His earth," [108] he was not announcing himself merely as a defender of religion or its protector. He identified his interest with the faith of Islam and treated the will of God as synonymous with his own aims.

Gradually, however, whether because of the fact that no powerful member of the ʿAlid house was ready to lead a rising, or due to Manṣūr's successful policy of blandishment or coercion, most of the *Ahl al-Ḥadīth* and jurists of Medina and Kūfa came to be reconciled with the caliphate. Eventually, willingly or unwillingly, they abandoned the ʿAlid cause and ranged themselves obediently under Manṣūr's orders.

Now, keeping in view this religio-political setting of events, we are better able to examine the re-emergence of the legitimist Imamate of the Ḥusaynid line under the leadership of Jaʿfar aṣ-Ṣādiq, and the role played by him in the midst of these circumstances. By an analysis of all that has been brought out above, one major and fundamental point is certain. All the successive claimants of the ʿAlid house based their claims on the principle that they were the rightful Imams due to their virtues and circumstances of birth, and that *the Imamate and the caliphate cannot be separated*: therefore it is exclusively their legitimist right as well as their religious duty to take the caliphate back from the usurpers, whether Umayyad or ʿAbbāsid. In other words, they thought it the function of the rightful Imam to run the caliphal administration, which is meant to establish the rule of justice and equality, and thus it is necessary for an Imam to be a caliph. This principle was accepted by the representative groups of the Muslim *Jamāʿa*—Muʿtazilites, Murjites, *Ahl al-Ḥadīth* and the jurists of Medina and Kūfa—which is evident from the wholehearted support given by them to the ʿAlid claimants and to their risings. On the other hand, the ʿAbbāsids too held the same view that the Imamate and the caliphate are inseparable, and a rightful Imam alone has the right to command the caliphal authority. But at the same time they disputed and rejected the claims of the ʿAlids for this office and asserted that only they themselves were the legitimist Imam-caliphs. Ultimately Manṣūr, however, succeeded in crushing the ʿAlids and gaining the submission of the representative groups of the *Jamāʿa*.

This meant the complete collapse and defeat of the ʿAlid claims to the Imamate, since, as they held, the Imamate was bound up with the caliphate, which they had failed to procure for themselves. This critical situation, however, required a fresh interpretation and elucidation of the whole concept of the Imamate.

It was at this point that the Imam Jaʿfar aṣ-Ṣādiq emerged with his comprehensive interpretation of the function of the Imamate. He differed categorically from the hitherto dominating view that an Imam should be a caliph as well, and put forward the idea of dividing the Imamate and the caliphate into two separate institutions until such time as God would make an Imam victorious. This Imam, who must be a descendant of the Prophet through ʿAlī and Fāṭima, derives his exclusive authority, not by political claims but by *Naṣṣ*, that is, explicit designation by the previous Imam, and he inherits the special knowledge of religion coming down in the family from generation to generation. Thus the sphere and domain of this Imam is chiefly religious leadership and the spiritual guidance of the community, not the temporal power. We shall see in detail in the following chapter how Jaʿfar elaborated this theory of the Imamate and the nature and function of an Imam. But let us make it clear here that Jaʿfar was by no means the originator of this theory of the Imamate. We have already pointed out that the idea of a legitimist Imam inspired with special knowledge had already been adopted by Zayn al-ʿĀbidīn, and then it was further advanced by Muḥammad al-Bāqir. It was, however, the time and circumstances which provided Jaʿfar with a most suitable and propitious opportunity to elaborate and explain the ideas propounded by his father and grandfather. This great opportunity therefore made Jaʿfar's Imamate crucial.

Before we close this chapter, two more points are to be noted in passing. One is the question whether Jaʿfar, by presenting the theory pertaining to his own and his father's Imamates, thought of establishing a sect, group, or party of his own, separated from the rest of the Muslims, or whether he wanted his Imamate with the above-mentioned prerogatives to be accepted and acknowledged by the whole body of the Muslim. The audience of Jaʿfar and the wide range of people whom he addressed and tried to convince is a sufficient proof that Jaʿfar himself did not intend to establish a separate sect which alone should follow his doctrine of the Imamate. But in the event, only those who had already a background of Shīʿī inclination of one sort or another accepted Jaʿfar's doctrine of the Imamate and ultimately became a section of the Muslim community distinguishable from the rest of it.

The second point is that the doctrine of the Imamate and the function of the Imam elaborated by Jaʿfar at this stage provided a basic authority for the later Twelver theologians and theorists to explain and solve many problems of the pre-Jaʿfar period. This was done by applying Jaʿfar's theory of the Imamate to the actions of the Imams of the House who came before him, for example, ʿAlī's acceptance of the first three caliphs, the abdication of Ḥasan, the inactive attitude of Ḥusayn and the quiescent policies of Zayn al-ʿĀbidīn and Muḥammad al-Bāqir. All these questions were solved in accordance with Ja'far's explanation that it is not necessary for a rightful Imam to combine the temporal power in his person or even claim the political authority—the caliphate—if the circumstances did not allow him to do so. On the other hand, it can also be said that Ja'far's theory of the Imamate was in fact a natural corollary of his family's past history and experience.

Notes to Chapter 10

[1] For the former date, see Ya'qūbī, *Ta'rīkh,* II, p. 381; Ibn Khallikān, I. p. 327; Ibn al-Jawzī, *Ṣafwa,* II, p. 93; 'Āmilī, *A'yān,* IV, p. 54; Muḥammad b. Ṭalḥa, *Maṭālib al-Su'ūl,* p. 89. For the latter, see Mas'ūdī, *Murūj,* III, p. 219; Sa'd al-Ash'arī, *Maqālāt,* p. 79; Kulaynī, *Kāfī,* p. 193; Majlisī, *Tadhkirat al-A'imma* p. 139. It is difficult to choose between these two dates, but the former is probably correct, since Ibn Khallikān and others record his birth in the *'Āmm al-Juḥāf,* the year of the flood in Mecca, which according to Ṭabarī, II, p. 1040, occurred in 80/699–700.

[2] Ibn Sa'd, V, p. 320; Ya'qūbī, II, p. 320; Qāḍī Nu'mān, *Sharḥ al-Akhbār,* MS. fol. 32a.

[3] Ibn Khallikān, I, p. 327; Qāḍī Nu'mān, loc. cit.

[4] Ṭabarī, III, p. 2509; Ya'qūbī, II, p. 381; Sa'd al-Ash'arī, *Maqālāt,* p. 79; Ibn Khallikān, loc. cit.; Kulaynī, *Kāfī,* p. 194; 'Āmilī, *A'yān,* IV, p. 452

[5] See Ibn Sa'd, V, p. 216; Ibn 'Imād, *Shadharāt,* I, p. 104; Ya'qūbī, III, p. 46; Kashshī, *Rijāl,* pp. 76–79; Abu Nu'aym, *Ḥilya,* III, p. 135

[6] Ibn Sa'd, V, pp. 189 ff.; Ṭabarī, II, p. 1183; Ibn 'Imād, *Shadharāt,* I, p. 62

[7] See Kulaynī, *Kāfī,* p. 193. His Imamate would have been of twenty-eight years' duration based on a birth date of 83/703–704; if 80/699–700 is accepted, his period in the Imamate would be thirty-one years.

[8] Ya'qūbī, II, p. 381

[9] Qāḍī Nu'mān, *Sharḥ al-Akhbār,* MS. fol. 42a

[10] ibid., fol. 39a

[11] Shahrastānī, *Milal,* I, p. 166

[12] S. Moscati, "Per Una Storia De la'Antica Šī'a," *RSO,* 1955, p. 251

[13] B. Lewis, *The Origins of Ismā'īlism,* p. 25

[14] Ḥusayn was also called "al-Mahdī, son of al-Mahdī", but this as yet had no messianic implications. See Ṭabarī, II, p. 546

[15] Balādhurī, V, p. 218; also see Ṭabarī, II, pp. 606 f., 633

[16] See Ibn Sa'd, V, p. 94

[17] Balādhurī, loc. cit.

[18] Ṭabarī, II, pp. 672–710; Balādhurī, V, p. 253. For the other titles which they were given, see Ṭabarī, II, p. 691; Balādhurī, loc. cit.

[19] For the name Kaysānīya there are a number of suggestions, and the person of Abū ʿAmra Kaysān has also been a great historical problem. For various suggestions and possibilities see Shahrastānī, *Milal,* I, p. 147; Baghdādī, *Farq,* p. 26; Balādhurī, V, p. 229; B. Lewis, *The Origins of Ismāʿīlism,* p. 27

[20] Ibn Saʿd, V, p. 115

[21] Ibn Khaldūn, *ʿIbar,* III, p. 172. Thus Abū Hāshim became recognized as the official head of this branch of the Shīʿa; see De Goeje, "Al-Balādhurī's *Ansāb*", *ZDMG,* 1884, p. 394

[22] See the verse of Kuthayyir in *Aghānī,* IX, p. 14, and the eulogy of Ibn al-Ḥanafīya by Al-Sayyid al-Ḥimyarī in *Aghānī,* VII, p. 227

[23] Kashshī, *Rijāl,* p. 314

[24] W. Ivanow, "Early Shīʿīte Movements", *JBBRAS,* 1939, p. 3

[25] ibid.

[26] Schacht, *An Introduction to Islamic Law,* p. 23

[27] Mubarrad, *Kāmil,* I, p. 710

[28] Jāḥiẓ. *Rasā'il,* "Kitāb Faḍl Banī Hāshim", p. 99; "Risāla fī Banī Umayya", p. 66. Also see the commentary on the Qur'ānic verse XVII, 50 in the *tafsīr* works.

[29] See Montgomery Watt, "Shīʿīsm Under the Ummayyads", *JRAS,* 1960, pp. 169 f.

[30] Ṭabarī, II, p. 1700

[31] Ṭabarī, loc. cit. For the use and meaning of the word *Rāfiḍī,* see Montgomery Watt, "The Rāfiḍites", *Oriens,* XVI (1963), p. 116

[32] Ṭabarī, loc. cit.

[33] Ṭabarī, II, p. 1709; Abū'l-Faraj, *Maqātil,* pp. 140 f.

[34] Jāḥiẓ, *Bayān,* I, p. 311–312

[35] ibid.

[36] Mubarrad, *Kāmil,* I, p. 260

[37] See Ṭabarī, II, p. 1774; Abū'l-Faraj, *Maqātil,* pp. 152 ff.

[38] Abū'l-Faraj, *Maqātil,* pp. 145 ff.

[39] See Jāḥiẓ, *Bayān,* I, p. 353; Abū'l-Faraj, *Maqātil,* pp. 233 ff.

[40] Abū Da'ūd, *Sunan,* II, p. 135

[41] See *Aghānī,* XII, p. 85

[42] Abū Da'ūd, *Sunan,* II, p. 135; Ibn Mājā, *Sunan,* II, p. 269

[43] Saʿd al-Ashʿarī, *Maqālāt,* pp. 74, 77; Nawbakhtī, *Firaq,* p. 59

[44] Saʿd al-Ashʿarī, *Maqālāt,* p. 77; Nawbakhtī, *Firaq,* p. 43

[45] Nawbakhtī, *Firaq,* p. 52; Baghdādī, *Farq,* pp. 36 ff.; Saʿd al-Ashʿarī, *Maqālāt,* p. 74

[46] Abū'l-Faraj, *Maqātil,* pp. 209 f., 292 ff.

[47] ibid.

[48] Ṭabarī, III, pp. 143 ff.; Abū'l-Faraj, *Maqātil,* pp. 206, 253

[49] Ṭabarī, III, p. 52; Abū'l-Faraj, *Maqātil,* pp. 209, 256. For Al-Abwa, see Yaqūt, *Muʿjam al-Buldān,* I, p. 79. According to another

report, this homage was paid at Suwayqa; see Abū'l-Faraj, *Maqātil*, pp. 293 ff.; *EI*[1] article "Muḥammad b. 'Abd Allāh"

[50] Abū'l-Faraj, *Maqātil*, pp. 208, 253, 178

[51] See, for example, Ṭabarī, III, p. 152

[52] Ṭabarī, III, pp. 143, 152; *EI*[1] article "Muḥammad b. 'Abd Allāh"

[53] Abū'l-Faraj, *Maqātil*, p. 209

[54] Abū'l-Faraj, *Maqātil*, pp. 207 f., 254 ff; *EI*[1] article "Muḥammad b. 'Abd Allāh"

[55] See *Aghānī*, XII, pp. 213 ff; Ṭabarī, II, pp. 1879, 1881; Montgomery Watt, "Shī'ism Under the Umayyads", p. 170

[56] Ṭabarī, II, pp. 1881, 1883, 1887

[57] See Montgomery Watt, "Shī'ism Under the Umayyads", p. 170

[58] See Montgomery Watt, *EI*[2] article "'Abbās b. 'Abd al-Muṭṭalib"

[59] Kashshī, *Rijāl*, pp. 56 f.

[60] See Kashshī, *Rijāl*, pp. 57 ff; Veccia Vaglieri, *EI*[2] article "'Abd Allāh b. 'Abbās"

[61] Mubarrad, *Kāmil*, I, p. 180

[62] See Abū'l-Faraj, *Maqātil*, p. 126; *Kāmil*, V, pp. 32–9; S. Moscati, "Testamento di Abū Hāshim", *RSO*, XXVII (1952), pp. 24–8

[63] Mas'ūdī, *Murūj*, III, p. 238; Abū'l-Faraj, loc. cit.; *Kāmil*, loc. cit.; Moscati, loc. cit.; Bernard Lewis, *EI*[2] article "Hāshimīya"

[64] Lewis, *EI*[2] articles "Hāshimīya" and "'Abbāsids"

[65] See Nawbakhtī, *Firaq*, pp. 28–29; Nashwān al-Ḥimyarī, *Ḥurr al-'Ayn*, pp. 159–60

[66] For the readiness of the Khurāsānians to follow any branch of the *Ahl al-Bayt*, see Ibn Qutayba, *'Uyūn al-Akhbār*, I, p. 204; Yāqūt, *Mu'jam al-Buldān*, II, p. 352

[67] Abū Muslim was adopted by Ibrāhīm as a member of the *Ahl al-Bayt*; see Ṭabarī, II, pp. 1937, 1949. For Abū Muslim himself, see Ibn Khallikān, III, pp. 145–55; Mas'ūdī, *Murūj*, III, p. 239; Ibn Qutayba, *Ma'ārif*, p. 145; Dīnawarī, p. 337; Ṭabarī, II, pp. 1949 f., 1987 ff; R. N. Frye, "The Role of Abū Muslim", *Muslim World*, January 1947

[68] See Wellhausen, *Arab Kingdom*, pp. 492–566; Lewis, *EI*[2] article "'Abbāsids"

[69] See Ṭabarī, III, pp. 25 ff., 42 ff., Dīnawarī, p. 357; Mas'ūdī, *Murūj*, III, p. 244

[70] Ṭabarī, III, p. 27; Mas'ūdī, *Murūj*, III, p. 253

[71] Jahshiyārī, *Al-Wuzarā' wa'l-Kuttāb*, p. 83; Mas'ūdī, *Murūj*, III, p. 253; Ibn Khallikān, III, pp. 148 f; Ṭabarī, III, pp. 27 f.; Ya'qūbī, II, pp. 345, 449

72 Masʿūdī, loc. cit.; Ṭabarī, loc. cit.; Wellhausen, *Arab Kingdom,* p. 544; S. Moscati, *EI*[2] article "Abū Salama"

73 Jahshiyārī, *Al-Wuzarā' wa'l-Kuttāb,* p. 86; Ṭabarī, III, p. 27

74 Jahshiyārī, loc. cit.; Ibn Tiqtaqa, *Al-Fakhrī,* p. 109

75 Masʿūdī, *Murūj,* III, p. 253 f.

76 See Yaʿqūbī, loc. cit.; Masʿūdī, loc. cit.; Jahshiyārī, loc. cit.

77 S. Moscati, *EI*[2] article "Abū Salama"

78 Yaʿqūbī, II, p. 345, gives the period of concealment as two months; Ṭabarī, III, p. 27, makes it forty days. Other sources do not mention the precise period.

79 See Lewis, *EI*[2] article "ʿAbbāsids"

80 Ṭabarī, III, pp. 28 ff.; Jahshiyārī, *Al-Wuzarā',* pp. 86 ff.; Yaʿqūbī, II, pp. 245 f; Masʿūdi, *Murūj,* III, pp. 255 f.

81 Ṭabarī, III, pp. 29 ff. Yaʿqubī, II, p. 350, says Abū'l-ʿAbbās did not speak at all because of fever. Masʿūdī, *Muruj,* III, p. 255 gives only a summary of the speech in two lines.

82 The speech of Dā'ūd is widely recorded, esp. Ṭabarī, III, pp. 31 ff.; Yaʿqūbī, II, p. 350. Masʿūdī, *Murūj,* III, p. 256 again only summarizes the main points.

83 See Ṭabarī, III, pp. 60 f.; Yaʿqūbī, II, pp. 352 f.; Masʿūdī, *Murūj,* III, p. 270; Ibn Khallikān, II, p. 196

84 See Ṭabarī, III, pp. 58 ff.; Masʿūdī, loc. cit.

85 Lewis, *EI*[2] article "ʿAbbāsids"

86 See Ṭabarī, III, pp. 75 f., 85; Maqrīzī *an-Nizaʿ,* p. 52

87 Yaʿqūbī, II, p. 369; Masʿūdī, *Murūj,* III, p. 295; Ṭabarī, III, pp. 151 ff.

88 See Ṭabarī, III, pp. 149 ff.

89 Ṭabarī, III, p. 199; Abū'l-Faraj, *Maqātil,* pp. 277 ff.

90 Ṭabarī, III, p. 200

91 Abū'l-Faraj, *Maqātil,* pp. 291 ff.

92 Ṭabarī, III, pp. 248, 252, 254; Abū'l-Faraj, *Maqātil,* pp. 248, 271; Shahrastānī, *Milal,* I, p. 156

93 Ṭabarī, III, pp. 291–300. For the names and details see Abū'l-Faraj, *Maqātil,* pp. 360 f., 365 ff.

94 Abū'l-Faraj, *Maqātil,* pp. 365 ff.

95 ibid., pp. 344 ff.

96 Baghdādī, *Farq,* pp. 36 ff., 148; Saʿd al-Ashʿarī, *Maqālāt,* p. 76

97 The name Rāwindīya is given to the sect which held that Abū Hāshim bequeathed the Imamate to Muḥammad b. ʿAlī (the ʿAbbāsid). See Lewis, *Origins of Ismāʿīlism,* p. 28

98 Manṣūr himself was a son of a slave-girl, and perhaps it was because of this that, though he was older than As-Saffāḥ, Ibrāhīm al-Imām did not appoint him as his successor.

99 Mubarrad, *Kāmil,* IV, pp. 114 f; Ṭabarī, III, pp. 209 ff.; Ibn Ṭiqṭaqa, *Al-Fakhrī,* pp. 225 ff.

[100] Ṭabarī, III, p. 189

[101] i.e., Fạṭima, the mother of Abū Ṭālib; Fāṭima, the mother of 'Alī; Fāṭima, the daughter of the Prophet; Fāṭima bint al-Ḥusayn, the mother of 'Abd Allāh al-Maḥḍ; and finally Hind bint Abī 'Ubayda, a descendant of 'Abd al-Muṭṭalib, the mother of An-Nafs az-Zakīya. See Abū'l-Faraj, *Maqātil*, p. 202. Manṣūr belittled this "descent through women", being himself a son of a slave-girl.

[102] *Qur'ān*, XXXIII, 40

[103] Ṭabarī, III, pp. 211 ff.; Mubarrad, *Kāmil*, IV, pp. 116 ff.

[104] Ṭabarī, III, p. 200

[105] Khaṭīb al-Baghdādī, *Ta'rīkh Baghdād*, XIII, p. 380; Abū'l-Faraj, *Maqātil*, pp. 366 ff., 365 ff.

[106] Khaṭīb al-Baghdādī, *Ta'rīkh Baghdād*, XIII, p. 422; Shahrastānī, *Milal*, I, p. 158. Abū'l-Faraj (*Maqātil*, pp. 367, 368) asserts that Abū Ḥanīfa was poisoned at the orders of the Caliph.

[107] Ṭabarī, III, p. 426. See Arnold, *The Caliphate*, p. 51. This principle was also stressed by the later 'Abbāsid caliphs; see Ṭabarī, III, p. 1565

[108] Ṭabarī, III, p. 426

Chapter 11

The Doctrine of the Imamate

It has been explained in detail in the preceding chapter how the activist claimants of the House of ʿAlī were crushed, their apparently popular movements collapsed one after the other, and the ʿAbbāsids finally managed to firmly establish themselves as the sole authority of both the state and religion. A process of assimilation was set into motion and most of the cross-currents represented by a number of politico-religious or religio-political groups were gradually being absorbed, under the patronage of the state authority, into a synthesis to be known as the *Jamāʿa*, which was supposed to support and in turn was supported by the ʿAbbāsid caliphate.

In this setting the strategic task of the Imam Jaʿfar aṣ-Ṣādiq was to save the basic ideal of Shīʿism from absorption by the emerging synthesis on the one hand, and to purify it from extremist and activist tendencies within itself on the other. Thus the circumstances in which the Imamate of Jaʿfar happened to fall afforded him a unique opportunity, denied to his father and grandfather, to firmly establish and explain the principles of legitimacy. The rudiments of the concept and function of the Imam had already been introduced by ʿAlī in his speeches, by Ḥasan in his letters to Muʿāwiya, and by Ḥusayn in his correspondence with the Shīʿīs of Kūfa and Baṣra, which we have discussed in the preceding chapters. After the death of Ḥusayn, the concept of legitimacy within the family of Muḥammad and of the function of the Imam restricted to religious and spiritual guidance of the community were laid down by Zayn al-ʿĀbidīn and Muḥammad al-Bāqir. Now, after the removal of other contenders from the scene, Jaʿfar enjoyed a strategically advantageous position, and it was his task to elucidate the doctrine of the Imamate and elaborate it in a definitive form.

In this attempt Jaʿfar put the utmost emphasis on two fundamental principles. The first was that of the *Naṣṣ*, that is, the Imamate is a prerogative bestowed by God upon a chosen person, from the family of the Prophet, who before his death and with the guidance of God, transfers the Imamate to another by an explicit designation (*Naṣṣ*). On the authority of *Naṣṣ*, therefore, the Imamate is restricted, through all political circumstances, to a definite individual among all the descendants of ʿAlī and Fāṭima, whether he claims the temporal rule for himself or not. Naturally, the transfer of the Imamate through *Naṣṣ* would be both incomplete and meaningless unless it could be traced back to the person of ʿAlī, who should have been entrusted with the office of the Imamate by the Prophet himself. The *Naṣṣ* thus initiated by the Prophet came down from ʿAlī to Ḥasan, from Ḥasan to Ḥusayn, and then remained strictly in the line of Ḥusayn until through successive *Naṣṣ* it reached Jaʿfar. This theory, as we shall see presently, distinguished Jaʿfar's Imamate from all other claimants, who did not claim a *Naṣṣ* from any preceding Imam. Zayd clearly denied that there was an explicit *Naṣṣ* or designation of ʿAlī by Muḥammad,[1] or that there was any designation of the next Imam by the preceding one. Nor did Muḥammad an-Nafs az-Zakīya or his brother Ibrāhīm ever resort to the principle of *Naṣṣ* from any preceding authority. On the contrary, as Ashʿarī points out,[2] the idea of *Naṣṣ* was the key trait of the *Rawāfiḍ*[3] as opposed to the supporters of Zayd and later on An-Nafs az-Zakīya. Ashʿarī's statement is in accordance with the unanimous reports given by the Twelver writers themselves, such as Nawbakhtī, Saʿd al-Ashʿarī, and Kashshī, of Muḥammad al-Bāqir's followers, who upheld him against Zayd as the only legitimist ʿAlid authority on the principle of *Naṣṣ*, though the doctrine of *Naṣṣ* was not yet fully elaborated in his time. A comparison between the traditions related from Al-Bāqir and those from Jaʿfar would demonstrate that Jaʿfar became increasingly clear and emphatic in his expositions on the doctrine of the *Naṣṣ* Imamate. As a result, a further comparison between the attitudes of the followers of these two respective Imams discloses a trend towards a clear acceptance of Jaʿfar as the

Imam largely on the principle of *Naṣṣ*. This is evident from the action of a group of the Kūfan Shīʿīs who, after the death of Al-Bāqir, adhered for some time to Zayd, but soon abandoned him and went over to Jaʿfar, whom they regarded as the representative of Al-Bāqir's claims.[4] Hodgson quotes Strothmann's suggestion, "that the story of the Kūfan Shīʿīs abandoning Zayd for Jaʿfar shows that they already accepted the idea of a line of Imams by inheritance."[5] The idea of the *Naṣṣ* Imamate, however, became such a common instrument that not only Jaʿfar, but a number of *ghulāt* (extremist Shīʿīs of Kūfa, who will be discussed later), such as Bayān, Abū Manṣūr, and Mughīra,[6] claimed inheritance from Al-Bāqir and achieved some short-lived success. There are numerous references in our sources to the effect that Jaʿfar repeatedly condemned those fanatics and warned his followers not to accept their traditions.

The second fundamental principle embodied in the doctrine of the Imamate as elaborated and emphasized by Jaʿfar was that of *ʿIlm*. This means that an Imam is a divinely inspired possessor of a special sum of knowledge of religion, which can only be passed on before his death to the following Imam. In this way the Imam of the time becomes the exclusively authoritative source of knowledge in religious matters, and thus without his guidance no one can keep to the right path.[7] This special knowledge includes both the external (*ẓāhir*) and the esoteric (*bāṭin*) meanings of the Qurʿān.[8] A close scrutiny of the traditions related from Al-Bāqir and then mostly from Jaʿfar on the subject of the Imamate will show that they rotate around these two principles of *Naṣṣ* and *ʿIlm*, which are not merely conjoined or added to one another, but are so thoroughly fused into a unitary vision of religious leadership that it is impossible to separate the one from the other. Hence *Naṣṣ* in fact means transmission of that special knowledge of religion which had been exclusively and legitimately restricted to the divinely favoured Imams of the House of the Prophet through ʿAlī, and which can only be transferred from one Imam to his successor as the legacy of the chosen family. Thus, for the adherents of Jaʿfar, his claim was not just that he was an Imam who ought to be a member of the ʿAlid family, but that he was the particular individual, from the descent of the Prophet, designated by his father and therefore inherently possessed of all the authority to guide believers in all religious matters.

As we shall see presently in the traditions of Al-Bāqir and Jaʿfar aṣ-Ṣādiq, this emphasis on the aspect of "special knowledge" having been possessed by the Imams of the House of the Prophet was a natural corollary of and a necessary response to the situation and tendencies of the epoch. This was the time when there was a wide search for *Ḥadīth* and a vigorous attempt was being made to construct total systems of the pious life in Islam. These efforts eventually issued in the formulation of a complete system of *Sharīʿa* law. It was the time of Mālik b. Anas and Abū Ḥanīfa, the Imams of *Fiqh* who were busy working out their legal systems in their respective centres of Medina and Kūfa. Jaʿfar aṣ-Ṣādiq, being the descendant of the Prophet and known for his and his family's learning in religious matters, was evidently looked upon by the community in general at least as an Imam of *Fiqh*, like that of Mālik and Abū Ḥanīfa, concerned with working out the proper details of how the pious should solve the various cases of conscience that might arise. So he appears in Sunnī traditions to a degree, and even, as has been pointed out earlier, Abū Ḥanīfa is reported to have been his pupil. But, unlike Mālik and Abū Ḥanīfa to the Sunnī Muslims, to the followers of the House of the Prophet Jaʿfar had a unique authority in these matters by virtue of his position as Imam by *Naṣṣ*; that is, to the Shīʿa his was the final decision on earth in these matters, whereas the others, as was indeed admitted, had no more legal authority in principle than any of their followers.[9]

> "This claim was perhaps initially less a matter of the knowledge he had (from his father) than of the authoritative use he could make of it, or in other words, his hereditary authority to decide cases. Any sovereign must be empowered to make the final decisions in any legal matter; hence the Imam's very claim that sovereignty was justly his could readily entail a claim to final authority in legal, and in this case all religious, matters. Such a claim would be readily transmuted to one of supernatural knowledge in many minds. But in an Imam where the authority was not in actual fact the sovereign, and his *ʿIlm* remained on a theoretical level, that discernment, that *ʿIlm* which should guide his decisions, took on a special sacredness and became a unique

gift inherited from Imam to Imam. Accordingly, as the exclusively authorized source of the knowledge of how to lead a pious life, the Imam had an all-important function whether he was a ruler or not." [10]

With the Imamate thus based on *Naṣṣ* and *'Ilm*, as explained by Ja'far, it should no longer be difficult for us to understand why Ja'far himself remained absolutely indifferent in all those struggles for power which took place in his lifetime. In his doctrine of the Imamate it was not at all necessary for a divinely appointed Imam to rise in rebellion and try to become a ruler. To him his place was above that of a ruler, who should only carry out what an Imam decides as a supreme authority of religion. It was on this basis that when Zayd came out with his claims, Ja'far raised no protest and even exalted Zayd's virtues before a delegation of Kūfan Shī'īs. But at the same time he said to Fuḍayl b. Rassān that had Zayd become a king, he would not have known how to act and fulfil his duties.[11] In this way he implied that Zayd had the right to political authority only. He made similar remarks when Muḥammad an-Nafs az-Zakīya rose to claim the Imamate. Ja'far emphatically denied any share in the religious leadership of the community for the descendants of Ḥasan,[12] from whom Ḥusayn inherited the Imamate, which then remained in the latter's progeny.

According to the traditions related in this connection, Al-Bāqir designated Ja'far as his successor in many ways. He called him "the best of all mankind in his time", and "the one in charge of the family of Muḥammad" (*Qā'im Āl Muḥammad*), and also trusted him with the books and scrolls and the weapons of the Prophet, which were in his possession.[13] These scriptures containing special knowledge of religion and the weapons of the Prophet must only come into the possession of the true Imam, who is designated by *Naṣṣ* by the previous Imam. Thus by declaring that they were in his trust, Ja'far denied the rights of An-Nafs az-Zakīya, who asserted that he had the sword of the Prophet.[14] Whether these family treasures were in the custody of Ja'far or were in the possession of the Ḥasanid claimants, the fact remains that Ja'far himself claimed the spiritual leadership of the community which he based on the same principles as Al-Bāqir, namely on *Naṣṣ*.

Jaʿfar explained that the Imamate is bequeathed from father to son, but not necessarily to the eldest son, for "as Daniel selected Solomon from among his progeny," so an Imam designates as his successor the son he considers really worthy of the office. Thus Jaʿfar could annul the appointment of his eldest son Ismāʿīl, who died before him, pass over the candidature of his next son, ʿAbd Allāh, and nominate the third, Mūsā al-Kāẓim.[15]

In explaining the position of the Imam, Jaʿfar made repeated declarations in unequivocal terms and proclaimed that the Imamate is a covenant between God and mankind, and recognition of the Imam is the absolute duty of every believer.[16] "Whoever dies without having known and acknowledged the Imam of his time dies as an infidel."[17] The Imams are the proofs (*Ḥujja*) of God on earth, their words are the words of God, and their commands are the commands of God. Obedience to them is obedience to God, and disobedience to them is disobedience to God. In all their decisions they are inspired by God, and they are in absolute authority. It is to them, therefore, that "God has ordained obedience"[18] (*Qur'ān* IV, 59).

Jaʿfar goes on to declare that the Imam of the time is the witness for the people and he is the gate to God (*Bāb Allāh*) and the road (*Sabīl*) to Him, and the guide thereto (*Dalīl*), and the repository of His knowledge, and the interpreter of His revelations. The Imam of his time is a pillar of God's unity (*tawḥīd*). The Imam is immune from sin (*khaṭā*) and error (*ḍalāl*). The Imams are those from whom "God has removed all impurity and made them absolutely pure" (*Qur'an*, XXXIII, 33); they are possessed of the power of miracles and of irrefutable arguments (*dalā'il*); and they are for the protection of the people of this earth just as the stars are for the inhabitants of the heavens. They may be likened, in this community, to the Ark of Noah: he who boards it obtains salvation and reaches the gate of repentance.[19] In another tradition, "God delegated to the Imams spiritual rulership over the whole world, which must always have such a leader and guide. Even if only two men were left upon the face of the earth, one of them would be an Imam, so much would his guidance be needed."[20]

In fact, according to the Imam Jaʿfar's explanation, there

are always two Imams, the actual or "speaking" Imam (*Nāṭiq*) and his son-successor, who during the lifetime of his father is "silent" (*ṣāmit*).[21] The silent Imam does not know of his exalted position until his father's death, for only then is he entrusted with the scriptures and the secrets of religion. When the father expires, his son immediately steps into his place and becomes the "proof" (*al-Ḥujja*) for mankind.[22]

As has been pointed out earlier, in order to prove his rights to the Imamate on the principle of *Naṣṣ* it was only logical that the utmost emphasis should be put first of all on ʿAlī's rights to the spiritual leadership of the community as the divinely favoured legatee of the Prophet. It was not a new thing, however. ʿAlī himself had put forward his claim time and again after the death of the Prophet until his own assassination; and thereafter Ḥasan, Ḥusayn, Zayn al-ʿĀbidīn, and Muḥammad al-Bāqir never missed an opportunity to pronounce ʿAlī's rights and superiority to the heritage of the Prophet. Jaʿfar, enjoying better circumstances than his predecessors, only elucidated and systematized concepts and ideals they had already introduced in rudimentary form. Thus he, as indeed did his father before him, quoted many verses of the Qur'ān which in his interpretation proved the appointment of ʿAlī to the Imamate. The numerous verses quoted in this connection by the Shīʿī sources[23] are among those which are accepted by all Muslims as the *Āyāt al-Mutashābihāt*: unclear verses which require interpretation (*tā'wīl*), as opposed to the *Āyāt al-Muḥkamāt*: clear or firm verses in which there is no room for any interpretation. In the Qur'ān we read:

> "God, it is He Who has sent down to you the Book. Some of its verses are perspicuous (*muḥkamāt*), these are the basis of the Book: others are unclear (*mutashābihāt*) . . . No one knows their interpretation except God, and those who are firm in their knowledge say, 'We believe therein, it is all from our Lord.'"[24]

It was at the time of Jaʿfar that such verses were being interpreted by the religious leaders of the community. Jaʿfar, by virtue of his birth and family background, perhaps had better claims to explain the Qur'ān than the other Muslims; and it was, therefore, quite natural for a section of the community adhering to the family of the Prophet to give more weight to Jaʿfar's interpretations than to those who only acquired knowledge through scholarship.

Like *Naṣṣ*, the "special knowledge" of religion (*ʿIlm*) which Jaʿfar declared for himself should also be traced back to ʿAlī, from whom it passed from Imam to Imam until it came into Jaʿfar's possession. Thus Jaʿfar said that the Prophet entrusted ʿAlī with the greatest name of God and the traditions pertaining to the knowledge of prophethood (*Āthār an-Nubuwwa*).[25] This is only one of numerous traditions recorded by the Shīʿī sources regarding the extraordinary knowledge with which ʿAlī distinguished himself among all those around the Prophet. There must, however, have been some substance to the fame and widespread reputation of the unparalleled knowledge of ʿAlī; not only the Shīʿī sources and Jaʿfar's traditions, but most of the Sunnī sources and their standard collections of *Ḥadīth*, have recorded a number of traditions in regard to ʿAlī's superior knowledge.[26] As has been pointed out earlier, the Caliph ʿUmar is frequently quoted as saying that "ʿAlī is the best of all the judges of the people of Medina and the chief of the readers of the Qur'ān."[27] Perhaps the most representative tradition of ʿAlī's erudite knowledge, recorded even by most of the Sunnī sources, is one which has the Prophet saying: "I am the city of knowledge (*ʿIlm*), and ʿAlī is its door."[28] With the overwhelming testimony coming down to us from both Sunnī and Shīʿī sources, there seems to be little doubt that ʿAlī was acknowledged as having extraordinary knowledge in religious matters. Inheritance of this knowledge thus became a source of the claim of special rights for the legitimist Imams of the House.

Another very relevant and rather difficult problem connected with Jaʿfar's claims to the *Naṣṣ* and inheritance of "special knowledge" was the question of the scope and applicability of the term *Ahl al-Bayt*. On the one hand, all the descendants of ʿAlī, whether through Fāṭima or not, were claiming membership of the "Sacred House". On the other hand, the ʿAbbāsids, being the descendants of Hāshim, also claimed the prerogative of the *Ahl al-Bayt* and were revered by their followers as God's inspired Imams and as the *Mahdī*. Jaʿfar thus put his utmost emphasis on a tradition from the Prophet which would limit the inclusive meaning of the

Qur'ānic verse referring to the people of the House "from whom [all kinds of] uncleanliness were removed" to ʿAlī, Fāṭima, and their progeny. This tradition is known as the *Ḥadīth al-Kisā* or as the *Ḥadīth Aṣḥāb al-Kisā*. The *ḥadīth* runs: "Muḥammad made ʿAlī, Fāṭima, Ḥasan, and Ḥusayn enter under his mantle (*kisā*) in the house of Umm Salima and then said: 'Every Prophet has his family (*ahl*) and his charge (*thaql*); these, O God, are my family and my charge.' Hearing this, Umm Salima asked: 'Am I not from the people of your House?' The Prophet replied: 'No, may you be well; only these under the mantle are the people of my House and my charge.'"[29]

The tradition is a long one. But perhaps the most important part of it is when the archangel Gabriel came down to announce the "Verse of the Purification"[30] for the "Five of the Mantle",[31] and Muḥammad introduced them to the angel saying: "There are, under the mantle, Fāṭima, her husband ʿAlī, and her two children Ḥasan and Ḥusayn." One can see clearly that the point of gravity is laid here not on ʿAlī, but on Fāṭima, with reference to whom ʿAlī, Ḥasan, and Ḥusayn are introduced. Pre-Islamic literature is not devoid of examples where people are introduced through their mothers or wives. In the case of Fāṭima, we have seen in the previous chapter that An-Nafs az-Zakīya in his letter to Manṣūr made special reference to his relationship to Fāṭima. The reference to her was also made essential even by the Zaydīs, who restricted the Imamate to only those ʿAlids who were Fāṭimids. But it was Jaʿfar who in his elaborations put extreme emphasis on this point. It had indeed an immense potential appeal for the claims of the legitimist Imams. Eventually Fāṭima came to be regarded, especially among the Twelver Shīʿīs, as one of the most respected figures.

Through such traditions, Jaʿfar in his own lifetime established for his line of Imams the sanctity of the *Ahl al-Bayt* as an inherited quality confined only to those of the children of Fāṭima who were ordained to be the Imams, and in this way rejected the claims of all other Hāshimites, whether ʿAlids or ʿAbbāsids.

Such an hereditary claim to the Imamate based on *Naṣṣ* and "special knowledge", as elaborated by Jaʿfar and his father Al-Bāqir, however, greatly exposed the claimants to the danger of persecution by the ʿAbbāsids, who also claimed spiritual leadership of the community. Thus arose the famous doctrine of *Taqīya* (dissimulation) on which Jaʿfar put the utmost emphasis, raising it almost to the status of a condition for Faith. It is interesting to note that there is not a single tradition on *Taqīya* from any Imam prior to Al-Bāqir, which is a sufficient proof that the doctrine of *Taqīya* was first introduced by him and was further elaborated by Jaʿfar, and that it was, in fact, a need of the time and the circumstances in which they were living and working out the tenets for their followers. One may see that the theory of *Taqīya* suits very well the theory of extraordinary knowledge embodied in the Imams, which should be limited to a few selected persons who inherited that knowledge through *Naṣṣ*. Thus Jaʿfar said:

> "This affair (*amr*) [the Imamate and the esoteric meaning of religion] is occult (*mastūr*) and veiled (*muqanna*) by a covenant (*mithāq*), and whoever unveils it will be disgraced by God."[32]

In a conversation with Muʿalla b. Khunays, one of the extremists of Kūfa whom Jaʿfar discredited, the Imam said:

> "Keep our affair secret, and do not divulge it publicly, for whoever keeps it secret and does not reveal it, God will exalt him in this world and put light between his eyes in the next, leading him to Paradise. O Muʿalla, whoever divulges our affair publicly, and does not keep it secret, God will disgrace him in this world and will take away light from between his eyes in the next, and will decree for him darkness that will lead him to the Fire. O Muʿalla, verily the *Taqīya* is of my religion and of the religion of my father, and one who does not keep the *Taqīya* has no religion. O Muʿalla, it is necessary to worship in secret as it is necessary to worship openly. O Muʿalla, the one who reveals our affairs is the one who denies them."[33]

The esoteric mysteries of religion were *Wilāyat Allāh*, which God entrusted to Gabriel, who brought them to Muḥammad. The Prophet, in turn, handed them over to ʿAlī, and they became the inheritance of the Imams, who are bound to keep them secret.[34] The duty, therefore, incumbent on the Faithful is that they should not impart their faith to those who do not share the same beliefs. Jaʿfar thus accused the Kaysānites of betraying religion when they spread its secrets among the common people: "Our secret continued to be preserved until it came into the hands of the sons of Kaysān (*wuld Kaysān*) [his followers] and they spoke of it on the roads and in the villages of the Sawād."[35]

A careful examination of the development of the concept and doctrine of the *Taqīya* would clearly reveal the fact that it was a natural corollary of the prevalent circumstances of the time and an inevitable necessity imposed by the danger of following certain religious or political views. To announce publicly that certain persons were divinely inspired Imams and therefore the sole object of obedience was a direct challenge to the authority of the ʿAbbāsid caliphs, who claimed to have combined in themselves both the temporal and religious sovereignty. Shīʿism thus had to find its own means to preserve itself in that difficult situation. This was accomplished through the introduction of the doctrine of dissimulation, but this, according to the pattern of the epoch, where the entire pattern of life was considered from a religious standpoint, must be supported by certain passages from the Qur'ān or a *Ḥadīth* indicating a precedent. According to Jaʿfar, both Joseph and Abraham practised *Taqīya* when they resorted to concealment of the truth: the first when he accused his brother of theft, and the second when he asserted that he was ill.[36] Muḥammad himself, accordingly, is reported to have practised *Taqīya* until the verse in which he was ordered to preach publicly was revealed. It reads: "O you Apostle, reveal the whole that has been revealed to you from your Lord; if you do it not, you have not preached His message and God will not defend you from wicked men."[37] Another verse which was used to support the doctrine of *Taqīya* reads: "And who disbelieves in God after believing in Him, except under compulsion, and whose heart is confident in faith."[38]

In Al-Bāqir's period the doctrine of *Taqīya* was established in Shīʿism, and we may attribute the rudiments of its theory to him. But it was left to Jaʿfar to give it final form and make it an absolute condition of true faith: "Fear for your religion and protect it [*lit.* veil it] with the *Taqīya*, for there is no faith (*Imān*) in whom there is no *Taqīya*."[39] Goldhizer traces the history of the doctrine of *Taqīya* and finds it practised without being announced as a principle even by Muḥammad b. al-Ḥanafīya, though in his findings, too, it was Jaʿfar who so elaborated *Taqīya* as one of the doctrines of Shīʿī faith out of the political needs of his time.[40]

It is, however, hardly disputable that the doctrine of *Taqīya*, thus made a necessary part of faith by Jaʿfar, ultimately served the Shīʿīs as a very useful instrument in the preservation of their doctrinal discipline during all unfavourable and rather hostile political circumstances. This is also evident from another tradition from Jaʿfar quoted by Ṣadūq in his Creed, where the Imam says: "Mix with the people [i.e., enemies] outwardly, but oppose them inwardly so long as the Amirate is a matter of opinion."[41] On another occasion, when Zakarīya b. Sābiq enumerated the Imams in the presence of Jaʿfar and reached Muḥammad al-Bāqir, he was interrupted by Jaʿfar's exclamation: "That is enough for you. God has affirmed your tongue and has guided your heart."[42] We may conclude from all these traditions that the real meaning of *Taqīya* is not telling a lie or falsehood, as it is often understood, but the protection of the true religion and its followers from enemies through concealment in circumstances where there is fear of being killed or captured or insulted.

There is another important point which must be discussed here briefly. A considerable number of traditions are to be found, especially in the earliest Shīʿī collection of *ḥadīth*, *Al-Kāfī*, which describe the Imams as supernatural human beings. What was the origin of these traditions, and to what extent are the Imams themselves responsible for them? These traditions are reported, as indeed are all Shīʿī traditions, on the authority of one of the Imams, in this case mainly from Al-Bāqir and Jaʿfar. But were these Imams really the authors of such traditions, which describe their supernatural character? The first thing which must be noted in this connection is that while Al-Bāqir and Jaʿfar themselves lived in Medina, most of their followers lived in Kūfa. This fact brings us to a crucial problem. Kūfa had long been a centre of *ghulāt* speculations and activities. Whether ʿAbd Allāh b. Sabāʾ,[43] to whom the history of the *ghulāt* is traced, was a real personality or not, the name *As-Sabāʾīya*[44] is often used to describe the *ghulāt* in Kūfa who believed in the supernatural character of ʿAlī. According to the heresiographers, Ibn Sabāʾ was the first to preach the doctrine of *waqf* (refusal to recognize the death of ʿAlī) and the first to condemn the first two caliphs in addition to ʿUthmān.[45] Baghdādī says that *As-Sabāʾīya* mostly consisted of the old Sabāʾīyans of South Arabia, who survived all vicissitudes until the time of Mukhtār and formed the nucleus of his "chair-worshippers".[46]

This early group of *ghulāt* seems to have been absorbed by the Kaysānīya, who believed in Muḥammad b. al-Ḥanafīya's Mahdism and followed his son Abū Hāshim ʿAbd Allāh. The death of Abū Hāshim was the turning point in the history of the *ghulāt*, for it caused the split in consequence of which they separated into two distinct groups. One upheld the various successors of Abū Hāshim and believed in his concealment and return and eventually transplanted themselves into Iran, where they grew into the Kharramite revolutionary movement towards the end of the Umayyad period. The other group overlapped the Kaysānite stage, remained in Kūfa, and somehow connected itself with the Ḥusaynid Imams. The most conspicuous names in this second group, who became the followers of Al-Bāqir and then of Jaʿfar aṣ-Ṣādiq, are Ḥamza b. ʿUmara al-Buraydī, Bayān b. Simʿān, Saʿīd an-Nahdī, Mughīra b. Saʿīd al-ʿIjlī, his co-tribesman Abū Manṣūr al-ʿIjlī, and Muḥammad b. Abī Zaynab Miqlāṣ b. Abīʾl-Khaṭṭāb. It would be too lengthy to even briefly describe their extremist teachings here; suffice it to say that they preached that the Imams were the incarnations of God, that the divine particle incarnate in ʿAlī b. Abī Ṭālib enabled him to know the unseen, foretell the future, and to fight against the infidels, that the power of the invisible angelic world was in ʿAlī like a lamp within a niche in a wall, and that God's light was in ʿAlī as the flame in a lamp.[47] In connection with these *ghulāt* and their teachings, here we will only point out that from Al-Bāqir onwards, all the subsequent Imams always cursed them and repeatedly warned their followers not to accept traditions from them.[48] Kashshī quotes Jaʿfar, who complains of Mughīra, for example, as misrepresenting Al-Bāqir, and adds that all the *ghuluw* ascribed to Al-Bāqir was from Mughīra.[49] In fact Jaʿfar and all the Imams who followed him were always unequivocal in violently cursing the *ghulāt* and condemning their teachings.

There was, however, another very active group in Kūfa, busy in advancing the cause of Al-Bāqir and Jaʿfar. The most important among them were people such as Jābir b. Yazīd al-Juʿfī,[50] Abū Ḥamza ath-Thumālī,[51] and Muʿādh b. Farra an-Naḥwī.[52] Paying only occasional visits to the Imams in Medina and enjoying their confidence, they severed their relations with the *ghulāt* of Kūfa. On behalf of the Imams they had doctrinal quarrels with the *ghulāt* and preached against the latter's excessive claims regarding the nature and function of the Imams. They did remain faithful to a certain doctrinal discipline, imposed by the Imams, while this was aggressively violated by the *ghulāt*. Yet, when we see the traditions related by Jābir and his associates in this group, it seems that they must have been influenced by some of the ideas propagated by the *ghulāt*, especially those of Bayān b. Simʿān and Mughīra b. Saʿīd.

Perhaps no follower of Al-Bāqir and Jaʿfar dared to go so far in his assertions as Jābir. It will suffice to quote here only one from a great number of traditions related by Jābir, which indicates his semi-*ghulāt* tendencies. Jābir related that Al-Bāqir said:

> "'O Jābir, the first beings that God created were Muḥammad and his family, the rightly guided ones and the guides; they were the phantoms of light before God.' I asked, 'And what were the phantoms?' Al-Bāqir said, 'Shadows of light, luminous bodies without spirits; they were strengthened by the Holy Spirit (*Rūḥ al-Quds*), through which Muḥammad and his family worshipped God. For that reason He created them forbearing, learned, endowed with filial piety, and pure; they worship God through prayer, fasting, prostrating themselves, enumerating His names, and ejaculating: God is great.'"[53]

If we compare the ideas of the *ghulāt* concerning God's light in ʿAlī, pointed out above, with Jābir's description of the Imams as the "shadows of light" and "luminous bodies", there seems to be a common trend of thinking between the two.

It is perhaps for this reason that later *ghulāt* groups accepted Jābir as their forerunner. This is indicated by the assertions of Abū'l-Khaṭṭāb and his successors, who claimed Jābir as their predecessor. Thus *Umm al-Kitāb* is said to contain the teachings of Al-Bāqir, Jābir b. ʿAbd Allāh al-Anṣārī, and Jābir al-Juʿfī.[54] Another religious writing, *Risālat al-Juʿfī*, containing Ismāʿīlī doctrines, is based mainly on the expositions of Jābir on the authority of Al-Bāqir.[55] Apparently neither the doctrine of *Umm al-Kitāb* nor that of *Risālat al-Juʿfī* represent the views of Al-Bāqir, and probably only little of what Jābir himself taught. It is nevertheless an important point that he was regarded as the spiritual forefather of the post-Khaṭṭābite *ghulāt*.

However, in spite of the fact that *ghuluw* was repeatedly condemned by Al-Bāqir, Jaʿfar, and the successive Imams of the Ḥusaynid line, a number of traditions containing some *ghulāt* ideas found their way into Shīʿī collections of *ḥadīth*. Most of these traditions are related from Jābir al-Juʿfī. But it is now by no means possible to ascertain whether Jābir himself was the author of these traditions or whether these were attached to his name by the later *ghulāt* and were circulated in the Imamite circles. In both the Sunnī and the Shīʿī science of *ḥadīth*, little attention was paid to the substance of a tradition: usually a *ḥadīth* was either accepted or rejected according to the credibility and trustworthiness of its transmitters. In the Shīʿī science of *ḥadīth*, the main criterion was that if a person was proven to have been a devoted and sincere adherent of the Imam of his time, his traditions were acceptable. Jābir, in spite of his semi-*ghulāt* tendencies and exaggerations, whether authentic or forged, nevertheless remained, throughout his life, faithful to Al-Bāqir and Jaʿfar. When Muḥammad b. Yaʿqūb al-Kulaynī (died 328/939) compiled the first collection of the Shīʿī traditions, *Al-Kāfī fī'l-ʿIlm ad-Dīn*, his purpose was to collect whatever came to him on the authority of those who were known as the adherents of any one of the Imams. In this way a great many traditions ascribing supernatural and superhuman characteristics to the Imams, propounded by the semi-*ghulāt* circles in Kūfa, crept into the Shīʿī literature.

There are, however, numerous traditions in *Kāfī* in which both Al-Bāqir and Jaʿfar clearly denied that they possessed supernatural powers and discounted the miracles attributed to them.[56] It is thus most unlikely that Jaʿfar was personally responsible for all those fantastic descriptions of the supernatural character of the Imams which were circulated in his name by his semi-*ghulāt* followers in Kūfa. Indeed, Jaʿfar did not excommunicate them as he did, for example, in the case of Abū'l-Khaṭṭāb, and as Al-Bāqir did in the cases of Bayān, Abū Manṣūr, and Mughīra. In *Kāfī* itself, there are many traditions from both Al-Bāqir and Jaʿfar aṣ-Ṣādiq in which they declared that they were simply God-fearing men, distinguished from others only because they were the Prophet's nearest relatives and thus became the custodians and trustees of his message. And by virtue of their devotion to God and because of the fact that perfect knowledge of God had come to them through *Naṣṣ* and *ʿIlm*, they were able to live their lives in complete obedience to the will of God.[57] Regarding the traditions pertaining to the supernatural character of the Imams, perhaps the most decisive and revealing is the statement of Jaʿfar himself in which he said: "Whatever is in agreement with the Book of God, accept it; and whatever is contrary to it, reject it."[58] When we recall that Jaʿfar aṣ-Ṣādiq was at least a century before the time of Bukhārī and Muslim, it is significant to find that it is the Imam Jaʿfar who is credited with establishing this criterion for testing *hādīth*, one which came to be regarded as the most important principle to observe in judging traditions.[59]

Moreover, the fact that the *ghulāt* or semi-*ghulāt* were attributing their own thoughts to the Imams and that the Imams were not responsible for these statements is further illustrated by a report given by Kashshī. A follower of the Imam ʿAlī ar-Riḍa once read before him certain *aḥādīth* which he had copied from the notebooks of those in Iraq who had taken down sayings of Al-Bāqir and Jaʿfar. The Imam strongly rejected the authenticity of those traditions and declared that Abū'l-Khaṭṭāb and his followers had contrived to have their lies accepted in those notebooks.[60] Similar traditions have been noted earlier wherein Jaʿfar complained of Mughīra misrepresenting Al-Bāqir.

We have so far been discussing the extremists and semi-extremists of Jaʿfar's circle and their excessive claims for the persons of the Imams. Not all of Jaʿfar's followers were fanatics, however. A considerable number of them were simply Shīʿīs distinguished from the other Muslims only by the higher degree of their devotion to the memory of ʿAlī and by their conviction that he was the best person after the Prophet for the combined office of the spiritual and temporal leadership of the community. Thus they considered the Imamate as the right of ʿAlī and his descendants, ordained to them by God. The best example of these forerunners of the Shīʿīs, later to become the Twelvers, is ʿAbd Allāh b. Abī

Yaʿfūr, a resident of Kūfa. He opposed his fellow Kūfans, such as Muʿalla b. Khunays, who asserted that the Imams were prophets. Ibn Abī Yaʿfūr objected to this and said that they were only pure, God-fearing, learned theologians entrusted with guiding the community on the path of God.[61] Very strict in his religious practices, he was highly favoured and respected by Jaʿfar.[62] He enjoyed the respect of the moderate traditionists' circles, and when he died during the lifetime of Jaʿfar, many of the *Ahl al-Ḥadīth* and pro-Shīʿī Murjites accompanied his bier.[63]

There was still another group among the followers of Jaʿfar, busy in the intellectual or dialectical questions of the day, along the lines of the Muʿtazila. It is indicative of Jaʿfar's leadership that he gathered around himself the men who could stand with remarkable vigour among those of the Muslim scholars who were speculating on the philosophical problems of the time. This group of the first Shīʿī speculative theologians, to be discussed presently, who provided the intellectual element in the Imamate of Jaʿfar, stand out from the Shīʿī extremists even in the hostile presentations of some of the heresiographers. Ashʿarī takes much interest in them and clearly distinguishes them from the extremists or semi-extremists among the Shīʿīs of Jaʿfar's following. It may also be noted here in passing that a close study of the heresiographical works, such as those of Ashʿarī and Baghdādī, enable us to discern the cross-currents and intermingling of ideas between the Shīʿī and Sunnī schools of thought at their evolutionary stages. However, the attachment of this group to the Imam marked a great advance in the development of Shīʿism in its own right. These speculative theologians of Jaʿfar's circle were later regarded as the élite of the Shīʿī *mutakallimūn*, though before the science of *kalām* became a definite branch of learning the early Shīʿī *mutakallimūn*, who formed the backbone of the future Twelver Shīʿa, were speculative theologians, traditionists, and jurists all at the same time.

In this group, mention should first be made of Abūʾl-Ḥasan b. Aʿyān b. Susan, better known by his *kunyā*, Az-Zurāra. He was a *mawlā* of the Banū Shaybān of Kūfa, and the grandson of an enslaved Greek monk who adopted Islam.[64] Zurāra originally belonged to the supporters of Zayd b. ʿAlī, for together with his brother Ḥumrān b. Aʿyān and Aṭ-Ṭayyār, he was a disciple of Al-Ḥakam b. ʿUtayba, a Zaydite and a great Muʿtazilite leader. This itself suggests that under Muʿtazilite influence Zurāra developed his interest in speculative theology. Zurāra and his two brothers later changed their allegiance and attached themselves to Al-Bāqir, Ḥumrān being the first to take this step.[65]

After the death of Al-Bāqir, Zurāra belonged to the circle of the closest adherents of Jaʿfar aṣ-Ṣādiq, who spoke of him with great appreciation: "Four men are the best beloved by me, whether alive or dead: Burayd b. Muʿāwiya al-ʿIjlī, Zurāra, Muḥammad b. Muslim, and Al-Aḥwal".[66] Ibn Abī ʿUmayr[67] said that he and his contemporaries were beside Zurāra "like children around their teacher".[68] It seems that because of his vehement activities in the cause of Jaʿfar, Zurāra met with some difficulties and even dangers. Thus, to spare him hardships, Jaʿfar, resorting to the principle of *Taqīya*, apparently disavowed him and even cursed him. Justifying this, he said that in order to save Zurāra, he had acted in the same way as the Prophet Khiḍr, when he sank a ship to save it from being taken from its owners by a tyrannous king.[69]

Zurāra, who only occasionally paid visits to Jaʿfar in Medina or met him in Mecca, lived in Kūfa and there had a large circle of disciples. Though Zurāra was also regarded as a traditionist, a lawyer, and a theologian, he attained his great renown in the fields of the science of tradition and in *kalām*. In fact, he was the founder of the Shīʿī school of speculative theology in the proper sense, and the first teacher of *kalām*[70] from within the circle of Jaʿfar.

Among Zurāra's pupils, who were all devoted followers of Jaʿfar, were his own sons Ḥasan,[71] Ḥusayn,[72] and ʿUbayd Allāh;[73] his brother Ḥurmān, the grammarian and one of the foremost companions of Al-Bāqir;[74] Hamẓa, the son of Ḥurmān;[75] Bukayr b. Aʿyūn[76] and his son ʿAbd Allāh;[77] Muḥammad b. al-Ḥakam;[78] Ḥumayd b. Rabbāḥ;[79] Muḥammad b. an-Nuʿmān al-Aḥwal, and Hishām b. Sālim al-Jawāliqī.[80] The circle of Zurāra was usually known as *Az-Zurārīya* or *At-Tamīmīya*,[81] and its intellectual activities in the field of scholastic theology greatly strengthened the cause of Jaʿfar and later that of Mūsā al-Kāẓim.[82]

Together with other theological and scholastic problems,

Zurāra and his disciples evolved the theory that the knowledge of God is an obligation on every believer and cannot be attained without an Imam designated by God, and thus complete obedience to the Imam is a religious duty. The Imams *by necessity* are endowed with special knowledge. Therefore, what other men can attain by discursive reason (*naẓar*), an Imam always knows owing to his special knowledge and his superior and unequalled power of reasoning. Zurāra and his circle promulgated their views on almost every question of what we now call scholastic philosophy, such as the attributes of God, His Essence and His Actions, His Intention or Will, and the human capacity.[83] The impression we get of Zurāra from the sources, especially from Kashshī, is that he played a very important role in the development of legitimist Shīʿī thought and contributed a great deal to the formation of the Imamite creed. He is one of the most frequently quoted authorities in all the major books of the Shīʿīs.

Abū Jaʿfar Muḥammad b. Nuʿmān al-Aḥwal was another striking personality among the speculative theologians of Kūfa who linked the question of the Imamate with other fundamental scholastic problems. His circle is described by the heresiographers as *An-Nuʿmānīya*, and he distinguished himself among all the adherents of Jaʿfar for his excellence in dialectics and learning in theology, as well as for the piquancy of his answers in disputes with his adversaries. An extremely committed Shīʿī, Al-Aḥwal was at first one of the most devoted adherents of Al-Bāqir, whose claims he defended against Zayd. He later became an equally ardent supporter of Jaʿfar aṣ-Ṣādiq and finally of Mūsā al-Kāẓim.

The greater part of his intellectual activities in promoting the Shīʿī cause was perhaps spent during the Imamate of Jaʿfar. He is counted among the most prominent companions of Jaʿfar, and was one of those who accepted Mūsā al-Kāẓim as their Imam immediately after the former's death, and without considering the candidature of any other son of Jaʿfar.[84] He is frequently reported to have held heated debates with the great jurist Abū Ḥanīfa, whom he despised for being a Murjite. Abū Ḥanīfa, on his part, treated him with scorn and contempt.[85] Al-Aḥwal is described as the most courageous and vociferous in his convictions regarding the rights of the legitimist Imams on rational grounds.[86] As a zealous supporter of the legitimist line, he upheld the dogma of the God-imposed duty of complete obedience to the Imams, and of the supreme knowledge possessed by them, necessary for the guidance of men. He is said to have been a prolific writer, and a number of his works are mentioned by various authorities. His writings include his *Kitāb al-Imāma*, his *Kitāb ar-Radd ʿalāʾl-Muʿtazila fī Imāmat al-Mafḍūl*, and a number of other treatises, probably of a polemical nature.[87] The titles of the books ascribed to him suggest that the question of the Imamate was one of the main issues between the Muʿtazila and the Shīʿī thinkers of that time. Kashshī records a number of controversial debates held by him in support of Jaʿfar's rights to the Imamate, and also quotes Jaʿfar as saying: "Al-Aḥwal is most beloved by me, whether alive or dead."[88]

Another foremost supporter of Jaʿfar in this circle was Hishām b. Sālim al-Jawāliqī, who was brought up in his childhood as a slave from Jurjān, and became a *mawlā* of Bishr b. Marwān. He also lived in Kūfa, earning his living as a seller of fodder (*ʿallāf*). Like his close friend Al-Aḥwal, he led a large circle of disciples and propounded his theories on all questions of the nature and attributes of God.[89]

Perhaps the greatest of all the Shīʿī thinkers of Jaʿfar's following were Abū Muḥammad Hishām b. al-Ḥakam[90] and ʿAlī b. Ismāʿīl al-Maythamī.[91] The former was originally a disciple of Jahm b. Safwān, the Jubrite, but converted to the Shīʿī doctrine and became a most devoted follower of Jaʿfar aṣ-Ṣādiq. He must have been quite young at that time, for he lived until the Imamate of ʿAlī ar-Riḍa and was one of his closest companions.[92]

The theories regarding God and other scholastic questions propounded by these five most important thinkers of Jaʿfar's period are too lengthy to be examined here. What mainly concerns us at present is their contribution to the doctrine of the Imamate, which they linked up with fundamental principles of a scholastic nature. A remarkable fact is that although these five thinkers often differ from each other on many questions, their teachings and ideas concerning the Imamate are almost the same. The essence of their doctrine of the Imamate is that the Prophet appointed ʿAlī to the

Imamate by an explicit designation (*naṣṣ*), and after him, his sons Ḥasan and Ḥusayn acceded to the Imamate in the same way. This appointment was based on the principle that mankind needs an Imam to lead it on the right path as much as an individual needs intelligence to co-ordinate the activities of his body and to guide him. To guide mankind and preserve it from straying, an Imam must be infallible. This is because the Imam, who is below the status of a Prophet, can receive no revelation from God. Therefore, since he is the infallible guide appointed through the Grace of God, obedience to him is synonymous with obedience to God, while disobedience is the same as infidelity.[93]

While so many speculative theologians from among the followers of Jaʿfar were busy working out the scholastic problems of the time, there were a good many in his circle who concentrated their efforts mainly on legal questions. It has been pointed out earlier that the distinction between jurists and traditionists at this stage, especially among the Shīʿīs, was not very clear. Nevertheless, there was a difference in their respective interests. Some were more interested in the traditions of a dogmatic and doctrinal nature, others in the traditions concerning practical problems. Thus most of the traditions dealing with legal matters are reported on the authority of Jamīl b. Darrāj, ʿAbd Allāh b. Miskān, ʿAbd Allāh b. Bukayr, Ḥammād b. ʿUthmān, Ḥammād b. ʿIsā, and Abān b. ʿUthmān.[94] All of them belonged to the close circle of Jaʿfar and are unanimously accepted by all the Twelver Shīʿī writers as the most authoritative transmitters of legal traditions and as the eminent jurists from among the disciples of Jaʿfar. Kashshī describes them as "the six most reliable authorities among all the followers of Jaʿfar on legal traditions; on their trustworthiness and profound knowledge of law there has been a complete consensus among the Shīʿī scholars."[95] Kashshī's statement is confirmed by examining Kulaynī's *al-Kāfī*, Ṣadūq's *Man Lā Yaḥḍuruhu'l-Faqīh*, and Ṭūsī's *Istibsār* and *Tahdhīb al-Aḥkām.* These "Four Standard Books" (*Al-Kutub al-Arbaʿ*) have the same importance for the Shīʿīs as the six canonical collections of Sunnī *Ḥadīth* (*Ṣiḥāḥ as-Sitta*) have for the Sunnīs.

To this list of the frequently quoted jurists of Jaʿfar's period must be added the name of Abān b. Taghlib b. Riyāḥ,[96] an important and outstanding jurist-traditionist, and formerly an associate of Zayn al-ʿĀbidīn and Al-Bāqir. When he died in 140/757, Jaʿfar is reported to have said, "I would love to have my Shīʿa like Abān b. Taghlib," and "his death grieved my heart."[97] Abān's name appears in a good number of traditions, mostly of a practical nature.

It is important to note that almost all these jurist-traditionists of Jaʿfar's circle were in continuous attachment to three or at least two generations of the legitimist Imams, either Zayn al-ʿĀbidīn, Al-Bāqir, and Jaʿfar, or Al-Bāqir, Jaʿfar, and Mūsā, while some others who joined Jaʿfar served the line of the legitimist Imams till ʿAlī ar-Riḍa.

From this brief summary of the activities of individuals and groups working under the leadership of the Imam Jaʿfar aṣ-Ṣādiq in all the fundamental branches of religious learning, we may deduce two conclusions. First, at that formative stage of Islamic thought and institutions, the contributions made by these people, based on the teachings of Jaʿfar and his predecessors, provided a solid foundation for the elaboration of the dogma and legal system of Imamite Shīʿism by the later Twelver theologians and jurists. Second, the fact that so many persons, working in various aspects of religious life, chose to gather around Jaʿfar with the acceptance of his Imamate on the Principle of *Naṣṣ*, set the Imamite stream of Shīʿism well on the way to its own distinct character within Islam.

There are many Shīʿī creeds preserved for us by the earliest Shīʿī sources, such as Kashshī, which explain the beliefs of the Imamite Shīʿīs during the lifetime of Jaʿfar aṣ-Ṣādiq. One of these creeds, pronounced by ʿAmr b. Ḥurayth before Jaʿfar, reads:

> "I would like to describe my religion (*dīnī*) and what I believe, so that you may confirm me in my faith. My religion is that I testify that there is no God but God, and Muḥammad is His Apostle and Servant. I testify that the coming of the Day of Judgement is not subject to doubt, and that God will resurrect those who are in their graves. I testify to the obligations of prayer, the paying of the *zakāt*, fasting in the month of Ramaḍān, and the duty of pilgrimage to the House (*Ka'ba*) for those who have the means for it. I testify to the *wilāya* of ʿAlī b. Abī Ṭālib, the commander of the faithful (*Amīr al-Mu'minīn*) after the Prophet of God, may the Blessings of God be upon them both, and the

> *wilāya* of Al-Ḥasan and Al-Ḥusayn, the *wilāya* of ʿAlī b. al-Ḥusayn and that of Muḥammad al-Bāqir, and after his, yours. I testify that you are the Imams. In this religion I live, and in this religion I shall die, and this is the religion by which I worship God."

Having heard this, Jaʿfar declared:

> "This, by God, is indeed my religion and the religion of my fathers, who worshipped God openly and in secret; so fear God and hold your tongue from saying anything except that which is good."[98]

Similar statements are recorded by Kashshī from Dawūd b. Yūnus and Khālid b. Bajalī.[99] A detailed account of the Twelver Shīʿī beliefs dealing with all articles of faith, whether fundamental (*uṣūl*) or non-fundamental (*furūʿ*), are given by Shaykh Ibn Babawayh al-Qummī, better known as Shaykh aṣ-Ṣadūq (died 381/991–2), in his creed entitled *Risālat al-ʿItiqādāt*. Shaykh Ṣadūq is universally acknowledged by the Twelver Shīʿa as one of their greatest authorities, and his *Risāla*, one of the earliest extant Shīʿī creeds, is accepted as the most authoritative statement of their beliefs. Comparing this Shīʿī creed with the standard Sunnī creeds, such as *Fiqh Akbar I*, *Fiqh Akbar II*, and the *Waṣiyat Abī Ḥanīfa*, one finds that except on the question of the Imamate the differences between the Sunnīs and the Shīʿīs are of the same nature as, say, the differences between the Ashāʿira and the Muʿtazila. The Shīʿī views are in most cases the same as those of the Muʿtazila, who certainly remained part of Sunnī Islam, though their rationalistic views were ultimately rejected by the *Jamāʿa*.

The question of the Qurʿān may serve as the best illustration of this fundamental unity. The Shīʿī belief, as stated by Shaykh aṣ-Ṣadūq, reads:

> "Our belief concerning the Qurʿān is that it is the Word of God, His revelation sent down by Him, His speech and His Book . . . 'Falsehood cannot come at it from before it or behind it. It is a revelation from the Wise, the Praiseworthy' (Qur'ān, XLI, 42) . . . And our belief is that God, the Blessed and Exalted, is its Creator and Revealer and Master and Protector and Utterer. Our belief is that the Qur'ān, which God revealed to His Prophet Muḥammad, is [the same as] the one between the boards

(*daffatayn*). And it is that which is in the hands of the people, and is not greater in extent than that. The number of Suras as generally accepted is one hundred and fourteen." [100]

In this statement of Ṣadūq on the Qurʿān, two points are worth noticing. First, the Shīʿa, like the Muʿtazila, believe that the Qurʿān is the created word of God, and not uncreated and eternal as taught by the Ashāʿira and officially accepted by Sunnī Islam. The second and more important point is that the text of the Qur'ān as it is to be found in the *textus receptus*, which is in the hands of everyone in the shape of a book, is accepted wholly by the Shīʿīs, just as it is by the Sunnīs. Thus the assertion that the Shīʿīs believe that a part of the Qur'ān is not included in the *textus receptus* is erroneous.

We are not, however, concerned here with the details of the Shīʿī creed or the development of the Shīʿī legal and theological systems, which took place in progressive stages, as indeed was also the case in Sunnī Islam. Nor is this work meant to discuss the contributions of the last six Imams after Jaʿfar aṣ-Ṣādiq, after which the Imamite Shīʿa came to be known as the *Ithna ʿAsharīya*, or the Twelvers. Our purpose has only been to trace the origins and early development of those religious inclinations through which the Shīʿīs eventually came to distinguish themselves from the rest of the Muslim community.

Keeping in view what has been discussed throughout this work, and looking at the activities of those who gathered around Jaʿfar aṣ-Ṣādiq, we may conclude that the Imamite Shīʿīs, by the time of Jaʿfar's death in 148/765, had acquired a distinct character of their own. The actual disagreements between the Shīʿīs and the Sunnīs in certain details of theology and legal practices were not as important as the "Spirit" working behind these rather minor divergences. This "Spirit", arising from the differences in the fundamental approach and interpretation of Islam, as discussed in Chapter 1, issued forth in the Shīʿī concept of leadership of the community after the Prophet. It is this concept of divinely-ordained leadership which distinguishes Shīʿī from Sunnī within Islam; and thus it has been on the emergence of this concept that our attention has been focused in these pages.

Notes to Chapter 11

[1] See Ibn Ḥazm's discussion in Friedlander, "The Heterodoxies of the Shīʿites in the Presentation of Ibn Ḥazm", *JAOS*, XXVIII (1907), p. 74

[2] Ashʿarī, *Maqālāt al-Islāmīyīn*, ed. Helmut Ritter (Istanbul, 1929), pp. 16–17

[3] A title with which the Sunnī heresiographers describe the Twelver Shīʿa. For the meaning and use of the term, see Watt, "The Rafidites: A Preliminary Study", *Oriens*, XVI (1963)

[4] Ṭabarī, II, p. 1700

[5] Hodgson, "How Did the Early Shīʿa Become Sectarian?", *JAOS* (1955), p. 10

[6] For such claims made by these *ghulāt*, see Nawbakhtī, *Firaq*, pp. 25, 30, 39, 52–55; Saʿd al-Ashʿarī, *Maqālāt*, pp. 33, 35, 37; Shahrastānī, *Milal*, I, pp. 178, 176. Saʿd al-Ashʿarī (*Maqālāt*, p. 37) writes that Bayān claimed the Imamate as the legatee of Abū Hāshim, and not as that of Al-Bāqir.

[7] Kulaynī, *Kāfī*, I, p. 208

[8] ibid., I, p. 261

[9] Hodgson, op. cit., p. 11

[10] ibid.

[11] Kashshī, *Rijāl*, p. 285

[12] Kulaynī, *Kāfī*, I, p. 274

[13] Kulaynī, *Kāfī*, I, p. 356

[14] ibid., pp. 265 f.; Kashshī, *Rijāl*, p. 427

[15] Kulaynī, *Kāfī*, I, p. 318

[16] Kulaynī, *Kāfī*

[17] ibid., p. 462

[18] ibid., pp. 214–220

[19] See Kulaynī, *Kāfī*, I, pp. 207 ff.; Ṣadūq, *Risālat al-Itiqādāt*, trans. A. A. A. Fyzee, *A Shīʿite Creed* (London 1942), p. 96

[20] Kulaynī, *Kāfī*, I, pp. 205, 207, 304 f.

[21] ibid., p. 205

[22] ibid.

[23] See Kulaynī, *Kāfī*, "Kitāb al-Ḥujja", *passim*; Mufīd, *Irshād*, I, pp. 304–13

[24] *Qur'ān*, III, 6

[25] Kulaynī, *Kāfī*, I, p. 262

[26] See Wensinck, *Handbook of Early Muḥammadan Tradition* (Leiden 1960), under the heading "ʿĀli"

[27] Ibn Saʿd, II, p. 101
[28] ibid.
[29] Kulaynī, *Kāfī*, I, pp. 330 f.
[30] "And God only wishes to remove from you [all kinds of] uncleanliness, O *Ahl al-Bayt* [of Muḥammad], and thoroughly purify you."
[31] See Thaʿlabī, *Tafsīr*, p. 402
[32] Kulaynī, *Kāfī*, II, p. 488
[33] ibid.
[34] ibid., p. 487
[35] ibid., p. 486
[36] Kulaynī, *Kāfī*, I, p. 483
[37] *Qur'ān*, v, 67
[38] *Qur'ān*, xvi, 106
[39] Kulaynī, *Kāfī*, I, p. 483
[40] "Das Prinzip der Takija im Islam", *ZDMG*, LX (1906), pp. 213–20
[41] Ṣadūq, *Creed*, p. 110
[42] Kashshī, *Rijāl*, p. 419
[43] See *EI*² article "ʿAbd Allāh b. Sabā'"
[44] Saʿd al-Ashʿarī, *Maqālāt*, p. 20; Nawbakhtī, *Firaq*, p. 22
[45] Saʿd al-Ashʿarī, loc. cit.; Nawbakhtī, loc. cit.
[46] *Farq*, p. 32
[47] Kashshī, *Rijāl*, p. 296; Shahrastānī, *Milal*, I, p. 152; Ashʿarī, *Maqālāt*, pp. 6–9
[48] See Kashshī, *Rijāl*, p. 148, *passim*; Nawbakhtī, *Firaq*, p. 34
[49] Kashshī, *Rijāl*, p. 223
[50] See Samʿānī, *Ansāb*, p. 113b; Kashshī, *Rijāl*, pp. 191 ff.; Najashī, *Rijāl*, pp. 93 f.
[51] See Chapter 9
[52] Ḥā'irī, *Muntahā*, pp. 202 f.; Ibn Nadīm, *Fihrist*, p. 66
[53] *Kāfī*, I, p. 279
[54] See Ivanow, "Notes sur Umm al-Kitāb", *REI*, 1932
[55] See E. E. Salisbury, "Translation of an Unpublished Arabic Risala", *JAOS*, 1853, pp. 167–93
[56] e.g., *Kāfī*, pp. 365 ff.; Kashshī, *Rijāl*, pp. 324 f.
[57] e.g., *Kāfī*, I, p. 308, *passim*
[58] Yaʿqūbī, II, p. 381; Kashshī, *Rijāl*, p. 224
[59] See Donaldson, *The Shīʿite Religion*, p. 135
[60] Kashshī, *Rijāl*, p. 224. See Hodgson, op. cit., p. 13
[61] Kashshī, *Rijāl*, p. 247
[62] ibid.
[63] ibid.
[64] Ṭūsī, *Fihrist*, pp. 141 ff.; Ḥāʿirī, *Muntahā*, pp. 135–6; Ḥillī, *Rijāl*, p. 76

[65] Ḥā'irī, *Muntaha*, p. 120

[66] Kashshī, *Rijāl*, p. 135; Ṭūsī, *Fihrist*, p. 146; Ḥā'irī, *Muntahā*, p. 136

[67] Abū Aḥmad Muḥammad b. Abī 'Umayr Ziyād b. 'Īsā, a traditionist and companion of Mūsā al-Kāẓim and 'Alī ar-Riḍa, who is said to have written four books. See Najāshī, p. 228; Ḥā'irī, *Muntahā*, p. 254

[68] Kashshī, *Rijāl*, p. 135

[69] Kashshī, *Rijāl*, p. 138. For the reference to Khiḍr, see *Qur'ān*, XVIII, 71

[70] Ibn Nadīm, *Fihrist*, p. 220; Ḥā'irī, *Muntahā*, p. 136

[71] Ḥā'irī, *Muntahā*, p. 93; Ibn Nadīm, loc. cit.

[72] Ḥā'irī, *Muntahā*, p. 110; Ibn Nadīm, loc. cit.

[73] Ḥā'irī, *Muntahā*, p. 99; Ibn Nadīm, loc. cit.; Ṭūsī, *Fihrist*, p. 202, referring to him as 'Ubayd b. Zurāra

[74] Ibn Nadīm, loc. cit.; Kashshī, *Rijāl*, p. 176

[75] Ḥā'irī, *Muntahā*, p. 131; Ṭūsī, *Fihrist*, p. 117

[76] Kashshī, *Rijāl*, p. 181; Ḥā'irī, *Muntahā*, p. 68; Ibn Nadīm, loc. cit.

[77] Ṭūsī, *Fihrist*, p. 188; Ḥā'irī, *Muntahā*, p. 182; Ibn Nadīm, loc. cit.

[78] A brother of Hishām b. al-Ḥakam; see Ḥā'irī, *Muntahā*, p. 271

[79] Ash'arī, *Maqālāt*, I, p. 43

[80] For the last two, see below, pp. 307–8

[81] Ash'arī, *Maqālāt*, I, p. 28, referring to At-Tamīmīya

[82] See a detailed account of the activities of Zurāra and his circle in Kashshī, *Rijāl*, pp. 133–61

[83] Detailed accounts can be found in Ash'arī, *Maqālāt*, II, pp. 36 f.; Baghdādī, *Farq*, p. 43; Shahrastānī, *Milāl*, I, p. 186

[84] Kashshī, *Rijāl*, pp. 185 ff.; Najāshī, *Rijāl*, p. 228; Sa'd al-Ash'arī, *Maqālāt*, p. 88; Ṭūsī, *Fihrist*, p. 223; Ibn Nadīm, *Fihrist*, p. 176; Ḥā'irī, *Muntahā*, p. 295; Ḥillī, *Rijāl*, p. 138

[85] Najashī, *Rijāl*, p. 228; Kashshī, *Rijāl*, p. 187

[86] See Kashshī, *Rijāl*, pp. 135 ff.; Ibn 'Abd Rabbih, *'Iqd*, II, p. 465

[87] See Ibn Nadīm, *Fihrist*, p. 176; Najāshī, *Rijāl*, p. 228; Shahrastānī, *Milal*, I, p. 187

[88] Kashshī, *Rijāl*, p. 185

[89] Kashshī, *Rijāl*, pp. 280 ff.; Najāshī, *Rijāl*, p. 305; Ṭūsī, *Fihrist*, p. 354; Ḥā'irī, *Muntahā*, pp. 323–4. For his ideas, also see Ash'arī, *Maqālāt*, I, p. 34; Baghdādī, *Farq*, p. 139; Shahrastānī, *Milal*, pp. 184 f.; Fakhr ad-Dīn ar-Rāzī, *I'tiqādāt*, p. 64; Nawbakhtī, *Firaq*, p. 66; Ibn Nadīm, *Fihrist*, p. 177

[90] A *mawlā* of Kinda, but often described as the client of the Banū Shaybān, because he attached himself to that tribe. See Kashshī,

Rijāl, pp. 475 ff.; Ṭūsī, *Fihrist*, p. 353; Najāshī, *Rijāl*, p. 304; Ibn Nadīm, *Fihrist*, p. 175; Ḥā'irī, *Muntahā*, pp. 322 ff.

91 A *mawlā* of the Banū Asad, he lived in Baṣra, where he frequented the circles of the local Muʿtazilite *mutakallimūn*. See Najāshī, p. 176; Ḥā'irī, *Muntahā*, pp. 207–8; Ṭūsī, *Fihrist*, p. 212; Kashshī, *Rijāl*, p. 213

92 Kashshī, *Rijāl*, p. 214

93 See Ashʿarī, *Maqālāt*, I, p. 48, and *index*; Shahrastānī, *Milal*, I, pp. 184 ff., and *index*

94 Kashshī, *Rijāl*, p. 375. For the biographical data and detailed information on them, see Kashshī, *Rijāl*, index; Najāshī, *Rijāl*, index; Ḥā'irī, *Muntahā*, *passim*

95 Kashshī, *Rijāl*, p. 375

96 See Kashshī, *Rijāl*, p. 330; Ḥā'irī, *Muntahā*, p. 17; Najāshī, *Rijāl*, pp. 7–10; Dhahabī, *Mīzān*, I, pp. 4–5

97 See Kashshī, *Rijāl*, p. 330

98 Kashshī, *Rijāl*, p. 418

99 See Kashshī, *Rijāl*, pp. 419 f.

100 Ṣadūq, *Creed*, pp. 84 f.

Bibliography

A. Primary Sources

ABŪ DĀ'ŪD, SULAYMĀN B. AL-ASHʿATH *Sunan al-Muṣṭafā* Cairo n.d.

ABŪ'L-FARAJ AL-IṢFAHĀNĪ *Kitāb al-Aghānī* Beirut 1973

—— *Maqātil aṭ-Ṭālibiyīn* Tehran 1949

ABŪ'L-MAḤĀSIN YŪSUF B. TAGHRĪBIRDĪ *An-Nujūm az-Zāhira* Cairo 1929 ff.

ABŪ NUʿAYM AL-IṢBAHĀNĪ *Ḥilyat al-Awliyā'* Cairo 1933

ABŪ YŪSUF YAʿQŪB B. IBRĀHĪM *Kitāb al-Kharāj* Cairo 1933

ʿALĪ AL-MUTTAQĪ *Kanz al-ʿUmmāl* Hyderabad 1364 AH

AL-ANBARĪ, ABŪ BAKR MUḤAMMAD B. QĀSIM *Sharḥ al-Qaṣā'id as-Sabʿa aṭ-Ṭiwāl al-Jāhiliyyāt* ed. ʿAbd as-Salām Hārūn; Cairo 1963

AL-ASHʿARĪ, ABŪ'L-ḤASAN ʿALĪ B. ISMĀʿĪL *Maqālāt al-Islāmiyyīn*, ed. Helmut Ritter; Istanbul 1929

AL-ASHʿARĪ, MUḤAMMAD B. YAḤYĀ B. ABĪ BAKR *At-Tamhīd wa'l-Bayān fī Maqtal ash-Shahīd ʿUthmān* ed. Maḥmūd Zāyid; Beirut 1964

AL-ASHʿARĪ, SAʿD B. ʿABD ALLĀH AL-QUMMĪ *Kitāb al-Maqālāt wa'l-Firaq* ed. Muḥammad Jawād Mashkūr; Tehran 1963

AL-AZRAQĪ, MUḤAMMAD B. ʿABD ALLĀH *Akhbār Makka* ed. Rushdī aṣ-Ṣāliḥ; Mecca 1352 AH

AL-BAGHDĀDĪ, ABŪ MANṢŪR ʿABD AL-QĀHIR *Al-Farq bayna'l-Firaq* ed. al-Kawtharī; Cairo 1948

—— *Uṣūl ad-Dīn* Istanbul 1928

AL-BALĀDHURĪ, AḤMAD B. YAḤYĀ B. JĀBIR *Ansāb al-Ashrāf* vol. I, ed. Muḥammad Ḥamīdullah, Cairo 1955; vol. IV A–B, ed. Max Schloessinger, Jerusalem 1938–1971; vol. V, ed. S. D. F. Goitein, Jerusalem 1936

—— *Futūḥ al-Buldān* trans. Philip K. Hitti, *Origins of the Islamic State* New York 1916

AL-BAYḌĀWĪ, ʿABD ALLĀH B. ʿUMAR *Anwār at-Tanzīl* ed. Fleischer; 1846–1848

AL-BAYHAQĪ, MUḤAMMAD B. IBRĀHĪM *Kitāb al-Maḥāsin wa'l-Masāwī* ed. Friedrich Schwally; Giessen 1902

AL-BUKHĀRĪ, MUḤAMMAD B. ISMĀʿĪL *Jāmīʿ aṣ-Ṣaḥīḥ* Cairo 1932

AD-DAMĪRĪ, KAMĀL AD-DĪN *Ḥayāt al-Ḥayawān* Bulaq 1284 AH

ADH-DHAHABĪ, ABŪ ʿABD ALLĀH MUḤAMMAD *Ta'rīkh al-Islām* Cairo 1367 AH

—— *Tadhkirat al-Ḥuffāẓ* Hyderabad 1333 AH

—— *Mīzān al-Iʿtidāl* n.d.

AD-DĪNAWARĪ, ABŪ ḤANĪFA AḤMAD B. DĀʾŪD *Kitāb al-Akhbār at-Tiwāl* Cairo 1960

AD-DIYĀRBAKRĪ, ḤUSAYN B. MUḤAMMAD *Taʾrīkh al-Khamīs* Cairo 1309 AH

FARAZDAQ *Dīwān* ed. ʿAbd Allāh Ismāʿīl aṣ-Ṣāwī; Cairo 1936

AL-ḤĀʾIRĪ, MUḤAMMAD B. ISMĀʿĪL *Muntahā al-Maqāl* Tehran 1302 AH

AL-ḤILLĪ, ḤASAN B. YŪSUF *Al-Bāb al-Ḥādī ʿAshar* trans. W. M. Miller; London 1928

—— *Minhāj al-Karāma fī Maʿrifat al-Imāma* Tehran 1880

—— *Kashf al-Yaqīn fī Faḍāʾil Amīr al-Muʾminīn* Tehran 1880

—— *Rijāl* ed. Muḥammad Ṣādiq; Najaf 1961

IBN ʿABD AL-BARR *Kitāb al-Istīʿāb* Cairo n.d.

IBN ʿABD RABBIH, AḤMAD B. MUḤAMMAD *Al-ʿIqd al-Farīd* ed. Aḥmad Amīn et al.; Cairo 1952–6

IBN ABĪ'L-ḤADĪD *Sharḥ Nahj al-Balāgha* ed. Muḥammad Abū'l-Faḍl Ibrāhīm; Cairo 1959

IBN ʿASĀKIR, ʿALĪ B. AL-ḤASAN *Tabyīn Kidhb al-Muftarī* Damascus 1347 AH

—— *At-Taʾrīkh al-Kabīr* Damascus 1347 AH

IBN AL-ATHĪR, ABŪ'L-ḤASAN ʿALĪ B. KARĪM *Al-Kāmil fi't-Taʾrīkh* Beirut 1975

IBN AL-ATHĪR, ʿALĪ B. MUḤAMMAD *Usd al-Ghāba* Cairo n.d.

IBN DURAYD, MUḤAMMAD B. AL-ḤASAN *Kitāb al-Ishtiqāq* ed. Ferdinand Wüstenfeld; Göttingen 1854

IBN AL-ḤABĪB, MUḤAMMAD B. ḤABĪB *Kitāb al-Muḥabbar* ed. Listenstater; Hyderabad 1942

IBN ḤAJAR, AḤMAD B. MUḤAMMAD AL-HAYTHAMĪ *Aṣ-Ṣawāʾiq al-Muḥriqa* ed. ʿAbd al-Wahhāb; Cairo 1375 AH

IBN ḤAJAR AL-ʿASQALĀNĪ *Lisān al-Mīzān* Hyderabad 1329 AH

—— *Tahdhīb at-Tahdhīb* Hyderabad 1325 AH

IBN ḤANBAL, AḤMAD B. MUḤAMMAD *Al-Musnad* Cairo 1895

IBN ḤAZM, ABŪ MUḤAMMAD ʿALĪ B. AḤMAD *Al-Faṣl fi'l-Milal wa'l-Ahwāʾ wa'n-Nihal* Cairo 1347 AH

IBN HISHĀM, ABŪ MUḤAMMAD ʿABD AL-MALIK *Sīrat Rasūl Allāh* ed. Muṣṭafā Saqqa et al., Cairo 1936; trans. Alfred Guillaume *The Life of Muhammad* Oxford 1967

IBN ʿIMĀD AL-ḤANBALĪ *Shadharāt adh-Dhahab* Cairo 1350 AH

IBN AL-JAWZĪ, ABŪ'L-FARAJ ʿABD AR-RAḤMĀN *Kitāb Ṣifwat as-Ṣafwa* Hyderabad 1355 AH

—— *Talbīs Iblīs* Cairo 1340 AH

IBN KATHĪR, ISMĀʿĪL B. ʿUMAR *Al-Bidāya wa'n-Nihāya* Cairo 1932 ff.

—— *Tafsīr al-Qurʾān al-ʿAẓīm* Cairo n.d.

IBN KHALDŪN, ʿABD AR-RAḤMĀN *Al-ʿIbar* Cairo 1867 ff.

—— *Al-Muqaddima* ed. ʿAlī ʿAbd al-Wāḥid Wafī

IBN KHALLIKĀN, AḤMAD B. MUḤAMMAD *Wafayāt al-Aʿyān* ed. Iḥsān ʿAbbās; Beirut 1972

IBN NADĪM, MUḤAMMAD B. ISḤĀQ *Kitāb al-Fihrist* ed. Gustav Flügel; Leipzig 1871

IBN NASHWĀN AL-ḤIMYARĪ *Ḥurr al-ʿAyn* ed. Kamāl Muṣṭafā; Cairo 1948

IBN QUTAYBA, MUḤAMMAD B. ʿABD ALLĀH *ʿUyūn al-Akhbār* Cairo 1925

—— *Kitāb al-Maʿārif* Cairo n.d.

—— *Al-Imāma wa's-Siyāsa* (attributed), Cairo 1957

IBN AṢ-ṢABBĀGH, NŪR AD-DĪN AL-MĀLIKĪ *Al-Fuṣūl al-Muhimma fī Maʿrifat al-A'imma* Persia 1886

IBN SAʿD, MUḤAMMAD *Kitāb aṭ-Ṭabaqāt al-Kubrā* Beirut 1957 ff.

IBN AṬ-ṬIQṬAQA, MUḤAMMAD B. ʿALĪ *Al-Fakhrī fī'l-Adab as-Sulṭānīya* Cairo 1921

AL-JĀḤIẒ, ABŪ ʿUTHMĀN ʿAMR B. BAḤR *Al-Bayān wa't-Tabyīn* ed. ʿAbd as-Salām Hārūn; Cairo 1960

—— *Rasāʾil al-Jāḥiẓ* ed. Ḥasan as-Sandūbī; Cairo 1933

AL-JAHSHIYĀRĪ, MUḤAMMAD B. ʿABDŪS *Kitāb al-Wuzarāʾ wa'l-Kuttāb* Cairo 1938

AL-JĪLĀNĪ, ʿABD AL-QĀDIR *Ghunyat aṭ-Ṭālibīn* Delhi 1300 AH

AL-KALBĪ, HISHĀM B. MUḤAMMAD *Kitāb al-Aṣnām* ed. Aḥmad Zakī Bāshā; Cairo 1914

AL-KASHSHĪ, ʿUMAR B. MUḤAMMAD *Maʿrifat Akhbār ar-Rijāl* Mashhad n.d.

KHALĪFA B. KHAYYĀṬ *Ta'rīkh* ed. Suhayl Zakkār; Cairo 1967

AL-KHATĪB AL-BAGHDĀDĪ *Ta'rīkh Baghdād* Cairo 1931

AL-KHAYYĀṬ, ʿABD AL-RAḤĪM *Kitāb al-Intiṣār* ed. Nyberg; Beirut 1957

AL-KULAYNĪ, MUḤAMMAD B. YAʿQŪB *Al-Uṣūl al-Kāfī* Karachi 1965

—— *Al-Furūʿ al-Kāfī* Tehran 1890

AL-KUMAYT *Al-Hāshimīyāt* ed. Aṣ-Ṣaydāwī; Cairo 1950

AL-MAʿARRĪ, ABŪ'L-ʿALĀʾ *Risālat al-Ghufrān* Cairo 1950

AL-MAJLISĪ, MUḤAMMAD BĀQIR *Biḥār al-Anwār* Persia 1301–1315 AH

MĀLIK B. ANAS *Al-Muwaṭṭā* Cairo 1862

AL-MAQRĪZĪ, AḤMAD B. ʿALĪ *An-Nizāʾ wa't-Takhāṣum bayna'l-Banī Umayya wa Banī Ḥāshim* Najaf 1368 AH

AL-MASʿŪDĪ, ʿALĪ B. ḤUSAYN *Murūj adh-Dhahab* Beirut 1966

—— *Kitāb at-Tanbīh wa'l-Ishrāf* Leiden 1894

AL-MINQARĪ, NAṢR B. MUZĀHIM *Waqʿat Ṣiffīn* Cairo 1365 AH

AL-MUBARRAD, MUḤAMMAD B. YAZĪD *Kitāb al-Kāmil* Cairo n.d.

AL-MUFAḌḌAL B. MUḤAMMAD *Al-Mufaḍḍaliyyāt* ed. Charles James Lyall; Oxford 1921

AL-MUFAḌḌAL B. ʿUMAR AL-JUʿFĪ *Kitāb al-Haft wa'l-Azilla* (attributed), ed. ʿĀrif Tamir; Beirut 1960

AL-MUFĪD, MUḤAMMAD B. MUḤAMMAD *Amālī* Najaf 1351 AH
—— *Kitāb al-Irshād* Tehran 1344 AH
MUḤAMMAD AL-KHAṬĪB *Mishkāt al-Maṣābīḥ* Lucknow 1924
MURTAḌA B. DĀʿĪ *Kitāb Tabṣirat al-ʿAwām* Tehran 1313 AH
MUSLIM, ABŪ'L-ḤUSAYN *Aṣ-Ṣaḥīḥ* Cairo n.d.
NĀBIGHA ADH-DHUBYĀNĪ *Dīwān* ed. Shukrī Fayṣal; Beirut 1968
AN-NAJĀSHĪ, AḤMAD B. ʿALĪ *Kitāb ar-Rijāl* Tehran n.d.
AN-NASĀ'Ī, AḤMAD B. SHUʿAYB *As-Sunan* Cairo 1894
AN-NAWBAKHTĪ, ḤASAN B. MŪSĀ *Kitāb Firaq ash-Shīʿa* Najaf 1959
QĀḌĪ NUʿMĀN, ABŪ ḤANĪFA *Sharḥ al-Akhbār* SOAS MS No. 25732
—— *Daʿā'im al-Islām* ed. A. A. A. Fyzee; Cairo 1951–61
AR-RĀZĪ, FAKHR AD-DĪN *Iʿtīqādāt al-Firaq al-Muslimīn wa'l-Mushrikīn* Cairo 1338 AH
—— *Mafātīḥ al-Ghayb* Cairo n.d.
SADŪQ, SHAYKH IBN BABWAYHI *Man Lā Yaḥḍuruhu'l-Faqīḥ* Persia 1342 AH
—— *Risālat al-Iʿtiqādāt* trans. A. A. A. Fyzee, *A Shīʿite Creed* Calcutta 1942
—— *ʿUyūn Akhbār ar-Riḍā* Persia 1858
AS-SAMʿĀNĪ, ʿABD AL-KARĪM B. MUḤAMMAD *Kitāb al-Ansāb* Leiden 1912
ASH-SHAHRĀSHŪB, MUḤAMMAD B. ʿALĪ *Manāqib Āl Abī Ṭālib* Najaf 1956
ASH-SHAHRASTĀNĪ, MUḤAMMAD B. ʿABD AL-KARĪM *Al-Milal wa'n-Nihal* ed. Muḥammad Sayyid Kaylānī; Cairo 1961
SHAMS AD-DĪN, MUḤAMMAD B. ṬŪLŪN *Al-A'immat al-Ithnā ʿAshar* ed. Ṣalāḥ ad-Dīn al-Munajjid; Beirut 1958
AS-SUBKĪ, ABŪ NAṢR ʿABD AL-WAHHĀB *Ṭabaqāt ash-Shāfiʿīya* ed. Aḥmad b. ʿAbd al-Karīm; Cairo n.d.
SUYŪṬĪ, JALĀL AD-DĪN *Ta'rīkh al-Khulafā'* Cairo 1351 AH
AṬ-ṬABARĪ, ABŪ JAʿFAR *Ta'rīkh ar-Rusul wa'l-Mulūk* ed. M. J. de Goeje et al; Leiden 1879–1901
—— *Al-Mukhtasar min Kitāb adh-Dhayl al-Mudhayyal* Cairo 1929
—— *Jāmiʿ al-Bayān fī Tafsīr al-Qur'ān* Cairo 1328 AH ff.
AṬ-ṬABARSĪ, FAḌL B. ḤASAN *Al-Iḥtījāj* Tehran 1302 AH
AṬ-ṬŪSĪ, NAṢĪR AD-DĪN MUḤAMMAD B. ḤASAN *Al-Istibsār* Najaf 1956
—— *Kitāb al-Fihrist* ed. A. Spranger; Calcutta 1855
—— *Tahdhīb al-Aḥkām* Najaf 1959 ff.
AL-YAʿQŪBĪ, AḤMAD B. ʿALĪ YAʿQŪB AL-WĀḌIH *At-Ta'rīkh* Beirut 1960
YĀQŪT, SHIHĀB AD-DĪN *Muʿjam al-Buldān* Beirut 1955
ZAYD B. ʿALĪ *Majmaʿ al-Fiqh* ed. Griffini, *Corpus Juris di Zaid Ibn ʿAlī* Milan 1919

B. Secondary Sources

ABBOTT, NABIA *Studies in Arabic Literary Papyri* Chicago 1957–72
ĀGHĀ BUZURG, TIHRĀNĪ *Adh-Dharīʿa ilā Taṣānīf ash-Shīʿa* Najaf 1936 ff.
ʿALĪ AL-WARDĪ *Waʿāẓ as-Salāṭīn* Baghdad 1954
AMEER ALI, SAYID *Muhammadan Law* London 1936
ʿĀMILĪ, MUḤSIN B. ʿABD AL-KARĪM AL-ḤUSAYNĪ *Āʿyān ash-Shīʿa* Damascus 1935 ff.
ARNOLD, SIR THOMAS W. *The Caliphate* Oxford 1924
BROCKELMANN, CARL *Geschichte der arabischen Litteratur* Leiden 1937 ff.
—— *History of the Islamic Peoples* London 1959
DONALDSON, D. M. *The Shīʿite Religion* London 1933
DURI, ABD AL-AZIZ "Al-Zuhrī: A Study on the Beginning of History Writing in Islam" *BSOAS* XIX (1957)
EGHBĀL, ʿABBĀS *Khāndāne Nawbakht* Tehran 1311 AH
The Encyclopaedia of Islam 1st edition 1913–38; New Edition 1960-proceeding
FRIEDLAENDER, I. "The Heterodoxies of the Shīʿites in the Presentation of Ibn Ḥazm" *JAOS* XXVII
FRYE, RICHARD N. "The Role of Abū Muslim in the ʿAbbāsid Revolt" *The Muslim World* XXXVII (1947)
FYZEE, A. A. A. "Shīʿī Legal Theories" *Law in the Middle East*, ed. Majid Khadduri and H. J. Liebesney; Washington 1955
GIBBON, EDWARD *History of the Decline and Fall of the Roman Empire* ed. J. B. Bury; London 1901
GOLDZIHER, I. *Muhammedanische Studien* trans. S. M. Stern and C. R. Barber; *Muslim Studies* London 1967–1972
—— "Das Prinzip der Takija im Islam" *ZDMG* LX (1906)
HAMIDULLAH, MUHAMMAD "The City State of Mecca" *IC* XII (1938)
—— *Ṣaḥīfah Hammām Ibn Munabbih* Hyderabad 1961
ḤASAN AṢ-ṢADR *Tāsīs ash-Shīʿa li-ʿUlūm al-Islām* Kazimain 1951
HIBAT AD-DĪN *Nuḍhat al-Ḥusayn* Najaf 1937
HITTI, PHILIP K. *History of the Arabs* London 1949
HODGSON, MARSHAL G. S. "How Did the Early Shīʿa Become Sectarian?" *JAOS* 1955
—— *The Order of the Assassins* Monton 1955
IVANOW, W. "The Early Shīʿite Movements" *JBBRAS* 1939
—— *A Guide to Ismāʿīlī Literature* London 1933
—— "Notes sur l'Ummu'l-Kitāb" *REI* 1932
KAḤḤĀLA, ʿUMAR RIḌĀ *Muʿjam Qabāʾil al-ʿArab* Damascus 1949
ḲHALĪF, YŪSUF *Ḥayāt ash-Shīʿr fīʾl-Kūfa* Cairo 1968
KHUDA BUKHSH *Politics in Islam* Lahore 1932
LANE, E. W. *An Arabic-English Lexicon* London 1863

LEWIS, BERNARD *The Arabs in History* London 1950
—— *The Origins of Ismāʿīlism* Cambridge 1940
MOSCATI, S. "Per Una Stiria Dell'Antica Šiʿa" *RSO* XXX (1955)
—— "Il Testamento di Abū Hāshim" *RSO* XXVII (1952)
MASSIGNON, L. "Explication du Plan de Kufa (Iraq)" *Opera Minora* Beirut 1963; Arabic trans. Taqī al-Maṣʿabī, *Khiṭaṭ al-Kūfa* Saida 1939
MOWDŪDĪ, ABŪ'L-ĀʿLA *Khilāfat wa Mulūkīyat* Lahore 1966
MUIR, SIR WILLIAM *The Caliphate* Edinburgh 1915
NICHOLSON, R. A. *A Literary History of the Arabs* Cambridge 1956
PETERSEN, E. L. *ʿAlī and Muʿāwiya in Early Arabic Tradition* Copenhagen 1964
AL-QAZWĪNĪ, MUʿIZZ AD-DĪN *Ansāb al-Qabā'il al-ʿIrāqīyya* Najaf 1918
RAMAḌĀN, LAWAND *Al-Imām aṣ-Ṣādiq* Beirut n.d.
RUSKA, J. "The History of Jābir Problem" *IC* XI (1937)
—— "Gābir Ibn Ḥayyān und seine Beziehungen zum Imām ʿGaʿfar al-Ṣādiqʿ" *Der Islam* XVI
SCHACHT, JOSEPH *An Introduction to Islamic Law* Oxford 1964
—— *The Origins of Muhammadan Jurisprudence* Oxford 1950
SERJEANT, R. B. "Ḥaram and Ḥawtah, the Sacred Enclave in Arabia" *Mélanges Taha Husayn* ed. Abdurrahman Badawi; Cairo 1962
—— "The Saiyids of Ḥaḍramawt" An Inaugural Lecture, *BSOAS,* London 1957
—— "Professor A. Guillaume's Translation of the Sīrah" *BSOAS* XXI (1958)
SEZGIN, URSULA *Abū Mikhnaf, ein Beitrag zur Historiographie der Umaiyadischen Zeit* Leiden 1971
SHAHĀBĪ, MAḤMŪD *Adwār Fiqh* Tehran 1329 AH
WATT, W. MONTGOMERY *Islam and its Integration of Society* London 1961
—— *Islamic Political Thought* Edinburgh 1968
—— *Muhammad at Mecca* London 1953
—— *Muhammad at Medina* London 1955
—— "The Muslim Yearning for a Saviour: Aspects of Early ʿAbbāsid Shīʿism" *The Saviour God* ed. S. G. F. Brandon; Oxford 1963
—— "The Rāfiḍites: A Preliminary Study" *Oriens* XVI (1963)
—— "Shīʿism under the Umayyads" *JRAS* 1960
WELLHAUSEN, JULIUS *The Arab Kingdom and Its Fall* Calcutta 1927
—— *Die religio-politischen Oppositionsparteien im alten Islam* trans. ʿAbdurraḥmān Badawī, *Al-Khawārij wa'sh-Shīʿa* Cairo 1958
WENSINCK, A. J. *A Handbook of Early Muhammadan Tradition* Leiden 1960
—— *The Muslim Creed* Cambridge 1932

Index

Abān b. Taghlib b. Riyāḥ, 309–10
Abān b. ʿUthmān, 30, 31, 309
al-ʿAbbās b. ʿAbd al-Muṭṭalib, 22, 70, 270–1, 279
ʿAbbās b. ʿAlī, 187–9 *passim*, 191, 206
ʿAbbās Mahmūd al-ʿAqqād, 204
ʿAbbāsids, 7, 211, 269, 270–4, 289
  claim to caliphate of, 277–9
  and Imams, 271–2, 298, 299
  and Shīʿa, 261
Abbot, Nabia, 30, 68
ʿAbd Allāh b. al-ʿAbbās, 31–2, 120, 131–4 *passim*, 140–1, 144, 148
  and ʿAlī, 271
  and Ḥusayn, 182, 203, 204
ʿAbd Allāh b. Abī Bakr, 30, 38
ʿAbd Allāh b. Abī Yaʿfūr, 304–5
ʿAbd Allāh b. al-Aḥmar, poet, 229
ʿAbd Allāh al-ʿAlā'ilī, 205
ʿAbd Allāh b. ʿĀmir, 143, 150–2 *passim*
ʿAbd Allāh b. Bukayr b. Aʿyān, 306, 309
ʿAbd Allāh b. Jaʿfar aṣ-Ṣādiq, 294
ʿAbd Allāh al-Maḥḍ (ʿAbd Allāh al-Muthanna b. al-Ḥasan b. ʿAlī al-Maḥḍ), 247, 266, 268–9, 273, 275
ʿAbd Allāh b. Masʿūd, 82, 109–10, 268
ʿAbd Allāh b. Miskān, 309
ʿAbd Allāh b. Muʿammar al-Laythī, 255
ʿAbd Allāh b. Muʿāwiya, 266, 268, 270
ʿAbd Allāh b. Nawfal b. al-Ḥārith, 150–152 *passim*
ʿAbd Allāh b. Sabā', 300
ʿAbd Allāh b. Saʿd b. Nufayl al-Azdī, 222, 232
ʿAbd Allāh b. ʿUmar b. al-Khaṭṭāb, 67, 131, 166, 175, 182
ʿAbd Allāh b. Wahb b. Sabāʿ, *see* Ibn as-Sawdā
ʿAbd Allāh b. Wālin at-Taymī, 223–4, 232
ʿAbd Allāh b. Yazīd al-Anṣārī, 227, 230
ʿAbd Allāh b. Zayn al-ʿĀbidīn, 238
ʿAbd Allāh b. Ziyād, 224
ʿAbd Allāh b. az-Zubayr, 131, 168, 175–177, 183
  death of, 242, 245
  revolt of, 198–9, 227, 230, 238
  and Zayn al-ʿĀbidīn, 238, 245
ʿAbd ad-Dār, 8
ʿAbd al-Malik b. Marwān, Caliph, 238, 250
ʿAbd Manāf, 8, 13, 271
ʿAbd al-Muṭṭalib, 8–9, 13, 17, 271
ʿAbd ar-Raḥmān b. Abī Bakr, 168, 175
ʿAbd ar-Raḥmān b. ʿAwf, 46, 64–5, 67, 70–1, 73–4, 84
ʿAbd ar-Raḥmān b. al-Muljam, 91
ʿAbd ar-Raḥmān b. Samra, 150–2 *passim*
ʿAbd ar-Raḥmān b. Umm al-Ḥakam, 143
ʿAbd ash-Shams, 7, 74, 150
ʿĀbis b. Abī Ḥabīb ash-Shākirī, 182
Abraham, 10, 14–15, 299
Abū 'l-ʿAbbās as-Saffāḥ, Caliph, 269, 272, 274–5, 277
Abū ʿAbd Allāh Muḥammad b. Saʿd, *see* Ibn Saʿd
Abū Aḥmad Muhammad b. Abī ʿUmayr Ziyād b. ʿĪsā, 306
Abū ʿAmra Kaysān, 263
Abū 'l-Aswad ad-Du'alī, poet, 93
Abū Ayyūb al-Anṣārī, 52
Abū Bakr Aḥmad b. ʿAbd al-ʿAzīz al-Jawharī, *see* al-Jawharī
Abū Bakr b. Muḥammad al-Ḥaḍramī, 251
Abū Bakr aṣ-Ṣiddīq, Caliph, 13–14 *passim*, 16, 17, 113
  accession of, 28–9, 32–3, 37, 42–51
  and 'Ali, 58, 60, 62–3, 73
  caliphate of, 58, 94, 252
  nomination of ʿUmar by, 63–4, 152
  and war of apostasy, 59–60, 67
Abū Baṣīr Layth al-Bakhtarī al-Murādī al-Asadī, 250
Abū Dā'ūd, 19, 32

Index

Abū Dharr b. Jundab al-Ghifārī, 52, 83–86 *passim*
Abū 'l-Faraj al-Iṣfahānī, 269
  on Ḥasan, 138, 142, 144–5, 147–8, 150, 152, 154
  on Hujr's revolt, 161, 162
  on Kerbela, 214–15
Abū Ḥamza Thābit b. Dīnār, 243
Abū Ḥamza ath-Thumālī, 250, 302
Abū Ḥanīfa an-Nu'mān, 255, 260, 267, 276, 280, 292, 307
Abū'l-Ḥasan b. A'yān b. Susan az-Zurāra, *see* az-Zurāra
Abū Hāshim 'Abd Allāh, 242, 246, 259, 263, 270–2, 274, 301
Abū Humayd, 273
Abū Ja'far 'Abd Allāh, 272
Abū Ja'far al-Manṣūr, *see* al-Manṣūr, Caliph
Abū Ja'far Muḥammad b. Nu'mān al-Aḥwal, 306, 307–8
Abū Jahl, 22
Abū Jahm, 273
Abū Khālid al-Kābulī, 242, 245
Abū 'l-Khaṭṭāb, 302–4 *passim*
Abū Manṣūr al-'Ijlī, 291, 301, 303
Abū Ma'shar, 36
Abu Mikhnaf Lūt b. Yaḥyā, 93
  on Ḥasan, 138–9, 144, 162
  on Kerbela, 193, 200, 211–16
  on the Saqīfa, 37, 39, 40, 47
  on *Tawwābūn*, 228
Abū Muḥammad Aḥmad b. A'tham al-Kūfī al-Kindī, *see* Ibn A'tham
Abū Muḥammad Hishām b. al-Ḥakam, 308
Abū Mūsā al-Ash'arī, 109, 122, 130, 271
Abū Muslim, 270, 272, 277, 278
Abū Salama Ḥafṣ, 272–5
Abū Sufyān, 13, 59, 70, 131
Abū Ṭalha al-Anṣārī, 68
Abū Ṭālib, 9, 17
Abū 'l-Ṭufayl 'Āmir b. Wā'ila, 263
Abū 'Ubayda b. al-Jarrāḥ, 35, 44–7 *passim*, 49, 73
'Adī b. Ḥātim al-Tā'ī, 106, 118–19, 122, 142
Aḍrūh, arbitration of, 91, 121–2, 130
Ahl al-'Āliya, 104, 107, 108
Ahl al-Bayt, 7, 15–16, 75, 133, 180–1
  and Abbāsids, 274, 277, 296
  and Mahdism, 265
  in poetry, 250
  sanctity of, 297
  Shī'ī cause of, 125, 137, 160, 182, 223–224, 228–9, 236
  Shī'ī concepts of, 269–70, 272, 296–7
Ahl al-Ḥadīth, see Aṣḥāb al-Ḥadīth
Ahl al-'Irāq, 95
Aḥmad b. Ḥanbal, Imām, 19, 21
Aḥmad b. Muḥammad b. Ayyūb, 41–2
Aḥmad b. Yaḥya b. Jābir al-Balādhurī, *see* al-Balādhurī
al-Aḥwal, *see* Ja'far Muḥammad b. Nu'mān al-Aḥwal
Āl, Ahl, 14, 15–16
'Ā'isha, 34, 90, 94–6 *passim*, 166
'Alī b. 'Abd Allāh b. al-'Abbās b. 'Abd al-Muṭṭalib, 270–1
'Ali b. Abī Ṭālib, Caliph, 1, 2, 16, 271, 274
  his attitude during first caliphates, 59–65, 72, 282
  caliphate of, 89–97
  his character, 72
  death of, 91, 130
  election of, 88, 119
  at Ghadīr Khum, 19–22
  and Imamate, 304, 308–9, 310
  in Kūfa, 90–1, 97, 106–7, 123–4
  and Mu'āwiya, 73
  Muḥammad's special favours to, 17–19, 58, 295–6
  opponents of, 95–6
  partisans of, 51–3, 86–7, 95–7, 105–6, 119, 121–2, 124–5
  at the Saqīfa, 37, 38, 42–5 *passim*, 47, 49, 50–1
  in the Shūrā, 67, 70–1
  superior knowledge of, 296, 301–2
  and 'Uthmān, 74, 75–6, 84–5, 87
'Alī b. al-Ḥusayn, Zayn al-'Ābidīn, 192, 194, 213–15 *passim*, 252
  death of, 246
  followers of, 242–6, 254, 259, 310
  and Imamate, 229–30, 282, 289, 311
  and Mukhtār, 236–7, 238–9, 240
  quiescence of, 229, 236, 262, 266, 282
  and Umayyads, 237–8
'Alī b. Ismā'īl al-Maythamī, 308
'Alī ar-Riḍa, Imam, 304, 308, 310
Alids,
  claim to caliphate by, 278–81
  factions within, 267, 269–70, 276–7
  and Fātimids, 297
'Alqama b. Muḥammad al-Ḥaḍramī, 251
al-A'mash, 267, 280
'Āmir b. Uḥaymir b. Bahdala, 5
'Ammār b. Yāsir, 52, 74, 76, 82, 84–6 *passim*, 109
'Amr b. al-'Ās, 95, 130, 154
'Amr b. al-Ḥāmiq al-Khuzā'ī, 153
'Amr b. al-Ḥurayth, 159–60, 224, 227, 310
'Amr b. 'Ubayd, 268–9
Ansāb al-Ashrāf, 36
Anṣār (helpers), 11, 67–8
  clan rivalries among, 48–9
  in Kūfa, 107, 109, 110
  partisans of 'Ali among, 51–3, 87, 94, 130–1

at the Saqīfa, 27, 29, 34–5, 37, 42–7 *passim*
apostasy, wars of, 59, 67, 110
Arabs, main groups of, 11–12; *see also* Nizārī; Yemenī
Arab society, 3–6
al-ʿasabīya, 3
Aṣḥāb al-Ḥadīth, 253–4, 261, 277, 279, 280
Ashāʿira, 311–12
al-Ashʿarī, Abū'l-Ḥasan ʿAlī b. Ismāʿīl, 290
al-Ashʿarī, Saʿd b. ʿAbd Allāh al-Qummī, 17, 305
al-Ashʿath b. Qays al-Kindī, 104, 118, 120–1, 123
ashrāf al-qabāʾil, 119, 122–3
ʿAwāna, 36, 139–40, 142–3, 215
Āyāt al-Mutashābihāt, 295
ʿAyn al-Warda, battle of, 231, 239, 240, 245
Azra b. Qays, 206

Badr, battle of, 18, 109
al-Baghdādī, Abū Manṣūr ʿAbd al-Qāhir, 248, 301, 305
Bakhamra, battle of, 276
al-Baladhuri, Ahmad b. Yaḥya b. Jabir,
  on Karbalā, 213
  on Kūfa, 108
  on the Saqīfa, 28, 29, 31, 36–7, 39, 40, 42–3, 45–6
  on Shūrā, 68
Banū ʿAbd al-Muṭṭalib, 17, 75
Banū ʿAbd al-Qays, 105, 107, 113
Banū ʿAbs, 107
Banūʿ Adī b. Kaʿb, 16
Banū Ahl al-Ḥajar, 105
Banū ʿAkk, 105
Banū Asad, 104, 107, 108, 113, 192, 196
Banū Ashʿar, 106, 107
Banū Aws, 3, 11, 12, 48
Banū Azd, 104, 107, 196–7
Banu Bajīla, 104, 107, 113
Banū Bakr, 103, 107, 113
Banū Ḍabba, 107
Banū Dhubya, 107
Banū Ḍubayʿa, 104
Banū Ghassān, 104
Banū Ghatfān, 104
Banū Ḥaḍramawt, 104, 106
Banū Hamdān, 104, 106, 107, 113, 144
Banū Ḥamrā, 105, 108, 115
Banū Hāshim, 8, 17, 65–7, 266
  Alids and Abbasids, 276–7
  and Banū Umayya, 65, 74
  and caliphate, 66, 69
  hereditary sanctity of, 7, 10, 13, 22, 58, 241
  at the Saqīfa, 37
  as supporters of ʿAlī, 86
Banū Hawāzin, 104, 196
Banū Ḥimyar, 104, 106, 113
Banū Iyād, 105, 113
Banu Jadīla, 104
Banū Kalb, 227
Banū Khathʿam, 104, 107
Banū Khazraj, 3, 11, 12, 48
Banū Kināna, 104, 107
Banū Kinda, 104, 106–8 *passim*, 113, 121, 196
  kings of, 7
Banū Madhḥij, 104, 106–8 *passim*, 113, 121, 196–7
Banū Mahar, 106, 107
Banū Makhzūm, 75
Banū Muḥārib, 104
Banū Nimr, 104, 113
Banū Qayla, 11
Banū Qays ʿAylān, 104, 107, 227
Banū Quḍāʿa, 104, 106
Banū Quraysh, 11, 46, 73, 120, 135
  clan rivalries among, 48, 66–7, 74
  in Kūfa, 104, 107, 113
Banū Rabīʿa, 107, 113, 144, 232
Banū Ribāb, 107
Banū Rihāb, 104
Banū Taghlib, 104, 107, 113
Banū Taym b. Murra, 16, 48
Banū Tamīn, 103, 104, 107, 108, 113, 115, 196
Banū Tayy, 105–6, 113
Banū Thaqīf, 196–7
Banū Umayya, 1, 7, 13, 70, 131, 271
  anti-Umayyad propaganda, 264, 270
  domination of, 80–1, 120, 241
  downfall of, 269
  rivalry with Banū Hāshim, 65, 74
  and ʿUthmān, 81–3, 88, 94
  and Zayn alʿĀbidīn, 237–8
al-Baraʿa b. ʿĀzib al-Anṣārī, 52, 109
Baṣra, 103, 107, 178, 197
  and Kūfa, 120
  rebellions in, 227, 276
  Shīʿa of, 227–8, 231, 232, 251
Baṣra school, 37
Bayan b. Simʿan, 249, 291, 301–2, 303
Bilāl, 3
Bishr b. Marwān, 308
Bukayr b. Aʿyūn, 306
al-Bukhāri, Muḥammad b. Ismāʿīl, 32
Burayd b. Muʿāwiya al-ʿIjlī, 250, 306
Busr b. Abī Arṭaṭ, 149
buyūtāt al-ʿArab (noble families), 113, 117
Buzurg at-Tehrānī, Agha, 39

Christian tribes, 113
Companions of the Prophet (Ṣahāba), 67, 82, 84, 87, 117, 130–1, 242

Ḍamra, poet, 4
Dā'ūd b. 'Alī, 274
Dā'ūd b. Yūnus, 311
Daylamites, 105, 114, 115
adh-Dhahabī, Abū 'Abd Allāh Muḥammad, 68
dhimma (protected people), 112
Dhū'l-Jaddayn b. 'Abd Allāh b. Ḥammām ash-Shaybānī, 7
Dhurrīya, 14–15
ad-Dīnawarī, Abū Ḥanīfa Aḥmad b. Dā'ūd, 138, 140, 143, 144, 149, 195, 196
dīwān system (distribution of stipends), 61, 110–11, 122, 184
Dūmat al-Jandal, 10

Fadak, 63
Farazdaq, poet, 93, 184, 243–4
Farewell pilgrimage, 19
Fāṭima, 16, 17, 50–1, 63, 95
  Alid descent from, 226, 228, 236, 244, 279, 297
  death of, 59
Fāṭima bint al-Hasan, 251
Fihrist, 39
Fiqh (jurisprudence), 250, 292
Fuḍayl b. Rassān, 293
al-Fuḍayl b. Yasār, 250
Furāt b. Aḥnaf al-'Abdī, 243

Ghadīr Khum, 19–21
ghulāt, 291, 300–4
Gibb, H., 212
Gibbon, Edward, 194–5
Goldziher, I., 11, 20, 299

Ḥabīb b. al-Muẓāhir, 177, 182, 189, 206
ḥadīth, 292, 299, 303, 304
  collections of, 296, 300, 309
Ḥadīth al-Kisā, 297
al-Hajjāj, 213
al-Ḥakam b. 'Utayba al-Kindī, 253, 306
Ḥākim b. Ḥazm, 22
Hammād b. 'Īsā, 263, 309
Ḥammād b. 'Uthmān, 309
Hamza b. Ḥumrān b. A'yān, 306
Hamza b. Muḥammad b. 'Abd Allāh aṭ-Ṭayyār, 249, 305
Hamza b. 'Umara al-Buraydī, 301
Hānī b. Hānī as-Sabi'ī, 179
Hānī b. 'Urwa, 183, 185, 196
ḥasab, 4
Ḥasan b. 'Alī, 16, 17, 84, 87
  abdication of, 101, 126, 140–7, 148–53, 282
  death of, 157, 158–9
  and Imamate, 293, 311
  in Medina, 157–8
  and Mu'awiya, 133–7, 289
  and Shī'ā, 155–7
  succession of, 130, 132–3
Ḥasan b. az-Zurāra, 306
Hāshim b. 'Abd Manāf al-Qurayshi, 7, 8, 10, 17, 74
Hāshimīya sect, 271–2
Ḥassān b. Thābit, poet, 20
hereditary sanctity, 7, 10, 12–15, 16, 22, 58, 92, 229, 241
Hilāl b. Ḥubāb, 267
al-Hīra, 102, 105, 117
Hishām b. 'Abd al-Malik, Caliph, 243–244, 266
Hishām b. Muhammad al-Kalbī, *see* Ibn al-Kalbī
Hishām b. Sālim al-Jawālīqī, 306, 308
historical research, 30–41, 199–200
Hitti, Philip, 211
Hodgson, Marshal G. S., 92, 236, 291
Horovitz, 20
al-Ḥubāb b. Mundhir, 47
al-Ḥudaybīya, treaty of, 109, 131
al-Ḥudhayfa b. Badr al-Fazārī, 7
Ḥudhaifa b. al-Yamān, 51, 86, 102, 109
Ḥujr b. 'Adī al-Kindī, 82, 101, 118, 121–122, 155, 157, 206
  revolt of, 159–63
Ḥumayd b. Rabbāḥ, 306
Ḥumrān b. A'yān, 249, 305
Ḥurr b. Yazīd at-Tamīmī al-Yarbū'ī, 186–7, 196, 197, 208–9, 210
Ḥusayn 'Alī Maḥfūz, 20
Ḥusayn b. 'Alī, 16, 17, 84, 87, 106, 135, 175
  delegations from Kūfa to, 166, 177–9
  and Imamate, 293, 311
  at Kerbela, 101, 187–92
  letters to 'Irāq, 179–81, 289
  motives for journey to Kerbela, 178–191, 199–205
  and Mu'āwiya, 157, 159, 166–7, 177
  supporters of, 177–8, 182, 184–5, 188, 195–7, 205–10
  travel to Kūfa, 184–6, 200
  and Walīd b. 'Utba, 176–7
  and Yazīd, 176–7, 181, 202
  and Zayn al-'Ābidīn, 239
Ḥusayn b. Naṣr, 214
Ḥusayn b. an-Numayr at-Tamīmī, 185, 186
Ḥusayn b. az-Zurāra, 306

Ibn 'Abbās, 13, 38, 66
Ibn 'Abd al-Barr, 19, 150
Ibn 'Abd Rabbith, Ahmad b. Muhammad, 20, 22, 41, 87
Ibn Abī'l-Hadīd, 39, 43, 62, 93, 138–9, 142, 144, 150, 154
Ibn Abī Sarḥ, 74, 81, 82

Ibn Abī ʿUmayr, *see* Abū Aḥmad Muḥammad b. Abī ʿUmayr
Ibn al-Ashʿath, 116, 213
Ibn Aʿtham al-Kūfī, 138–9, 144–6 *passim*, 150, 152
Ibn al-Athīr, Abū'l-Hasan ʿAlī b. Karīm, 41, 68
Ibn al-Athīr, ʿAlī b. Muḥammad, 19
Ibn Babaway al-Qummī, Shaykh, *see* as-Sadūq, Shaykh
Ibn al-Ḥanafīya, *see* Muḥammad b. al-Ḥanafīya
Ibn Ḥazm, Abū Muḥammad ʿAlī b. Aḥmad, 248
Ibn Hishām, Abū Muḥammad ʿAbd al-Malik, 9, 20, 41, 216
Ibn Isḥāq, Muḥammad b. Isḥāq b. Yasār, 28–31, 38, 40–2 *passim*, 68–9
Ibn al-Kalbī, Hishām b. Muḥammad, 36, 139, 212, 214, 215
Ibn Kathīr, Ismāʿīl b. ʿUmar, 20, 194, 213, 214
Ibn Khaldūn, ʿAbd ar-Raḥmān, 10
Ibn Khallikān, Aḥmad b. Muḥammad, 255
Ibn Māja, 19, 32
Ibn Nadīm, Muḥammad b. Isḥāq, 39, 138
Ibn Saʿd, Muḥammad, 9, 20, 28, 32–6, 37, 39, 45
  on period of Rāshidūn, 60, 109, 113
Ibn Saʿd, *see* ʿUmar b. Saʿd
Ibn as-Sawdā, 86
Ibn Ziyād, *see* ʿUbayd Allāh b. Ziyād
Ibn az-Zubayr, *see* ʿAbd Allāh b. az-Zubayr
Ibrāhīm b. ʿAbd Allāh al-Maḥḍ, 275–6, 280, 290
Ibrāhīm al-Imām, 269, 272–3
Ibrāhīm b. Muḥammad b. Ṭalḥa, 227
Imamate,
  and caliphate, 278–83
  doctrine of, 290–312
  of Jaʿfar aṣ-Ṣādiq, 261, 280–3
  legitimist, 248–9, 251, 254, 280–1, 307–308
  of Muḥammad al-Baqir, 247–55
  of Muḥammad b. al-Ḥanafīya, 236, 240–2, 247
  nature of, 179–81, 236, 239–40
  principle of ʿIlm, 291, 292–3, 296, 304
  principle of Naṣṣ, 248, 290–1, 292–6, 304
  religious function of, 247, 249, 282, 289, 293
  supernatural character of, 300–4
  of Zayn al-ʿĀbidīn, 229–30, 239, 242–246, 247
Imāmīya (Imamate), 237
imārat al-bayt, 9
inheritance, 63
ʿirāfa (distribution group), 110–11, 184
ʿIrāq, Iraqis,
  and ʿAli, 80, 90, 120
  conquest of, 101
  and Hasan, 131–3, 140, 144–7, 155
  and Mahdism, 241–2
  and Syrian control, 80, 131, 195, 263
ʿirq, 6
Ishmael, 10, 14
Ismāʿīlīya sect, 249
isnād (chain of transmitters), 29
al-Istibsār, 309
Ithnā-ʿasharīya, see Twelver Shīʿa

Jābir b. ʿAbd Allāh al-Anṣārī, 242, 302
Jābir b. Yazīd al-Juʿfī, 301–3
Jaʿfar b. ʿAlī Ṭālib, 270
Jaʿfar Muḥammad b. Nuʿmān al-Ahwal, 306, 307
Jaʿfar aṣ-Ṣādiq, Imam, 39, 76, 248, 250–1, 253, 255, 263
  descent and childhood of, 259–60
  his doctrine of *Taqīya,* 298–300
  followers of, 301–2, 305–12
  and *ghulāt,* 301–3
  Imamate of, 261, 280–3, 289–92
  his interpretations of Qur'ān, 295–7
  his learning, 260–1
  and an-Nafs az-Zakīya, 275–6
  quiescence of, 266–7, 269
  and supernatural powers of Imam, 303–4
al-Jāḥiẓ, Abū ʿUthmān b. Baḥr, 20, 43
Jahm b. Safwān, 308
al-Jahshiyārī, Muḥammad b. 'Abdūs, 273
Jalūlā', battle of, 101, 114
Jamāʿa (community), 60, 72, 92, 156, 277, 289
  religious and political principles of, 137
Jamājim, battle of, 116
al-Jamal, battle of, 88, 90, 93, 95, 96, 120, 178
Jamīl b. Darrāj, 309
Jarīr b. ʿAbd Allāh, 104, 120
al-Jarrāḥ b. Sinān al-Asadī, 145
al-Jawharī, Abū Bakr Aḥmad b. ʿAbd al-ʿAzīz, 39
jizya (poll-tax), 116
Jubayr b. Muṭʿim, 245
Juʿda bint al-Ashʿath, 158

Kaʿb b. ʿAbda an-Nahdī, 86
Kaʿba, 9-10
  burning of, 262, 264
  guardianship of, 9, 10
  pilgrimage to, 7, 18
al-Kāfī fī'l-ʿIlm ad-Dīn, 300, 303, 309
kalām (scholasticism), 305, 306–9

Karbalā, Kerbela, battle of, 181, 182, 187–93, 231, 262
historical attitudes to, 198–200, 201–2
rajaz at, 205, 209–10, 211, 214
supernatural stories about, 215–16
Umayyad army at, 182–98, 206, 209
victims at, 196–7, 240
al-Kashshī, 'Umar b. Muḥammad, 253, 263, 290, 301, 304, 307–10 *passim*
Kaysanites, Kaysānīya, 255, 263, 265, 267, 270, 277, 298–9, 301
Khadīja, 17
Khālid b. Bajalī, 311
Khālid b. Sa'īd, 53
kharaj (land tax), 116
Kharijites, 91, 96, 122, 123
and Hasan, 144, 155, 158
Kharramite movement, 301
Kwawalī b. Yazīd al-Aṣbaḥī, 192
Khawārij, see Kharijites
Khaybar, battle of, 18, 63
Khuzayma b. Thābit, 51–2
Kitāb al-Futūḥ, 138–9
Kitāb al-Imāma, 308
Kitāb al-Jamal, 93
Kitāb ar-Radd 'alā'l-Mu'tazila, 308
Kitāb at-Tabaqāt al-Kabīr, 32, 37
Kitāb Waq'at Ṣiffīn, 93
Kūfa,
Abbāsids in, 272–3
'Alī in, 90–1, 97, 106–7, 114, 120, 123–124
development phases of, 119
founding of, 101–2
ghulāt in, 300–3
and Ḥasan, 140, 142
and Ḥusayn, 166, 177–9, 182–4, 195
Ibn Mu'āwiya's rising in, 270
and Ibn az-Zubayr, 227
Mahdism in, 241, 262
organisation of, 103–8, 120
population, number and composition in, 108–9, 111–16
power struggle in, 117–24
pro-Alids in, 272
Shī'a in, 101, 117, 157, 159–63, 166, 177–9, 182–4, 240–1, 252–3, 305
Shī'ī revolt (51/671) in, 159–61
stipend system in, 110–11
Tawwābūn in, 227
tribal leaders in, 121, 123, 125–6, 153, 161–2, 224
Kūfa school, 37, 82, 253
al-Kumayt b. Zayd al-Asadī, poet, 20, 93, 250, 254
Kuthayyir, poet, 93, 241, 263

legal traditions, 309–10

al-Madā'in, 101, 113, 142–7 *passim*, 150
Shī'a of, 227–8, 231, 232
al-Madā'inī, 36–9 *passim*, 138–9, 144, 150, 154, 214–15
Mahdism, 237, 241, 261–5, 267–8, 275–6
al-Majlīsī, Muḥammad Bāqir, 41
Mālik b. Anas, 260, 275, 280, 292
Mālik b. A'yān, 251
Mālik b. Ḥabīb ath-Tha'labī, 86
Mālik b. al-Ḥārith al-Ashtar an-Nakhā'ī, 82, 92, 118, 119, 121–2, 153
al-Manṣūr, Caliph, 275, 277–80
Maqtal al-Ḥusayn, 212–15
al-Māriqūn, 96
Ma'rūf b. Kharrabūdh, 250
Marwān b. al-Ḥakam, Caliph, 60, 84, 88, 166, 176, 227, 238
Marwān II b. Muḥammad, Caliph, 272–273
Maskin, 134, 142–3, 146, 147, 150
Mas'ūd b. Kudam, 276
al-Mas'ūdi, 'Alī b. Husayn, 28, 41, 68, 149, 273
mawālī (clients), 114–16, 123, 125, 232
and Mahdism, 262–3
and Shī'a, 239–40, 241
mawlā, 19, 21
Mecca, 131–2
aristocracy of, 7–10, 94, 119–20
Mu'āwiya in, 168–9
tribal society in, 11, 103
Medina, 2–3, 27, 131–2
group conflicts in, 49
Mu'āwiya in, 168
an-Nafs az-Zakīya's rising in, 275
and prophetic traditions, 245–6, 260
revolt (35/656) in, 87, 94, 119
revolt (62/681) in, 238
sack of, 264
school of, 31–2, 37, 245–6, 253
tribal society in, 103
al-Miqdād b. 'Amr, 52, 75, 76, 85, 86
Mītham b. Yahyā at-Tammār, 86
Moscati, S., 261, 273
Moses, 18
Mu'ādh b. Farra an-Naḥwī, 302
Mu'alla b. Khunays, 298, 305
Mu'āwiya b. Abī Sufyān, Caliph, 182
accession of, 153
and 'Alī, 73, 90, 95, 120, 123
death of, 174–5
and Ḥasan, 133–7, 140–53 *passim*
in Hijāz, 168–9
and Ḥujr's revolt, 159–66
and Kūfa tribal leaders, 121, 123, 125–126, 153
nomination of Yazīd by, 158–9, 167–9, 175, 181
and Shī'a, 166–7
Mu'awiya II, 227
Muḍar tribes, 104, 113, 232
al-Mufīd, Shaykh Muḥammad b. Muḥammad, 213, 214

al-Mughīra b. Sa'īd al-'Ijlī, 249, 268, 291, 301–2, 303–4
al-Mughīra b. Shu'ba, 143, 159, 167
muhājirūn (emigrants),
  in Kūfa, 109, 110
  in Mecca, 120
  and nomination of 'Umar, 65
  partisans of 'Alī among, 52–3, 87, 130–131
  at the Saqīfa, 27, 29, 35, 42, 44–5, 47, 49
Muḥammad, the Prophet, 3, 93, 299
  his ancestry, 7–10
  inheritance of, 63
  his special favours to 'Ali, 17–22, 58, 295–6
  status of, 1–2
  succession to, 11, 13–17, 22–3, 27–8
Muḥammad b. Abī Bakr, 87
Muḥammad b. Abī Ḥudhayfa, 87
Muḥammad b. Abī Zaynab Miqlāṣ b. Abī'l-Khaṭṭāb, 301
Muḥammad b. 'Alī b. 'Abd Allāh, 271
Muḥammad al-Baqir, Imam, 243, 245, 246
  death of, 254–5
  followers of, 248–54, 265, 290, 301–2, 306, 307, 310
  and *ghulāt*, 301–3
  Imamate of, 247–54, 282, 289, 292, 311
  and nomination principle, 248, 293
  quiescence of, 249, 265, 282
  and supernatural powers of Imam, 303–4
  and Taqīya principle, 298, 299
Muḥammad b. al-Ḥakam, 306
Muhammad b. al-Hanafiya, 182, 228–9, 236–7, 239–42, 245, 246, 270
  Mahdism of, 228, 237, 240–1, 261–3, 301
  and Taqīya, 299
Muḥammad b. Iṣḥāq b. Yasār, *see* Ibn Iṣḥāq
Muḥammad b. Jubayr b. Mut'im, 242
Muḥammad al-Mahdī b. Manṣūr, 268
Muḥammad b. Marwān al-Baṣrī, 251
Muḥammad b. Minkadir, 255
Muḥammad b. Muslim b. Riyāḥ aṭ-Ṭā'ifī, 250, 306
Muḥammad an-Nafs az-Zakīya, 247, 267–70, 290
  and Imamate, 293, 297
  and Manṣūr, 277–8, 297
  rebellion of, 275–6, 280
Muḥammad b. Ṭalḥa, 87, 131
Muḥammad b. Ya'qūb al-Kalaynī, 303
mukarrib, 7
al-Mukhtār b. Abī 'Ubayda ath-Thaqafī, 216, 236–7, 272
  and Ibn al-Hanafīya, 240–1
  and Mahdism, 262–3, 301
  revolt of, 101, 198–9, 211, 228–9, 232, 235, 245
  and Zayn al-'Ābidīn, 238–9
Murji'ites, Murji'a doctrine, 32–3, 39, 261, 281, 305, 307
Mūsā al-Kāẓim b. Ja'far aṣ-Ṣādiq, Imam, 294, 306, 307, 310
al-Musayyab b. Najaba al-Fazārī, 118, 177, 222–3, 232
Muslim b. 'Aqīl, 32, 179, 182, 183–4, 185, 191, 195–6, 200
Muslim b. Awsaja, 177–8, 189, 207
Muslim b. 'Uqba, 238
al-mutakallimūn, 305
Muthannā b. al-Ḥāritha, 105
al-Muthannā b. Mukharriba al-'Abdī, 224, 228
Mu'tazilites, 251–2, 265, 267, 268, 275–6, 281, 305–6, 311–12
al-Muṭṭalib, 8
Muzāḥim b. Ḥurayth, 210

Nābigha adh-Dhubyānī, poet, 4
Nāfi' b. Azraq, 255
Nāfi' b. Hilāl al-Jamalī, 209–10
Nahrawān, battle of, 123
an-Najāshi, Aḥmad b. 'Alī, 39
Najrān, 113
an-Nākithūn, 96
an-Nasā'ī, Aḥmad b. Shu'ayb, 19, 32
Naṣr b. Muẓāhim al-Minqarī, 72, 93, 214
naṣṣ (nomination), 248, 290–1, 292–3, 298, 309, 310
an-Nawbakhtī, Ḥasan b. Mūsā, 17, 255, 290
Nicholson, R. A., 11
Nihāwand, battle of, 111, 114
Nizārī (Northern Arabs), 103, 105, 113, 117, 161–2, 232
Noah, 14, 15
Nukhayla, 230–1
Nu'mān b. Bashīr, 179
Nu'mān b. al-Mundhir, King of Hīra, 5

Persia, wars with, 111
Persians in Kūfa, 112, 113–16
prophets, hereditary sanctity of, 14–15, 16

al-Qādisīya, 158, 185, 186
  battle of, 101, 102, 105, 106, 108, 110–113 *passim*
Qanbar b. Kadam, 86
Qāsim b. 'Awf, 242
Qāsim b. Ḥasan b. 'Alī, 189, 191
Qāsim b. Muḥammad b. Abī Bakr, 36, 259
al-Qāsitūn, 96
Qatāda b. Di'āma, 255

Qays b. Mushīr aṣ-Ṣaydāwī, 185, 201, 205–6
Qays b. Sa'd b. 'Ubada al-Ansārī, 133, 140–3, 146–8, 153
Qu'rān, the, 2, 9, 14–16, 18, 93, 311–12
Quraysh al-Biṭāḥ, 3
Quraysh aẓ-Ẓawāḥir, 3
Qurbā, 16
qurrā, (Qur'ān readers), 82, 85, 87, 89–90, 119, 122, 232
Quṣayy, 8, 22

Rabb al-Ka'ba, 6
Rāfiḍa, 266, 290
rajaz, 205, 209–10, 211
ar-Rāshidūn (rightly guided caliphs), 60, 72, 181, 264
rawādif (newcomers), 111
Rawāfid, *see* Rāfiḍa
Rawandites, 277
religion, pre-Islamic, 6–7, 12
'return' (*raj*'a), 263
ridda, see apostasy, wars of
ar-rifāda, 8, 9
Rifā'a b. Shaddād al-Bajalī, 177, 223–4, 232
Risālat al 'Itiqadāt, 311
Risālat al-Ju'fī, 302
Rub' al-Khālī, 11

as-Sabā'īya, 300–1
Sa'd b. 'Abd Allāh al-Ḥanafī, 207
Sa'd b. Abī Waqqās, 65, 67, 74, 101–4, 107, 108, 131
Sa'd b. Ḥudhayfa al-Yamān, 224, 228
Sa'd b. Mas'ūd ath-Thaqafī, 145
Sa'd b. Qays, 120
Sa'd b. 'Ubāda, 42, 45, 47, 48
as-Sadūq, Shaykh, 311–12
as-Saffāh, *see* Abū'l-'Abbās
Ṣahāba, *see* Companions of the Prophet
Sahl b. Hunayf, 52
Sa'īd b. 'Abd Allāh al-Ḥanafī, 179, 182
Sa'īd b. al-'Ās, 82, 119
Sa'īd b. al-Jubayr, 242–3
Sa'īd b. al-Manṣūr, 251
Sa'īd b. al-Musayyib, 31, 245–6
Sa'īd an-Nahdī, 301
Sa'īd b. Qays al-Hamdānī, 118, 142
sanctuaries, guardianship of, 6
Salmān al-Fārisī, 3, 52, 102, 109
as-Samāwī, 196
Saqīfa, assembly of the, 11, 22, 27–48, 226
as-Sarrāj, 263
Ṣa'ṣa'a b. Ṣuḥan al-'Abdī, 119
Sassanian feudal system, collapse of, 114, 115
Sawād of Kūfa, 112, 134, 270
Sayyid al-Ḥimyarī, poet, 85, 93, 241, 263
Schacht, Joseph, 264
scholasticism, *see kalām*
schools of law, 75, 250, 292
Sezgin, Ursula, 212, 215
Sha'ban, M. A., 138–9
ash-Sha'bi, 114
ash-Shahrastānī, Muḥammad b. 'Abd al-Karīm, 248, 255, 260
Shamir (Shimr) b. Dhū'l-Jawshan, 187, 189–91 *passim*
ash-Shaqshiqīya, 61, 71, 91
sharaf, 6
Sharī'a, 292
ash-Sharīf, ar-Raḍī, 61–2
Shī'a, Shī'ism, 21, 39, 137
  during 'Ali's caliphate, 89–97
  development of, during first caliphs, 58–76, 80
  extremist, 267–8, 270, 274, 276, 291, 301–5
  Four Pillars of, 53
  and *ḥadīth, see ḥadīth*
  during Hasan's caliphate, 155–7
  and Husayn's martyrdom, 211, 222
  and Imamate, *see* Imamate
  in Kūfa, *see* Kūfa
  legitimist, 132, 236–7, 247–8, 251, 254, 266, 289, 307
  and Mahdism, 241–2, 261–2
  martyrology of, 166
  during Mu'awiya's caliphate, 159–67
  mutakallimūn branch of, 305–8
  nature of, 1–2
  origin of, 17, 27, 53, 211
  political and religious motives in, 182, 195–6, 205–11, 226
  principle of first two caliphs, 181, 252–254, 265–6
  schools of law, 75, 250, 292
  split in, 236–7, 267, 269–70, 276–7
  and Tawwābūn, 222, 233
Shī'at 'Alī, 95–6, 126
  categories of, 97
  and Hasan, 150, 153, 155–7
Shī'at Banī 'Abbās, 275
Shūrā (electorate body) 58, 67–74, 75, 131, 226
Shurayḥ b. 'Awf al-'Absī, 82
Shurayḥ b. Ḥārith, qāḍī, 164
Ṣiffīn, battle of, 90, 93, 97, 121–2, 130, 178
Sinān b. Anas b. 'Amr, 192
as-siqāya, 8, 9, 279
Sīra (life of Prophet), 30
Sīrat Rasūl Allāh, 28
Sufyān ath-Thawrī, 267, 276, 280
Sulaymān b. 'Abd al-Malik, Caliph, 271
Sulaymān b. Ṣurad al-Khuzā'ī, 82, 159, 177, 182, 222–5, 227–8, 230–2, 240
Sunna, 5–6, 10, 137, 180–1, 227
Sunnīs, 1, 20, 27–8, 137
  on Imamate, 248
  and Qur'ān, 312

on the Saqīfa, 39
schools of law, 75, 292
Sunnī authorities, 19–20
as-Suyūtī, Jalāl ad-Dīn, 41
Syria, 120
civil war in, 277
domination of, 80, 131, 195, 263

aṭ-Ṭabari, Abū Ja'far Muhammad b. Jarīr, 20, 28, 29, 31, 105, 108, 273
on Abbasids, 274
on Ḥasan's abdication, 138, 139, 142, 149, 152
on Ḥujr's revolt, 162
on Ibn Mu'āwiya, 270
on Kerbela, 196–7, 212, 215
on the Saqīfa affair, 39, 40–1, 47, 48
on the Shūrā, 68
Tābi'ūn, 30
at Tabrāsī, Faḍl b. Ḥasan, 41
Tabūk, 18, 33
Tā'if, 103
Ṭalḥa b. 'Ubayd Allāh, 42, 64, 67, 70, 74, 89–90, 94–5
as supporter of 'Alī, 84, 85, 87
Taqīya, principle of, 252, 298–300, 306
Tawwābūn (penitents), 101, 196, 197, 211, 216, 222–33, 235–6, 239
and Imamate, 229–30, 245, 269
at-Ṭayyār, *see* Hamza b. Muḥammad b. 'Abd Allāh aṭ-Ṭayyār
Ṭirimmāh b. 'Adī at-Tā'ī, 106, 200–1
at-Tirmidhī, 19, 32
trade caravans, 10
tribe, the, 3–7
and Islamic authority, 109–10, 117–18, 126
sacerdotal lineages, 6–7
tribal groupings in Kūfa, 104–8
see tribal names under Banū
at-Turābīya, 96
aṭ-Ṭūsī, Nasīr ad-Dīn Muḥammad b. Ḥasan, 39, 309
Twelver Shi'a, 237, 243, 282, 290, 305, 309–11 *passim*

'Ubayd Allāh b. al-'Abbās, 142–3, 147–8
'Ubayd Allāh b. 'Abd Allāh b. 'Utba b. Mas'ūd, 31, 38
'Ubayd Allāh al-Murrī, 225–6
'Ubayd Allāh b. Ziyād, 86, 183–5, 187, 193–4, 195, 205–6
death of, 238
expulsion of, 227
and *Tawwābūn*, 230
'Ubayd Allāh b. az-Zurāra, 306
Ubayy b. Ka'b, 52
'Ukāz, fair of, 7, 10
'Umar b. 'Alī Zayn al-'Ābidīn, 273
'Umar b. al-Khaṭṭab, Caliph, 13, 16, 29, 33, 49, 113, 279
and 'Alī, 60–1, 62–3, 72
appointment of Shūrā, 67–71
and Banū Hāshim, 66, 69
caliphate of, 58, 65, 67, 94, 252
and Kūfa, 101, 102, 104, 108, 109–11, 117–18
nomination of, 63–5
at the Saqīfa, 34–5, 38, 40, 41–6
'Umar b. Sa'd, 187–8, 192, 197, 206
Umma, 69
composition of, 2–3, 11
and Ḥasan, 131–2
leadership principles of, 13–14
Umm al-Kitāb, 302
Umm Salima, 239, 268, 297
'Urwa b. az-Zubayr b. al-'Awwām, 30, 31
Usayd b. Ḥuḍayr, 42, 48
'Uthmān b. 'Affān, Caliph, 60, 64–5
assassination of, 87–9, 94
caliphate of, 74, 81–5, 118
in Shūrā, 67, 70, 73, 75–6
'Uthmān b. Ḥunayf, 52

Vaglieri, Veccia, 21, 61, 213

Wahb b. Munabbih, 30
walāya, 180–1
al-Walīd b. 'Uqba, 81–2, 111, 118–19
al-Walīd b. 'Utba, 175–7
al-Walīd b. Yazīd, Caliph, 268
waqf, doctrine of, 300
wārith (heir), 92–3, 180
wāṣi (legatee), 92, 97, 278
Wāṣil b. 'Aṭā', 251–2, 265, 268
Wellhausen, Julius, 11, 137, 212, 231
Wüstenfeld, Ferdinand, 215

Yaḥyā b. Umm aṭ-Ṭiwāl, 242, 245
Yaḥyā b. Zayd, 266–7
al-Yaman, 10, 12, 21
al-Ya'qūbi, Aḥmad b. 'Alī Ya'qūb al-Wāḍih, 28, 38–40, 46, 255
on 'Alī's accession, 92
on Ḥasan's abdication, 138, 140, 142–143, 147, 149
on Shūrā, 68
Yāqūt, Shihāb ad-Dīn, 108
Yarmūk, battle of, 110
Yazīd b. Qays al-Arḥabī, 86, 118
Yazīd b. Mu'āwiya, Caliph
caliphate of, 174–6, 181, 202–3, 238
death of, 224, 227
and Ḥusayn's death, 194
nomination of, 158–9, 167–9
Yemenī (Southern Arabs), 103, 113, 117, 125, 161–2, 232

Yūsuf b. 'Umar, 250

Zaḥr b. Qays, 194
Zakarīya b. Sābiq, 300
Zamzam, well of, 9–10, 278
Zayd b. 'Ali Zayn al-'Abidin, 247–8, 251–4
  revolt of, 255, 265–6, 293
  supporters of, 249, 253, 270, 290–1, 305
Zayd b. al-Arqam, 109, 193
Zaydīya sect, 248–9, 251, 253, 267, 275–6, 297
Zayn al-'Ābidīn, *see* 'Alī b. al-Ḥusayn
Zaynab bint 'Alī, 192–3, 194
Ziyād b. Abī Sufyān, 107, 159–65, 167, 181
az-Zubayr b. al-'Awwām, 42–3, 52–3, 67, 70, 74, 89–90, 94–5
  as supporter of 'Alī, 84, 85, 87
Zufar b. al-Ḥārith, 231
Zuhayr b. al-Qayn, 187, 189, 206–7, 208, 210
Zuhra b. Ḥawiya, 105
az-Zuhrī, 29–31 *passim*, 37, 38, 42, 139–142, 246
az-Zurāra, b. A'yān b. Susan, 249–50, 254, 305–7